ANNUAL EDITIONS

Western Civilization

Volume 1—The Earliest Civilizations Through the Reformation

Sixteenth Edition

EDITOR

Robert L. Lembright
James Madison University

Robert L. Lembright taught World Civilization, Ancient Near East, Byzantine, Islamic, and Greek/Roman history at James Madison University. He received his BA from Miami University and his MA and PhD from The Ohio State University. Dr. Lembright has been a participant in many National Endowments for the Humanities Summer Seminars and Institutes on Egyptology, the Ancient Near East, Byzantine History, and the Ottoman Empire. He has written several articles in the four editions of *The Global Experience*, as well as articles in the *James Madison Journal* and *Western Views of China and the Far East*. His research has concentrated on the French Renaissance of the sixteenth century, and he has published reports in the *Bulletins et memoires, Societé archaeologique et historique de la Charente*. In addition, Dr. Lembright has written many book reviews on the ancient world and Byzantine and Islamic history for *History: Reviews of New Books*.

McGraw Hill — Connect Learn Succeed™

The McGraw-Hill Companies

Mc
Graw
Hill

Connect
Learn
Succeed™

ANNUAL EDITIONS: WESTERN CIVILIZATION, VOLUME 1, SIXTEENTH EDITION

Published by McGraw-Hill, a business unit of The McGraw-Hill Companies, Inc., 1221 Avenue
of the Americas, New York, NY 10020. Copyright © 2012 by The McGraw-Hill Companies, Inc.
All rights reserved. Previous edition(s) 2012, 2009, and 2007. No part of this publication may be
reproduced or distributed in any form or by any means, or stored in a database or retrieval system,
without the prior written consent of The McGraw-Hill Companies, Inc., including, but not limited
to, in any network or other electronic storage or transmission, or broadcast for distance learning.

Some ancillaries, including electronic and print components, may not be available to customers
outside the United States.

Annual Editions® is a registered trademark of The McGraw-Hill Companies, Inc.

Annual Editions is published by the **Contemporary Learning Series** group within the
McGraw-Hill Higher Education division.

1 2 3 4 5 6 7 8 9 0 QDB/QDB 1 0 9 8 7 6 5 4 3 2 1

ISBN 978-0-07-805110-4
MHID 0-07-805110-X
ISSN 0735-0392 (print)
ISSN 2158-415X (online)

Managing Editor: *Larry Loeppke*
Developmental Editor II: *Debra A. Henricks*
Permissions Coordinator: *DeAnna Dausener*
Marketing Specialist: *Alice Link*
Senior Project Manager: *Joyce Watters*
Design Coordinator: *Margarite Reynolds*
Buyer: *Susan K. Culbertson*
Media Project Manager: *Sridevi Palani*
Cover Designer: *Kristine Jubeck*

Compositor: Laserwords Private Limited
Cover Image: © Image Source/PunchStock (inset); The Palma Collection/Getty Images (background)

Editors/Academic Advisory Board

Members of the Academic Advisory Board are instrumental in the final selection of articles for each edition of ANNUAL EDITIONS. Their review of articles for content, level, and appropriateness provides critical direction to the editors and staff. We think that you will find their careful consideration well reflected in this volume.

EDITOR

Robert L. Lembright
James Madison University

ACADEMIC ADVISORY BOARD MEMBERS

Frederic J. Baumgartner
Virginia Polytechnic Institute

Beverly A. Blois
Northern Virginia Community College—Loudoun Campus

Morgan R. Broadhead
Jefferson Community and Technical College

Manuel G. Gonzales
Diablo Valley College

Wendel Griffith
Okaloosa Walton Community College

Timothy Hack
Salem Community College

Anthony Heideman
Front Range Community College

Bernard M. Klass
Los Angeles Pierce College

Charles R. Lilley
Northern Virginia Community College—Woodbridge Campus

George E. Munro
Virginia Commonwealth University

Tracy Musacchio
John Jay College/CUNY

Teresa Mushik
Park University

Michelle Anne Novak
Houston Community College—Southeast

Fred Siegel
The Cooper Union

Don Sine
American Public University

Eric Strahorn
Florida Gulf Coast University

Paul R. Waibel
Belhaven College

Preface

What does it mean to say that we are attempting to study the history of Western civilizations? A traditional course in Western civilization was often a chronological survey in the development of European institutions and ideas, with a slight reference to the Near East and the Americas and other places where Westernization has occurred. Typically, it began with the Greeks, then the Romans, and on to the medieval period, and finally to the modern era, depicting the distinctive characteristics of each stage, as well as each period's relation to the preceding and succeeding events. Of course, in a survey so broad, from Adam to the atomic age in two semesters, a certain superficiality was inevitable. Main characters and events galloped by; often there was little opportunity to absorb and digest complex ideas that have shaped Western culture.

It is tempting to excuse these shortcomings as unavoidable. However, to present a course in Western civilization that leaves students with only a scrambled series of events, names, dates, and places, is to miss a great opportunity. For the promise of such a broad course of study is that it enables students to explore great turning points or shifts in the development of Western culture. Close analysis of these moments enables students to understand the dynamics of continuity and change over time. At best, the course can give a coherent view of the Western tradition and its interplay with non-Western cultures. It can offer opportunities for students to compare various historical forms of authority, religion, and economic organization; to assess the great struggles over the meaning of truth and reality that have sometimes divided Western culture; and even to reflect on the price of progress.

Yet, to focus exclusively on Western civilization can lead us to ignore non-Western peoples and cultures or else to perceive them in ways that some label as "Eurocentric." But contemporary courses in Western history are rarely, if ever, mere exercises in European tribalism.

Indeed, they offer an opportunity to subject the Western tradition to critical scrutiny, to asses its accomplishments and its shortfalls. Few of us who teach these courses would argue that Western history is the only history that contemporary students should know. Yet it should be an essential part of what they learn, for it is impossible to understand the modern world without some specific knowledge in the basic tenets of the Western tradition.

When students learn the distinctive traits of the West, they can develop a sense of the dynamism of history. They can begin to understand how ideas relate to social structures and social forces. They will come to appreciate the nature and significance of innovation and recognize how values often influence events. More specifically, they can trace the evolution of Western ideas about such essential matters as nature, humans, authority, the gods, even history itself; that is, they learn how the West developed its distinctive character.

Of course, the articles collected in this volume cannot deal with all these matters, but by providing an alternative to the summaries of most textbooks, they can help students better understand the diverse traditions and processes that we call Western civilization.

This book is like our history—unfinished, always in process. Comments and criticisms are welcome from all who use this book. For that, an article rating form is included at the back of the book. Please feel free to recommend articles for the next edition. With your assistance, this anthology will continue to improve.

Robert L. Lembright
Editor

iv

Contents

Preface   iv

Correlation Guide   x

Topic Guide   xi

Internet References   xiii

UNIT 1
The Earliest Civilizations

Unit Overview   xvi

These articles discuss some of the attributes of early civilizations. The topics discuss the role of dogs, Egypt, law, ancient wonders, and ancient empires.

1. **More than Man's Best Friend,** Jarret A. Lobell and Eric A. Powell, *Archaeology,* September/October 2010

   Whenever or wherever dogs were first *domesticated* they have left mementos all over the archaeological world. The authors explore *the roles dogs played in past cultures and how the ancients celebrated them.*   2

2. **Uncovering Secrets of the Sphinx,** Evan Hadingham, *Smithsonian,* February 2010

   American archaeologist Mark Lehner has been working for many years to discover aspects and meaning of the *Sphinx.* He believes that *Pharaoh Khafre* built the Sphinx to honor his father, *Khufu* and it served to harness the sun's power to *resurrect the soul of the pharaoh.*   7

3. **Journey to the Seven Wonders,** Tony Perrottet, *Smithsonian,* June 2004

   Though only one of the *Seven Wonders of the Ancient World* still stands, they still intrigue our imagination. Author Tony Perrottet details the *Pyramids, the Lighthouse of Alexandria, the Temple of Artemis at Ephesus, the Mausoleum at Halicarnassus, the Colossus of Rhodes, the Hanging Gardens of Babylon, and the Statue of Zeus at Olympia.* Why do these monuments still capture our thoughts after 2,000 years?   11

4. **The Coming of the Sea Peoples,** Neil Asher Silberman, *Military History,* Winter 1998

   About 1200 B.C. a new military force swept southward across the Aegean Sea and into Asia Minor, Cyprus and Canaan—and even reached the borders of Egypt. Where were the *"sea peoples,"* and how did their weapons and tactics launch a *military revolution* in the ancient world?   15

5. **I, Pillar of Justice,** Frank L. Holt, *Saudi Aramco World,* May/June 2009

   The major focus of this article is *Mesopotamia* in the time of *Hammurapi* and discusses the *Law Code.* There are 282 laws enumerated and the conditions and penalties for various offenses.   22

6. **Before Tea Leaves Divination in Ancient Babylonia,** William W. Hallo, *Biblical Archaeology Review,* March/April 2005

   William Halo discusses the use of *hepatoscopy (a form of divination involving the inspection of animal livers)* by the *Assyrian kings.* He sees parallels between ancient liver inspections and modern intelligence.   25

The concepts in bold italics are developed in the article. For further expansion, please refer to the Topic Guide.

UNIT 2
Greece and Rome: The Classical Tradition

Unit Overview   **28**

These articles focus on Greek and Roman society. Sports, crime, politics, military conquests, women in Etruscan society, and Cleopatra are discussed.

7. **Troy's Night of the Horse,** Barry Strauss, *The Trojan War,* March 2007

   There have been many theories as to the reality of the Trojan War, but most historians are convinced that the **Trojan Horse** was a fiction. However, Barry Strauss suggests that we think of the fall of Troy as an **example of unconventional warfare**—Bronze Age style, and that the Greeks **must have used** some kind of **deceit** to take the city.   **30**

8. **The Historical Socrates,** Robin Waterfield, *History Today,* January 2009

   The popular image of **Socrates** as a man of **immense moral integrity** was largely the **creation of his pupil Plato.** If we study the evidence of his trial, says the author, a different picture emerges, of a **cunning politician opposed to Athenian democracy.**   **34**

9. **Good Riddance, I Say,** Frank L. Holt, *Saudi Aramco World* July/August 2008

   Frank L. Holt uses a **bit of broken pottery** to enlighten us about **daily life** in fifth century **Athens.** He explains how the **political banishment called ostracism** was used between two Athenian statesmen—**Themistocles and Aristeides the Just.**   **38**

10. **Outfoxed and Outfought,** Jason K. Foster, *Military History,* January/February 2007

    Jason K. Foster recounts how the superior-trained Athenian Hoplites **(heavily armed soldiers)** and new battle tactics overwhelmed the ancient world's greatest empire, Persia. Had Athens been defeated, **democracy, art, culture, and philosophy** might have been lost forever.   **42**

11. **Mighty Macedonian: Alexander the Great,** Richard Covington, *Smithsonian,* November 2004

    His victories on the battlefield earned him the title **Alexander the Great,** but what were his motives? Was it his motivation to **surpass his father, Philip II,** or to **win his mother Olympias' love,** which enabled him to conquer the **Persian Empire?**   **45**

12. **Etruscan Women: Dignified, Charming, Literate and Free,** Ingrid D. Rowland, *Archaeology Odyssey,* May/June 2004

    The author tells us that the Etruscan Women's **freedom of action, appetite for wine, and their loose morals** were scandalous to the Greeks and later, to the Romans. They were powerful, dignified, elegant, and aristocratic, and seemed to be equal to men.   **50**

13. **Rome's Craftiest General: Scipio Africanus,** James Lacey, *Military History,* July/August 2007

    Publius Cornelius Scipio "Africanus" learned the art of war at a very young age against Rome's greatest enemy, **Hannibal Barca.** Although Scipio and the Romans were first defeated, he eventually gained a command to take Spain from Carthage and then met Hannibal at Zama in 202 B.C. The latter was the crowning achievement of his career and gave him the title, **"Africanus" or "victor of Africa,"** but it was to be his last important command.   **53**

The concepts in bold italics are developed in the article. For further expansion, please refer to the Topic Guide.

UNIT 3
The Judeo-Christian Heritage

Unit Overview   56
The articles in this section examine the Hebrew religion, Jesus, and Mary Magdalene.

14. **Did Captured ARK Afflict Philistines with E.D.?,** Aren M. Maeir,
    Biblical Archaeological Review, May/June 2008
    What did the Bible mean by the statement that God afflicted the **Phillistines** with
    'opalim' which is usually translated as "hemorrhoids." The author contends that the real
    meaning had to do with **sexual function.**   58

15. **Who Wrote the Dead Sea Scrolls?,** Andrew Lawler, *Smithsonian,* January 2010
    There is a controversy fueled by the thoughts of Israeli archaeologist, Yuval Peleg, who
    does not believe in the traditional view that the **Dead Sea Scrolls** were written by an
    ascetic group called the **Essenes.** He contends that Jews, fleeing from the **Roman
    War** 66–70 A.D. hid documents in the Qumran caves to keep them safe. His and other
    theories are discussed.   60

16. **From Jesus to Christ,** Jon Meacham, *Newsweek,* March 28, 2005
    How did the **Jesus** of history, whom many in his time saw as a failed prophet, come to
    be viewed by billions as the **Christ of faith?** What were the **Jewish traditions** incorpo-
    rated into Christianity? And why did **Christianity succeed** where many other religious
    movements failed?   63

17. **An Inconvenient Woman,** Jonathan Darman, *Newsweek,* May 29, 2006
    Was **Mary Magdalene a saint or sinner?** Most of her history remains a mystery but
    Jonathan Darman says that she was **faithful to Jesus' message of love and hope.**   68

UNIT 4
Muslims and Byzantines

Unit Overview   74
These selections discuss the Byzantine civilization as well as important political and scientific
methods in the Muslim world.

18. **The Elusive Eastern Empire,** Dionysios Stathakopoulos, *History Today,*
    November 2008
    The author recounts the history of the **Byzantine Empire** which began with **Constan-
    tine the Great** and lasted until the capital, **Constantinople,** was captured by the **Otto-
    man Turks in 1453.** Great emperors such as **Justinian and Heraclius** are detailed
    along with the many problems in religion and foreign attackers.   76

19. **The Lost Secret of Greek Fire,** Bruce Heydt, *Military History,* April 2006
    Greek Fire was a terrifying weapon which protected the **Byzantine Empire** for centu-
    ries, but there are many secrets which the modern world would like to know. What was
    the **chemical makeup, how was it discharged, and when was the secret lost?** The
    author says that perhaps some day we may find the answers in a forgotten archive.   80

20. **Islam's First Terrorists,** Clive Foss, *History Today,* December 2007
    The **Kharijites** emerged in the late seventh century and caused chaos during the Arab
    civil wars. Although they flourished in chaotic times and were able to set up a few states,
    none of these states lasted. Their insistence on **democracy** undermined a strong lead-
    ership, while their **fanaticism** led to internal splits.   85

21. **Al-Kimiya Notes on Arabic Alchemy,** Gabriele Ferrario, *Chemical Heritage,*
    Fall 2007
    Alchemy meant a **method by which base metals could be transmuted into noble
    (gold or silver) ones.** The experiments and writing of Arabic scientists gave us words
    in chemistry for **alcohol, elixir, distillation, and solvents.** These alchemists transmitted
    the legacy of the ancient and Hellenistic knowledge to the West.   89

The concepts in bold italics are developed in the article. For further expansion, please refer to the Topic Guide.

UNIT 5
The Medieval Period

Unit Overview 94

These selections examine the medieval world. Topics include the church, education, military conquests, trade, and culture.

22. **The Church in the Middle Ages,** Marius Ostrowski, *History Review,* December 2006

When the Roman Empire fell in the fifth century, it was the Christian church which gained immense power and held it for a millennium. The church brought together ***politics, religion, warfare, and culture*** which lasted until the Reformation. **96**

23. **What Did Medieval Schools Do for Us?,** Nicholas Orme, *History Today,* June 2006

When the Roman Civilization evaporated in England during the fifth century, learning inclined more into/toward the monasteries, where Latin Grammars were developed to teach those who knew no Latin. By the twelfth century, school became what we would call ***modern:*** they ***moved away from the monasteries, had full-time teachers, and they were more in number.*** Many more children—boys and girls—were literate. **101**

24. **1215 and All That,** James Lacey, *Military History,* May 2010

After signing the ***Magna Carta, which limited King John's powers and protected the nobles rights,*** one might have hoped for peace. However, the barons got drunk and ***proclaimed John a disgrace,*** while the king turned to ***vengeance.*** **105**

25. **The Fourth Crusade and the Sack of Constantinople,** Jonathan Phillips, *History Today,* May 2004

What caused the knights of the ***Fourth Crusade*** to sack Constantinople and establish a Latin Empire, which lasted from 1204 to 1261? Jonathan Phillips says that it was a ***clash of cultures***—the Byzantines saw themselves as superior to the West and the Westerners saw the Byzantines as effeminate and duplicitous. **109**

26. **Monsoons, Mude and Gold,** Paul Lunde, *Saudi Aramco World,* July/August 2005

The ***global economy*** of the Middle Ages was created by taking advantage of the monsoons to link the Indian Ocean with the West. The Venetians sent ***mude,*** or convoys of ships, to the East for luxury items. This trade meant finding new sources of gold needed to pay for the goods as well as maps of the routes. **113**

27. **How a Mysterious Disease Laid Low Europe's Masses,** Charles L. Mee Jr., *Smithsonian,* February 1990

The great ***Bubonic plague*** of the fourteenth century destroyed a third of Europe's population and had profound psychological, social, religious, economic, and even artistic consequences. Charles Mee spells out the causes, symptoms, and effects of the epidemic that altered ***medieval life.*** **119**

UNIT 6
Renaissance and Reformation

Unit Overview 124

The following articles discuss, the Renaissance, politics, war, culture, and the importance of religion in Western Europe.

28. **Joan of Arc,** Kelly DeVries, *Military History,* January/February 2008

Kelly DeVries says that ***Joan of Arc's*** fame comes from ***her skill at leading men into battle against great odds.*** She inspired later generals to adopt her tactics, such as ***direct engagements and frontal assaults.*** These things later made her celebrated and a saint. **126**

The concepts in bold italics are developed in the article. For further expansion, please refer to the Topic Guide.

29. **Christian Humanism: From Renaissance to Reformation,** Lucy Wooding, *History Review,* September 2009

Christian Humanism had key features such as ***internationalism*** or traveling scholars, ***correspondence*** between scholars, one language—***Latin,*** a sound ***biblical*** knowledge, and a desire for ***education.***   **131**

30. **The Luther Legacy,** Derek Wilson, *History Today,* May 2007

Martin Luther has been seen as an advocate of ***individual freedom, intellectual repression, nationalism, spirituality, and secularism.*** But, as Derek Wilson says, this did not make Luther a dry philosopher but a flesh-and-blood fallible human being. He was a ***theologian who lived his theology.***   **136**

31. **Explaining John Calvin,** William J. Bouwsma, *The Wilson Quarterly,* New Year's Edition 1989

John Calvin's image in history is well established. The religious reformer has been credited with—or blamed for—promoting the ***capitalist work ethic, individualism,*** and ***Puritanism.*** His biographer, William Bouwsma, says our image of Calvin as a cold, inflexible moralist is mistaken. According to the author, Calvin's life and work were full of "the ambiguities, contradictions, and agonies" of a troubled time.   **139**

32. **Who Was Henry VIII and When Did It All Go Wrong?,** Suzannah Lipscomb, *History Today,* April 2009

The author says that what we know today of ***King Henry VIII*** is a false picture. We take our understanding of Henry in his last days and use it as a blueprint for his life and his reign—his ***character flaws were not manifest until much later.***   **144**

33. **Women in War,** John A. Lynn, *Military History,* October 2007

In the armies of sixteenth century Europe, there was a woman for every man. The tasks performed by camp women were ***prostitution, laundry, meal preparation, commerce, and heavy camp labor.*** The import of women in the field is recounted by John A. Lynn.   **148**

Test-Your-Knowledge Form   **152**
Article Rating Form   **153**

The concepts in bold italics are developed in the article. For further expansion, please refer to the Topic Guide.

Correlation Guide

The *Annual Editions* series provides students with convenient, inexpensive access to current, carefully selected articles from the public press. **Annual Editions: Western Civilization, Volume I: The Earliest Civilization through Reformation, 16/e** is an easy-to-use reader that presents articles on important topics such as *ancient Greece, Islam, medieval society,* and many more. For more information on *Annual Editions* and other *McGraw-Hill Contemporary Learning Series* titles, visit www.mhhe.com/cls.

This convenient guide matches the units in **Western Civilization, Volume I, 16/e** with the corresponding chapters in one of our best-selling McGraw-Hill history textbooks by Sherman/Salisbury.

Annual Editions: Western Civilization, Volume I, 16/e	The West in the World, Volume I: To 1715, 4/e by Sherman/Salisbury
Unit 1: The Earliest Civilizations	**Chapter 1:** The Roots of Western Civilization: The Ancient Middle East to the Sixth Century B.C.E.
Unit 2: Greece and Rome: The Classical Tradition	**Chapter 2:** The Contest for Excellence: Greece, 2000–338 B.C.E. Timeline: The Big Picture **Chapter 3:** The Poleis Become Cosmopolitan: The Hellenistic World, 336–150 B.C.E. **Chapter 4:** Pride in Family and City: Rome from Its Origins through the Republic, 753–44 B.C.E.
Unit 3: The Judeo-Christian Heritage	**Chapter 5:** Territorial and Christian Empires: The Roman Empire, 31 B.C.E. to 410 C.E.
Unit 4: Muslims and Byzantines	**Chapter 6:** A World Divided: Western Kingdoms, Byzantium, and the Islamic World, ca. 376–1000
Unit 5: The Medieval Period	**Chapter 7:** The Struggle to Bring Order: The Early Middle Ages, ca. 750–1000 **Chapter 8:** Order Restored: The High Middle Ages, 1000–1300 **Chapter 9:** The West Struggles and Eastern Empires Flourish: The Late Middle Ages, ca. 1300–1500
Unit 6: Renaissance and Reformation	**Chapter 10:** A New Spirit in the West: The Renaissance, ca. 1300–1640 **Chapter 11:** "Alone before God": Religious Reform and Warfare 1500–1648

Topic Guide

This topic guide suggests how the selections in this book relate to the subjects covered in your course. You may want to use the topics listed on these pages to search the web more easily.

On the following pages a number of websites have been gathered specifically for this book. They are arranged to reflect the units of this Annual Editions reader. You can link to these sites by going to www.mhhe.com/cls.

All the articles that relate to each topic are listed below the bold-faced term.

Animals
1. More than Man's Best Friend

Archaeology
1. More than Man's Best Friend
2. Uncovering Secrets of the Sphinx
3. Journey to the Seven Wonders
5. I, Pillar of Justice
7. Troy's Night of the Horse
9. Good Riddance, I Say
12. Etruscan Women: Dignified, Charming, Literate and Free
14. Did Captured Ark Afflict Philistines with E.D.?
15. Who Wrote the Dead Sea Scrolls?

Art
3. Journey to the Seven Wonders
18. The Elusive Eastern Empire

Babylonia
6. Before Tea Leaves Divination in Ancient Babylonia

Bible
14. Did Captured Ark Afflict Philistines with E.D.?
15. Who Wrote the Dead Sea Scrolls?
16. From Jesus to Christ
17. An Inconvenient Woman

Byzantium
18. The Elusive Eastern Empire
19. The Lost Secret of Greek Fire
25. The Fourth Crusade and the Sack of Constantinople

Christianity
16. From Jesus to Christ
17. An Inconvenient Woman
22. The Church in the Middle Ages
29. Christian Humanism: From Renaissance to Reformation
30. The Luther Legacy
31. Explaining John Calvin

Culture
3. Journey to the Seven Wonders
6. Before Tea Leaves Divination in Ancient Babylonia
8. The Historical Socrates
9. Good Riddance, I Say
12. Etruscan Women: Dignified, Charming, Literate and Free
18. The Elusive Eastern Empire
19. The Lost Secret of Greek Fire
20. Islam's First Terrorists
21. Al-Kimiya Notes on Arabic Alchemy
22. The Church in the Middle Ages
23. What Did Medieval Schools Do for Us?
29. Christian Humanism: From Renaissance to Reformation
33. Women in War

Disease
27. How a Mysterious Disease Laid Low Europe's Masses

Education
23. What Did Medieval Schools Do for Us?
29. Christian Humanism: From Renaissance to Reformation

Egypt
2. Uncovering Secrets of the Sphinx

England
24. 1215 and All That
32. Who Was Henry VIII and When Did It All Go Wrong?

Europe
22. The Church in the Middle Ages
23. What Did Medieval Schools Do for Us?
24. 1215 and All That
25. The Fourth Crusade and the Sack of Constantinople
26. Monsoons, Mude and Gold
27. How a Mysterious Disease Laid Low Europe's Masses
28. Joan of Arc
29. Christian Humanism: From Renaissance to Reformation
30. The Luther Legacy
31. Explaining John Calvin
33. Women in War

Greece, ancient
3. Journey to the Seven Wonders
8. The Historical Socrates
9. Good Riddance, I Say
10. Outfoxed and Outfought
11. Mighty Macedonian: Alexander the Great

France
28. Joan of Arc

Islam
20. Islam's First Terrorists
21. Al-Kimiya Notes on Arabic Alchemy
25. The Fourth Crusade and the Sack of Constantinople
26. Monsoons, Mude and Gold

Italy
26. Monsoons, Mude and Gold

Jews and Judaism
14. Did Captured Ark Afflict Philistines with E.D.?
15. Who Wrote the Dead Sea Scrolls

Medieval society
22. The Church in the Middle Ages
23. What Did Medieval Schools Do for Us?
24. 1215 and All That
25. The Fourth Crusade and the Sack of Constantinople
26. Monsoons, Mude and Gold
27. How a Mysterious Disease Laid Low Europe's Masses

Middle East

20. Islam's First Terrorists
21. Al-Kimiya Notes on Arabic Alchemy
25. The Fourth Crusade and the Sack of Constantinople
26. Monsoons, Mude and Gold

Military

4. The Coming of the Sea Peoples
7. Troy's Night of the Horse
10. Outfoxed and Outfought
11. Mighty Macedonian: Alexander the Great
13. Rome's Craftiest General: Scipio Africanus
19. The Lost Secret of Greek Fire
24. 1215 and All That
25. The Fourth Crusade and the Sack of Constantinople
28. Joan of Arc

Persia, ancient

10. Outfoxed and Outfought

Reformation

29. Christian Humanism: From Renaissance to Reformation
30. The Luther Legacy
31. Explaining John Calvin

Religion

14. Did Captured Ark Afflict Philistines with E.D.?
15. Who Wrote the Dead Sea Scrolls
16. From Jesus to Christ
17. An Inconvenient Woman

22. The Church in the Middle Ages
28. Joan of Arc
29. Christian Humanism: From Renaissance to Reformation
30. The Luther Legacy
31. Explaining John Calvin

Roman civilization

13. Rome's Craftiest General: Scipio Africanus
18. The Elusive Eastern Empire

Science

19. The Lost Secret of Greek Fire
21. Al-Kimiya Notes on Arabic Alchemy

War

4. The Coming of the Sea Peoples
7. Troy's Night of the Horse
10. Outfoxed and Outfought
11. Mighty Macedonian: Alexander the Great
13. Rome's Craftiest General: Scipio Africanus
18. The Elusive Eastern Empire
19. The Lost Secret of Greek Fire
25. The Fourth Crusade and the Sack of Constantinople
33. Women in War

Women

12. Etruscan Women: Dignified, Charming, Literate and Free
28. Joan of Arc
33. Women in War

Internet References

The following Internet sites have been selected to support the articles found in this reader. These sites were available at the time of publication. However, because websites often change their structure and content, the information listed may no longer be available. We invite you to visit www.mhhe.com/cls for easy access to these sites.

Annual Editions: Western Civilization, Volume 1

General Sources

Archaeological Institute of America (AIA)
www.archaeology.org

Review this site of the AIA for information about various eras in human history. It presents news about the activities and research of the AIA, AIA/IAA-Canada, and other archaeological research institutions and organizations around the world.

The History of Costumes
www.siue.edu/COSTUMES/history.html

This distinctive site illustrates garments worn by people in various historical eras. Clothing of common people is presented along with that worn by nobility. Provided by C. Otis Sweezey, the site is based on a history of costumes through the ages that was originally printed between 1861 and 1880.

Library of Congress
www.loc.gov

Examine this website to learn about the extensive resource tools, library services/resources, exhibitions, and databases available through the Library of Congress in many different subfields of historical studies.

Smithsonian Institution
www.si.edu

Access to the enormous resources of the Smithsonian, which holds some 140 million artifacts and specimens in its trust for "the increase and diffusion of knowledge," is provided at this site.

UNIT 1: The Earliest Civilizations

Archaeology
archaeology.org

A publication of the Archaeological Institute of America. Visit this site for the latest news, videos, reviews, interviews, and more.

Biblical Archaeology Review
Bib-arch.org8

Deals with anything related to Judaism or Christianity from all periods.

Hypertext and Ethnography
www.umanitoba.ca/faculties/arts/anthropology/tutor/aaa_presentation.html

This site will be of great value to people who are interested in culture and communication. Brian Schwimmer addresses such topics as multivocality and complex symbolization.

NOVA Online/Pyramids—The Inside Story
www.pbs.org/wgbh/nova/pyramid/

Take a virtual tour of the pyramids at Giza through this interesting site. It provides information on the pharaohs for whom the tombs were built.

The Oriental Institute/University of Chicago
www.oi.uchicago.edu/OI/default.html

Open this site to find information on ancient Persia, Mesopotamia, Egypt, and other topics in ancient history.

UNIT 2: Greece and Rome: The Classical Tradition

Diotima/Women and Gender in the Ancient World
www.stoa.org/diotima/

This site features a wide range of resources on women and gender in the ancient and classical world.

Exploring Ancient World Cultures
http://eawc.evansville.edu

This electronic, college-level textbook has been designed by a worldwide team of scholars. Especially useful are the links to related websites. Learn about Greece and Rome, the pyramids of Egypt, and many more eras and topics.

WWW: Classical Archaeology
www.archaeology.org/wwwarky/classical.html

Useful information and links regarding ancient Greek and Roman archaeology are provided at this site.

UNIT 3: The Judeo-Christian Heritage

Biblical Archaeological Review
bib-arch.org

Deals with anything related to Judaism or Christianity from all periods.

Institute for Christian Leadership/ICLnet
www.iclnet.org

This site of the Institute for Christian Leadership, a Christian organization, presents documents and other resources of use in the study of early Christianity. Internet links are provided.

Newsweek
www.newsweek.com

Visit this site for the latest information on politics, business, environment, technology, culture, world news, health, trends, and more.

Internet References

Selected Women's Studies Resources/Columbia University
www.columbia.edu/cu/libraries/subjects/womenstudies/

Click on extensive links to information about women in religion and philosophy and a wealth of other topics.

Smithsonian.com
www.smithsonianmag.com

Visit this site for arts and culture, science and nature, history and archaeology, travel, photos, videos, and more.

UNIT 4: Muslims and Byzantines

ByzNet: Byzantine Studies on the Net
www.thoughtline.com/byznet/

This website offers a brief historical overview of the Byzantine Empire, a collection of maps, and a comprehensive list of emperors.

Chemical Heritage Magazine
www.chemicalheritage.org/magazine

Visit this site for interesting news and information that fosters an understanding of chemistry's impact on society.

History Today
www.historytoday.com

Visit this site for online content as well as a unique archive of interesting articles.

Islam: A Global Civilization
www.templemount.org/islamiad.html

This site presents information on Islamic history. It chronicles the basic tenets of the religion and charts its spread, including the period of the Umayyad Dynasty in Spain.

Military History
www.historynet.com/military-history

Visit this site for engaging military history articles by award-winning writers and historians.

UNIT 5: The Medieval Period

EuroDocs: Primary Historical Documents from Western Europe
http://eudocs.lib.byu.edu

This collection is a high-quality set of historical documents. Facsimiles, translations, and transcriptions are included as well as links to information on Medieval and Renaissance Europe, Europe as a Supernatural Region, and individual countries.

Feudalism
www.fidnet.com/~weid/feudalism.htm

Feudalism is covered in great detail at this site, which offers subjects such as feudal law, agriculture, development in Europe during the feudal period, and feudal terms of England, as well as primary source material.

The Labyrinth: Resources for Medieval Studies
www.georgetown.edu/labyrinth/

Labyrinth provides easy-to-search files in medieval studies. As a major site for topics in medieval history and lore, make it a primary stop for research.

History Review
historytoday.com/archive/history-review

Visit this site to peruse history articles dating back to 1995.

History Today
historytoday.com

Visit this site for online content as well as a unique archive of interesting articles.

Military History
www.historynet.com/military-history

Visit this site for engaging military history articles by award-winning writers and historians.

Saudi Aramco World
saudiaramcoworld.com

Anything dealing with Islam—history, culture, art, literature—is covered. Very good for listings of exhibitions of Islamic or African culture around the globe.

Smithsonian
smithsonian.com

Visit this site for arts and culture, science and nature, history and archaeology, travel, photos, videos, and more.

The World of the Vikings
www.worldofthevikings.com

For information on Viking ships and travel—and other aspects of Viking life—visit this site from Past Forward Ltd.

UNIT 6: Renaissance and Reformation

1492: An Ongoing Voyage/Library of Congress
http://lcweb.loc.gov/exhibits/1492/

This site provides displays examining the causes and effects of Columbus' voyages to the Americas and explores the mixture of societies coexisting in five areas of the Western Hemisphere before the arrival of the Europeans. It then surveys the Mediterranean world at a turning point in its development.

Burckhardt: Civilization of the Renaissance in Italy
www.idbsu.edu/courses/hy309/docs/burckhardt/burckhardt.html

Jacob Burckhardt's famous book on the Renaissance is available, chapter by chapter, on the net at this site.

Elizabethan England
www.springfield.k12.il.us/schools/springfield/eliz/elizabethanengland.html

Prepared by senior literature and composition students in Springfield High School (Illinois), this unusual site covers Elizabethan England resources in some detail: Historical Figures and Events, Everyday Life, Arts and Architecture, Shakespeare and His Theatre, and Links to Other Sources.

History Net
www.historynet.com/

The National Historical Society site provides articles on a wide range of topics, with emphasis on American history, book reviews, and special interviews.

Internet References

The Mayflower Web Pages

www.mayflowerhistory.com/

These Web pages represent thousands of hours of research, organization, and typing. The site is a merger of two fields: genealogy and history.

Sir Francis Drake

www.mcn.org/2/oseeler/drake.htm

Sir Francis Drake and, in particular, his "famous voyage"—the circumnavigation of the world during the reign of Queen Elizabeth I—are the focus of this site. It is provided by Oliver Seeler's site, The History Ring.

Society for Economic Anthropology Homepage

http://sea.org.ohio-state.edu/

This is the home page of the Society for Economic Anthropology, an association that strives to understand diversity and change in the economic systems of the world. The site presents data on the organization of society and culture, a topic of interest to students of the Renaissance and Reformation.

UNIT 1

The Earliest Civilizations

Unit Selections

1. **More than Man's Best Friend,** Jarret A. Lobell and Eric A. Powell
2. **Uncovering Secrets of the Sphinx,** Evan Hadingham
3. **Journey to the Seven Wonders,** Tony Perrottet
4. **The Coming of the Sea Peoples,** Neil Asher Silberman
5. **I, Pillar of Justice,** Frank L. Holt
6. **Before Tea Leaves Divination in Ancient Babylonia,** William W. Hallo

Key Points to Consider

- Explain the various treatments of dogs in the ancient world.

- What was the purpose of the Sphinx?

- Name the Seven Wonders of the ancient world and explain why they capture our thoughts even after 2,000 years.

- Who were the "Sea Peoples" and how did their weapons and tactics launch a military revolution in the ancient world?

- List the methods by which kings in Mesopotamia used to learn about the future and discuss any parallels in today's world.

- Why would most criminals would not wish to be punished according to the Law Code of Hammurapi?

Student Website

www.mhhe.com/cls

Internet References

Archaeology
archaeology.org
Biblical Archaeology Review
Bib-arch.org8
Hypertext and Ethnography
www.umanitoba.ca/faculties/arts/anthropology/tutor/aaa_presentation.html
NOVA Online/Pyramids—The Inside Story
www.pbs.org/wgbh/nova/pyramid/
The Oriental Institute/University of Chicago
www.oi.uchicago.edu/OI/default.html
Smithsonian
Smithsonianmag.com
Saudi Aramco World
saudiaramcoworld.com

Civilization is a relatively recent phenomenon in human experience. What exactly is civilization? How do civilized people differ from those who are not civilized? How is civilization transmitted?

Civilization, in its contemporary meaning, describes a condition of human society marked by an advanced stage of artistic and technological development and by corresponding social and political complexities. Thus, civilized societies have developed formal institutions for commerce, government, education, and religion— activities that are carried out informally by pre-civilized societies. In addition, civilized people make much more extensive use of symbols. The greater the complexity of civilized life, the greater the requirement for a much wider range of specialized activities.

Symbolizations, specialization, and organization enable civilized societies to extend greater control over their environments. Because they are less dependent than pre-civilized societies upon a simple adaptation to a particular habitat, civilized societies are more dynamic. Indeed, civilization institutionalizes change. In sum, civilization provides us with a wider range of concepts, techniques, and options to shape our destinies.

In the West, the necessary preconditions for civilization first emerged in the great river valleys of Mesopotamia and Egypt. There we find the development of irrigation, new staple crops, the introduction of the plow, the invention of the wheel, mathematics, science, improved sailing vessels, and metallurgy (see "Before Tea Leaves Divination in Ancient Babylonia"). These developments revolutionized society. Population increased, became more concentrated and complex. The emergence of cities or "urban revolution" marked the beginning of civilization.

Civilization combines complex social, economic, religious, and political structures with a corresponding network of ideas and values. The Sumerians organized themselves in city-states that were headed by kings who acted in the name of the local patron deity. The Egyptians developed the first centralized and authoritarian system based on loyalty to divine pharaohs (see "Uncovering Secrets of the Sphinx"). The Assyrians used force and intimidation to shape an international empire.

These early civilizations allowed for little individualism or freedom of expression. As historian Nels M. Bailkey notes in *Readings in Ancient History: Thought and Experience from Gilgamesh to St. Augustine* (2002), "their thought remained closely tied to religion and found expression predominantly in religious forms." Elaborate myths recounted the deeds of heroes, defined relations between humans and the gods, and generally justified the prevailing order of things. Thus, myths reveal something of the relationship between values and the social order in ancient civilizations.

We are inclined to make much of the limitations of ancient systems of thought and authority. Yet, the record of the

© Glen Allison/Getty Images

Mesopotamians and Egyptians demonstrates the civilizations' potential for innovation and collective accomplishment from the beginning. They developed mathematics, monumental architecture, law, astronomy, art, timekeeping and monetary systems, and literature rich in diversity and imagination. The records of ancient civilization note not just the cruelty and destruction of the age but also the awakening concern for justice (see "I, Pillar of Justice") and moral righteousness. These early civilizations are also notable for their heroic efforts to bring nature under human control.

For a time, the great river valleys remained islands of civilization in a sea of barbarism. The spread of civilization to rain-watered lands required the outlying areas to find the means to produce a food surplus and to develop the social mechanisms for transferring the surplus from farmers to specialists. The first condition was met by the diffusion of plow agriculture; the second by cultural contacts that came through conquest, trade, and migration.

Several satellite civilizations evolved into great empires. Such enterprises grew out of conquest; their initial success and later survival typically depended upon their relative capacity to wage war. "The Coming of the Sea Peoples" describes how an ancient military revolution affected the balance of power in the Near East and furthered cultural exchange between diverse and dispersed societies. The problem of governing scattered and often hostile subjects required that the conquerors create new patterns of authority. The growth of the Assyrian and Persian empires was not mere acts of conquest; it was innovations in government and administration. The earliest efforts to impose and maintain imperial hegemony must have been both crude and cruel.

More Than Man's Best Friend

Dogs have been an integral part of human culture for 15,000 years . . . sometimes in unexpected ways.

JARRETT A. LOBELL AND ERIC A. POWELL

Today there are some 77 million dogs in the United States alone. But as late as 20,000 years ago, it's possible there wasn't a single animal on the planet that looked like today's beloved (at least in some cultures) *Canis lupus familiaris*. Just how and when the species first became recognizably "doggy" has preoccupied scientists since the theory of evolution first gained widespread acceptance in the 19th century. The idea that dogs were domesticated from jackals was long ago discarded in favor of the notion that dogs descend from the gray wolf, *Canis lupus,* the largest member of the Canidae family, which includes foxes and coyotes. While no scholars seriously dispute this basic fact of ancestry, biologists, archaeologists, and just about anyone interested in the history of dogs still debate when, where, and how gray wolves first evolved into the animal that is the ancestor of all dog breeds, from Neapolitan mastiffs to dachshunds. Were the first dogs domesticated in China, the Near East, or possibly Africa? Were they first bred for food, companionship, or their hunting abilities? The answers are important, since dogs were the first animals to be domesticated and likely played a critical role in the Neolithic revolution. Recently, biologists have entered the debate, and their genetic analyses raise new questions about when and where wolves first developed into what we today recognize as dogs.

It can be very difficult to distinguish between wolf and dog skeletons, especially early in the history of dogs, when they would have been much more similar to wolves than they are today. What are perhaps the earliest dog-like remains date to 31,700 years ago and were first excavated in the 19th century at Goyet Cave in Belgium. Paleontologist Mietje Germonpré of the Royal Belgian Institute of Natural Sciences recently led a team that studied a canid skull from the cave and concluded that it had a significantly shorter snout than wolves from the same period. This dog-like wolf could represent the first step toward domestication and would make the Paleolithic people we call the Aurignacians, better known as the first modern humans to occupy Europe, the worlds first known dog fanciers. But the analysis is controversial, and there is a large gap between the age of the Goyet Cave "dog" and the next oldest skeletons that could plausibly be called dog-like, which date to 14,000 years ago in western Russia. Perhaps the Goyet Cave wolf represents an isolated instance of domestication and left no descendants. But based on finds of dog skeletons throughout the Old World, from China to Africa, we know that certainly by 10,000 years ago dogs were playing a critical role in the lives of humans all over the world, whether as sentries, ritual sacrifices, or sources of protein.

The archaeological record suggests dogs were domesticated in multiple places at different times, but in 2009, a team led by Peter Savolainen of the Royal Institute of Technology in Stockholm published an analysis of the mitochondrial DNA of some 1,500 dogs from across the Old World, which narrowed down the time and place of dog domestication to a few hundred years in China. "We found that dogs were first domesticated at a single event, sometime less than 16,300 years ago, south of the Yangtze River," says Savolainen, who posits that all dogs spring from a population of at least 51 female wolves, and were first bred over the course of several hundred years. "This is the same basic time and place as the origin of rice agriculture," he notes. "It's speculative, but it seems that dogs may have first originated among early farmers, or perhaps hunter-gatherers who were sedentary."

But this year a team led by biologist Robert Wayne of the University of California, Los Angeles, showed that domesticated dog DNA overlaps most closely with that of Near Eastern wolves. Wayne and his colleagues suggest that dogs were first domesticated somewhere in the Middle East, then bred with other gray wolves as they spread across the globe, casting doubt on the idea that dogs were domesticated during a single event in a discrete location. Savolainen maintains that Wayne overemphasizes the role of the Near Eastern gray wolf, and that a more thorough sampling of wolves from China would support his team's theory of a single domestication event.

University of Victoria archaeozoologist Susan Crockford, who did not take part in either study, suspects that searching for a single moment when dogs were domesticated overlooks the fact that the process probably happened more than once. "We have evidence that there was a separate origin of North American dogs, distinct from a Middle Eastern origin," says Crockford. "This corroborates the idea of at least two 'birthplaces.' I think we need to think about dogs becoming dogs at different times in different places."

As for how dogs first came to be domesticated, Crockford, like many other scholars, thinks dogs descend from wolves that gathered near the camps of semi-sedentary hunter-gatherers, as well as around the first true settlements, to eat scraps. "The process was probably driven by the animals themselves," she says. "I don't think they were deliberately tamed; they basically domesticated themselves." Smaller wolves were probably more fearless and curious than larger, more dominant ones, and so the less aggressive, smaller wolves became more successful at living in close proximity to humans. "I think they also came to have a spiritual role," says Crockford. "Dog burials are firm evidence of that. Later, perhaps they became valued as sentries. I don't think hunting played a large role in the process initially. Their role as magical creatures was probably very important in the early days of the dog-human relationship."

Whatever the reasons behind their domestication, dogs have left their pawprints all over the archaeological record, sometimes literally, for thousands of years. Over the following pages, we explore not only the roles dogs played in past cultures throughout the world, but how ancient artists celebrated our oldest companions.

Constant Companions

As they were talking, a dog that had been lying asleep raised his head and pricked up his ears. This was Argos, whom Odysseus had bred before setting out for Troy. . . . As soon as he saw Odysseus standing there, he dropped his ears and wagged his tail, but he could not get close up to his master [and] Argos passed into the darkness of death, now that he had seen his master once more after 20 years.

—Homer, Odyssey, Book 17

As anyone who has ever had a dog knows, there is little to compare to its faithful companionship. Evidence for love of dogs in the ancient world is abundant, from Homer's account of Argos waiting for his master to return from the Trojan War to the careful burials of cherished pets all over the world. And, as many owners also know, dogs live for treats. Even in the afterlife, their owners liked to spoil them. Behind the Stoa of Attalos, the main public building of the ancient Athenian market, a fourth-century grave was found containing the skeleton of a dog with a large beef bone near his head. And the Chiribaya people of Peru (A.D. 900–1400) also made sure that their pets had something to snack on after death. In 2006, archaeologists working in an ancient cemetery near the city of Ilo in southern Peru found the well-preserved

remains of 80 dogs interspersed with the burials of about 2,000 people ("Peru's Mummy Dogs," January/February 2007). Each dog had its own grave next to its owner, some were wrapped in finely woven llama-wool blankets, and many had llama and fish bones near their noses. The dogs ranged in age from puppies to adults, and most died from natural causes. Sonia Guillén, director of the Mallaqui Center in Ilo and the leader of the excavation, believes that these dogs were not only pets, but also were used to herd llamas and alpacas, which explains why they were highly valued even after death. Guillén is working to establish a link between these centuries-old breeds and modern Peruvian herding dogs.

The ancient Egyptians also cherished their dogs, not only as deities (see The Dog Catacomb), but also as companions in this life—and the next. A mummy of a small dog that dates to the fourth century B.C. was found in the sacred Egyptian city of Abydos in 1902 alongside that of a man identified on his coffin as Hapi-Men. Both mummies are now in the University of Pennsylvania Museum of Archaeology and Anthropology. Hapi-Men and his companion, "Hapi-Puppy," were recently part of a project to reexamine several mummies from the museum's collection. Hapi-Puppy was taken to the University of Pennsylvania Hospital for a CT scan that confirmed he was indeed a dog (not a cat, as was also thought possible.) According to anthropologist Janet Monge, who led the scan study, Hapi-Puppy died at about two years of age, more like an adolescent than a baby, and had the same size, stockiness, and power of a Jack Russell terrier. "Hapi-Men must have loved his dog, and after his death, it seems that the dog pined away and died soon enough to have been mummified and buried with his master," says Salima Ikram of the American University in Cairo. According to Ikram, this practice was not uncommon. "There are much earlier Middle Kingdom (2080–1640 B.C.) tombs that depict a man and his dog, and both are named so that they can survive into the afterworld together," she says.

Studying the remains of dog burials, even those from thousands of years ago, often has an emotional impact on researchers. "Perhaps of all the archaeological cases for pets I can think of," says Michael MacKinnon, an archaeologist from the University of Winnipeg, "I believe the Yasmina 'sick' dog is the most poignant." Along the north wall of the Roman-era Yasmina cemetery in the city of Carthage in Tunisia, excavations led by Naomi Norman of the University of Georgia uncovered a third-century A.D. burial of an adolescent/young adult in a carefully made grave topped with cobbles and tiles, and with the skeleton of an elderly dog at its feet. The dog was also buried with one of the few grave goods found in the cemetery, a glass bowl carefully placed behind its shoulder.

The Yasmina dog, which probably resembled a modern Pomeranian, is an example of a toy breed, and one of the earliest specimens to be identified as a Maltese. But what is more remarkable about the dog is that, despite a host of physical problems including tooth loss that likely required it to eat soft foods, osteoarthritis, a dislocated hip, and spinal deformation that would have limited mobility, the dog survived into its mid-to-late teens. It was clearly well cared for, and even death could not separate it from his owner, according to MacKinnon. "Whether the dog represents a sacrifice [perhaps meant to 'heal' the sick person in the afterlife] or just companionship is unknown, but these two aspects need not be mutually exclusive," he says. "There is a great connection between humans and animals in Roman antiquity. To me, this aspect of animals garnering sentimental value and being treated like humans is a key aspect of Roman culture."

Sacrificial Dogs

Patroclus had owned nine dogs who ate beside his table. Slitting the throats of two of them, Achilles tossed them on the pyre.

—Homer, Iliad, Book 23

Sacrificing dogs to appease supernatural forces has been a part of religious traditions as different as those of ancient Greece, where the Spartans slaughtered dogs to ensure victory in battle, and Shang Dynasty China. Some inscribed oracle bones dating to this period (1766–1050 B.C.) mention the rite of *ning,* which involved dismembering a dog to honor the winds. Often sacrificed dogs were single offerings, as was the case of the dog killed at the Minoan site of Monastiraki in Crete, where excavation director Athanasia Kanta last year found a small bench with a skeleton of a dog (missing its head) and several conical cups arranged around it. Kanta interpreted the find as a sacrifice to appease the gods following a large earthquake—there are collapsed walls and fire damage throughout the site.

At the site of Sardis in Turkey, once the capital of the Lydian Empire (680–546 B.C.), excavators uncovered 26 small pits, each containing four pots—a cooking jug, deep cup, shallow bowl, and small pitcher, all used for common meals—along with an iron knife and the bones of a puppy. According to one of Sardis's long-time excavators, Crawford Greenewalt Jr. of the University of California, Berkeley, the burials are the remains of a ritual meal, perhaps dedicated to the Lydian version of the god Hermes. "I do not believe these deposits are evidence of cynophagy [eating dogs], which was not part of the normal ancient Mediterranean diet," he says.

Some dog sacrifices are on a more massive scale. In 1937, archaeologists excavating in the Agora, the main marketplace of ancient Athens, made a stunning discovery—a well containing bones from hundreds of people, including approximately 450 newborns, and from more than 100 dogs. According to Lynn M. Snyder, who is re-examining the animal bones from the well, the infants likely died of natural causes. But she believes the dogs were "most likely sacrificed as part of a purification ritual after a birth, whether successful or not." Several ancient Greek sources identify dogs as the victims of choice to cleanse the pollution caused by both death and childbirth.

But dogs weren't just sacrificed in antiquity. In Hungary, a team excavating a site in the medieval town of Kaná just outside Budapest, discovered more than 1,000 dog bones, about 12 percent of all the mammal bones at the site. From these, Márta Daróczi-Szabó, an archaeozoologist at Eöetvöes Loránd University in Budapest identified five puppies, buried in pots, that were sacrificed and placed into the construction trenches of several buildings. Daróczi-Szabó believes that the puppies and several other dog burials at the site were intended to ward off evil, a custom that survived in Hungary into the 20th century. Although similar sacrifices have been found at other Hungarian excavations, especially of religious sites, Daróczi-Szabó was surprised by the pots from the domestic contexts at Kaná. "From these kinds of sacrificial pots, dog remains are very rare," she says. "More often eggs or chicken bones are found. So I was very excited by these finds." Daróczi-Szabó believes they suggest the practice of dog sacrifice was quite common during the Middle Ages in Hungary. "Despite the formal institution of Catholicism by the first Hungarian king, István I (1000–1038), who banned pagan rituals, it shows that part of the population still maintained these rituals in spite of the ideological dominance of Christianity."

Dogs of Roman Britain

"There were quite a lot of dogs here, and in Roman Britain in general," says Michael Fulford, director of the excavations at Silchester, the site of the large Roman town of Calleva Atrebatum in southern England. Decades of excavations have uncovered dozens of dogs of all types, ranging from terrier- to Labrador- and even greyhound-sized. Some were stillborn or died at birth, while others lived to ripe old ages. And although a few dogs show clear signs of having been killed deliberately, at least one was very well treated. Although the dog was rendered permanently lame by multiple leg fractures, it bore no trace of infection, suggesting that its paw was cleaned and immobilized, allowing it to heal properly. "What's interesting too is that dogs were treated both as rubbish and also reverentially," says Fulford. His team found an early third-century A.D. pit with the remains of a puppy that was killed (the team is not sure how), two other dogs, a raven, and two doubly-pierced pot sherds. The dogs were also buried with a knife that was probably used as a razor and had an ivory handle in the form of two coupling dogs. According to Nina Crummy, the excavation's finds specialist, the burial of the knife, an expensive object that had been made on the continent, would not have been lightly undertaken. "It should be interpreted as a deliberate burial, either as a kind of grave gift accompanying the burial of a pair of valued dogs, or a votive offering connected with the ritual life of the inhabitants [of this area of the city]," she says.

The dogs from Silchester are also evidence that in the Roman world, small dogs were favored over larger ones. According to University of Winnipeg archaeologist Michael MacKinnon, the spread of toy breeds by the Romans represents shifting attitudes toward pet-keeping, or an ardent effort to incorporate pet ownership into the more regular uses of dogs, such as herding and guarding. "It seems to be a Roman phenomenon that I suspect ties in with conspicuous consumption by the elite and other attempts at wealth and showiness," says MacKinnon. Archaeological evidence from the Roman world, including Silchester, also suggests that they may have been breeding for smaller dogs. "Bow-legged animals occur [starting in the] early Romano-British period, as does the absence of the lower third molar and crowding of the premolars," says Kate Clark, the Silchester team's bone specialist. "These conditions are due to the rapid diminution of the species whereby jaw size decreases faster than tooth size."

One of the most charming signs of dog life at Roman villas, farms, and military camps across Britain are the pawprints left in drying building tiles. There are dozens of these tiles from Silchester, and hundreds from Roman Britain—perhaps as many as one percent of all the tiles produced there according to Fulford—proof that it is not just modern dogs who stick their paws where they may not belong.

Dogs as Food

The Indians came forth in peace and gave them corn, although little and many hens, and a few little dogs, which are good food. These are little dogs that do not bark, and they rear them in the house for food.

—Rodrigo Rangel, Personal Secretary to
Hernando De Soto, 1540

When the Spanish explorer Hernando de Soto came to the southeast United States, he brought with him his own war dogs, animals similar to greyhounds and mastiffs, but he also seems to have enjoyed an occasional dog barbecue courtesy of the Native Americans he met on his travels. Whether by habit, preference, or necessity, dogs have been a part of many cultures' diets. Evidence for the large-scale breeding of dogs as food has been found at the late Iron Age (ca. 450–100 B.C.) site of Levroux in central France. Excavations at the site of Porden Point, Devon Island, Canada, have revealed that the people of the Thule culture (ancestors of the modern Inuit) were using dogs both for work and food from the 12th to 15th centuries. The Aztecs, whose ancestors were called the Chichimec, or "Dog People," are known to have bred a hairless dog they called a Xoloitzcuintle to serve at royal feasts. And at Halliday, a site near Cahokia, the mound center north of modern-day St. Louis, which was the largest pre-Columbian city north of Mexico from A.D. 1050 to 1400, butchered dog bones have been found in great quantities, suggesting they formed a significant part of the diet of the Mississipian culture.

Some of the best evidence for dog consumption in antiquity comes from the Olmec culture, often thought of as a precursor to the Maya ("Beyond the Family Feud," March/April 2007). The Olmec flourished in the lowlands along the Gulf of Mexico from about 1400 to 400 B.C. Although they had an abundance of food at their disposal, the Olmec ate dogs as part of their regular diet. At San Lorenzo, an Olmec city that has been excavated since the 1970s, archaeologists have found the remains of dogs and other animals used for food, including birds, deer, and fish, in the middens. Amber VanDerwarker of the University of California, Santa Barbara, has worked on several Olmec sites, including two farming villages within 40 miles of San Lorenzo. VanDerwarker has a fascinating theory about how the Olmec of the Early Formative Period (1900–1000 B.C.), when San Lorenzo was occupied, may have used dogs. "At the farm sites, we mostly find lower limb fragments like feet and also skulls in the middens. These are not the meaty parts of dogs," says VanDerwarker. "But at the elite sites like San Lorenzo, we find bones from all the meaty sections. This suggests that the farmers were raising dogs (and crops such as maize) to give to their leaders at certain times of the year as a kind of tax payment." Carbon isotope analysis of the dog bones allowed scholars to reconstruct their diet. The study shows that the Olmec dogs only ate maize, whereas humans ate a diverse range of foods. Perhaps the dogs were being deliberately fattened up to make them a more valuable form of tribute.

Dogs were also part of daily meals for one of the peoples who had close contact with the Olmec, the inhabitants of the Soconusco region on the Pacific coast of Chiapas, Mexico. "Unlike in the Old World, where you have many different domesticated animals, in the New World, dogs are one of the only domestic animals that can provide a ready source of animal protein," says anthropologist Robert Rosenswig of the University at Albany. He also thinks that "dogs were consumed for nutritional and ceremonial reasons, unlike wild animals whose numbers cannot be counted on for large gatherings." Rosenswig believes there may have been a change in the use of dogs at approximately 1400 B.C. Prior to this, dogs were buried along with humans—one dog burial that he excavated at the Cuauhtémoc site about six miles from the Guatemalan border contained grave offerings similar to those in human burials, including a pot that looks like a dog's bowl. After this point, all known dog remains indicate that they were consumed as food, since the bones are only found in garbage middens, not in graves with people. "The changing use of dogs was one aspect of new cultural practices on the Pacific coast at this time that also included the use of Olmec-style pottery and figurines," he says. "It indicates more intensive connection between peoples from distant regions of Mesoamerica."

The Dog Catacomb

In 1897, French Egyptologist Jacques De Morgan published a map of the necropolis of Saqqara, the burial place of Egypt's first capital city, Memphis. The map includes the only known plan of the "Dog Catacombs" at the site, but no information about the date or circumstances of their discovery. In fact, virtually nothing is known of these catacombs.

Last year, I began a Cardiff University-Egypt Exploration Society mission to the catacombs, which date from the Late and Ptolemaic Periods (747–30 B.C.), the last dynasties before the Romans conquered Egypt. We hope to learn if the De Morgan plan is accurate and see if we can find any clues to the early history of the catacombs' exploration. Right now we are completely remapping the catacombs and looking for clues to the circumstances of their discovery, such as travelers' graffiti and lamps from earlier explorers. The first catacomb, one of two main locations for dog burials at Saqqara, was the subterranean element of the Temple of Anubis—the jackal-headed god of the dead—a little to the south. According to the map, the temple had a long corridor that was probably a ceremonial route and numerous shorter tunnels on each side filled with thousands of mummified dogs and animal remains. The majority of these animals would have been votive offerings by pilgrims who hoped that the deceased animals would intercede with the deity on their behalf. Others, however, may have been representatives of the god and lived within the temple compound. Some of the dogs that were buried in special niches in the tunnel walls, rather than being piled in the great mass of remains, may be those animals. Many seem to have lived to considerable age, while other animals met their deaths after only a few months.

But the question remains—are they really all dogs, as the catacombs' name suggests? Preliminary examination by the American University in Cairo's Salima Ikram, the project's animal bone specialist, suggests that many of the mummified animals, now mostly lacking their wrappings, are indeed dogs. But according to Ikram, "Anubis was a kind of super-canid, so it is likely that jackals, foxes, and maybe even hyenas were mummified and given as offerings to Anubis." There is also still debate about exactly what kind of canid Anubis was meant to represent. Although the concept of dog breeds is a modern one, we hope to discover more information about the species, types, ages, and genders of the animals in the catacombs to understand how the god was perceived. —Paul Nicholson, Director, Cardiff University-Egypt Exploration Society Mission to the Dog Catacombs

Guardians of Souls

Run on the right path, past the two brindled, four-eyed dogs. . .guardian dogs, the four-eyed keepers of the path, who watch over men.

Farewell to a Dead Man from the Rig Veda,
10.12.10–10.14.10

Many ancient people assumed they would encounter dogs in the afterworld, from readers of the *Rig Veda,* the Vedic Sanskrit hymns composed in India in the second millennium B.C., to Greeks and Romans reared on tales of Cerberus, the three-headed hound who guards the entrance to Hades. The Aztecs even believed that the dead ascend to the afterworld by holding on to the tail of the dog god Xolotl, who also first brought people into this world when he dug a hole into the lower world. For many cultures, dogs likely served a critical role as *pyschopomps,* a Greek word meaning "guide of souls."

Dody Fugate, a curator at the Museum of Indian Arts and Culture in Santa Fe, New Mexico, has studied more than 700 dog burials in the Southwest, and believes that for many ancient Americans following shamanic ways, dogs were spiritual escorts to the afterlife. "Dogs have been a part of our lives for so long, they are hooked into our brains," she says, noting that rock art in Utah shows figures interpreted as shamans accompanied by dogs. But by about A.D. 1300, when organized religion along with the katchina cult began to replace shamanic beliefs in much of the Southwest, dogs disappear from grave sites. Fugate thinks that in the new belief systems dogs were no longer considered spiritual escorts to the next world, and were reduced to the simple role of companions in this one.

Uncovering Secrets of the Sphinx

Who built it? Why? And how? After decades of research, American archaeologist Mark Lehner has answers.

Evan Hadingham

When Mark Lehner was a teenager in the late 1960s, his parents introduced him to the writings of the famed clairvoyant Edgar Cayce. During one of his trances, Cayce, who died in 1945, saw that refugees from the lost city of Atlantis buried their secrets in a hall of records under the Sphinx and that the hall would be discovered before the end of the 20th century.

In 1971, Lehner, a bored sophomore at the University of North Dakota, wasn't planning to search for lost civilizations, but he was "looking for something, a meaningful involvement." He dropped out of school, began hitchhiking and ended up in Virginia Beach, where he sought out Cayce's son, Hugh Lynn, the head of a holistic medicine and paranormal research foundation his father had started. When the foundation sponsored a group tour of the Giza plateau—the site of the Sphinx and the pyramids on the western outskirts of Cairo—Lehner tagged along. "It was hot and dusty and not very majestic," he remembers.

Still, he returned, finishing his undergraduate education at the American University of Cairo with support from Cayce's foundation. Even as he grew skeptical about a lost hall of records, the site's strange history exerted its pull. "There were thousands of tombs of real people, statues of real people with real names, and none of them figured in the Cayce stories," he says.

Lehner married an Egyptian woman and spent the ensuing years plying his drafting skills to win work mapping archaeological sites all over Egypt. In 1977, he joined Stanford Research Institute scientists using state-of-the-art remote-sensing equipment to analyze the bedrock under the Sphinx. They found only the cracks and fissures expected of ordinary limestone formations. Working closely with a young Egyptian archaeologist named Zahi Hawass, Lehner also explored and mapped a passage in the Sphinx's rump, concluding that treasure hunters likely had dug it after the statue was built.

No human endeavor has been more associated with mystery than the huge, ancient lion that has a human head and is seemingly resting on the rocky plateau a stroll from the great pyramids. Fortunately for Lehner, it wasn't just a metaphor that the Sphinx is a riddle. Little was known for certain about who erected it or when, what it represented and precisely how it

related to the pharaonic monuments nearby. So Lehner settled in, working for five years out of a makeshift office between the Sphinx's colossal paws, subsisting on Nescafé and cheese sandwiches while he examined every square inch of the structure. He remembers "climbing all over the Sphinx like the Lilliputians on Gulliver, and mapping it stone by stone." The result was a uniquely detailed picture of the statue's worn, patched surface, which had been subjected to at least five major restoration efforts since 1,400 B.C. The research earned him a doctorate in Egyptology at Yale.

Recognized today as one of the world's leading Egyptologists and Sphinx authorities, Lehner has conducted field research at Giza during most of the 37 years since his first visit. (Hawass, his friend and frequent collaborator, is the secretary general of the Egyptian Supreme Council of Antiquities and controls access to the Sphinx, the pyramids and other government-owned sites and artifacts.) Applying his archaeological sleuthing to the surrounding two-square-mile Giza plateau with its pyramids, temples, quarries and thousands of tombs, Lehner helped confirm what others had speculated—that some parts of the Giza complex, the Sphinx included, make up a vast sacred machine designed to harness the power of the sun to sustain the earthly and divine order. And while he long ago gave up on the fabled library of Atlantis, it's curious, in light of his early wanderings, that he finally did discover a Lost City.

The sphinx was not assembled piece by piece but was carved from a single mass of limestone exposed when workers dug a horseshoe-shaped quarry in the Giza plateau. Approximately 66 feet tall and 240 feet long, it is one of the largest and oldest monolithic statues in the world. None of the photos or sketches I'd seen prepared me for the scale. It was a humbling sensation to stand between the creature's paws, each twice my height and longer than a city bus. I gained sudden empathy for what a mouse must feel like when cornered by a cat.

Nobody knows its original name. Sphinx is the human-headed lion in ancient Greek mythology; the term likely came into use some 2,000 years after the statue was built. There are hundreds of tombs at Giza with hieroglyphic inscriptions dating back some 4,500 years, but not one mentions the statue. "The Egyptians didn't write history," says James Allen, an Egyptologist at Brown University, "so we have no solid evidence for what its builders thought the Sphinx was.. . .Certainly something divine, presumably the image of a king, but beyond that is anyone's guess." Likewise, the statue's symbolism is unclear, though inscriptions from the era refer to Ruti, a double lion god that sat at the entrance to the underworld and guarded the horizon where the sun rose and set.

The face, though better preserved than most of the statue, has been battered by centuries of weathering and vandalism. In 1402, an Arab historian reported that a Sufi zealot had disfigured it "to remedy some religious errors." Yet there are clues to what the face looked like in its prime. Archaeological excavations in the early 19th century found pieces of its carved stone beard and a royal cobra emblem from its headdress. Residues of red pigment are still visible on the face, leading researchers to conclude that at some point, the Sphinx's entire visage was painted red. Traces of blue and yellow paint elsewhere suggest to Lehner that the Sphinx was once decked out in gaudy comic book colors.

For thousands of years, sand buried the colossus up to its shoulders, creating a vast disembodied head atop the eastern edge of the Sahara. Then, in 1817, a Genoese adventurer, Capt. Giovanni Battista Caviglia, led 160 men in the first modern attempt to dig out the Sphinx. They could not hold back the sand, which poured into their excavation pits nearly as fast as they could dig it out. The Egyptian archaeologist Selim Hassan finally freed the statue from the sand in the late 1930s. "The Sphinx has thus emerged into the landscape out of shadows of what seemed to be an impenetrable oblivion," the *New York Times* declared.

The question of who built the Sphinx has long vexed Egyptologists and archaeologists. Lehner, Hawass and others agree it was Pharaoh Khafre, who ruled Egypt during the Old Kingdom, which began around 2,600 B.C. and lasted some 500 years before giving way to civil war and famine. It's known from hieroglyphic texts that Khafre's father, Khufu, built the 481-foot-tall Great Pyramid, a quarter mile from where the Sphinx would later be built. Khafre, following a tough act, constructed his own pyramid, ten feet shorter than his father's, also a quarter of a mile behind the Sphinx. Some of the evidence linking Khafre with the Sphinx comes from Lehner's research, but the idea dates back to 1853.

That's when a French archaeologist named Auguste Mariette unearthed a life-size statue of Khafre, carved with startling realism from black volcanic rock, amid the ruins of a building he discovered adjacent to the Sphinx that would later be called the Valley Temple. What's more, Mariette found the remnants of a stone causeway—a paved, processional road—connecting the Valley Temple to a mortuary temple next to Khafre's pyramid. Then, in 1925, French archaeologist and engineer Emile Baraize probed the sand directly in front of the Sphinx and discovered yet another Old Kingdom building—now called the Sphinx Temple—strikingly similar in its ground plan to the ruins Mariette had already found.

Despite these clues that a single master building plan tied the Sphinx to Khafre's pyramid and his temples, some experts continued to speculate that Khufu or other pharaohs had built the statue. Then, in 1980, Lehner recruited a young German geologist, Tom Aigner, who suggested a novel way of showing that the Sphinx was an integral part of Khafre's larger building complex. Limestone is the result of mud, coral and the shells of plankton-like creatures compressed together over tens of millions of years. Looking at samples from the Sphinx Temple and the Sphinx itself, Aigner and Lehner inventoried the different fossils making up the limestone. The fossil fingerprints showed that the blocks used to build the wall of the temple must have come from the ditch surrounding the Sphinx. Apparently, workmen, probably using ropes and wooden sledges, hauled away the quarried blocks to construct the temple as the Sphinx was being carved out of the stone.

That Khafre arranged for construction of his pyramid, the temples and the Sphinx seems increasingly likely. "Most scholars believe, as I do," Hawass wrote in his 2006 book, *Mountain of the Pharaohs,* "that the Sphinx represents Khafre and forms an integral part of his pyramid complex."

But who carried out the backbreaking work of creating the Sphinx? In 1990, an American tourist was riding in the desert half a mile south of the Sphinx when she was thrown from her horse after it stumbled on a low mud-brick wall. Hawass investigated and discovered an Old Kingdom cemetery. Some 600 people were buried there, with tombs belonging to overseers—identified by inscriptions recording their names and titles—surrounded by the humbler tombs of ordinary laborers.

Near the cemetery, nine years later, Lehner discovered his Lost City. He and Hawass had been aware since the mid-1980s that there were buildings at that site. But it wasn't until they excavated and mapped the area that they realized it was a settlement bigger than ten football fields and dating to Khafre's reign. At its heart were four clusters of eight long mud-brick barracks. Each structure had the elements of an ordinary house—a pillared porch, sleeping platforms and a kitchen—that was enlarged to accommodate around 50 people sleeping side by side. The barracks, Lehner says, could have accommodated between 1,600 to 2,000 workers—or more, if the sleeping quarters were on two levels. The workers' diet indicates they weren't slaves. Lehner's team found remains of mostly male cattle under 2 years old—in other words, prime beef. Lehner thinks ordinary Egyptians may have rotated in and out of the work crew under some sort of national service or feudal obligation to their superiors.

This past fall, at the behest of "Nova" documentary makers, Lehner and Rick Brown, a professor of sculpture at the Massachusetts College of Art, attempted to learn more about construction of the Sphinx by sculpting a scaled-down version of its missing nose from a limestone block, using replicas of ancient tools found on the Giza plateau and depicted in tomb paintings. Forty-five centuries ago, the Egyptians lacked iron or bronze tools. They mainly used stone hammers, along with copper chisels for detailed finished work.

Bashing away in the yard of Brown's studio near Boston, Brown, assisted by art students, found that the copper chisels

The Way it Was?

Egyptologists believe the Sphinx, pyramids and other parts of the two-square-mile Giza complex align with the sun at key times, reinforcing the pharoah's role in sustaining the divine order.

Lehner's vision of the restored Sphinx after the 15th century B.C. includes a statue of Thutmose IV's father, Amenhotep II, atop an engraved granite slab.

became blunt after only a few blows before they had to be resharpened in a forge that Brown constructed out of a charcoal furnace. Lehner and Brown estimate one laborer might carve a cubic foot of stone in a week. At that rate, they say, it would take 100 people three years to complete the Sphinx.

Exactly what Khafre wanted the Sphinx to do for him or his kingdom is a matter of debate, but Lehner has theories about that, too, based partly on his work at the Sphinx Temple. Remnants of the temple walls are visible today in front of the Sphinx. They surround a courtyard enclosed by 24 pillars. The temple plan is laid out on an east-west axis, clearly marked by a pair of small niches or sanctuaries, each about the size of a closet. The Swiss archaeologist Herbert Ricke, who studied the temple in the late 1960s, concluded the axis symbolized the movements of the sun; an east-west line points to where the sun rises and sets twice a year at the equinoxes, halfway between midsummer and midwinter. Ricke further argued that each pillar represented an hour in the sun's daily circuit.

Lehner spotted something perhaps even more remarkable. If you stand in the eastern niche during sunset at the March or September equinoxes, you see a dramatic astronomical event: the sun appears to sink into the shoulder of the Sphinx and, beyond that, into the south side of the Pyramid of Khafre on the horizon. "At the very same moment," Lehner says, "the shadow of the Sphinx and the shadow of the pyramid, both symbols of the king, become merged silhouettes. The Sphinx itself, it seems, symbolized the pharaoh presenting offerings to the sun god in the court of the temple." Hawass concurs, saying the Sphinx represents Khafre as Horus, the Egyptians' revered royal falcon god, "who is giving offerings with his two paws to his father, Khufu, incarnated as the sun god, Ra, who rises and sets in that temple."

Equally intriguing, Lehner discovered that when one stands near the Sphinx during the summer solstice, the sun appears to set midway between the silhouettes of the pyramids of Khafre and Khufu. The scene resembles the hieroglyph *akhet,* which can be translated as "horizon" but also symbolized the cycle of life and rebirth. "Even if coincidental, it is hard to imagine the Egyptians not seeing this ideogram," Lehner wrote in the *Archive of Oriental Research.* "If somehow intentional, it ranks as an example of architectural illusionism on a grand, maybe the grandest, scale."

If Lehner and Hawass are right, Khafre's architects arranged for solar events to link the pyramid, Sphinx and temple. Collectively Lehner describes the complex as a cosmic engine, intended to harness the power of the sun and other gods to resurrect the soul of the pharaoh. This transformation not only guaranteed eternal life for the dead ruler but also sustained the universal natural order, including the passing of the seasons, the annual flooding of the Nile and the daily lives of the people. In this sacred cycle of death and revival, the Sphinx may have stood for many things: as an image of Khafre the dead king, as the sun god incarnated in the living ruler and as guardian of the underworld and the Giza tombs.

But it seems Khafre's vision was never fully realized. There are signs the Sphinx was unfinished. In 1978, in a corner of the statue's quarry, Hawass and Lehner found three stone blocks, abandoned as laborers were dragging them to build the Sphinx Temple. The north edge of the ditch surrounding the Sphinx contains segments of bedrock that are only partially quarried. Here the archaeologists also found the remnants of a workman's lunch and tool kit—fragments of a beer or water jar and stone hammers. Apparently the workers walked off the job.

The enormous temple-and-Sphinx complex might have been the pharaoh's resurrection machine, but, Lehner is fond of saying, "nobody turned the key and switched it on." By the time the Old Kingdom finally broke apart around 2,130 B.C., the desert sands had begun to reclaim the Sphinx. It would sit ignored for the next seven centuries, when it spoke to a young royal.

According to the legend engraved on a pink granite slab between the Sphinx's paws, the Egyptian prince Thutmose went hunting in the desert, grew tired and lay down in the shade of the Sphinx. In a dream, the statue, calling itself Horemakhet—or Horus-in-the-Horizon, the earliest known Egyptian name for the statue—addressed him. It complained about its ruined body and the encroaching sand. Horemakhet then offered Thutmose the throne in exchange for help.

Whether or not the prince actually had this dream is unknown. But when he became Pharaoh Thutmose IV, he helped introduce a Sphinx-worshiping cult to the New Kingdom (1550–1070 B.C.). Across Egypt, sphinxes appeared everywhere in sculptures, reliefs and paintings, often depicted as a potent symbol of royalty and the sacred power of the sun.

Based on Lehner's analysis of the many layers of stone slabs placed like tilework over the Sphinx's crumbling surface, he believes the oldest slabs may date back as far as 3,400 years to Thutmose's time. In keeping with the legend of Horemakhet, Thutmose may well have led the first attempt to restore the Sphinx.

When Lehner is in the United States, typically about six months per year, he works out of an office in Boston, the headquarters of Ancient Egypt Research Associates, a nonprofit organization Lehner directs that excavates the Lost City and trains young Egyptologists. At a meeting with him at his office this past fall, he unrolled one of his countless maps of the Sphinx on a table. Pointing to a section where an old tunnel had cut into the statue, he said the elements had taken a toll on the Sphinx in the first few centuries after it was built. The porous rock soaks up moisture, degrading the limestone. For Lehner, this posed yet another riddle—what was the source of so much moisture in Giza's seemingly bone-dry desert?

The Sahara has not always been a wilderness of sand dunes. German climatologists Rudolph Kuper and Stefan Kröpelin, analyzing the radiocarbon dates of archaeological sites, recently concluded that the region's prevailing climate pattern changed around 8,500 B.C., with the monsoon rains that covered the tropics moving north. The desert sands sprouted rolling grasslands punctuated by verdant valleys, prompting people to begin settling the region in 7,000 B.C. Kuper and Kröpelin say this green Sahara came to an end between 3,500 B.C. and 1,500 B.C., when the monsoon belt returned to the tropics and the desert reemerged. That date range is 500 years later than prevailing theories had suggested.

Further studies led by Kröpelin revealed that the return to a desert climate was a gradual process spanning centuries. This transitional period was characterized by cycles of ever-decreasing rains and extended dry spells. Support for this theory can be found in recent research conducted by Judith Bunbury, a geologist at the University of Cambridge. After studying sediment samples in the Nile Valley, she concluded that climate change in the Giza region began early in the Old Kingdom, with desert sands arriving in force late in the era.

The work helps explain some of Lehner's findings. His investigations at the Lost City revealed that the site had eroded dramatically—with some structures reduced to ankle level over a period of three to four centuries after their construction. "So I had this realization," he says, "Oh my God, this buzz saw that cut our site down is probably what also eroded the Sphinx." In his view of the patterns of erosion on the Sphinx, intermittent wet periods dissolved salt deposits in the limestone, which recrystallized on the surface, causing softer stone to crumble while harder layers formed large flakes that would be blown away by desert winds. The Sphinx, Lehner says, was subjected to constant "scouring" during this transitional era of climate change.

"It's a theory in progress," says Lehner. "If I'm right, this episode could represent a kind of 'tipping point' between different climate states—from the wetter conditions of Khufu and Khafre's era to a much drier environment in the last centuries of the Old Kingdom."

The implication is that the Sphinx and the pyramids, epic feats of engineering and architecture, were built at the end of a special time of more dependable rainfall, when pharaohs could marshal labor forces on an epic scale. But then, over the centuries, the landscape dried out and harvests grew more precarious. The pharaoh's central authority gradually weakened, allowing provincial officials to assert themselves—culminating in an era of civil war.

Today, the Sphinx is still eroding. Three years ago, Egyptian authorities learned that sewage dumped in a nearby canal was causing a rise in the local water table. Moisture was drawn up into the body of the Sphinx and large flakes of limestone were peeling off the statue.

Hawass arranged for workers to drill test holes in the bedrock around the Sphinx. They found the water table was only 15 feet beneath the statue. Pumps have been installed nearby to divert the groundwater. So far, so good. "Never say to anyone that we saved the Sphinx," he says. "The Sphinx is the oldest patient in the world. All of us have to dedicate our lives to nursing the Sphinx all the time."

EVAN HADINGHAM is senior science editor of the PBS series "Nova." Its *"Riddles of the Sphinx"* was to air January 19.

Journey to the Seven Wonders

Though only one of the ancient marvels still stands, they still engage our imagination—and launch a thousand tours—more than two millennia later.

Tony Perrottet

Visitors to the Lobby of the Empire State Building in Midtown Manhattan are often surprised to find a series of pictorial stained-glass panels. Added in the 1960s, they were meant to link the great skyscraper to other engineering triumphs. These triumphs, however, are not the great symbols of American modernity you might expect—other massive steel-and-concrete structures like the Hoover Dam or the Panama Canal—but the Seven Wonders of the Ancient World.

The colorful lobby paintings make no attempt at accuracy. Rather, they echo fantasies of the ancient monuments that have been current since the Renaissance—but they are mysteriously inspiring all the same: the Pyramids of Giza, the Pharos of Alexandria, the Temple of Artemis in Ephesus, the Mausoleum at Halicarnassus, the Colossus of Rhodes, the Hanging Gardens of Babylon, the Statue of Zeus at Olympia.

Why should a collection of monuments more than two millennia old still capture the imagination—especially when six of the seven are no longer standing?

"It's that word 'wonder,' " says David Gilman Romano, professor of classics at the University of Pennsylvania. "If you just called them the Seven Architectural Marvels, it wouldn't have the same impact." Then, too, the one that does survive—the Pyramids of Giza—is sufficiently stunning to convince us that the ancients weren't exaggerating the splendor of the other six.

It's also our passion for ordering the world. "We are living in a time very much like that of the Hellenic period," says Larissa Bonfante, professor of classics at New York University. "The Greeks loved to have things categorized—they loved anything out of the ordinary—and so do we." In our chaotic age, bombarded as we are with new technologies and rapid cultural change, we still seem to yearn for the security of mutually acknowledged "greats"—whether it be Impressionist painters, *Citizen Kane,* the Washington Monument, Cartier-Bresson photographs or the Hanging Gardens of Babylon.

One of the first-known lists of wonders was drawn up in the third century B.C., when a Greek scholar at the Library of Alexandria, Callimachus of Cyrene (305–240 B.C.), wrote a treatise called "A collection of wonders in lands throughout the world."

The essay has been lost, but his choices may have become the basis for later selections, such as the famous list attributed to the engineer Philo of Byzantium around 250 B.C. Of course, the whole idea of Seven Wonders started with antiquity's fondness for the number seven: being indivisible, it gave each of its elements equal status and so enjoyed a privileged position in numerology.

The list also reflected a shift in Western attitudes toward the world, as thinkers began to celebrate man-made creations along with those of the gods. In the wake of Alexander the Great's conquests of the Persian Empire and parts of India (334–325 B.C.), Greeks marveled at their own achievements. "Like the sun," raves Philo of the Hanging Gardens, "beauty dazzling in its brilliance."

From their inception, the ancient Wonders were also rooted in human curiosity. In fact, the sites originally were not called "Wonders" at all, but *theamata,* "things to be seen," preferably in person. In the Hellenic era, wealthy and erudite Greeks traveled by land and sea around the cultural centers of the eastern Mediterranean, broadening their education firsthand. Although the lands conquered by Alexander the Great had dissolved into separate kingdoms by the time Philo compiled his list, they were still ruled by Greek-speaking dynasties, and while travel was not yet as safe as it would become under the Roman Empire, the network of Greek culture extended far and wide, offering an open invitation to explore.

Today one can follow the itinerary of an ancient traveler as he—a peripatetic Greek scholar of that time was almost always male—sought out the magnificent Seven. Along the route, he would find passable highway inns and cheap roadside restaurants. At the sites themselves, professional tour guides called *exegetai,* or "explainers," jostled for commissions ("Zeus protect me from your guides at Olympia!" prayed one first-century B.C. antiquarian worn down by their harangues). There were papyrus guidebooks to consult before departing and vendors with whom to haggle over souvenirs: a cheap glass vial engraved with an image of the Pharos of Alexandria has been found by archaeologists as far away as Afghanistan.

The Statue of Zeus at Olympia

Departing in the Shadow of the Acropolis from Athens, the traditional center of ancient learning, a scholar-tourist of 250 B.C. would likely have set off on his grand tour with a couple of servants and a pair of pack mules to carry the luggage. The first and easiest Wonder to visit was the great sculptor Phidias' (c. 485–425 B.C.) Statue of Zeus (completed around 435 B.C.) at Olympia, a religious sanctuary in southern Greece and the site of the Olympic Games. An energetic walker could cover the 210 miles in ten days. Arriving at Olympia, visitors beheld a walled enclave where a trio of Doric temples, 70 altars and hundreds of statues of past Olympic victors created a dazzling sculpture garden. The most impressive of the structures was the Temple of Zeus, built between 466 and 456 B.C. and resembling the Parthenon in Athens. Through its grand bronze doors, a constant stream of travelers passed into the flickering torchlight, there to behold a glowering, 40-foot-high, gold-and-ivory figure of the King of the Gods seated on a throne, his features framed by a leonine mane of hair.

"It seems that if Zeus were to stand up," wrote the Greek geographer Strabo, who visited the statue early in the first century B.C., "he would unroof the temple." Beyond its stunning size, viewers were struck by the majesty of the image's expression—even stray dogs were said to be cowed. The sculptor had captured both Zeus' invincible divinity and his humanity. Roman general Aemilius Paullus (c. 229–160 B.C.), an earlier visitor, "was moved to his soul, as if he had beheld the god in person," while the Greek orator Dio Chrysostom wrote that a single glimpse of the statue would make a man forget his earthly troubles.

The Colossus of Rhodes

From Olympia, our intrepid traveler would have caught a merchant ship from the isthmus of Corinth, sailing eastward some 300 miles across the pellucid waters of the Aegean. Since there was no exclusive passenger service, one simply negotiated a price with the ship's captain and took a place on deck. One's servants would arrange the creature comforts, leaving the traveler to enjoy the view and make small talk with fellow passengers.

Arriving a few days later at their destination, the bustling island of Rhodes, the travelers would have been greeted with a breathtaking sight. There, towering majestically above the island's port, so crowded with ships' masts that it was said to resemble a field of wheat, stood a 110-foot-high Colossus—a gleaming bronze statue of the Greek sun god Helios. It was long believed that the statue straddled the harbor entrance, but modern archaeologists say this would not have been possible with the bronze-casting techniques available to the sculptor, Chares of Lindos, when he erected it between 294 and 282 B.C. While not even a drawing of the statue survives, scholars theorize the Colossus was an upright figure holding a torch aloft in one hand not unlike the Statue of Liberty; Helios' face was quite possibly modeled after Alexander the Great's. Yet, for all its majesty, the Colossus turned out to be the most fragile Wonder of them all—standing for only 56 years before collapsing in an earthquake in 226 B.C. "Even lying on the ground, it is a marvel," wrote Roman scholar Pliny the Elder in the first century A.D. "Few people can even put their arms around the figure's thumb, and each of its fingers is larger than most statues."

The Temple of Artemis in Ephesus

The Colossus would have made an appropriate introduction to the opulence of Asia Minor (modern Turkey), where the temple of Artemis mixed Oriental splendor and Hellenic artistry. Size mattered in the ancient world, and in the ostentatious port of Ephesus, citizens built their greatest temple to tower above the city skyline. Though the Parthenon of Athens was regarded as the most perfectly proportioned of all buildings, the Temple of Artemis overwhelmed it in scale. Estimates suggest the interior was about 425 feet long and 255 feet wide, making it nearly as cavernous as New York City's Grand Central Terminal. One hundred twenty-seven columns, painted in gaudy colors, supported its huge ceiling; some visitors felt lost in the dizzying forest of pillars, as imposing as sequoia trunks. Guides warned tourists not to stare at the temple's polished white-marble walls lest they be struck blind by their brilliance. Swathed in clouds of incense, a statue of the mother goddess beckoned with open arms. This was not the svelte, athletic huntress Artemis of Greek lore but a majestic, maternal creation from the East, whose multiple breasts hung like papayas from her torso. Among eunuch priests offering sacrifice at the statue's feet, silversmiths peddled souvenir miniatures of the temple and goddess for the pagan faithful. "Only in Heaven has the Sun ever looked upon its equal," gushed Greek author Antipater around 100 B.C.

The Mausoleum at Halicarnassus

No less splendor graced the Mausoleum, rising 140 feet into the air like a gigantic wedding cake above the turquoise harbor of Halicarnassus, now the modern port of Bodrum on the so-called Turkish Riviera, about 60 miles from the Colossus. Built, legend has it, around 350 B.C. for King Mausolos, the ruler of Caria, by his grief-stricken sister-wife, Artemisia, the Mausoleum was an art lover's fantasy whose tiers teemed with more than a hundred statues of heroes, kings and Amazon warriors, carved by the five greatest Greek sculptors of the day. "Even today," noted Pliny the Elder in 75 A.D., "the hands of the sculptors seem to vie with one another in artistry" The glittering confection was topped with a statue believed to be of the dead king and his wife riding a golden chariot.

The Lighthouse of Alexandria

Sailing south to Egypt, a journey of several days, travelers up to 50 miles out to sea could spot the fifth—and the only practical—ancient Wonder: the Pharos, or lighthouse, of Alexandria, whose orange flame guided ship pilots along the Nile

Delta's treacherous coastline. Looming above Alexandria's busy Eastern Harbor and surrounded by palm trees and statues of the Pharaohs, the 445-foot, three-tiered limestone tower was taller than the Statue of Liberty. At its pinnacle, a giant burning brazier topped by a statue of Zeus provided a suitably theatrical arrival to the city where Europe, Africa and Asia met. Once ashore, visitors hastened to Alexandria's Great Library to observe the scientists, astronomers and geographers who labored in what amounted to the first government-funded think tank, the Mouseion. It was these learned men who had produced the lighthouse.

The Pyramids of Giza

Eventually, our Seven Wonders tourist would likely have torn himself away from Alexandria's pleasures to sail up the Nile and gaze upon the oldest and most impressive wonder of them all—the Pyramids of Giza, three pyramids that rise, even to this day, from the undulating sands of the Giza Plateau. (For thousands of years, the Great Pyramid of Giza was the tallest and most precise stone building in the world.) The pyramids were especially dazzling in the Greek era when they were still sheathed in white limestone and covered by hieroglyphics and graffiti, glistening brilliantly in the desert sun. Surrounding the pyramids, the remains of ancient temples dating back to the Old Kingdom—the apogee of Egyptian military power and artistic skill circa 2500 B.C.—dotted the landscape. Shaven-headed priests, acting as tour guides, pretended to translate the pyramids' hieroglyphics, which they said described the construction of the monuments, including even what the Egyptian workmen who built them, between around 2580 and 2510 B.C., ate on the job.

The Hanging Gardens of Babylon

The final site on our traveler's itinerary would have been the most difficult to visit. He would have had to sail to Antioch, in Syria, then follow 500 miles of desert tracks, either on horseback or by carriage, to gaze upon the gardens' splendor. Babylon, lying some 45 miles south of modern Baghdad, was once widely regarded as the most intoxicating urban center in the world. Travelers entered the city through the Ishtar Gates, inlaid with blue glazed bricks bearing images of lions, bulls and dragons, only to behold a forest of towering ziggurats, obelisks and smoking altars by the Euphrates River.

The Hanging Gardens—a rooftop paradise of sculpted terraces, shade, and perfumed flowers—rose majestically above the human sprawl, watered by a hydraulic irrigation system. ("A work of art of royal luxury . . . suspended above the heads of spectators," noted Greek engineer Philo around 250 B.C.) The gardens had been built by King Nebuchadnezzar II (604–562 B.C.) for his wife, a princess from Media, a fertile kingdom by the southern Caspian Sea, who was homesick for greenery; it was said Alexander the Great gazed upon them from his deathbed in the royal palace in 323 B.C.

But much about the gardens is unknown, including their exact location. "The Hanging Gardens, by their very nature, cannot be definitively found," says Richard A. Billows, professor of history at Columbia University "They would not leave a very clear footprint that says 'this must have been the spot.' This isn't helped by the fact that there is no clear idea of what the gardens looked like."

Though only one of the Seven Wonders survives, it and the sites of the six others still launch a thousand package tours each year. Fascination with the Pyramids of Giza is certainly understandable; even stripped of their gleaming limestone—Arab conquerors used it as building material in the Middle Ages—the pyramids' majesty, antiquity and bulk continue to astonish visitors, even if their first glimpse is from a crowded Cairo suburban highway.

But our fascination with the "missing" Wonders is harder to explain. Two of them exist only as fragments on display in museums; others have been scorched entirely from the earth. And yet, they remain curiously compelling. Phidias' Statue of Zeus at Olympia was taken to Constantinople in the fourth century A.D. and was later destroyed in a palace fire, but the sanctuary itself—near the first Olympic Stadium through overgrown ruins buzzing with bees—remains one of the most visited attractions in Greece. All that is left of the Temple of Zeus is its foundation, but the spot where the statue stood has been identified. In 1958, archaeologists found, some 50 yards from the temple ruins, the workshop in which the artist Phidias sculpted the statue in the fifth century B.C.—including pieces of ivory and the base of a bronze drinking cup engraved with the words "I belong to Phidias" in classical Greek.

In Rhodes, hordes of tourists cluster each summer at Mandraki Harbor, where the Colossus is thought to have stood. Around A.D. 650, more than eight centuries after its collapse, it was broken up by Arab plunderers and sold as scrap metal. Today, not a toenail remains, though local entrepreneurs peddle souvenir T-shirts, spoons and cups emblazoned with the statue's image. (In 1999, the citizens of Rhodes announced a memorial to be built on the site, though work has yet to begin.)

As for the two Wonders of Asia Minor—the Temple of Artemis and the Mausoleum—they were devastated by earthquakes, barbarians and vengeful Christians. Scraps of both lie in the British Museum in London, but their sites are hauntingly bare. In an ironic genuflection to the cycles of history, chunks of the Mausoleum's original masonry were used to refortify the Castle of St. Peter at Bodrum, which was restored in the 1970s as a museum dedicated to underwater archaeology.

And, as the city of Alexandria reminds us, there is always hope for finding "lost" Wonders. In 1994, Asra el Bakri, an Egyptian filmmaker creating a documentary about Alexandria's Eastern Harbor, noticed some huge stone blocks just below the water's surface off Fort Qait-Bey; on a promontory at the heart of the old city. Within a year, French marine archaeologists had catalogued just under 3,000 chunks of masonry, some of which is thought to be the lighthouse, scattered about the ocean floor. Soon they were raising the magnificent statues that once stood by its side. The sculptures are believed to have fallen there during earthquakes that struck the region from late antiquity to the 14th century A.D.

"As a news story, it was definitely very sexy" says Colin Clement, spokesman for the Centre d'Etudes Alexandrines (CEA), the French organization leading the work. "It seemed like everyone wanted to film or photograph what we were doing." More recently, marine archaeologists discovered the frame of a nearly 40-foot-high double door that was once part of the lighthouse. Using computer graphics, CEA archaeologists are now piecing together how the edifice would have looked and functioned. "Little by little, from campaign to campaign, we have more results," says Jean-Yves Empereur, director of the CEA, emphasizing that he is attempting to reconstruct all of ancient Alexandria graphically, not just a single monument.

One tour company, ignoring warnings that the harbor's untreated sewage may cause typhoid, offers recreational diving to the lighthouse stones as well as to two dozen fragmented sphinxes on the sea bottom. For its part, the Egyptian government has floated plans for an underwater marine park, which tourists would visit in glass-bottomed boats. "Why not?" says Clement. "What's the point of doing the work if it's just for a few academics reading fusty obscure journals?"

Of course, one Wonder has dropped off today's grand tour entirely—the Hanging Gardens. "Things have been going very badly for Babylon over the last 20 years," says Harriet Crawford, chairman of the British School of Archaeology in Iraq. Saddam Hussein's "reconstruction" program, begun in 1987, devastated the Mesopotamian city's venerable ruins. As a self-styled new Nebuchadnezzar, Hussein built a luxurious palace on a hill above the excavations of the original royal palace, then ordered the ancient edifice rebuilt using bricks stamped with his name. The Hanging Gardens—Babylon's trademark feature—played a key role in this farce: courtyards and passageways were built to integrate the supposed site of the gardens into the reconstruction. Ironically new research carried out by Stephanie Dalley and others of the Oriental Institute at Oxford University suggests the gardens may not have been in Babylon at all, but in Nineveh, the ancient capital of Assyria in what is now northern Iraq. Nor are they thought to have been built by Nebuchadnezzar, but an Assyrian king, Sennacherib.

Misguided though it was, the work in Babylon shows the power of the past to shape the present. In seeking to connect himself to Iraq's most glorious era, "Hussein saw the significance of Babylon," says Crawford. "He used it as a symbol of national identity and triumph, to unite all the factions in Iraq."

The fate of the original Seven Wonders has long provoked a wide spectrum of reactions, from melancholy meditations on human vanity to the transience of man's achievements. But if their most obvious lesson is that our finest creations will one day turn to rubble, it is a lesson that we resolutely refuse to learn. Which is only as it should be, as the ancient Wonders' durability if only in our imagination—so eloquently testifies.

Travel writer **TONY PERROTTET** is the author of *Pagan Holiday: On the Trail of Ancient Roman Tourists* (Random House, 2002).

The Coming of the Sea Peoples

A low-tech revolution in Bronze Age battlefield tactics changed the history of the Western world.

Neil Asher Silberman

In the long annals of Western military history, one important group of battlefield innovators—whose archaeological traces have been uncovered from mainland Greece to the coasts of Lebanon and Israel—has often been overlooked. Around 1200 B.C., a wave of sword-wielding warriors streamed southward across the Aegean and eastward toward Asia Minor, Cyprus, and Canaan. By around 1175, some of them had reached the borders of Egypt, where they were finally repulsed by the land and sea forces of Pharaoh Ramesses III. Yet in their stunning military successes throughout the region, these warriors exerted an enormous impact on the development of ancient warfare and proved instrumental in the transformation of Mediterranean society. In subsequent centuries, the rising kingdoms of Israel and Phoenicia and the city-states of Classical Greece all adopted their tactics, arms, and strategic mentality.

Who were these invading forces and where did they come from? What was it about their weapons and tactics that proved to be so deadly to the great Late Bronze Age empires—and so influential in shaping the societies that succeeded them? For the past 150 years, historians have recognized that the twelfth century B.C. was a time of great upheaval, in which ancient empires were toppled and new societies were born. They have ascribed this dramatic transformation not to innovations in warfare but to vast population movements, spearheaded by a coalition of northern tribes and ethnic groups who are mentioned repeatedly in ancient Egyptian inscriptions—and whom nineteenth-century scholars dubbed the "Sea Peoples" or the "Peoples of the Sea." These Sea Peoples were not simply Bronze Age Vikings but were a haphazard collection of farmers, warriors, and craftspeople, as well as sailors who originated in the highlands of the Balkans and the coastlands of Asia Minor. Their only common trait seems to have been their movement across the Mediterranean toward the centers of trade and agriculture of the Near East.

Their impact on the Near Eastern empires was dramatic, though scholars are deeply divided on the reasons. Some maintain that the Sea Peoples were displaced from their homelands by famine, natural disasters, or political breakdown and were able to overcome the sophisticated, cosmopolitan empires of the Mediterranean by their sheer barbarian savagery. Others suggest that a closer analysis of the historical records and archaeological remains from this period can pinpoint a more specific agent of change connected to the era's vast population movements. There is reason to believe that only a small, specialized class of professional warriors, in the midst of the much more massive migratory waves, was responsible for the military attacks of the Sea Peoples. As a skilled caste of mercenary foot soldiers who drifted southward to find employment in kingdoms throughout the region, this group of Sea Peoples had both the tactical know-how and the weaponry to recognize—and demonstrate—just how pitifully vulnerable the great Late Bronze Age powers had become. The civilization of the Late Bronze Age (c. 1550 to c. 1200 B.C.), to which these northern mercenary contingents gravitated, was typified by grand monuments, opulent palace cultures, and some of the most complex administrative and accounting systems the Mediterranean world had ever seen. In Egypt, the powerful pharaohs of the New Kingdom resided amid the splendor of Thebes in Upper Egypt. There they prospered from the rich agricultural produce of the Nile valley and enjoyed the luxury goods acquired from a far-flung trade network reaching from Africa and the southern coast of Arabia to the islands of the Aegean Sea. To the north of Egypt, in the city-states of Canaan, on the island of Cyprus, and at the cosmopolitan port of Ugarit, local dynasties ruled over docile peasant populations and vied with one another for diplomatic or commercial advantage. In the vast continental expanse of Asia Minor, the Hittite empire maintained its feudal rule from the stronghold of Hattusas. And across the Aegean Sea, on mainland Greece, Crete, and the islands, a unique palace-based civilization of regional rulers, with their coteries of servants, craftsmen, priests, and mercenary forces, comprised the chivalric society that was at least partially reflected in the physical details of Homer's *Iliad*.

Despite these differences in styles and traditions, all the empires of the Late Bronze Age were united in their dependence on a single military technology. No self-respecting kingdom could exist for long without attack forces based on the light battle chariot, which was then the most sophisticated and reliable vehicle of war. The chariots of this period were constructed with

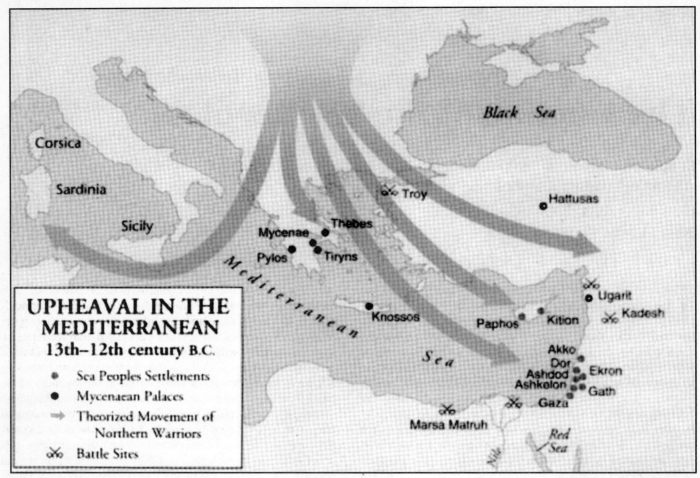

UPHEAVAL IN THE MEDITERRANEAN
13th–12th century B.C.

● Sea Peoples Settlements
● Mycenaean Palaces
➡ Theorized Movement of Northern Warriors
✗ Battle Sites

Geosystems, Columbia, MD

Not long after appearing in Egypt, Sea People warriors fought for the Egyptians at Kadesh (c. 1275 B.C.). They would become agents of radical change, likely bringing down Mycenaean civilization and enfeebling the great empires of the ancient world.

considerable skill—and at considerable cost—from sturdy yet highly flexible laminates of wood and bone that enabled them to travel at high speed and with great maneuverability. Propelled by a specially bred and trained two-horse team, the chariot was manned by a professional driver and a combat archer, whose composite bow, also constructed of laminated materials, could launch arrows with extraordinary accuracy and force. These factors all added up to make the light chariot a high-powered, highly mobile weapons delivery system that could swoop down on static infantry forces with frightening speed and velocity.

The figure of the charioteer—as an embodiment of individual skill and courage—became, in many respects, a symbol for the age. The firepower of the new-style chariots was so overwhelming on the battlefield that no ruler who hoped to maintain his throne against his local or regional rivals could afford to be without them—any more than any truly modern nation can afford to be without an effective air force. As a result, Bronze Age kings, pharaohs, and princes scrambled to assemble chariot forces. And just as the kings and potentates of other eras strutted in the guise of knights-errant, cavalry officers, or naval commanders, Late Bronze Age Egyptian pharaohs and Mycenaean, Hittite, and Canaanite kings were all grandly depicted on their monuments in the pose of triumphant charioteers. Yet as the chariot buildup continued through the fourteenth and thirteenth centuries B.C., and as chariot formations gradually rendered infantry battles obsolete in conflicts between rival city-states or empires, a costly arms race began to get out of control.

By the time of the Hittite-Egyptian confrontation at the battle of Kadesh in Syria in 1275 B.C., relatively modest chariot corps of a few dozen vehicles had expanded to enormous contingents. At Kadesh, the Hittite chariot corps alone numbered at least 3,500 vehicles. This placed a strain on even the wealthiest kingdoms. The cost of chariots and horses was substantial. And the skilled craftsmen, chariot drivers, archers, and horse trainers required to maintain the battle-readiness of a kingdom's chariot force could—and did—demand lavish personal support, generous land grants, and conspicuously privileged status at each court they served. Thus, at times of shortage brought about by drought, flood, disease, or poor crop yields, the demands of the charioteers and their staffs could force individual kingdoms toward the breaking point. And yet the Late Bronze Age powers had all become dangerously dependent on this method of warfare. Little wonder, then, that when its tactical vulnerability was discovered, the whole edifice came tumbling down.

The result was one of the great turning points in history dubbed by some the Great Catastrophe. Within the span of just a few decades before and after 1200 B.C., the Bronze Age civilizations of Greece and Asia Minor were shattered, and Egypt gradually lost its role as a regional superpower. At the same time, the sudden arrival and settlement of new peoples on Cyprus and along the coast of Canaan ushered in a new era of small kingdoms and city-states.

Just beyond the confines of the civilized regions of the Mediterranean world, in the mountainous areas of the Balkan peninsula and in the rugged hinterlands of western and southern Asia Minor, the chariot had no power. It was suited only to action on the relatively level battlefields of the lowlands and the plains. On the occasions when the great empires felt the need to mount punitive expeditions against the inhabitants of the highlands, they dispatched infantry forces for brief, brutal demonstrations of force. For the most part, however, the highlanders were left alone as long as they handed over the demanded tribute and did nothing to interfere with the main routes of trade. Among the tribal societies of these regions, internal disputes were settled in contests of single combat between experienced professional warriors. Archaeological finds from warriors' tombs across western and central Europe, from Scandinavia to the Black Sea, have provided evidence of this mobile, deadly kind of hand-to-hand warfare, waged with long, two-edged swords that could be swung with enough momentum to decapitate an opponent or cut off a limb. Small round shields seem also to have been used to deflect rapid parries. Helmets of various designs and light body armor of many shapes and materials were also common in this individualistic style of war. In terms of weaponry and personal aggressiveness, the warriors of the frontier areas were much more formidable than the typical infantries of the Mediterranean empires, whose members were usually conscripted from the local peasantry, poorly trained, and armed only with short daggers, spears, or clubs.

The reason for the neglect of the infantry by the Mediterranean empires was the overwhelming importance accorded to chariot forces, which comprised the main tactical elements. Lines of chariots would charge against each other like modern tank forces, and, having penetrated or outflanked the opposing formation, would wheel around quickly and charge against the opposing chariots again. Foot soldiers were used in the decidedly secondary capacities of guard duty, road escort, frontier patrols, and routine police work. The only battlefield function reserved for foot soldiers was as "runners" who raced behind and among the chariots, snatching up fallen enemy booty and finishing off wounded enemy chariot crews. This mopping-up function was of little tactical significance. But by the time of the battle of Kadesh, the appearance of a new kind of runner proved to be an omen of the way that subsequent wars in the Mediterranean region would be waged—and won.

In a provocative new book entitled *The End of the Bronze Age: Changes in Warfare and the Catastrophe, ca. 1200 B.C.,* Robert Drews, a professor of ancient history at Vanderbilt University, argues that the arrival of northern-style warriors in the Mediterranean upset the unquestioned domination of the chariot. By so doing, it undermined the foundations of the regimes the chariots were meant to defend. Drews notes that barely ten years before the battle of Kadesh, Egyptian hieroglyphic reliefs recorded the ominous movements of a people named the "Sherden," who had arrived "in their warships from the midst of the sea." Wearing trademark horned helmets and armed with long swords and small round shields, they obviously made a profound impression on the Egyptians. By the time the Egyptian chariot forces moved north to confront the Hittites, contingents of Sherden had been recruited by the Egyptians to serve as bodyguards and particularly deadly "runners" among the chariots.

In contrast to the usual runners, who merely mopped up after the chariot charges, the Sherden apparently became an independent offensive force. They are shown in the reliefs of the battle of Kadesh using their weapons to slash, hack, and dismember enemy charioteers. Their weapons, which were originally designed for individual combat, made Sherden warriors far more mobile and adaptable to changing battlefield conditions than the traditional formations of infantry. And with significant numbers of aggressive, northern-style warriors swarming among the chariots, deflecting arrows with their shields and pouncing on disabled vehicles with long swords swinging, they would have posed a sudden, unexpected threat to the firepower and mobility of even the most impressive concentrations of chariotry. While the traditional Bronze Age foot soldiers marched together in relatively slow-moving formations and used weapons such as clubs and spears, which had only a limited radius of effectiveness, the Sherden seem to have ranged widely, pouncing on vulnerable chariot crews.

No less important, they possessed weapons far more effective in combat than those of standard Bronze Age foot soldiers. Ancient pictorial representations of Sherden runners suggest that they were also skilled in the use of the hunting javelin, commonly used in this period for felling wild game. In combination with the long sword, the hunting javelin would have been especially deadly. Drews makes a persuasive—if admittedly speculative—case for suggesting that these new weapons could transform units of runners into an effective battlefield strike force. "For the 'hunting' of chariot horses the javelin must have been ideal," Drews writes, "although it seldom would have killed the horse that it hit, the javelin would have surely brought it to a stop, thus immobilizing the other horse, the vehicle and the crew."

The battle of Kadesh ended in a stalemate between the Egyptians and the Hittites, ushering in a brief period of military balance between the two powers. But by the middle of the thirteenth century B.C., new groups of northern warriors armed with long swords and javelins were drawn in increasing numbers toward the centers of the Late Bronze Age empires, where they were destined to upset the delicate geopolitical balance. Initially, they found employment as mercenaries just as the Sherden had done. Among the names mentioned in Egyptian records and in the archives of Ugarit and the Hittite empire were—in addition to the Sherden—groups known as the Shekelesh, Tursha, Lukka, Shardana, and Ekwesh. Linguistic analysis of these names has enabled scholars to identify them with peoples mentioned in classical and biblical literature: Sicilians, Tyrrhenians, Lycians, and Achaean Greeks. The Sherden have been identified as a group originating on the island of Sardinia, or, according to some scholars, as its eventual conquerors.

It is important to recognize, however, that these Sea Peoples mentioned in the ancient records were not entire nations displaced from their homelands, but a particular military caste represented by warriors from many ethnic groups. Like the pirates and freebooters of the seventeenth-century Caribbean, their many separate nationalities were as conspicuous as the threatening uniformity of their weapons and hand-to-hand fighting techniques.

Archaeologists are generally agreed that the relative tranquility of the Late Bronze Age world following the battle of Kadesh was rocked sometime after 1250 B.C. by a great wave of destructions and upheavals that seems to have begun in the Aegean basin. The Mycenaean palace of Thebes in Boeotia was destroyed and abandoned. The flourishing city of Troy, guarding the trade routes to the Black Sea, was likewise destroyed in a great conflagration, to be succeeded by a much more modest settlement. There is suggestive evidence that these destructions may not have resulted from normal clashes between chariot forces. The hasty construction of a great fortification wall across the Isthmus of Corinth and the strengthening of the defenses around other Mycenaean palace complexes may reflect apprehensions about a far more pervasive danger, perhaps a threat by potential attackers that Bronze Age chariotry would have been unable to withstand. And those apparent fears of attack and conquest seem to have been justified, for by the middle of the next century, the destruction of all the Mycenaean palace complexes was virtually complete.

There may, of course, have been many specific, local reasons for this wave of upheaval. In some places, rivalries between regional centers could have led to the violence. In others, widespread social unrest caused by growing inequalities in late Bronze Age society may have led to local uprisings and the overthrow of the palace elite. Yet in a thought-provoking hypothesis that has already aroused considerable scholarly discussion, Drews pulls together tactical analysis, archaeological evidence, and the colorful testimony of heroic Greek myth to offer a novel reconstruction of the events. He suggests that the legendary accounts of the attacks against Thebes by a coalition of champions (immortalized by Aeschylus in his play *Seven Against Thebes*) and Homer's epic poem about the sack of Troy by Agamemnon's forces preserve memories of the first dramatic triumphs of free-lance northern infantry concentrations, fighting in the new style.

The gradually increasing scope of such encounters may suggest that news of the vulnerability of chariot forces spread among northern mercenary contingents. And in this very period, a wave of northern warriors now made their way southward in search of plunder, not employment. In looking anew at Homer's poetic metaphors about the epic battle between Achaeans and Trojans, it may well be—as Drews suggested—that the repeated description of the Achaean hero Achilles as "fleet-footed," and the characteristic description of the Trojans as "horse-taming," preserve memories of an epic clash between foot soldiers and horse-powered troops. Even though the *Iliad* was set down in writing several centuries later, at a time when chariot warfare had long been abandoned, the vivid image of Achaean soldiers streaming from the Trojan Horse may eloquently express, at least in mythic language, the sudden emergence of a new style of infantrymen—whose hidden power was revealed in an age of horse-based warfare. In their conquest of Troy, the Achaean foot soldiers departed from the empty wooden horse, thereby symbolically leaving behind the horse (and chariot) as the preferred weapons platforms of the age.

The violent events in the Aegean do not seem to have affected the great capitals and emporia of the Near East—at least not immediately. International commerce continued throughout the thirteenth century B.C., and a certain measure of prosperity was enjoyed in the royal courts of the Near East. New Kingdom Egypt (where at least some Sea People had gone to find work as mercenary runners) therefore beckoned as a tempting target for plundering attacks. The aging pharaoh Ramesses II (c. 1279–c. 1212 B.C.), after having emerged from the battle of Kadesh in a military stalemate with the Hittites, still presided over a vast territory and trade network extending from Canaan, south to Nubia, and as far west as Libya. Excavations at Late Bronze Age port cities and recovered cargoes from sunken merchant ships of this period throughout the eastern Mediterranean have emphasized the volume of international trade—and the extent of interaction between nations, cultures, and ethnic groups during this cosmopolitan age. Only recently have excavations uncovered the ruins of a once busy Late Bronze Age trade depot—littered with sherds of pottery from Mycenaean Greece, Egypt, Cyprus, and Canaan—on a sandy island known as Bates's Island off the coast of Egypt's western desert, about 120 miles east of the modern border with Libya.

It was surely no coincidence or accident that the first major attack by northern warriors on Egypt was launched from this direction. Far from being an isolated wilderness, Libya was connected to Egypt by land and sea trade routes. At a time of reported famine, it was a Libyan leader named "Meryre, Son of Did," who instigated the first major operation in which a coalition of northern warriors played a prominent role. Scholars have always puzzled over how and why Libyans forged a coalition with the various Sea Peoples. Yet the archaeological evidence of an offshore trade depot so close to Libya indicates that it was not a cultural backwater but on one of the main routes in the movement of people and goods. It is entirely conceivable that Meryre was aware of events going on elsewhere in the eastern Mediterranean, possibly through the contact his subjects had with the polyglot gangs of sailors, stevedores, and workers who were drawn into the networks of long-distance trade. More important, he seems to have been keenly aware of the recent—one might even say revolutionary—developments in the art of warfare. Indeed if Meryre had heard about recent successes achieved by northern warriors in direct assaults on chariot forces in Greece and Asia Minor, his subsequent actions in recruiting Sea People warriors for his own campaign would suddenly be understandable.

Why else would he contemplate an invasion of Egypt with only foot soldiers? If he were planning a less organized infiltration of the border lands, he would not have needed to form the grand coalition he did. Yet soon after the death of Ramesses II around 1212 B.C., Meryre began to organize a campaign against the western Nile Delta, for which he gained the cooperation of a number of warrior bands. Later Egyptian records note that they came from "the northern lands"—which could indicate an origin in any of the territories along the northern shores of the Mediterranean. The specific mention of Ekwesh, Lukka, Sherden, Shekelesh, and Tursha (identified as Achaeans, Lycians, Sardinians, Sicilians, and Tyrrhenians) suggests that Meryre's appeal attracted recruits from many lands. He promised them a share of the fertile territory and booty to be gained in attacking the forces of the new pharaoh, Merneptah, the long-lived Ramesses' already elderly son. Seen in the context of the times, Meryre thus made an audacious tactical gamble: in recruiting tens of thousands of northern-style foot soldiers along with his own sizable infantry contingents, he was confident that he could overcome the Egyptian chariotry.

As things turned out, Meryre lost his gamble but proved to be a strategist ahead of his time. Merneptah's chariots met the advancing Libyan-Sea People coalition in midsummer 1208 B.C. in the western desert, at a site probably not far from the later and also fateful battlefield of El Alamein. The Egyptian forces reportedly slew 6,000 Libyans and more than 2,200 of the invading Ekwesh, with significant casualties suffered by the other Sea Peoples as well. Yet the list of spoils taken in the battle by the Egyptians gives a clear indication of the novel nature of the encounter: more than 9,000 long swords were captured from the invaders—with only an utterly insignificant twelve Libyan chariots being seized. For the time being, the pharaoh's chariots had prevailed over massed formations of swordsmen and javelineers. But new troubles were not long in coming for the pharaoh. Frontier populations in other regions were growing restless, and Merneptah soon had to undertake a punitive campaign into Canaan, where he was forced to reassert his control over some important cities and pacify the highlands. In typically bombastic prose he reported one of the most gratifying outcomes of the encounter: "Israel is laid waste; his seed is not!" The clear, if mistaken, implication was that this people had been so thoroughly defeated that they or their descendants would never appear on the stage of history again.

The quotation, which comes from Merneptah's so-called Victory Stele at the Temple of Karnak, contains this earliest mention of the people of Israel outside the Bible, and it may also indicate the extent of the tactical revolution spreading throughout the Mediterranean world. For in the hill country of Canaan at precisely this period, c. 1250–c. 1200 B.C., archaeologists have discovered the sudden establishment of scores of hilltop villages throughout the modern area of the West Bank. Being far from the lowland Canaanite urban centers and outposts of Egyptian presence in fortresses along the coast and major trade routes, they represent the earliest settlements of the Israelites. Their defense against outside powers was not based on chariot warfare but most likely on coordinated militia campaigns. Certainly the biblical books of Joshua and Judges are filled with references

to the defeat of the Canaanite kings and the destruction of their chariot forces. Although many historians have come to question the historical reliability of the story of the Israelite Exodus from Egypt, the vivid scriptural account of the drowning in the Red Sea of the pharaoh's pursuing army—and its great chariot corps—might preserve in dreamlike narrative an indelible historical memory of an era of great victories over chariotry.

The threats by northern-style raiders against Egypt and the other great centers of the Bronze Age civilization continued to intensify in this period, with port cities, fortresses, temples, and trade depots throughout the region put to the torch, and in some cases never fully reoccupied again. It is likely that in the spreading chaos, movements of people grew more frequent. Warriors and mercenaries were on the move, of course, but so were other groups formerly serving as craftsmen, servants, or functionaries in the palace centers that had been destroyed by hostile attacks. All of these groups were the "Sea Peoples," both the victims and the perpetrators of the spreading wave of violence. In certain places on Cyprus and along the coast of Canaan, settlers from the Aegean world arrived to establish new communities in the ruins of destroyed Late Bronze Age cities. And the characteristic Mycenaean-style pottery they produced at sites such as Ashkelon, Ekron, and Ashdod in Canaan clearly indicates that whether they themselves were marauders or refugee craftsmen and officials from the destroyed palace-centers of the Aegean, the course of their lives and communities had been disrupted by upheavals throughout the Mediterranean world.

Although it is impossible to follow precisely the sequence of raids, conquests, and refugee colonizations in Greece, Cyprus, Egypt, and Canaan, there is suggestive evidence that the use of new weapons and tactics by the invaders continued to play a crucial role. In the rubble of the great trading emporium of Ugarit on the coast of modern Syria, for example, excavators have found a number of hunting javelins scattered in the destruction ruins. And the discovery of several newly cast long swords (one even bearing the royal cartouche of Merneptah!) hidden away in hoards at the time of the city's destruction may reflect a desperate, last-ditch effort by some local commanders to equip their forces with the same deadly weapons borne by the marauding Peoples of the Sea.

The last and greatest of attacks by contingents of northern warriors against the centers of Bronze Age civilization is memorialized in exacting detail on the outer walls of the Egyptian temple of Medinet Habu in Upper Egypt, built by Pharaoh Ramesses III, who ruled from c. 1186 to c. 1155 B.C. The Medinet reliefs depict what was one of the most notable events of Ramesses' reign: thousands of Egyptian foot soldiers, sailors, and archers are shown engaged in battles on land and sea against a bizarrely costumed coalition of invaders, who include—in addition to the Sherden and the Shekelesh of the earlier invasions—people known as the Tjekker, Denyen, Weshesh, and Peleset (whom scholars have identified as the biblical Philistines).

This invasion was apparently different and far more threatening than earlier actions. The tone of Ramesses III's official inscription accompanying the pictorial representations conveys an atmosphere of deep crisis that gripped Egypt when word arrived that seaborne and overland coalitions of northern warriors "who had made a conspiracy in their islands" were approaching. Although the precise origin of these warrior bands has never been pinpointed, the mention of "islands" suggests that the threat came from the direction of the Aegean Sea. Ramesses' chronicle goes on to trace the progress of the invaders across the region, in which many separate actions seem to have been combined for rhetorical purposes to heighten the drama of the events.

"All at once the lands were removed and scattered in the fray," reported the inscription in tracing the path of the invaders southward from the Hittite empire, through the cities of Cilicia, Cyprus, and Syria, toward Canaan, which was also known as Amor. "No land could stand before their arms from Hatti, Kode, Carchemish, Arzawa, Alayshia on, being cut off at one time. A camp was set up in one place in Amor. They desolated its people, and its land was like that which has never come into being. They were coming forward to Egypt, while the flame was being prepared before them," the inscription continued. "They laid their hands upon lands as far as the circuit of the earth, their hearts confident and trusting, 'Our plans will succeed!' "

In retrospect, we can see that Pharaoh Ramesses III was placed in an impossible situation in the Great Land and Sea Battles of 1175 B.C. When this last and greatest wave of Sea Peoples' invasions burst upon Egypt, Ramesses was forced to confront forces that had proved they could successfully overcome chariots—which remained the backbone of the Egyptian defense. In response, he apparently tried to change radically the fighting capabilities of his forces—as many desperate, doomed warlords have attempted to do throughout history. Indeed, as analysis of the Medinet Habu reliefs suggests, the vaunted Egyptian chariotry played almost no role in the fighting. Ramesses III's inscriptions can be seen as a commemoration of the heroism of his own infantry. He boasted that the Egyptian foot soldiers—once scorned as insignificant tactical factors—had fought "like bulls ready on the field of battle" and that the militiamen who engaged the enemy in hand-to-hand fighting aboard their ships "were like lions roaring on the mountaintops." No less significant is the fact that in one scene Ramesses himself is depicted as an unmounted archer—not a charioteer—with his two royal feet firmly planted on the bodies of fallen Sea People enemies.

Yet in discarding the ethos and discipline of chariot warfare on which his empire had become so dependent—and in mobilizing his foot soldiers to fight on the same terms and with the same weapons as the invaders—Ramesses sealed the fate of New Kingdom Egypt as surely as a defeat at the hands of the Sea Peoples would have done. For even though the Sea Peoples' invasion was repulsed, and some of the Sea Peoples, like the Philistines, were permitted to settle peacefully in colonies along the nearby coast of Canaan, Egypt would never regain its former strength. The Egyptian Empire—like all other Late Bronze Age kingdoms—had been built and maintained over hundreds of years as a towering social pyramid in which the king, his court, officers, and chariot forces reserved the pinnacle for themselves. The new method of marshaling units of highly mobile, highly motivated infantry against chariot forces required unprecedentedly large numbers of trained fighters. Egypt was never a society that viewed its general population as much more than beasts of burden; to accord peasant recruits respect and intensive training within the armed forces was something that the highly stratified society of New Kingdom Egypt found extremely difficult to do. The strict hierarchy began to crumble, and the growing power of mercenary units and local infantry bands caused widespread social unrest. By the end of the twelfth century, the power of New Kingdom Egypt was ended, and the country entered a new dark age. In contrast, the new world that unfolded in the centuries after the appearance of the Sea Peoples in Greece, Cyprus, Asia Minor, and Canaan drew its strength from the new cultural pattern, which was based on the solidarity and military might of local levies of foot soldiers, not elite units of courtly charioteers.

Chariot forces would again be used on the field of battle—as in the later campaigns of the Assyrian empire in the ninth and eighth centuries B.C.—but only in a supporting role to the infantry. And with the development of effective tack and stirrups during the subsequent centuries, the chariot could be dispensed with altogether, except perhaps as a battlefield conveyance for generals and kings. The Sea People warriors themselves were eventually assimilated into the general populations of the refugees from the great upheavals. Along the coast of Canaan and on Cyprus, new societies derived from Mycenaean models and led by descendants of refugees were born. Even in the rising kingdoms of Israel, Phoenicia, Aramea, Cilicia, Phrygia, and the city-states of Greece, where new forms of military and social organization emerged after the end of the Bronze Age, the legacy of the Sea Peoples—though dramatically transformed—could still be perceived. Just as the fleet-footed Achaean warrior Achilles became the role model for the citizen soldier of the archaic Greek polis, the image of the young David, surrounded by his band of mighty men of war, remained a cherished biblical symbol of national solidarity. And there were to be even more far-reaching developments in the use of large infantry formations as the kingdoms of Assyria and Babylonia swelled into great empires with enormous populations. Eventually, the massive formations of infantry units evolved into the Macedonian phalanx and the Roman legion.

The sweeping scenario of scattered contingents of Sea People warriors streaming together from their distant islands and hill country homes to overcome the elite chariot forces of the Bronze Age Mediterranean has not been without its critics. Scholars who still favor explanations such as natural disasters, generalized social breakdown, or the gradual cultural shift from Bronze Age chariot empires to Iron Age infantry kingdoms are skeptical of a single military cause. But without minimizing the possibility that natural or economic crises may indeed have undermined the political order and intensified social tensions, there is much to be said for the contention that only something as dramatic as the introduction of new weapons and tactics could have triggered violent upheavals on such a massive scale.

And there is, even beyond the specific questions of this remote period, a far more basic historical point. We must not merely see the episode of the "Sea Peoples" as a bizarre and bloody episode that took place in a far-off region more than

3,000 years ago. The long swords, javelins, and body armor of the invading Sea Peoples may seem quaintly rustic to us in a day of Stealth fighter-bombers and Tomahawk missiles. Yet they offer an important object lesson in the way that complacent dependency by great powers on expensive and complex military technology can suddenly be undermined. The grand catastrophe of the end of the Bronze Age and the role of the Sea Peoples in it should show us how unexpectedly simple weapons in the hands of committed warriors can topple great empires. Societies in any age can become dangerously presumptuous about the invulnerability of their advanced military technologies. Over centuries or even decades the society molds itself, in its religion, political order, and social hierarchy, to conform to the dominant technology. If that technology is undermined by groups with little stake in preserving the existing system, the results can be catastrophic. Today we speak of terrorists with homemade bombs and shoulder-fired missiles, but at the end of the Late Bronze Age in the eastern Mediterranean, it was northern warriors with long swords and hunting javelins who laid the groundwork for a dramatic transformation of society.

NEIL ASHER SILBERMAN is an author and historian specializing in the ancient history of the Near East. He is a contributing editor to *Archaeology* magazine.

I, Pillar of Justice

Frank L. Holt

Look at you looking at me. Your brow wrinkles into lines of cuneiform as your brain races to remember what makes this big black rock the pride of modern paris. Admit it: you don't have a clue what basalt really is. You can't identify the two figures carved on my face, and I seriously doubt that you can read a word of my ancient Akkadian. You probably arrived at the Louvre, like eight million others every year, more familiar with *The Da Vinci Code* than with the Code of Hammurapi. Well, c'est *la vie,* as they say around here. I can fix that—as I have fixed so much else for your struggling species. Now, try again: What should you know about me? Here's a clue: *Rock Rules!*

I, Pillar of Justice, mark an evolutionary triumph in the long, long history of stone. Before my time, for hundreds of millions of years, my lithic ancestors managed little more than the shaping and shifting of continents. After several fits and starts, a single-continent Pangaea finally divided itself into the separate land masses of our planet's present era. Along the way, my forebears learned to fashion themselves into mountains, valleys and vomiting volcanoes. Some made fossils, a magician's trick of mineralization with no real purpose but to pass the time. Only when rocks perfected the second act—erosion—before an astonished audience—you humans—did our idle fossilizing find true meaning, first as myths about giant men and then as the means to study dinosaurs. Somewhere between Pangaea and paleontology, we cultivated a brief Stone Age during which, for about 2.5 million years, my progenitors taught your progenitors the technology of tools and weapons. Men trusted in stone to capture, kill and carve their prey; to divide and defend their lands with makeshift walls and to arbitrate every dispute with spears and slings.

Then, my kind evolved and changed everything forever. I, Pillar of Justice, Pillar of Strength, showed rock a bolder way to mediate human conflict. I formed of my stony flesh something new: *words,* not weapons; *rules,* not tools. Thus, of all the things that rock has become (tabletops, T-Rex, temples, tombs), it is I who am by far the most advanced. On other branches of my phylogenetic tree, you will find obelisks—beautiful but not brainy—striving to be me. I overshadow in mind if not mass both the pyramids and the Parthenon. Mosaics? Dainty little pictures, to be sure, but I have progressed beyond gravel, to gavel. I am, after all, the rock of sages, the world's most famous code of law.

My story begins in Mesopotamia just a few millennia ago. There, after relying on rock for everything, some of your species foolishly tried to leave the Stone Age behind and start something of their own called *civilization.* This meant that men and women settled into cities, increased their crop yields through irrigation, opened trade routes to distant lands, divided themselves into different occupations and castes and invented writing to keep track of the whole experiment. Good old stone gave way to bronze for all their weapons, providing a keener edge for mutual slaughter. And, by golly, your ancestors sure did a lot more of *that* once they regressed into civilization. More people, more possessions, more inequality: It all added up to more conflict, mediated by muscle and metallurgy instead of stuff like me. War, crime and slavery inevitably increased as the role of rock declined. If your kind were to survive, stone would have to step up and lay down the law. I am the result of that evolutionary imperative.

I arrived on the scene as no more than a giant block of black basalt, a hard igneous rock cooled ages earlier from fiery magma. To save humankind, I took as my partner a member of your species named Hammurapi. (Some of you spell him Hammurabi. Humans cannot agree on anything.) He was a decent man descended from Amorites who had wandered from the western deserts into the little town of Bab-ilim ("Gateway of the God"), which you now call Babylon. In time, the immigrants became kings and, in 1792 BC, Hammurapi, the sixth in their dynasty, succeeded to the rule of their small realm. During his reign of 42 years, the new ruler of Babylon used both battle and diplomacy to extend his power over all of Mesopotamia. He secured his place among the great empire-builders of antiquity, making him the envy of such modern-day leaders as Saddam Hussein, who vaunted the "Hammurapi Division" of his Republican Guard and who, as a precondition for oil-export deals, often demanded my return from France. Hammurapi himself had no armored divisions, but his forces more than matched those of his rivals in Elam, Assyria, Larsa and Mari. For the next thousand years, Babylon would be the region's most renowned city in this new experiment called civilization.

That fame would eventually have as much to do with culture as with conquest. Gifted in mathematics, astronomy and engineering, the Babylonians built with precision, worked out square and cube roots, devised complex calendars and employed the Pythagorean theorem a full millennium before the Greeks "discovered" it. Every time you calculate an angle or glance at a clock, you pay homage to the Babylonians' choice of 60 as their base unit of measure, the foundation of the so-called sexigesimal system they adapted from the earlier Sumerians. In literature, the great Babylonian creation epic *Enuma Elish (When on High...)* mirrors the ascendancy of Babylon over Mesopotamia, and of the city's patron deity, Marduk, over the older gods Anu and Enlil. Hammurapi the Warrior, Hammurapi the Wise, cultivated the arts and sciences with a lavish hand as he led his armies to victory. A rock like me can appreciate these rare qualities in a man.

My 282 Legal Rulings Constitute the Literal Bedrock of Judicial History.

Near the end of Hammurapi's reign, I made him more illustrious than ever. I, Pillar of Justice, crowned his achievements by publishing a set of laws to govern the lives of his quarrelsome subjects. I was not the first to try this, but my success speaks for itself. All prior attempts by lesser men, using such lesser materials as crumbly clay tablets, show my superiority. Thanks to me, the name of Hammurapi would henceforth and forever be linked with the rule of law—the saving grace of human society Human, I say specifically, because if you look inside any comparable city built by bees or ants, you will never find a little stone pillar like me listing the rules that maintain insect order. No hive needs a Code of Hammurapi to prevent apiary anarchy. People, I'm afraid, are the problem.

To get everyone's attention, I knew I had to make a strong impression. I let the king polish me into a freestanding pillar called a *stele,* the ultimate message board of ancient Mesopotamia. I stand 2.25 meters (over 7') tall, my rounded conical shape topped with an arresting bas-relief carved into my basaltic face. To awe my onlookers, this image projects both earthly and heavenly power. Enthroned on the right sits Shamash the sun-god, the "Incorruptible Judge" whose piercing light exposes crime. Menacing flames rise from his shoulders. Receiving the deity's instruction, Hammurapi stands on the left. He raises his right hand to his mouth in a gesture of obeisance, just as all Babylonians did in turn when they encountered their king. This picture put people in the correct frame of mind to receive the extraordinary words cut into the remaining surfaces of my body, some 3800 lines of cuneiform covering me front and back.

As a lavish prologue, my first section pays homage to Hammurapi and his solicitude for gods and men. Some of what I say here about my partner has the ring of propaganda, I freely admit, but a certain amount of pomp was necessary at the time. This prologue enumerates at length the benefactions made by Hammurapi, "the exalted Prince of Babylon," to the many deities worshiped in his polytheistic empire. I gush that he enriched temples and cities, increased the harvest, heaped up sacrificial offerings, smote bandits, pardoned enemies, protected slaves and, not least, established peace. I call him "the King of Righteousness" and "the Salvation-Bearing Shepherd" whose mission was "to destroy the wicked, punish evil-doers and ensure that the strong no longer harmed the weak."

Next comes the important part: a collection of at least 282 legal rulings *(di-nat sharim)* that constitutes the literal bedrock of judicial history. This is our greatest gift to humankind since the Stone Age. Using mostly conditional "if-then" statements, I answer evil with punishment: "If anyone accuses another of a capital offense but fails to prove his case, then that accuser shall be put to death." This judgment is among the first five in the code, all dealing right at the start with the serious problem of bearing false witness. After all, any legal system is only as good as the evidence it allows. That is why my fifth ruling fines and removes from the bench any judge whose incompetence leads to a wrongful decision. Following these safeguards for judicial probity, my text then turns to matters of theft, land tenure, leases, loans, wages, family disputes, inheritance, personal injury and professional misconduct. In other words, I tackle the myriad ills arising from the day-to-day drama of people interacting with people.

Some of what I decree you moderns will find quite familiar, such as my prohibition of incest, adultery, kidnapping and slander. What you might consider exotic, however, are my many rules governing aspects of life no longer commonplace in your world. For example, I have an inordinate amount to say about oxen. What should be done if a person rents an ox and then somehow harms the animal? I list specific judgments for each kind of injury to the beast's neck, horns, eyes, tail or muzzle, as well as for those extreme cases where, say, the ox is eaten by a stray lion. Conversely, I cover disputes arising when the ox itself does the hurting. (Hint: The whole matter hinges on whether the owner knew his ox was dangerous and took appropriate measures to protect the public.) Dowries, debt slavery and sorcery require my attention, plus the occasional missing plow and defective irrigation ditch. On the subject of grain, I am a virtual encyclopedia.

My laws brim with decisions involving concubines, slaves and the rights of multiple wives within aggregate Mesopotamian families. I refuse to let a husband abandon an ill wife when he marries another, or let a husband sell a slave given to him by a wife once that servant has borne him children. I protect both husbands and wives from debts incurred by their mates before marriage. I put few obstacles in the way of divorce, except for grave concerns about the fair division of property and the welfare of any small children. Meanwhile, what must be done if a woman remarries while her husband is a prisoner of war? How many times must a father forgive a serious fault in his son? Can a prostitute bequeath her inheritance as she pleases? To be honest, I never imagined the amount of trouble humans could make for themselves—and thus for me.

My penalties for misconduct might sometimes astonish you, especially the recurring sentence of death. I execute thieves, liars, harborers of runaway slaves, tavern-keepers who do not arrest conspirators meeting in their establishments and neglectful wives. I must point out that Mesopotamian civilization organized itself into three distinct classes, and the punishments meted out differed accordingly. The *awilum* (upper class) fared better than the *mushkenum* (subordinate free class), who in turn enjoyed many obvious social and legal advantages over the *wardum* (slaves). Between Babylonians of equal rank, I followed the principle of retaliatory justice: An eye for an eye, a tooth for a tooth, a life for a life. But, if an *awilum* should blind the eye of a *mushkenum,* then the noble keeps his (more valuable) eye and instead pays a fine to his victim. Injuries to a *wardum* draw a fine payable to the slave-owner. I allow physicians to charge more for performing the same operation on an *awilum* than on patients of a lower class, but the consequences for malpractice are commensurately greater: Botch the medical procedure on an *awilum* and the doctor loses the incompetent hand that held the scalpel. In some rulings, my devotion to reciprocity may appear extreme. For example, when the builder's shoddy work causes the death of a homeowner's son, then I decree the death not of the builder but of the builder's own son in return. Some offenses warrant impaling (for a cheating wife who murders her husband), drowning (for a father caught having sex with his son's wife), burning at the stake (for incest with your mother), removal of the tongue (for a prostitute's son impugning his foster parents) or court-ordered mastectomy (for a wet-nurse secretly swapping one child for another). My discipline may seem hard as stone, but I felt compelled to set stern examples at this critical early stage of your social development.

I, Pillar of Justice, put a heavy premium on reliable witnesses and well-written contracts. Still, your ancestors occasionally left me no choice but to resort to trial by ordeal. If, for example, a wife were accused of adultery but was not actually caught in the act, then to remove her from suspicion, I ordered her thrown into the Euphrates. If innocent, she swam to the other side; if guilty, she drowned. This method allowed the gods to determine her fate. Before you protest—I've heard it all before—let me remind you that, for a penal system placed under the nominal authority of Shamash, I afford the gods a minimal role in Mesopotamian justice. I am not really a very religious rock, although I do take into account the beliefs and superstitions of those I evolved to help. Whatever your own religion might be, give me credit for the good I have done under difficult circumstances. I set up a system of legal recourse for rich and poor, free and slave. I spelled out a person's rights and responsibilities. I protected one human from another by declaring: *Let any person wronged by another bring his case before me, Pillar of Justice, and heed the judgments inscribed thereon. Let my laws bring order and put his mind at rest.*

I Protected One Human From Another by Declaring: "Let Any Person Wronged by Another Bring His Case Before Me, Pillar of Justice . . . Let My Laws Bring Order and Put His Mind At Rest."

In the final section of my massive cuneiform text, I again praise my partner Hammurapi. Of course, I mention me in this epilogue, too. Mostly, I call down curses upon any who might dare deface me. I warn that the sky—god Anu will destroy the scepter of any king who corrupts my words in any way. I swear that Babylon's great god Marduk will likewise bring him famine, that incorruptible Shamash will crush his troops, that Sin the moon—god will fill his shortened life with heavy sighs and sorrows, that the storm—god Adad will dry up the rivers and springs, plus all of the usual maledictions about barren wombs, raging fevers, incurable diseases and frightening omens of a dreadful future. On the other hand, I do include a more pleasant promise in the name of the gods that all subsequent rulers who respected me would surely prosper. Call it "good cop-bad cop," Mesopotamian style.

And so for 600 years I stood in Hammurapi's temple of the sun-god Shamash within the city of Sippar, known today as Abu Habbah, southwest of Baghdad. Empires rose and fell until there ruled a king who did not honor me. An Elamite conqueror, he was named Shutruk-Nahunte. Reigning from about 1185 to 1155 BC, he captured Sippar and carried me off to Susa among the spoils of war. He ordered me flayed and branded with some pompous inscription boasting of his own power—an unforgivable crime against the greatest rock in the world. His minions began their painful sacrilege—you can still observe the scars they inflicted at my base-but then they stopped. I'd like to think that one of my attackers spied in my epilogue the curses on all who defaced me and obediently laid down his chisel. Whatever the reason, I bear no inscription of Shutruk-Nahunte (whose infamy is a touchstone of the 2002 movie "The Emperor's Club," or so I am told). In time, my new home at Susa succumbed to other foreigners and I, broken in two pieces, fell silent in the courts of humankind. For 3000 years, as I lay lost, other codes built on what I had begun. Laws changed, but the need for laws never did.

Excavated beginning in 1901 by the Frenchman Jacques De Morgan, I came to live in the Louvre.

In December of 1901, one of my fragments emerged from the soil. A few weeks later in 1902, the other half came to light. I had been excavated by a team of archeologists led by the Frenchman Jacques de Morgan. I, Pillar of Justice, was immediately hailed as the most complete code of ancient Mesopotamian laws ever discovered. Scholars eagerly sought in me parallels to the Hebrew Old Testament, even though our similarities do not really run very deep, and they studied scrupulously all I had to say about life in early Babylonia. Naturally, I came to live in the Louvre, surrounded by adoring crowds hard-pressed to notice the 30,000 other objects sharing this ornate palace with me. Granted, many visitors like you may not at first recall everything you should about me, but the light of Shamash soon dawns.

Now, modern-day *mushkenum,* you may go, but do obey all the posted rules on your way out-NO Flash Photography; Do Not Touch the Artworks; Smoking is Prohibited; No Food or Drink in the Galleries—or else I might have to toss you into the Seine, just for old times' sake. Rock Rules.

FRANK L. HOLT (fholt@uh.edu) is a professor of history at the University of Houston and most recently author of *Into the Land of Bones: Alexander the Great in Afghanistan.* He is writing another book on ancient Afghanistan. This is his seventh article in the "I Witness History" series.

Before Tea Leaves Divination in Ancient Babylonia

The administration was determined to go to war, but it lacked the necessary public support. Fortunately there was timely intelligence, especially from southern Iraq, that victory was assured. Am I referring to the CIA and Washington in 2003 C.E.?

WILLIAM W. HALLO

No, this is Nineveh in 652–648 B.C.E., the administration was headed by King Ashurbanipal, and the intelligence came from a diviner who had studied the liver of an animal slaughtered for that purpose. This common practice is the subject of Danish Assyriologist Ulla Koch-Western-holz's *Babylonian Liver Omens,* which is primarily a scholarly translation and presentation of cuneiform texts devoted to hepatoscopy, or divination by means of the liver, the favored organ for extispicy (divination from sheep entrails).

Here's the diviner's report: "[If the omen for] the decimation of the army is situated on the right side of the 'head lift' of the liver: It is an omen of Shamash-shum-ukkin who waged war against Aššurbanipal the beloved of the great gods and defeat seized him in the midst of battle and before Aššurbanipal the king of the world he [. . .]: It is not favorable for Shamash-shumukkin" (CT 35:38:14–17) [a collection of cuneiform tablets in the British Museum]. According to Koch-Westenholz, the "if-clause" (known in Assyriology as the protasis) was realistic (based on the actual shape of the liver), but the prediction was fabricated to please the king of Assyria in his great war against his rebellious brother, who ruled Babylonia.

There are other parallels between ancient liver divination and modern intelligence. For one thing, it was expensive, involving not only the fee to the diviner but the sacrificial slaughter of possibly of two or even three animals so that the total number of omens obtained from their entrails would result in a decisive majority of answers on one side of the question or the other. As a result, the use of liver divinations was largely confined to the royal administration, which had at its disposal the necessary resources, while private persons mostly resorted to less expensive and less sophisticated methods. A second reason for the limited use of liver divination was that its predictions were never wrong: If events turned out other than foretold, the fault lay not with the prediction but with the protasis—that is, inadequate account had been taken of ancillary phenomena surrounding the actual taking of the omens and this would be duly considered in the future. As a result, increasingly elaborate handbooks of omens were produced to cover all possible (and many impossible) contingencies. Third, even if the king could at times encourage the production of omens favorable to his plans, more often he stood in awe of the learned specialists on whom he depended for the interpretation of their secret lore. So, for example, Esarhaddon, who extended the Assyrian Empire in the seventh century B.C.E. to its farthest limits, was nevertheless so much under the spell of his diviners (and physicians) that he left a whole dossier of inquiries to the Sun god Shamash and lived his whole life in fear of an early demise, which indeed came to pass. His son Ashurbanipal also followed his example.[1]

In ancient Israel, the Mesopotamian king was an object of ridicule for his dependence on divination. In Ezekiel 21:21–23, Jerusalem's fate hangs in the balance as the king of Babylon halts his army on its westward march through Syria to await divination not only by the liver (hepatoscopy) but also by arrows (belomancy) and *teraphim* (perhaps, small household idols) before deciding which road to take for his next conquest. As it was expressed by Balaam, that quintessential Mesopotamian diviner from Petor on the Euphrates, "Lo, there is no augury in Jacob, no divining in Israel: Jacob is told at once, yea Israel, what God has wrought" (Numbers 23:23). For Israel, the place of the diviner was taken by the seer and then the prophet—though less to predict the future than, in Martin Buber's terms, "to confront man with the alternatives of decision." As the first of the literary prophets declared, "Indeed, my Lord God does nothing without having revealed His purpose to His servants the prophets" (Amos 3:7).

Not that all forms of divination were forbidden to Israel. The *Urim* and *Thummim* widely resorted to by both Saul and David represented a binary sort of psephomancy (from the Greek words meaning divining from pebbles) that essentially provided only yes-or-no answers, with *Thummim* probably standing for yes and *Urim* for no. (When Saul prays *hava thammim* [1 Samuel 14:41], the text should probably be emended to *hava thummim*—give a yes!)[2] The cup that Joseph employed for divining (Genesis 44:5) constituted a form of lecanomancy—that is, interpretation by the shape of oil in water. The words that Jonathan used to determine whether God would deliver the Philistine garrison into his hands (1 Samuel 14:10), or earlier the words by which Abraham's servant decided he would know the right bride for his master's son (Genesis 24:12–14), represent legitimate forms of cledonomancy or divination by a (chance) word.

All these simple and inexpensive methods were also known in Mesopotamia, but they were not deemed worthy of ancient scholarly attention, and no handbooks were created to catalogue their interpretations. Handbooks were reserved for divination by such phenomena as the heavenly bodies (astrology), freak births among humans and animals (teratoscopy) and dreams (oneiromancy). Particular attention was paid to the ingredients in a food offering to a deity: incense (libanomancy), flour (aleuromancy), oil (lecanomancy) and especially the entrails of sacrificial sheep (extispicy).[3]

It is to this last technique that Koch-Westenholz has dedicated her book, but so vast is the cuneiform literature devoted to this particular technique of divination that in nearly 600 pages and plates (the latter are expertly drawn hand copies of the cuneiform texts), she was able to cover only three of the ten "chapters," comprising 27 of the estimated 100 tablets that once made up the canonical series, together with their commentaries, extract texts and other ancient scholarly apparatus. Between these chapters, more than 3,000 individual omens are presented, painstakingly reconstructed from more than 200 discrete cuneiform tablets and fragments of tablets (many of them published here for the first time).

All these omens are of the form: "if (the configuration of a given part of the liver is such and such), then this presages (such and such an outcome)." The "then-clause" is known in Assyriology as the apodosis. Since **BAR** readers are not exclusively veterinarians, they may be spared the protases, with their detailed descriptions of a dozen parts of sheep livers and gall bladders. Instead a brief overview of the predictions in the apodoses will suffice.

The great majority of the predictions deal with the royal house, the kingdom or the commonweal. There are references to the outcome of campaigns, battles or sieges, the health and welfare of the king (often referred to as "the prince") and other members of the royal family and its entourage, to the weather, the success or otherwise of the harvest or the flocks, and the interactions between the monarchy and its subjects. Some omens refer specifically to great kings of the past. For example, "Omen of Sargon whose troops were shut in by rainstorm and exchanged weapons among themselves." Or "Destruction: omen of Ibbi-Sin, king of Ur." Private concerns are far rarer

---

Glossary

astrology: study of heavenly bodies
teratoscopy: study of freak births among humans and animals
oneiromancy: divination based on dreams
libanomancy: study of incense offered to deities
aleuromancy: study of flour offered to deities
lecanomancy: study of oil offered to deities
extispicy: study of entrails of sacrificial sheep
psephomancy: divination based on pebbles
belomancy: study of arrows
hepatoscopy: study of animal livers
cledomancy: divination by a chance word

---

in the apodoses; examples include the prediction that "a snake will bite a man" and that "the patient will continue to waste away but will live." There are also omens that have a double signification, one for the king and another for the "commoner" (Akkadian *muškenu;* compare Hebrew *misken,* Arabic *miskin,* French *mesquin*), as for example "If (the extispicy) concerns the campaign, the enemy will defeat me. If it is a commoner's sacrifice: Attack."[4]

Only a relatively few omens concern women, and then mainly in their relationships to children or husbands. For example: "The man's wife will bear a son;" "A woman who does not [has not] give[n] birth easily will give birth easily;" or "A man's wife will write again and again about killing her husband: 'Kill my husband and marry me!'"

How can we explain the ancient Mesopotamian fascination with extispicy? I have long ago suggested an economic motive: It was inspired, at least in part, by an aversion to wastefulness. For the individual, offering up a sheep or ram from his own flock meant true sacrifice, not only in the literal sense of "making holy" that which was to be offered to or at least shared with the deity, but also in the modern sense of giving up something dear and precious to oneself. The edible parts of the animal could be consumed by the deity in the form of its statue, and what the deity deigned to leave uneaten (in effect, everything) was available for the priest and ultimately for the worshiper. But the entrails and certain organs were considered inedible. So what better use to make of organs such as the lung and liver than for divination? The king was constrained by no such economies, but he took over the practice and extended it to decision-making in all realms of public policy, which explains the public character of the great majority of the liver omens. And if enough of them predicted a favorable outcome, for an impending battle, for instance, they tended to become a self-fulfilling prophecy: Armies became fired up with the enthusiasm imparted by the favorable prognosis.

And how to explain the Israelite disdain for extispicy? Sacrifice took an entirely different form in ancient Israel. The deity was not worshiped in the form of a statue, but was unseen. The meat sacrifice was divided among worshiper, priest and deity,

Cuneiform Tablets: Who's Got What?

There is no official tally of the number of ancient Mesopotamian cuneiform tablets held by the world's museums, but experts agree that there are roughly half a million. The largest collection by far is in the possession of the British Museum, in London, which has approximately 130,000 of them. Next, in roughly descending order, are Berlin's Vorderasiatisches Museum, the Louvre in Paris, the Museum of Ancient Orient in Istanbul, the Baghdad Museum and Yale University's Babylonian Collection, which, with 40,000 tablets, has the largest holding in the United States. A close second is the University of Pennsylvania's Museum of Archaeology and Anthropology. Many tablets have lain in these collections for a century without being translated, studied or published.

with the deity's portion "wholly burnt" so that it went up (hence Hebrew *'olah,* literally "that which goes up"; translated in the Greek Septuagint as *holokaustos,* literally "burnt whole") in smoke whose odor was pleasant or soothing (*rei'ach nichoach*) to God. In Israel, there was no squeamishness about, nor prohibition against, eating the liver, hence no reason for with-holding it from the sacrifice and no economic motive to use it instead for divination.

Babylonian Liver Omens provides a fascinating, panoramic look at a world and a worldview that shares the Biblical stage with Israel yet differs from it so fundamentally that it silhouettes the latter by contrast as vividly as other aspects of that world highlight it by positive comparison.

Notes

1. Compare Ivan Starr, *Queries to the Sungod: Divination and Politic in Sargonid Assyria* (State Archives of Assyria 4, 1990), especially pp. 187–199, 255–257; and Simo Parpola, *Letters from Assyrian and Babylonian Scholars* (State Archives of Assyria 10, 1993), pp. 253–270.

2. On the frequent references to receiving a "firm yes" (*annu kinu*) in extispicy, see Starr, *Queries,* p. xvi; for a different view, see Cornelis van Dam, *Then Urim and Thummim: a Means of Revelation in Ancient Israel* (Winona Lake; In: Eisenbrauns, 1997), especially pp. 197–214.

3. Ulla Jeyes, "Divination as a Science in Ancient Mesopotamia," *Jaar-bericht Ex Oriente Lux* 32 (1991–1992), pp. 23–41, especially p. 23.

4. Found on p. 283, line 17 of the book under review; see also note 702 for a list of these from other divination series.

UNIT 2

Greece and Rome: The Classical Tradition

Unit Selections

7. **Troy's Night of the Horse,** Barry Strauss
8. **The Historical Socrates,** Robin Waterfield
9. **Good Riddance, I Say,** Frank L. Holt
10. **Outfoxed and Outfought,** Jason K. Foster
11. **Mighty Macedonian: Alexander the Great,** Richard Covington
12. **Etruscan Women: Dignified, Charming, Literate and Free,** Ingrid D. Rowland
13. **Rome's Craftiest General: Scipio Africanus,** James Lacey

Key Points to Consider

- Explain why the Greeks invented the story of the Horse in the Trojan War.

- Why do we not have a really good knowledge of Socrates?

- Explain how the Athenians win over the Persians at Marathon.

- Discuss the motives behind Alexander the Great's victories which enabled him to conquer the Persian Empire.

- Explain why the Etruscan Women were scandalous to the Greeks and Romans.

- Explain why Publius Cornelius Scipio is famous in Roman history.

Student Website
www.mhhe.com/cls

Internet References

Diotima/Women and Gender in the Ancient World
    www.stoa.org/diotima
Exploring Ancient World Cultures
    http://eawc.evansville.edu
WWW: Classical Archaeology
    www.archaeology.org/wwwarky/classical.html

It has been conventional to say that, for the West, civilization began in Mesopotamia and Egypt, but that civilization became distinctly Western in Greece. These matters no longer go undisputed; witness recent academic debates of Martin Bernal's thesis that Greek civilization derived its culture from the older cultures of Egypt and the Eastern Mediterranean.

Those disputes aside, the Greek ideals of order, proportion, harmony, balance, and structure—so pervasive in classical thought and art—inspired Western culture for centuries, even into the modern era. Their humanism, which made humans "the measure of all things," not only liberated Greek citizens from the despotism of the Near East, but also encouraged them, and us, to attain higher levels of creativity and excellence.

Though the Greeks did not entirely escape from the ancient traditions of miracle, mystery, and authority, they nevertheless elevated reason and science to new levels of importance in human affairs, and they invented history, as we know it. It was their unique sociopolitical system—the polis—that provided scope and incentives for Greek culture. Each polis was an experiment in local self-government. But to many modernists, the Greek order was tainted because it rested on slavery and excluded women from the political process.

For all its greatness and originality, classical Greek civilization flowered only briefly. After the great Athenian victory over the Persians at Marathon (see "Outfoxed and Outfought"), the weaknesses of the polis system surfaced during the Peloponnesian Wars. After the long conflict between Athens and Sparta, the polis ceased to fulfill the lives of its citizens as it had in the past. The Greeks' confidence was shaken by the war and subsequent events.

But it was not the war alone that undermined the civic order. The Greek way of life depended upon unique and transitory circumstances—trust, smallness, simplicity, and a willingness to subordinate private interests to public concerns. The postwar period saw the spread of disruptive forms of individualism and the privatization of life.

Eventually, Alexander the Great's conquests and the geographical unity of the Mediterranean enabled the non-Greek world to share Greek civilization (see "Mighty Macedonian:

Athens Academy, Greece

© Image Source/PunchStock

Alexander the Great"). Indeed, a distinctive stage of Western civilization, the Hellenistic age, emerged from the fusion of Greek and Oriental elements. At best, the Hellenistic period was a time when new cities were built on the Greek model, a time of intellectual ferment and cultural exchange, travel and exploration, scholarship and research. At worst, it was an era of amoral opportunism in politics and derivative art styles.

Later, the Greek idea survived Rome's domination of the Mediterranean. The Romans themselves acknowledged their debt to "conquered Greece." Modern scholars continue that theme, often depicting Roman culture as nothing more than the practical application of Greek ideals to Roman life. In addition, the Roman Republic invented an effective system of imperial government and a unique concept of law, which was carried on during the reign of the Empire.

The Romans bequeathed their language and law to Europe and preserved and spread Greek thought and values. The Greeks provided the basis for cultural unity of the Mediterranean; and the Romans provided the political unity. Between them, they forged and preserved many of the standards and assumptions upon which our traditions of civilization are built—the classical ideal.

Troy's Night of the Horse

The Trojans got tricked, but did the Greeks need a wooden horse?

BARRY STRAUSS

He is the last Greek at Troy. Pale in the morning light, he looks like a weak, ragged runaway. But looks can deceive. Sinon, as he is called, claims to be a deserter—the only Greek remaining when the entire enemy and its cursed fleet had suddenly departed. But can he be trusted? His name, Sinon, means "pest," "bane" or "misfortune" in Greek, leading some historians to consider it a nickname, like "the Desert Fox" for German General Erwin Rommel, or a generic name, like "Bones" for a military doctor. Sinon played a key role in the plot to take Troy, although he is often forgotten, overshadowed by the most famous trick in Western civilization.

The famous horse may be imagined as a tall and well-crafted wooden structure, towering over the wildflowers of the Scamander River plain. Its body is made of the pine of Mount Ida, a tree known today as Pinus equi troiani, "Trojan Horse Pine" and renowned since antiquity as a material for shipbuilding. The horse's eyes are obsidian and amber, its teeth ivory. Its crest, made of real horsehair, streams in the breeze. Its hooves shine like polished marble. And hidden inside are nine Greek warriors.

Everyone knows the story. The Greeks are said to have packed up their men, horses, weapons and booty, set fire to their huts, and departed at night for the nearby island of Tenedos, where they hid their ships. All that they left behind was the Trojan Horse and a spy, Sinon, pretending to be a deserter.

The Trojans were amazed to discover that after all those years, the enemy had slunk home. But what were they to do with the Horse? After a fierce debate, they brought it into the city as an offering to Athena. There were wild celebrations. The Trojans underestimated the cunning of their adversaries. That night, the men inside the horse sneaked out and opened the city's gates to the men of the Greek fleet, who had taken advantage of Troy's drunken distraction to set back from Tenedos. They proceeded to sack the city and win the war.

Everyone knows the story, but nobody loves the Trojan Horse. Although scholars disagree about much of the Trojan War, they nearly all share the conviction that the Trojan Horse is a fiction. From Roman times on, there have been theories that the Trojan Horse was really a siege tower, or an image of a horse on a city gate left unlocked by pro-Greek Antenor, or a metaphor for a new Greek fleet because Homer calls ships "horses of the sea," or a symbol of the god Poseidon, who destroyed Troy in an earthquake, or a folk tale similar to those found in Egyptian literature and the Hebrew

Bible. There has been every sort of theory about the Trojan Horse except that it really existed.

Many of these theories sound convincing, particularly the horse-as-siege engine, since Bronze Age Assyrians named their siege towers after horses, among other animals. But sometimes a horse is just a horse. Although epic tradition might exaggerate the details of the Trojan Horse and misunderstand its purpose, that the object existed and that it played a role in tricking the Trojans into leaving their city without defenses might just be true.

More about the Horse presently: In the meantime, back to the spy whom the Greeks had left behind. Although Sinon is less dramatic than the famous Horse, he was no less effective as an agent of subversion, and he inspires far more confidence as a genuine historical figure. The Trojan Horse is unique and improbable, although not impossible. But Sinon plays a well-attested role in unconventional warfare as it was waged in the Bronze Age.

In Virgil's retelling in the Aeneid, Sinon pretends to be a deserter in order to work his way into Troy. He testifies that the Greeks have left for good and argues that the Trojan Horse is a genuine gift and not some trick. Eventually, after a stormy debate, the Trojans decide to bring the Horse into the city.

Deceit is not unique to the Trojan saga; it was a fundamental ingredient in Hittite military doctrine. Consider some examples: A king broke off the siege of a fortress at the approach of winter, only to send his general back to storm the unsuspecting city after it had gone off alert. A general sent agents into the opposing camp before battle, where they pretended to be deserters and tricked the enemy into letting down his guard. Another king attacked a neighbor via a roundabout route to avoid enemy scouts. Nor were the Hittites alone in their use of trickery. For example, the siege of one Mesopotamian city by another involved sneak attacks at night and the impersonation of an allied unit of soldiers in an attempt to lull the besieged into opening their gates. (It failed.)

Think of the fall of Troy not as a myth about a Horse but as an example of unconventional warfare, Bronze Age style. The Trojan Horse might be better known as the Trojan Red Herring. Everyone focuses on the Horse, but the real story lies elsewhere. In fact, it would be possible to leave out the Trojan Horse and yet tell a credible and coherent narrative of the capture of Troy much as the ancients told it.

Without the Trojan Horse, the story might go like this: The Greeks decided to trick the Trojans into thinking they had gone

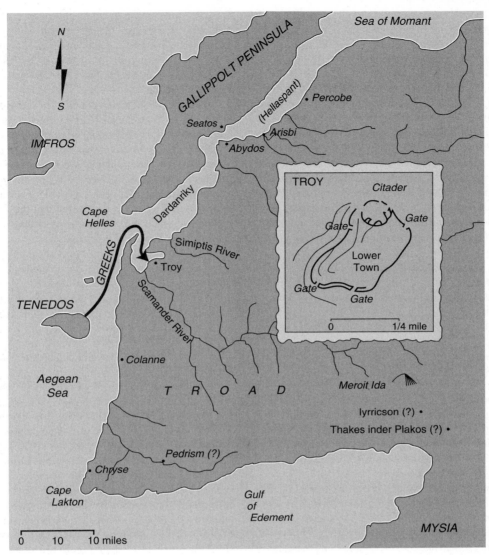

Tricking the Trojan defenders, the Greeks likely withdrew to the island of Tenedos, some seven miles away, before springing their surprise attack.

home when, in fact, they had merely retreated to Tenedos. Once they had lulled the enemy into dropping his guard, they planned to return in a surprise attack—at night. To know when to move, the Greeks would look for a lighted-torch signal, to be given by a Greek in Troy who had pretended to turn traitor and desert. Signals were used often in ancient battles, most famously at Marathon (490 BC), when a Greek traitor in the hills flashed a shield in the sunlight to communicate with the Persians. In the clear skies of the Mediterranean, fire signals could be seen from far off. They were visible as smoke signals during the day and as beacons at night. Tests show that the signals were visible between mountaintops up to a distance of 200 miles.

At the sign, the Greeks would row back rapidly to Troy. The final part of the plan required a few men inside Troy to open the city gate. These men might either have been Trojan traitors or Greeks who had sneaked into the city. With the emergency supposedly over, Troy's gatekeepers would not have proved difficult to overcome.

Compare the set of tricks by which the south Italian port city of Tarentum was betrayed in turn to Hannibal and then to the Romans.

In 213 BC a pro-Carthaginian citizen of Tarentum arranged for Carthaginian soldiers to come back with him from a nighttime hunting expedition. The soldiers wore breastplates and held swords under their buckskins; they even carried a wild boar in front, to appear authentic. Once the city gate was opened to them, they slaughtered the guards, and Hannibal's army rushed in. Four years later, the Romans under Fabius Maximus recaptured the city by having a local girl seduce the commander of Hannibal's garrison. He agreed to guide Roman troops over the walls at night while Fabius' ships created a distraction at the harbor wall on the other side of town. Although these events took place 1,000 years after the Trojan War, they could easily have been carried out with Bronze Age technology.

The Greek plan at Troy was to trick the enemy into dropping his guard. It worked: the Trojans relaxed. At that point, one Greek inside the city lit a signal fire to bring the Greek fleet back and then others opened a gate.

The island of Tenedos (now Bozcaada) lies about seven miles (six nautical miles) from the Trojan harbor. The Greeks might have

31

moored their ships in one of the sheltered coves on the island's east coast, near Troy but out of sight. At a rate of about five knots (about that of a 32-oared Scandinavian longship traveling 100 miles), they could have covered the distance in little more than an hour. That is, in daylight; the trip would no doubt have taken longer at night. But the Sack of Ilium claims it was a moonlit night, and, anyhow Bronze Age armies knew how to march by night. So the trip from Tenedos took perhaps no more than two hours. From the Trojan harbor it was another five miles by land to Troy. It was nighttime, and the road was primitive, but the Greeks knew it well. They could have covered the distance in three hours. Athenian sources claim the month was Thargelion, roughly modern May. At that time of year, sunrise at Troy is 5:30–6 A.M., sunset 8–8:30 P.M. If the Greeks left Tenedos at, say, 9 P.M., and if everything went without a hitch, they would have arrived at Troy between 2 and 3 A.M., that is, about three hours before sunrise. A forced march may have gotten the Greeks to Troy an hour or so earlier.

To carry out their plan, the Greeks had had to infiltrate a small group of soldiers into the city. But they did not need the Trojan Horse to do so. Odysseus had already sneaked in and out of the city on two separate occasions shortly before. People came and went through the gates of Troy throughout the period of the war, making it all the easier now to trick the gatekeepers into letting in a handful of disguised Greek warriors.

Once inside the city, all the Greeks needed was arms, which a determined man would not have found difficult to get. Hardened commandos could easily have overpowered a few Trojan soldiers and seized their shields and spears. Ancient cities under attack were also often betrayed from within. Not even weapons could stand up to "dissatisfaction and treachery," says an Akkadian poem. Troy no doubt had its share of Trojans who preferred dealing with the Greeks to prolonging the misery of war.

But if the Trojan Horse was not strictly necessary to the Greeks' plan, it might well nonetheless have been part of it. The Trojan Horse would certainly be more believable if ancient history recorded another occasion on which a similar ruse was employed. But how could it? The Trojan Horse was such a famous trick that it could have been used only once.

According to Homer, it was Odysseus who conceived of the idea and Epeius, known otherwise as the champion boxer at the funeral games of Patroclus, who built the Horse. Certainly the Greeks had the technology to build it. Ancient fleets usually sailed with shipwrights because wooden ships constantly need repairs, and Linear B texts (ancient inscribed clay tablets) refer both to shipwrights and carpenters as professions. There would have been no shortage of men in the Greek camp to do the job.

And there would have been no question about whether or not a statue of an animal would catch the Trojan king's fancy. Bronze Age monarchs liked animal imagery. A Babylonian king of the 1300s BC, for example, had specifically asked the pharaoh for a gift of realistic figures of wild animals, with lifelike hides, made by Egyptian carpenters. But which animal should the Greeks build at Troy? A Trojan Dog would have been insulting; a Trojan Lion frightening; a Trojan Bull or Cow would have thrown Greek cattle raids in the enemy's teeth. But a horse symbolized war, privilege, piety, popularity and Troy itself.

Horses are expensive, and in the' Bronze Age they were usually used in military context, rarely as farm animals. Rulers of the era often sent horses as a gift between kings, while ordinary Trojans might cherish a figure of a horse. In the Late Bronze Age,

horse figurines, made of baked clay, were collected throughout the Near East. Excavators recently found a clay model of a horse in Troy of the 1200s BC. Finally, there was the religious connotation: As a votive offering, the horse was all but an admission of Greek war guilt, a symbolic submission to the gods of the horse-taming Trojans.

The Horse could have been used to smuggle a small number of Greek soldiers into the city, but the chances of detection were very high. Although the traditional story of the Trojan Horse cannot be ruled out, it seems more probable that, if the Horse did exist, it was empty. There were simpler and less dangerous ways of smuggling soldiers into the city. The Horse's main value to the Greeks was not as a transport but as a decoy, a low-tech ancestor of the phantom army under General George Patton that the Allies used in 1944 to trick the Germans into expecting the D-Day invasion in the area of Pas de Calais instead of Normandy.

Epic tradition has some Trojans accepting the Horse as a genuine sign that the Greeks had given up while others remain skeptical. The debate lasted all day, according to Virgil, or three days, according to Homer. The Sack of Ilium identifies three camps: those who wanted to burn the Horse, those who wanted to throw it down from the walls and those who wanted to consecrate it to Athena. The length of the debate was in direct proportion to the stakes. The safety of the city as well as individual careers were hanging on the decision.

Virgil makes much of Priam's daughter Cassandra, an opponent of the Horse who enjoyed the gift of prophecy but suffered the curse of being ignored. This story does not appear in Homer, or what we have of the Epic Cycle. One person who does feature in the tradition is the Trojan priest Laocöon, a staunch opponent of the Greeks, who wanted to destroy the Horse. In Virgil, the debate over the Horse comes to an end when Laocöon and his sons are strangled by two snakes from the sea. The Sack of Ilium apparently places this event after the Horse had already been brought into town. Surely the snakes are symbolic; surely Laocöon and his boys were killed not by a sea snake but by a member of the pro-Greek faction, and so, therefore, by someone perceived as a tool of a signifier of evil like a snake.

Laocöon's snakes may well be rooted in Anatolian Bronze Age religion, local lore of the Troad, or both. Hittite literature made the snake a symbol of chaos and the archenemy of the Storm God. It makes sense for a snake to foil the Storm God's servant, the Trojan priest who was trying to save his city. The Troad, meanwhile, is rich in fossil remains of Miocene animals such as mastodons and pygmy giraffes, and these objects might have made their way into myth. For example, an Iron Age Greek painter probably used a fossilized animal skull as a model for a monster that Heracles is supposed to have defeated on the shore of Troy. So the story of Laocöon's murder by monsters from the sea may well have Trojan roots.

Laocöon's fate convinced Aeneas and his followers to leave town; they withdrew to Mount Ida in time to escape the Greek onslaught. Virgil famously tells a different story, in which Aeneas stays in Troy, fights the Greeks and then at last escapes the burning city while carrying his elderly father, Anchises, on his back. But the account in the Sack of Ilium, which records Aeneas' departure, strikes a more credible note. Aeneas would not have been eager to die for Priam, a king who had never given Aeneas the honor that he felt he was due. His homeland was south of the city, in the valley of Dardania beside the northern slopes of Mount Ida. What better place to regroup if Aeneas believed that Troy was doomed?

Helen played a double game. She had helped Odysseus on his mission to Troy and learned of his plan of the Horse. Now she tried to coax the Greeks out of the Horse, but Odysseus kept them silent—or perhaps the Horse was empty. Helen is supposed to have gone back home that night and prepared herself for the inevitable. She had her maids arrange her clothes and cosmetics for her reunion with Menelaus.

Whether or not there was a Trojan Horse, and whether or not the Trojans brought it into town and dedicated it to Athena, it is easy to imagine them celebrating the end of the war. They treated themselves to a night of partying, according to the Sack of Ilium. It was now, when the Trojans were occupied, that Sinon supposedly gave the prearranged torch signal. Once watchers on Tenedos saw it, the expedition to take Troy rowed rapidly back to the mainland.

Surprise, night and Trojan drunkenness would have given the Greeks substantial advantages, but taking Troy would require hard fighting nonetheless. Experienced warriors, the Trojans would have recovered quickly after their initial shock. If the battle began in darkness it no doubt would have continued into the daylight hours. The epic tradition offers a few details of Trojan resistance. The Greek Meges, leader of the Epeans of Elis, was wounded in the arm by Admetus, son of Augeias. Another Greek, Lycomedes, took a wound in the wrist from the Trojan Agenor, son of Antenor.

But what the tradition highlights, of course, is Greek victory. Admetus and Agenor, for instance, did not savor their successes, because that same night one was killed by Philoctetes and the other by Neoptolemus. A Greek named Eurypylus, son of Euaemon, killed Priam's son Axion. Menelaus began his revenge by killing Helen's new husband, Deïphobus, brother of Paris and son of Priam. But the Greek with the reputation for scoring the most kills during the sack of Troy is Achilles' son, Neoptolemus. Among his victims, besides Agenor, were Astynous, Eion and Priam himself, either at the altar of Zeus—no doubt the Storm God, where the Trojan king had sought shelter—or, as some say, at the doors of the palace because, not wanting to violate a god's altar, Neoptolemus was careful to drag his victim away first.

As for the Trojan women, tradition assigns Andromache to Neoptolemus and Cassandra to Agamemnon. Locrian Ajax had attempted to seize Cassandra but violated the altar of Athena or a Trojan goddess, which made the Greeks loath to reward him and thereby earn divine enmity.

Prudent Bronze Age warriors knew better than to insult an enemy's god. For example, when Hittite King Shuppiluliuma I conquered the city of Carchemish around 1325 BE, he sacked the town but kept all his troops away from the temples of Kubaba and Lamma. He bowed to the goddesses instead.

Priam's daughter Polyxena was, according to the Sack of Ilium, slaughtered at the tomb of Achilles as an offering to the hero's ghost. Little Astyanax, Hector's son, was murdered by Odysseus—thrown from the walls, in one version—lest he grow up and seek vengeance.

And then there was Helen. The Little Iliad states that Menelaus found her at home, in the house of Deïphobus. Menelaus' sword was drawn to seek vengeance on the agent of his humiliation and suffering, but Helen had merely to undrape her breasts to change his mind. It is the sort of story that we can only wish is true.

So much for the epic tradition. What do other Bronze Age texts and the archaeological excavations tell us about the sack of Troy?

Bronze Age documents show that however brutal the sack of Troy may have been, it would have conformed to the laws of war. Cities that did not surrender would, if they were captured, be destroyed. This role goes as far back as the first well-documented interstate conflict, the border wars between the two Sumerian city-states of Lagash and Umma between 2500 and 2350 BC.

When the Greeks sacked the city, they put Troy to the torch. Archaeology discloses that a savage fire destroyed the settlement level known as Troy VIi (formerly referred to as Troy VIIa). Blackened wood, white calcined stone and heaps of fallen building material were found in a thick destruction layer of ash and dirt that varied from about 20 inches to 6 feet deep. That inferno can be dated, according to the best estimate, sometime between 1230 and 1180 BC, more likely between 1210 and 1180.

The flames must have spread fast. One house in the lower city tells the story: A bronze figurine, as well as some gold and silver jewelry, was left abandoned on the floor of a room. The inhabitants had clearly fled in panic.

Imagine Troy's narrow streets clogged, and imagine the cries of disoriented refugees, the wailing of children; the growls and snorts, bleating, high-pitched squeals and relentless howls and barks of terrified barnyard animals (in the Bronze Age, typically kept within the town walls at night). Imagine too the clatter of arms, the clang and whistle of cold bronze, the cheers of the avengers, the whiz of javelins in flight, the reverberation of a spear that has found its mark, the holler and thud of street fighting, the surge of wails and curses, the gush and choking of pain, and much of it muffled by a fire burning fast and furious enough to sound like a downpour.

Archaeology draws a picture that is consistent with a sack of Troy. Outside the doorway of a house on the citadel, for example, a partial human male skeleton was discovered. Was he a householder, killed while he was defending his property? Other human bones have been found in the citadel, scattered and unburied. There is also a 15-year-old girl buried in the lower town; the ancients rarely buried people within the city limits unless an attack prevented them going to a cemetery outside town. It was even rarer to leave human skeletons unburied—another sign of the disaster that had struck Troy.

Two bronze spear points, three bronze arrowheads, and two partially preserved bronze knives have been found in the citadel and lower town. One of the arrowheads is of a type known only in the Greek mainland in the Late Bronze Age. The lower town has also yielded a cache of 157 sling stones in three piles. Another supply of a dozen smooth stones, possibly sling stones, was found on the citadel, in a building beside the south gate that looked to the excavators like a possible arsenal or guardhouse.

None of this evidence proves beyond doubt that Troy was destroyed in a sack. The fire that ravaged the city could have been caused by accident and then been stoked by high winds. If Troy was destroyed by armed violence, were the Greeks responsible? The archaeological evidence is consistent with that explanation but does not prove it.

This article is excerpted from Barry Strauss' book *The Trojan War*, published by Simon & Schuster in 2006.

The Historical Socrates

The popular image of Socrates as a man of immense moral integrity was largely the creation of his pupil Plato. If we examine evidence of his trial, argues **Robin Waterfield,** a different picture emerges, of a cunning politician opposed to Athenian democracy.

ROBIN WATERFIELD

T he great Athenian philosopher Socrates is widely lauded as one of history's wisest men, a reputation forged by his pupil Plato.

In the course of his *Apology of Socrates.* Plato tells a curious story. The Apology consists of the speeches that, according to Plato, Socrates delivered at his trial in Athens in 399 BC, and at one point Socrates feels he needs to explain why he has a certain reputation for wisdom. He says that his close and impulsive friend Chaerephon once paid a visit to the Pythia, the oracle in Delphi, to ask whether Socrates was the wisest man alive. The oracle proclaimed it so.

As a humble man, Socrates was puzzled by this, and set about questioning anyone he could buttonhole who had a reputation for wisdom or expertise in any area. He discovered that none of the so-called experts really deserved their reputation; they were incapable of giving coherent definitions of the concepts fundamental to their areas of expertise. He concluded that the Pythia was correct, at least in the sense that he, Socrates, was the only one who knew he did not know, the only one who did not suffer from a false conceit of wisdom.

The story has a kind of internal plausibility. It would indeed have been a life-changing event to have the oracle at the most important sacred site in Greece publicly declare that Socrates was the wisest man alive. It would have been somewhat like the Pope declaring one a candidate for future sainthood; it could well have impelled Socrates on his mission of questioning people. There's only one snag: the story is false, a fiction created by Plato for his own purposes.

Why should Chaerephon have approached the oracle with his question in the first place? In order for it to make sense to ask whether there was anyone wiser than Socrates, Socrates must already have had a reputation for wisdom. He was never famous as anything other than the person who questioned people to find out if they could define the moral and other concepts they claimed to work with. This enterprise had started around 440 BC, and had brought him notoriety by the end of the decade, when he first started to receive scathing attention from the comic poets. But this is precisely the kind of questioning that, according to Plato, was supposed to have been triggered by the oracle; it was not supposed to be taking place beforehand.

Another good reason for supposing the oracle a fiction is that there is no other reference to it throughout Plato's voluminous Socratic writings (he would surely have made hay with it), nor anywhere else in Greek literature, apart from a derivative mention in Xenophon's *Apology,* his version of the defence speeches. It would have been a famous tale, one that would have made Socrates' fellow Athenians proud of him, or would have been mocked by the comic poets.

What Plato was doing with this story is rather subtle. Throughout his life Plato wanted to establish philosophy, as he understood it, as the one valid form of higher education, and in order to do so he used his writings to puncture the claims of rivals—educators, poets, statesmen, orators and other experts. So this is what Plato has his character 'Socrates' do in the early dialogues: question such experts and find them lacking. This was Plato's mission, and his Socrates was the mouthpiece for it. But this is precisely the project summarised in Plato's *Apology* in the oracle story. Plato made up the story, then, as a way of introducing his own mission, the one he would give to the character Socrates who was to appear in his works.

Since Xenophon knew Socrates, he knew that Plato's Socrates was fictional. He was in a position to recognise that Plato's description of Socrates' philosophy was actually a clever way of outlining and introducing Plato's own. So Xenophon did the same: he used the same story for the same purpose, and merely tweaked it to suit his own ends. The chief difference between the oracle story in Plato and the version in Xenophon is that in Xenophon the oracle states that there is no one more free, upright and prudent than Socrates. Xenophon's sought to make Socrates a paragon of conventional virtue (and to explore what inner conditions are required for such virtue), and so his Socrates is 'free, upright and prudent', rather than 'wise'. Xenophon avoids mentioning wisdom because its corollary was Socratic ignorance: Plato's Socrates was wiser than anyone else because he was the only one who was aware of his ignorance. But ignorance is not one of the traits of Xenophon's Socrates, who spends most of his time advising others what to do, rather than ironically questioning them, as Plato's Socrates often does. Plato used the oracle story to establish his mission in writing, and Xenophon, recognising that this is what Plato had done, did the same for his own particular concerns.

We have reached the heart of what scholars call the 'Socratic Problem'. We are blessed by having more extant words written about Socrates than any other man of his time, and cursed by the fact that we cannot tell which, if any, of these words are true. We can be certain that Plato and Xenophon were not committed to factual reporting; nor, no doubt, were the other Socratics who wrote about their teacher, though their work has not survived. The Socratics were writing a kind of imaginative quasi-fiction: what Socrates might have said if he were talking with so-and-so on such-and-such a topic, in such-and-such a situation?

And this tenuous factual element is further diluted by each Socratics commitment to his own agenda. Hence Plato used the Chaerephon story for his purposes, and Xenophon used it for his. Consider the fact that not only Plato and Xenophon, but others of their contemporaries too, wrote *Apologies of Socrates.* If they were writers of historical truth, there would have been no need for more than one or two reproductions of his actual speeches. They were writing what, in their opinion, Socrates could or should have said, and this is what characterises the whole genre of Socratic writings.

Socrates himself wrote nothing, and the work of his immediate followers, after his death, is not historically reliable. Is the historical Socrates condemned to invisibility? We do have a witness to Socrates from his own lifetime. The comic playwright Aristophanes wrote a play called *Clouds,* in which Socrates was one of the main characters. The play was first produced in 423 BC, but the text we have is a revised version from a few years later. But the play is farce, not satire: it is no kind of evidence for the historical Socrates. In it, the character called Socrates is a portmanteau philosopher, combining in ridiculous forms the three most prominent intellectual trends of the period. He is portrayed as a scientist who believes in weird gods and employs highly imaginative speculation; as a quibbling, logic-chopping wiseacre; and as an ascetic moral teacher. It was not Aristophanes' purpose to report Socrates' views and attitudes. He chose him as his protagonist for no better reason than that Socrates was a highly visible Athenian, and Aristophanes was writing for an Athenian audience.

Socrates wrote nothing, and the work of his followers is not historically reliable

Our only contemporary witness, then, is of no help. In the face of these difficulties, the historical Socrates seems to recede ever further beyond our reach. This situation was so intolerable to generations of classical scholars that, even though not all of them acknowledged the ahistorical nature of the enterprise, and some positively argued for its historicity, they chose to privilege

Plato's portrait over Xenophon's or anyone elses. And so the Socrates who is likely to be familiar to readers of this magazine is Plato's Socrates: the merciless interrogator, committed to nothing but the truth, and determined, by means of incisive argument, to lay his own and our moral lives on a foundation of knowledge rather than opinion; a specialist in moral philosophy and moral psychology; a man of immense moral integrity, who was unjustly put to death, aged sixty-nine or seventy, by the classical Athenian democracy under which he lived.

But the uncomfortable truth is that little or nothing of this picture of Socrates may be accurate. Nevertheless, we do not have to despair altogether. There is another way to recover a true impression of the historical Socrates, and test the truth of the Platonic picture, by paying attention to the historical record and to historical plausibility.

Unfortunately, Socrates has for too long been in the hands of philosophers, and they are capable of overlooking the most stark pieces of historical evidence. I shall outline a slightly revisionist view of Socrates, one that emerges from the historical record as well as from judicious use of the extant literary evidence. The pivotal historical facts are as follows:

1. We know that the elderly philosopher was put on trial, and we know the charges that were brought against him.
2. We know what the Athenians themselves thought the trial was about.
3. We know what people's expectations were of moral philosophy at the time, and what kind of work Socrates was doing.
4. We know that Socrates stayed in Athens during the regime of the Thirty in 404-403 BC.

These points are all interconnected, and in what follows I will discuss them more or less at once.

This indictment and affidavit is sworn by Meletus Meletou of Pitthus, against Socrates Sophroniscou of Alopece. Socrates is guilty of not acknowledging the gods the city acknowledges, and of introducing other new divinities. He is also guilty of subverting the young men of the city. The penalty demanded is death.'

Preserved by a later biographer, these were the charges brought against Socrates in the spring of 399 BC. There are two aspects of these charges: Socrates was accused of impiety, *asebeia,* an offence under Athenian law, and of passing his impiety on to the young men who formed his circle.

The first oddity to us is that impiety should even be punishable. The reason that it was a punishable offence under Athenian law is significant. The gods permeated all aspects of Athenian life, private and public. The gods would not abandon the city as long as the citizens, collectively and individually, did not abandon them, and so it was one's duty as a citizen to perform the public and private rituals that preserved the gods' favour. By the same token, it was the duty of the democratic executive, the popular Assembly, to make sure that the city prospered in all respects. Shared rituals and beliefs bound the community together. Athens had become enormously powerful and prosperous, beyond the wildest imaginings of earlier generations, and the Assembly would punish those who seemed to rock the boat. One bad apple could turn the gods' favour from the city. Piety, then, was a political notion, using the term 'political' in the capacious Greek sense, to refer to the entire public life of the community.

This is borne out by what we know of other impiety trials in classical Athens. All of them reveal a strong political agenda. And this fact in turn is further corroborated by the trials, or suspicion, of intellectuals earlier than Socrates. If any intellectual got into trouble, he was likely to be accused of impiety, but that happened only if he had made himself politically undesirable on other grounds. To repeat: impiety was recognisably a political charge.

The classical Athenian legal system was open to wide interpretation. On all social charges, such as impiety, the laws were deliberately phrased vaguely without substantive definitions of the crime to guide the thinking of the *dikasts* (roughly, 'jurors'). The *dikasts* themselves implicitly revised the definition of the crime on the day. The laws were regarded more as instruments of persuasion than as the system of regulations on the basis of which a verdict should be reached.

Likewise, accusers and defendants hardly appealed to what we might regard as evidence; they slandered one another, each trying to prove that he was a model citizen compared with his rival. One could say the most outrageous or innuendo-laden things about one's opponent and his ancestors and friends. The most popular accusations included foreign or servile birth, low social status and deviant sexual behaviour. There was hardly any need to prove these slurs, and they were introduced whether or not they were relevant to the case.

It was up to the community itself to bring the prosecution (by means of one or two concerned citizens; there was no public prosecutor), and to interpret and apply its moral code in reaching a verdict and choosing a penalty. Hence the jury consisted of large numbers of men (probably 501 in Socrates' case), to ensure that the will of the people was done. There was no judge to advise these *dikasts*, and no appeal once their verdict had been reached. They were already the sovereign people: to whom else could an appeal have been made?

In short, all Athenian trials on charges such as those Socrates faced were potentially or evidently political. Undercurrents and subtexts were usual, and these undercurrents were political, at least in the sense that it was up to the *dikasts* to decide whether the defendant was a good citizen, and whether condemnation or acquittal would best serve the city, as much as whether he was guilty of the particular crime with which he was charged. 'Impiety' was exactly the kind of amorphous charge that opened up the texture of the Athenian legal system. The vagueness of its definition placed it squarely among those kinds of charges where it was expected, even required, that *dikasts* would assess the man as much as the crime.

All the historical evidence, then, suggests that Socrates' trial was a political trial. He was accused, in effect, of 'un-Athenian activities'. The historical context suggests this too. Athens had recently lost a long and catastrophic war. This proved that the gods had withdrawn their favour from the city; the bad apples needed to be eliminated.

We can go further: the trial was probably political in a more narrow sense as well. In the course of his speech 'Against Timarchus', the politician Aeschines referred to Socrates' trial, saying that the Athenian people condemned him for having been the teacher of Critias. Aeschines was speaking in 345 BC, fifty-four years after Socrates' trial. Aeschines was an educated man, the rival of Demosthenes in a kind of Gladstone-Disraeli battle for political supremacy in Athens. His reference to Socrates is as reliable as Tony Blair's claim to have attended football matches in Newcastle played before he was born.

Critias was one of the leaders of the Thirty Tyrants, the oligarchic junta which Sparta imposed on the Athenians in 404 BC after defeating them in the Peloponnesian War. The Thirty aspired to turn Athens into a hierarchical, Spartan-style society. They restricted the number of citizens to 3,000, disarmed everyone else, awarded themselves the power of life or death over all non-citizens, and expelled all non-citizens from living within the city itself. Non-citizens were to be the farmers, manufacturers and merchants for the elite 3,000, while all political power was effectively vested in the Thirty and their henchmen. In order to see through their radical programme of social reform, and in order to raise much needed cash (the city had been bankrupted by the war), they murdered about 1,500 people in a few weeks. Many more fled into exile.

Critias was a leader of the Thirty not just because he was one of the most ruthless, but also because he was an intellectual, their ideologue. He saw the slaughter as a way of purging Athens of undesirable elements, of returning power to the aristocrats who were divinely authorised to wield it, of turning back the clock to a time before democracy. His quest was a moral quest—but then tyranny always begins with the belief that you know better than others what is right for them.

The Thirty were soon defeated. Critias was killed and the rest fled or were allowed to leave. But Critias had long been a friend and student of Socrates, who had became tainted by the association. Nor was Critias the only democratically undesirable member of Socrates' circle. Socrates had been particularly close to Alcibiades, whose attempt to make himself the leader of an oligarchic coup in 411 BC only narrowly failed, and who was thought to want to set himself up as sole ruler of the city. He was the teacher of Xenophon, who was exiled for his anti-democratic leanings. He was close to others among the Thirty or their immediate cohorts, and in general he and his circle had long been suspected of favouring a Spartan-style society over Athenian democracy.

Socrates chose to stay in Athens during the regime of the junta. Plato and Xenophon are fairly reliable witnesses to Socrates' political views because they both agreed with him, and it is clear that Socrates too wanted to see the moral regeneration of Athens. Unless he was simply blind or foolish, he tolerated even the excesses of the Thirty because he was, at least to a degree, sympathetic to their aims, if not their methods. Many will find this a harsh thing to say about Socrates, who over the centuries has acquired a saintly aura, but it is the inevitable conclusion to which the historical facts point.

It seems harsh above all because our picture of Socrates, derived chiefly from Plato, is of a man who was primarily concerned with ethics and practical morality; his work was to encourage others if they evinced a desire to improve themselves. But the very nature of moral philosophy in those days suggests a qualification to this picture. Morality was not, or not just, an individual quest, a personal struggle against opposing desires and temptations. In Socrates' day, almost all Greek thinkers assumed or argued that the polis, the community, was the correct and only environment for human moral flourishing—that a good *polis* created goodness in its citizens. So Plato occupied himself in *Republic* with imagining an ideal state in which all members of society would be good to the best of their abilities, while for Aristotle education in moral goodness was a product of the right constitutional environment, and thorough ethical enquiry entailed also describing the state that would best allow its citizens to find and retain goodness.

As a moral philosopher, then, Socrates was also a political philosopher. And the initial plausibility of the view that Socrates was concerned with the political environment that would enable its citizens to fulfil their moral potential is confirmed by a vein of the evidence from Plato's and Xenophon's Socratic works. Time and again, Socrates accepts students expressly so that he can train them to be future leaders of Athens. They were to be as close as possible to morally perfect themselves, so that they would know what goodness was and how to bring it about in their community; then they could create a political environment within which all could flourish to the best of their abilities. No wonder people linked Socrates so closely with Critias: their aims, if not their methods, were very similar.

At the end of the nasty little civil war that brought about the downfall of the Thirty, everyone who had chosen to stay in Athens was offered the chance to leave. Many, especially if they had been members of the inner circle, seized the opportunity for exile. Others, especially if, like Socrates, they had been more loosely associated, took the risk of staying. But Socrates was famous, a figurehead. His continued residence in Athens seemed to be cocking a snook at the restored democracy. It was only a matter of time; even at his advanced age, a trial was inevitable. And two of his three prosecutors were prominent democrats.

There can be no doubt, then, that Socrates' trial was politically motivated, and there can be no doubt that, from the point of view of the Athenian democracy, he was guilty as charged. He was no true citizen of the democracy. There can be no doubt, either, that attention to the historical facts surrounding the case must lead us to qualify the Platonic-Xenophontic portrait of Socrates. He was put on trial as a political undesirable, and his radical political vision was indeed anti-democratic. This is not the Socrates with whom we are comfortably familiar, but it is more likely to be closer to the truth than the fictions that permeate the literary evidence.

Further Reading

Christopher Taylor, *Socrates: A Very Short Introduction* (Oxford University Press, 1998); Ryan Balot, *Greek Political Thought* (Blackwell, 2006); Thomas Brickhouse and Nicholas Smith (eds), *The Trial and Execution of Socrates: Sources and Controversies* (Oxford University Press, 2002); Debra Nails, *The People of Plato: A Prosopography of Plato and Other Socratics* (Hackett, 2002); Stephen Todd, *The Shape of Athenian Law* (Oxford University Press, 1993).

ROBIN WATERFIELD's *Why Socrates Died: Dispelling the Myths* is published this month by Faber and Faber. He is also the author of *Athens: A History* (Macmillan, 2004) and *Xenophon's Retreat: Greece, Persia and the End of the Golden Age* (Faber and Faber, 2006), and has translated numerous ancient Greek works for Oxford World's Classics and Penguin Classics.

Good Riddance, I Say

FRANK L. HOLT

Listen up, folks. Some old chiselers have given you the wrong idea about history. Just because something gets written on a big rock does not mean that it's . . . well, etched in stone. I say there are different ways of looking at the world, and most of them are not from a 25-meter height, like that pompous obelisk in Rome. To hear him tell it, nothing matters but the high and mighty. Well, I never met a pharaoh or a king; I never had armies of slaves and such setting me up or knocking me down. I never went to the Circus and had a clown like Nero race around me in his chariot. So what? I may not look like much, but I did something a lot more important. Hear me out if you want to know how a scrap of everyday trash got rescued from a garbage heap to change the course of human history.

Pardon my language, but I come from what Greek folks call *hoi polloi*—the common people, the working class, the lower crust. I don't know much about anything high, whether it's society, class, brow, fashion or falutin'. It's another world up there, a place for emperors and obelisks, but not for me. I like it down here where little things make big differences. A pot means as much to the poor as pillars and palaces mean to some Caesar who thinks he's a god.

From my beginning to my end, I always kept close to the ground. I am a humble son of earth and water, a foster child of fire. Born in the potters' quarter of Athens—still called Kerameikos ("Ceramicsville") today—I grew up hard and fast. Only hours out of the kiln, I stood on a rough-hewn shelf, my mouth wide open in awe of my surroundings. Swearing craftsmen of every description were spinning their pots and their yarns. I listened to their colorful shoptalk and watched as their muddy fingers taught the clay to become fancy things with frilly names that I struggled to pronounce: the shapely *loutrophoros* for ritual bathing, the slender *lekythos* for storing oil, the deep *krater* for mixing water and wine, the big-handled *kantharos* for serious drinking and the pitcher-like *oinochoe*, with a spout for pouring. Talented painters turned many of these pots—excuse me, *vases*—into the masterpieces you see in books and museums today. Not me. I never got glazed or painted. Even the old redneck crocks had more class than me. Since nobody bothered to make me beautiful, I knew right away what to expect. I'd never earn an ode from some famous poet, or make it into a museum. No, I was the workaday ware of every kitchen and storeroom in bustling Athens, the kind bought, used and broken in bulk, mourned for a moment—but only because of what I spilled—then immediately forgotten and replaced. All too soon, I joined the sweepings of some poor man's house, a vessel wrecked on a sandy floor.

Castoffs like me had no cause to hope for second chances. I was Humpty Dumpty, you might say, without the fuss of all the king's horses and men. Shattered, I waited in the household trash for that last journey out to the bottom of some deep, dark well or a smelly garbage pile beyond the city. Until then, I had nothing to do but pass my final days in idle trash-talk with other scraps of pottery. Some bits bragged of vases they had spotted in this fine shop or that; others put on airs about the jobs they had once had—say, preparing food for a wedding feast or funeral. Most of us, however, fantasized about one last chore before the grave. We wanted to become something called an *ostracon,* a piece of busted pot you could write on with something sharp. This was all the rage back then.

> **Most of us fantasized about one last chore before the grave: we wanted to become something called an *ostracon,* a piece of busted pot you could write on with something sharp.**

Sure, massive stone pillars may seem like the ultimate memo pad, but you need a swarm of stonecutters just to jot down a note or two. Not very practical for most people. That's why your daily life leaves a *paper* trail, not a desk drawer full of obelisks. Back in my day, even paper (in the form of imported papyrus) could be too pricey for the average Greek. In Athens, a grocery list would have cost more than the groceries! For simple folk, some other cheap, available item had to serve for the lists and tallies of everyday living. That explains why Athenians sometimes fumbled through their trash to find shards of shattered crockery like me. On us, a Greek could scratch a useful line or two, just as you might do today on the back of an old envelope.

But I didn't start this squabble with an obelisk just to brag about becoming a shopping list. Give a fellow more credit than that! Talk about dreams coming true: Scratched on me were three and a half words—not much, you think, right? But you can thank me later, because those words saved what you folks now call Western Civilization. Think I'm joking? Let me finish my story.

You see, the Athenian house where I lived belonged to a citizen. That made the man somebody special, even though you couldn't pick him out in a crowd of slaves or foreign workers. All the poor pretty much dressed and talked alike. In fact, the rich often complained that in the streets of Athens you couldn't tell a free man from a slave, making it hard to know who you could shove out of your way without breaking the law. My owner didn't care a lot about appearances (maybe that's why he bought me in the first place), but he sure was proud to be a registered citizen with the right to vote. He had no education, yet he attended the peoples' *ecclesia*—the assembly—whenever he could. There he voted on everything having to do with how the government was run. Imagine that: a commoner in charge of war, strategy, finances, religion—you name it. He even helped make all the laws! His politics (they called it this because he lived in a Greek *polis,* or city-state) depended on what he heard in the great public debates, and on the gossipy news that constantly bounced around the *agora,* or marketplace. It seemed to me that he lived an exciting life where the people (not including women, foreigners or slaves) decided everything for themselves. He called it a democracy.

I remember moving into this man's trash at a very scary time—not just for me, but for the whole city. Day after day my owner came home from the ecclesia and agora with terrifying talk of a Persian invasion. Persia, I learned, was the biggest power on Earth. Its empire stretched from the edges of Greece all the way to the other side of the world where only monsters lived. The Persians were unbelievably rich, powerful and angry—at Athens in particular. They accused us of meddling in their empire, which was true enough, but my owner said it couldn't be helped on account of our duty to spread democracy. Only eight years earlier, the Athenians had beaten off a large military force sent by Persia's King Darius to punish the city. The decisive battle, fought at Marathon, was already the stuff of legend: The soldiers who won it were considered heroes, our greatest generation. But everybody knew the Persians would try again. Year after year the tension grew, until finally, in what you folks call 482 BC, we went on red alert. Darius's son Xerxes, Persia's new "king of kings," made no secret that he intended to destroy Athens once and for all.

I remember moving into this man's trash at a very scary time, not just for me, but for the whole city.

But the news was not all bad. From my place in the jumble of cracked pottery heaped in the kitchen trash, I overheard my owner one day crowing like a rooster that he was suddenly rich. Apparently, state miners, digging on public land, had discovered a bonanza of pure silver. The find was worth a fortune. Word on the street was that every citizen should expect to receive an equal cut of the proceeds. And why not? What poor Athenian would want this silver tucked away in the state treasury instead of his very own pocket? "Easy come, easy *keep,*" my excited owner agreed.

So did a famous politician named Aristeides, one of the heroes of Marathon and a leader so honest and wise that the people called him "Aristeides the Just." This fine man proposed that the city should parcel out fair shares of the silver to every citizen just as soon as the miners (all of them state slaves) could be lashed into action.

But of course, this was democratic Athens, where even a no-brainer had to be debated. For days my owner fretted around the city, worried that some fool in the ecclesia or agora would come up with some different scheme for the money. And sure enough, somebody did. The man was named Themistocles—although some called him more colorful names. This guy had the nerve to propose that, instead of keeping the money, the people should let *him* spend it on a bunch of warships. You know how expensive those things are? You should have heard my owner howl at such an idea! *Boats?* No *navy* saved Athens last time at Marathon. That was our boys in the infantry. And didn't we already have a bigger fleet than most any other city-state anyway? And if Athens really did need more ships for some reason, didn't our laws say that the wealthiest Athenians had to cover these expenses through special taxes? What kind of leader picks the pockets of the poor to spare the rich?

Obviously, most citizens made fun of Themistocles, but the man simply would not shut up. Crowds showed up at his speeches just to boo him, but all they got was an earful back. Themistocles went on and on about the many dangers faced by our seaside city, starting with the powerful island of Aegina, visible just offshore, to that armada of Xerxes's massing farther to the east. Listening to him, you'd think the sky was falling as he warned that the future of Athens depended on its navy, not on the desire of every shortsighted buffoon to buy a bunch of brand new pots with a pocketful of silver. As you can imagine, the debate got pretty heated.

At first, my owner hung all the arguments of Themistocles on a familiar hook: "Pure politics, nothing more." After all, Themistocles had never in his life missed an opportunity to oppose anything Aristeides stood for, so why should this distribution of silver be any different? Whatever one said, the other could not say the opposite fast enough. They hated each other so much that Athens, folks sighed, wasn't big enough for both of them. They attacked each other in the courts and turned the ecclesia into a continual battleground. Many citizens naturally dismissed Themistocles's witless proposal as no more than a sad outgrowth of this tiresome feud. The man of my house assured us all that the costly fleet proposed by Themistocles had only one mission: to sink the ambitions of his rival Aristeides.

Aristeides and Themistocles hated each other so much that Athens wasn't big enough for both of them.

When you're waiting out your last days in a trash pile, you follow a drama like this very closely, just hoping to be around long enough to see how it finally ends. I thought I had this one all figured out, but, boy, was I wrong. You see, one afternoon my owner came home not so sure about the witlessness of Themistocles's idea. Some people, even the poor ones like my owner, were starting to change their minds. Day by day they found it more difficult to ignore Themistocles, who sounded less and less preposterous, while Aristeides started to seem more like a cheap panderer. What if it was true after all that Athens could not defend itself with the ships it already had? How could even the rich possibly cough up enough money to build hundreds more right away? Look at the big picture, my owner finally said. Face up to the patriotic duty of every good man to put aside self-interest and give up his share of the mining revenues for military defense. Yes, here with me lived an uneducated man who could nonetheless actually think *for* himself, and not just about himself. Somehow, in all the fire and smoke of Athenian politics, this commoner had settled on the notion of the greater good at the expense of personal gain. He wanted a free country more than free cash. I never felt prouder to be in his house.

I was not there for long. A showdown came between the new supporters of Themistocles and the remaining followers of Aristeides. Something had to be done fast, so all of us broken pots got together, and we decided the fate of the silver, the city and, as it turns out, of Western Civilization, too. It happened when my owner fished me from the garbage and used me to write down his vote in a special kind of election named (in my honor) an *ostracism*. This was an election you wouldn't want to win, because if you did, you were given 10 days to get lost. Every year, the Athenians could do this. In the winter, they met in the ecclesia and voted whether to ostracize anyone or not. If they decided to go ahead with it, they got together in the spring to choose a "winner." On that occasion, every registered citizen (like my owner) showed up at the agora with a piece of pottery. There, each voter scratched onto his ostracon the name of any one person he wanted gone, and then he pitched this ballot into a pile to be counted. If at least 6000 people voted, then the guy who got his name written down the most had to leave Athens for a decade. The person ostracized did not lose his property or his citizenship. This wasn't exile—more like a decade-long time-out. After that he could return to the city and pick up where he left off, no hard feelings.

My owner used me to write down his vote in a special kind of election named (in my honor) an ostracism. This was an election you wouldn't want to win.

Okay, folks, I know this sounds pretty much like mob justice. Nobody's name was off limits, and the fellow ostracized had no right to defend himself or appeal. But, truthfully, don't you wish you could occasionally vote to send someone away—a president, senator, judge, teacher, talk-show host, movie star, noisy neighbor, nosy relative. . .? Your choice, your reasons. The Athenians knew the system could be abused (and I hear

it later was), but they felt a lot safer if they could defend their new democracy against dangerous individuals. An annoying neighbor was not going to rack up enough votes to get ostracized, but a guy who tried to take over the city just might get the boot. Good riddance, I say. Or some stubborn leader who refused to compromise might have to leave. Good riddance to him, too. That's exactly what I went to the agora to do—to tell either Themistocles or Aristeides that, sure enough, Athens was not big enough for both of them. I left it up to my owner to decide which name I would carry into the voting box, and then to my grave.

As you can imagine, there was a lot of politicking going on at the last minute. Supporters of both sides worked the crowd, and I worried that my owner might suddenly change his mind again. He was clearly nervous, too, because he cradled me to my grave with trembling hands: He could barely read or write. Trying to hide this fact, he did his best to scratch the right letters on his ballot. All crooked but correct, he etched along my upper edge the letters A-R-I-S-T-E-I-D-E-S. This first part he managed okay, probably because he practiced it from the very day he decided to support the naval proposal of Themistocles. But then his memory failed. What should have come next was the name of Aristeides's father, Lysimachus, to make sure people knew exactly who he meant. My owner sweated through the first four letters and quit. Completely stumped, he gave up on that word and tried something else—the name of the district in Athens where Aristeides's family was from, Alopekethen. He worked at this for a while, ending up with A-L-O-P-E-K-E-E-I. Sensing a problem, he tried to change the last E to something different but never could decide how to fix it. He needed help.

My owner did not struggle alone, of course. Plenty of hoi polloi found it hard, if not impossible, to write down even a simple thing like a name. That doesn't make them dumb, just uneducated, and nobody should look down on them for it. I'm proud to say that Aristeides didn't, even though in the end he got enough of their votes to "win" the ostracism. Fact is, he even helped one illiterate citizen write out a vote against him! The story goes that the poor voter didn't recognize Aristeides when he asked him how to spell the name. Aristeides showed the guy without letting on who he was, then out of curiosity asked why he disliked Aristeides so much. "Never met him," admitted the voter, "but I'm sick and tired of people calling him 'The Just' all the time."

Something similar happened to my owner and me. I don't know who it was (surely not Aristeides again), but a fellow voter helped straighten us out. He looked at what had been done to me and shook his head. He grabbed me and roughly crossed out everything but the first word, Aristeides. Then, smooth and sure, he scratched down the father's name, Lysimachus, straight across my lower edge, and walked away.

I was done, tattooed with the three and a half words that tell the story of my incredible life. With a proud man's determination and a stranger's help, I made a difference. I counted in the historic vote that ostracized Aristeides the Just. This broke the deadlock over the silver. Themistocles got to stick around and supervise the building of the fleet, and those very warships really did save Athens and its democracy a few years later, defeating the invading armada of Xerxes. Otherwise, Western Civilization as you know it would never have existed. Without little old me, even that gigantic obelisk in Rome wouldn't be the same. Help his highness do the math: No cheap pot, no pottery scrap; no scrap, no ostracon; no ostracon, no ostracism; no ostracism, no money for ships; no ships, no victory; no victory, no Athens; no Athens—well, no telling what sort of "Modern Ones" he'd be talking to.

Of course, I missed seeing most of the good I did. After I got rid of Aristeides, government workers buried me and a bunch of other ballots near the agora. Some of us had voted for Aristeides or Themistocles, and some for various other fellows. We had no idea, at the time, about the great sea battle, or that years later Themistocles would be ostracized, too. No, we didn't see daylight again for 2500 years. Archeologists finally dug us up and recognized right away who we were. I got a special new name: P5976. I got my picture put in books, and, by golly—talk about luck!—I ended up in a museum (the Agora Museum) after all. If only my swanky-vase cousins could see me now, the grubby poor kid from the Kerameikos who changed the world.

FRANK L. HOLT (fholt@uh.edu) is a professor of history at the University of Houston and most recently author of *Into the Land of Bones: Alexander the Great in Afghanistan* (2005) and *Alexander the Great and the Mystery of the Elephant Medallions* (2003), both published by the University of California Press.

Outfoxed and Outfought

Why Darius' superior Persian army and navy lost to the Athenians at Marathon.

JASON K. FOSTER

On the morning of September 17, 490 BC, some 10,000 Greeks stood assembled on the plain of Marathon, preparing to fight to the last man. Behind them lay everything they held dear: their city, their homes, their families. In front of the outnumbered Greeks stood the assembled forces of the Persian empire, a seemingly invincible army with revenge, pillage and plunder on its mind.

The Athenians' feelings are best expressed by Aeschylus, who fought in the Persian wars, in his tragic play The Persians: "On, sons of the Hellenes! Fight for the freedom of your country! Fight for the freedom of your children and of your wives, for the gods of your fathers and for the sepulchers of your ancestors! All are now staked upon the strife!"

The two sides faced each another directly, waiting for the fight to start. The Athenians stalled for days, anticipating reinforcements promised by Sparta. But they knew they could not wait for long. The Persians, expecting as easy a victory as they had won against enemies so many times before, were in no hurry.

The Greeks, knowing the time for battle had come, began to move forward. Ostensibly, they advanced with focus and purpose, but beneath this firm veneer, as they looked on a vastly larger enemy—at least twice their number—many must have been fearful of what was to come. The Persian archers sat with their bows drawn, ready to loose a barrage of arrows that would send fear and confusion through the Greek ranks.

"The Athenians advanced at a run towards the enemy, not less than a mile away," recounted the historian Herodotus. "The Persians, seeing the attack developed at the double, prepared to meet it, thinking it suicidal madness for the Athenians to risk an assault with so small a force—rushing in with no support from either cavalry or archers."

Had the Persian archers been allowed to loose their bows, the battle might have ended before it had truly begun. Fighting their doubts and fears, the Athenians seized the initiative and rushed the Persians. Confronted by such a bold move and realizing their infantry would be pressed into action sooner than expected must have shaken Persian confidence.

The two Athenian commanders, Callimachus and Miltiades (the latter having fought in the Persian army himself), used their knowledge of Persian battle tactics to turn the tide further in their favor. As the clatter of spears, swords and shields echoed through the valley, the Greeks had ensured that their best hoplites (heavily armed infantry) were on the flanks and that their ranks were thinned in the center. Persian battle doctrine dictated that their best troops, true Persians, fought in the center, while conscripts, pressed into service from tribute states, fought on the flanks. The Persian elite forces surged into the center of the fray, easily gaining the ascendancy. But this time it was a fatal mistake. The Persian conscripts whom the Hellenic hoplites faced on the flanks quickly broke into flight. The Greeks then made another crucial decision: Instead of pursuing their fleeing foes, they turned inward to aid their countrymen fighting in the center of the battle.

By then, the Persians were in a state of utter confusion. Their tactics had failed, their cavalry was absent and their archers were useless. Their more heavily armed and armored opponents, who could sense that victory was close, were attacking them from three sides and pushing them into the sea. The Persians fled back to their ships. Many of the Athenians, buoyed by their success, dragged several of the Persian vessels to shore, slaughtering those on board.

When the day was over, the Greeks had won one of history's most famous victories, claiming to have killed about 6,400 Persians for the loss of only 192 Athenians. The Spartans eventually arrived, but only after the battle was long over. To assuage their disbelief in the Athenians' victory, they toured the battlefield. To their amazement, they found the claim of victory was indeed true. The Athenians had defeated the most powerful empire in the Western world.

Around the 5th century BC, the Persians under Cyrus the Great had rapidly expanded their domain. By the time of Darius I, the Persian empire covered most of southwest Asia and Asia Minor, reaching as far as the easternmost boundaries of Europe. The Persians demanded tribute and respect from all they dominated. The Greek cities in Asia Minor eventually decided to throw off the Persian yoke. Through those revolts, the assistance of the Athenians and the ensuing Battle of Marathon, the wheels had been set in motion to end Persian domination.

How did this sequence of events come to pass? From the time he ascended the throne, Darius, like all the kings before him, needed to conquer and add to the empire that his forebears had passed to him, to establish his worth as a ruler and maintain control. Establishing and retaining authority over such a vast dominion required thousands upon thousands of troops. To pay for the soldiery and to maintain the grandeur of the Persian capital, Persepolis (which Darius built to demonstrate his greatness), he needed more than the tribute from subjugated states. He needed to conquer more cities and territory to expand his treasury.

To the east of ancient Persia (modern-day Iran and Iraq) lay India and the Orient; expansion there held unknown dangers. To take this route, Darius would risk overextending his empire. To the west lay the inhospitable Libyan desert. To the north were the barbarian lands of the Scythians. Expansion into Europe seemed the most promising option, but the scattered city-states of Greece constituted a major roadblock to Darius' ambitions.

Before he could move on Greece, Darius had to achieve complete submission within his existing territories, and an empire of Persia's size was impossible to control centrally. Therefore, the Persians had established local governors or satraps, whose main role was to oversee the day-to-day functioning of their provinces and to ensure that all tribute was collected and sent to the capital. Many of these satraps ruled as tyrants. Understandably, the Greek cities east of the Aegean Sea would become restless and desire change when they cast a glance westward at the seeds of democratic society planted in Athens.

Dissent first began to appear on the island of Naxos, which revolted in 502 BC. The Naxians appealed to the despot of the Ionian city of Miletos, Aristagoras, for assistance. He agreed, meaning to take control of the island once the revolt had been crushed. For his plan to succeed, he enlisted the aid of Artaphernes, Darius' brother and the satrap of Lydia (modern-day Turkey). Aristagoras' tangled web fell apart when the plot against the Naxians failed. Owing the Persian emperor and his brother money and promised conquests, Aristagoras had no option but to incite his own people to revolt.

The revolt of Miletos led other cities to follow suit. The Ionian Greeks had also maintained strong trade and cultural ties with their kin on mainland Greece. Forced to pay tribute to a distant king, feeling the tyrannical push of the Persian governors and encouraged by the Athenians, many of these city-states decided to revolt. Athens sent 20 triremes (oar-propelled warships) to Ephesus. Their hoplites and the citizens of Miletos marched on the Lydian capital of Sardis and sacked it. On hearing of this in Persepolis, Darius was infuriated; according to legend, he instructed one of his servants to remind him three times daily of this Athenian outrage so he would never forget it.

The revolts in Ionia and an excuse to wreak vengeance on Athens gave Darius the perfect pretext to implement his plans of expansion in Europe. When he looked toward mainland Greece, he must have seen a disjointed conglomeration of city-states that bickered and fought among themselves. It must have seemed unlikely that such cities would form any lasting alliances and be capable of repelling a powerful foe. As the ruler with the largest army in the world, and with the success of his predecessors on which to build, Darius must have thought that one way or another victory would be assured.

In 492 BC, Darius gave Mardonius, his satrap in Thrace (northern Greece), command of 600 ships that sailed across the Hellespont (the Dardanelles) and along the coast. As it rounded Mount Athos, however, the fleet was destroyed by a freak storm, an event that would prove to have great significance. The Greeks took it as an encouraging omen that the gods must surely be on their side. Herodotus claims—with questionable accuracy—that the storm destroyed 300 ships and killed 20,000 men.

Two years later, Darius sent another 600 ships in a second attempt. Expecting little resistance, he sent emissaries to the cities of Greece asking for their submission and demanding offerings of earth and water. Most cities in the north and in Macedonia submitted to his demands. But war became inevitable when the Athenians refused, and the Spartans went even further and killed the Persian envoy.

A second Persian expedition was launched under the command of Datis and Darius' nephew, Artaphernes. As they moved across the Aegean, they subdued many of the island cities such as Naxos and Delos. Eventually they reached Eritrea, a large island off the Attic coast, and made their way to Marathon. Herodotus explains why the Persians chose to land at Marathon: "The part of Attic territory nearest Eritria—and also the best ground for cavalry to maneuver in—was at Marathon. To Marathon, therefore, Hippias directed the invading army, and the Athenians, as soon as the news arrived, hurried to meet it."

Marathon was also chosen to draw the Athenians away from Athens. While the hoplites were engaged on the field, the Persians planned to send their ships around the coast and easily capture the undefended city. The Persian plan was twofold: They knew that if the Athenian army was defeated outside of Athens, the city's civilian inhabitants would have no choice but to submit.

Almost immediately after hearing the news of the Persian landing, the Athenians sent a runner named Pheidippides to Sparta to ask for their assistance. The Spartans promised to send aid, but with a major qualification: No help would be forthcoming until the Carneia (a religious festival) was over. The Spartan refusal to commit troops before then left the Athenians with three choices: march out and meet the Persians at Marathon; defend the pass at Pallini; or stay in the city and defend its walls.

The Athenians chose Marathon. There were several reasons for this. The food supplies they would need to survive a protracted siege came from the surrounding countryside of Attica, which could easily be cut off by the encamped Persian army. The soon-to-be-vaunted Athenian navy was at that time little more than a flotilla and had no chance of defeating the Persian fleet. If the Persians were able to blockade both the land and sea, Athens could not withstand a sustained siege. The pass at Pallini was high in the mountains, but the Persians had sufficient forces to continue to attack pass defenders until Pallini fell.

Confronting the Persians at Marathon offered the Greeks several tactical possibilities. As stated by Herodotus, the geography of the plain of Marathon was significant in the Persian decision-making. Measuring approximately 10 miles long and three miles wide, it was flanked by boggy marshlands. A large, flat plain, it was perfect for the use of the Persians' main strike weapon: cavalry.

When the Athenians reached Marathon, they found the Persians camped along the coast. Obviously, the Greeks needed to take the high ground. Both sides sat encamped for nine days, each waiting for the other to make the first move. The Persians believed that the longer they stayed, the greater the fear that would rattle their opponents.

The outnumbered Athenians and their Plataean allies played for time in hopes that the Spartan hoplites would join them—not only to strengthen their numbers but because Spartan military renown stretched all the way to Persepolis, and a Spartan presence would surely dent Persian confidence. On the other hand, the longer the Persians stayed, the more cities would submit to them, lowering the confidence of the Athenian troops.

A meeting was held in the Greek camp to resolve the issue. The 10 Athenian generals (each of the original tribes that had first formed Athens had an elected general) voted, with five in favor of immediate battle and five voting to wait for the Spartans' arrival. According to Herodotus, it was the influence of Miltiades that swayed the decision. "With you it rests, Callimachus," he allegedly said, "either to lead Athens to slavery or, by securing her freedom, to leave behind to all future generations a memory far beyond even those who made Athens a democracy. For never since the time the Athenians became a people were they in so great a danger than now." Whether Miltiades was as influential as Herodotus made him out to be is uncertain; however, Callimachus voted in favor of starting the battle. Herodotus also stated that while each general normally took a daily turn in overall command, many of the lesser generals handed their turn over to Miltiades.

With approximately 1,000 Plataeans bolstering the Athenian ranks, the Hellenic forces mustered some 10,000 hoplites. The Persians may have numbered as high as 48,000. Familiar with the tactics and strengths of their enemy, the Greeks knew the Persian cavalry had to be taken out of the calculations. The Persians could not use the cavalry on one side because of the marshland. Nor could they use it on the opposite flank, as the Athenians had buried large stakes in the ground. It seems likely that the Persians, even without the use of either flank, would have used their premier weapon, but for whatever reason, the Persian cavalry was away from the battlefield. Miltiades may well have learned of the Persian cavalry's absence and then decided it was time to attack.

The absence of Persian cavalry is one of the reasons for the Greek victory. The second is that the Persians were completely unprepared for and unable to adapt to the Greeks' tactics. Persian battle tactics that previously had served them well entailed stationing their archers at the front to fire volley after volley of arrows into the enemy ranks, wreaking havoc and instilling fear. Once that objective was achieved, Persian infantry would move in to slaughter the confused opposition, with cavalry used only to complete the task when the enemy was routed.

The Greeks held an advantage at Marathon in the equipment of their infantry. An Athenian hoplite carried a heavy, 9-foot spear, wore a solid breastplate and carried an almost body-length shield. The Persian infantryman, in contrast, wore little more than robes and carried a shorter sword and a wicker or cane shield. Therefore, close-quarter combat favored the Athenians. The Persian disadvantage was exacerbated by the Greek use of the phalanx formation—an eight-hoplite by eight-hoplite square. The hoplites at the from would interlock their shields, as would the men to the side, forming an almost impenetrable barrier. Because of their lesser numbers, the Greeks had to thin their formation out, but even that would eventually further serve their purpose.

Although they had won a great victory, the Athenians knew the Persian threat had not passed, and they quickly marched back to prepare the defense of Athens from the attack they were certain would come. In an amazing feat of strength and endurance, they marched at double time directly from the battlefield and managed to reach the city before the Persian ships arrived.

With time of the essence, the Athenians dispatched Pheidippides to inform Athens' populace of their victory before the troops arrived. The tale goes that after running the 26 miles from Marathon to Athens, Pheidippides exclaimed: "Rejoice! We conquer!" then died from exhaustion. Whether true or not, that is the source of the modern-day marathon race; the distance of the modern race reflects the distance Pheidippides ran.

Even though the future battles of Salamis and Plataea were fought against a greater Persian threat, had Marathon ended in defeat, those later battles would never have occurred. Themistocles, who fought at Marathon, saw that Athens had been lucky the first time, and had the Persians conducted their campaign differently, the outcome might well have been different. Hence, soon after Marathon he successfully petitioned to have Athens build a stronger navy, which led to its success at Salamis.

Marathon smashed the myth of Persian invincibility, an achievement that lent a critical measure of confidence to the Greeks who fought the Persians again at Salamis and Plataea. It meant that many of the same commanders who served at Marathon were at the later battles and had knowledge of the Persian mind, and in the longer term, it would lead Alexander the Great on his conquest of Asia and the eventual decline and downfall of the Persian empire.

While most credit the second installment of the Persian wars with the birth of the Athenian renaissance, one could argue that Marathon was the catalyst for, and much of the reason behind, the Athenians' belief that they were on par with the Spartans— which allowed them to flourish. Had Marathon been a defeat and Athens annihilated, the Western democracy, culture, art and philosophy that developed from this period in history might have been lost, and the Western world today could be very different.

JASON K. FOSTER is a London-based teacher and historian specializing in ancient Rome, Greece and Egypt.

For further reading, he recommends: *The Histories,* by Herodotus; and *Plutarch's Rise and Fall of Athens.*

From *Military History,* January/February 2007, pp. 57–63. Copyright © 2007 by Weider History Group. Reprinted by permission.

Mighty Macedonian
Alexander the Great

RICHARD COVINGTON

Taking measured steps around a lush garden terrace in ancient Egypt, Anthony Hopkins as the Macedonian general Ptolemy dictates his memoirs of helping Alexander the Great conquer the world. While he strolls beneath the palm trees of the ancient library in Alexandria—in reality, a sprawling movie set at Shepperton Studios outside London—the aged ruler of Egypt delivers a bombshell. "We killed him," Ptolemy says.

Literally? Or metaphorically? With Oliver Stone writing and directing, you never know for sure, even though the notion that Alexander was poisoned by his generals is "as dead as doornails," says Robin Lane Fox, a British biographer of Alexander who worked as a consultant on the movie. Stone, after all, defended the multiple-gunmen conspiracy theory of the Kennedy assassination in his 1991 movie, *JFK*.

In the library scene, Ptolemy, portrayed by Hopkins as a world-weary old soldier, says that if Alexander's men didn't literally poison his body, their refusal to follow him deeper into India surely poisoned his spirit. "I never believed in his dream," he says. "The dreamers exhaust us."

True enough, no conqueror ever dreamed so exhaustively as Alexander the Great. In the fourth century B.C., the Macedonian warrior-king attacked the Persian Empire, the most powerful realm in the world, with almost 50,000 soldiers—then ranged across three continents for more than a decade, subduing tens of millions of people. By the time Alexander died in June 323 B.C., six weeks shy of his 33rd birthday, his empire stretched from the Balkans to the Himalayas—an unprecedented kingdom that spanned what is now Greece, Turkey, Lebanon, Syria, Jordan, Israel, Egypt, Iraq, Kuwait, Iran, Afghanistan, Pakistan and parts of India, Turkmenistan, Uzbekistan and Tajikistan.

Despite his imperialist accomplishments, Alexander has always seemed a melancholy figure, possessed by what the ancient Greeks called *pothos,* a passionate yearning. Once, when court philosopher Anaxarchus described the infinite number of worlds in the universe to him, Alexander broke down crying. "There are so many worlds," he lamented, "and I have not yet conquered even one."

It was this pothos, as much as his military genius, that would make him a romantic hero—to the 17th-century English poet John Dryden, to Sigmund Freud, to world leaders from Julius Caesar and Napoleon to Dwight David Eisenhower. Others, such as St. Augustine and Dante, reviled him as a murdering, plundering bandit. Frank Holt, an Alexander authority at the University of Houston, estimates that more than 2,000 books and articles have been written about him in the past 40 years.

Yet the truth about Alexander remains elusive. For one thing, as Cambridge University's Paul Cartledge (author of *Alexander the Great: The Hunt for a New Past*) points out, none of his actual words was recorded verbatim. Although there were several written eyewitness accounts of Alexander's campaigns, they survive only as fragments written down centuries later by sympathetic interpreters. Other writers suppressed or distorted events to make him look heroic or demonic, depending on their agendas.

Historians' verdicts vary. Some view Alexander as a charismatic, visionary leader intent on constructing a fusion of East and West, while others condemn him as a cruel and unstable megalomaniac, an ancient Stalin or Hitler who cared less about unifying mankind than consolidating control over as much territory as he could grab. A third camp credits Alexander with bringing Western notions of civilization to the East, using methods that seem brutal by today's standards but were acceptable in their time. Perhaps historians are divided because the man himself was divided—swinging wildly from blind wrath to acts of selfless generosity.

Historical novelists like Mary Renault and Valerio Manfredi have eagerly mined the Alexander legend, but few filmmakers have tackled the subject. Director Robert Rossen's 1956 *Alexander the Great,* with Richard Burton, was a heavy-handed dud. Since the success of *Gladiator* in 2000, however, "swords-and-sandals" epics—last in vogue with *Ben-Hur* in 1959 and *Spartacus* in 1960—are back, and at least three Alexander films are in the works—by Baz Luhrmann (director of *Strictly Ballroom* and *Moulin Rouge*), due out next year; by Ilya Salkind (producer of *Superman*); and by Stone, whose $150 million juggernaut with Colin Farrell in the title role is due to open across the country this month.

"Basically, I wanted to do the film as an experiment," says Stone, "to see if Alexander's motivations hold up today." Taking a break from editing the movie at a studio west of Paris in June, the director sounded more like a star-struck fan than notorious

Hollywood maverick. "He was the Sun God, the star of all time, Joe DiMaggio, Mickey Mantle rolled into one," Stone says. "Some historians put him down . . . in a class with Genghis Khan and Attila the Hun, but they miss the point. No tyrant ever gave back so much. His life was not about money for himself, but about his growing curiosity, engaging and fulfilling his intellect, his consciousness."

There's substantial agreement on one issue: Alexander's military prowess. "He would've made mincemeat of any Roman who came over the hill," says biographer Lane Fox.

"Julius Caesar would've gone straight back home as fast as his horse could carry him." And Napoleon? "Alexander would've wiped him out too. Napoleon only fought dodos."

Alexander personally spearheaded his attacks, suffering severe arrow, lance, sword and knife wounds. As Roman historian Arrian said of Alexander around A.D. 150, "The sheer pleasure of battle, as other pleasures are to other men, was irresistible." Once, when he found himself stranded without a ladder atop a fortress surrounding Multan in present-day Pakistan, he jumped straight down alone into the midst of the enemy, instead of leaping outside the walls to safety. Managing to fend off his attackers until help arrived, he received a nearly fatal arrow wound that may have punctured his lung. When his doctor insisted that officers hold him down to keep him from squirming, Alexander waved them away, sitting stoically as the surgeon sliced the deeply embedded barb out of his chest. "As a warrior and strategist," Lane Fox says, "no one compares to Alexander."

Born in July 356 B.C. in Pella, near the Aegean coast in then Macedonia (now Greece), Alexander was the only son of the ruthless King Philip II and the hot-tempered Olympias. (After Philip died, she killed Philip's last wife, Eurydice, and Eurydice's baby daughter, Europa.) At the time of Alexander's birth and right up until Philip's assassination 20 years later, Alexander's father was preoccupied with consolidating the Macedonian Empire through diplomacy, political marriage, intrigue and war—particularly against the rebellious Greeks to the south. Although Macedonians spoke Greek and regarded themselves as Greek, the Athenians, Thebans and citizens of other Greek city-states dismissed them as culturally inferior hicks.

According to Peter Green, professor emeritus of classics at the University of Texas at Austin, Olympias spoiled her son outrageously; he idolized her in return. The love-hate relationship that Alexander had with his father, says Green, was "an ambivalent blend of genuine admiration and underlying competitiveness." From his father, Alexander is believed to have inherited courage, quickness of decision and intellectual perceptiveness. His mother, who may have tried to turn their son against his father, gave him a will stronger than Philip's, as well as fervent religiosity.

When the prince was a young boy, he eyed a black stallion, Bucephalas, that neither the king nor anyone else could control. As the horse stymied rider after rider, Alexander noticed that he reared at the sight of his own shadow. When Alexander's turn came, he calmly stroked the animal, turned his head into the sun so that he could not see his shadow and galloped off in triumph. "My boy, you must find a kingdom big enough for your ambitions," Philip declared. "Macedonia is too small for you." Alexander rode Bucephalas until the war horse died in 326 B.C. fighting elephant-mounted brigades in present-day Pakistan.

During his early teens, Alexander was taught by Aristotle, who inspired the prince's lifelong interest in biology, medicine and zoology. Ultimately, Alexander broke ranks with his tutor on an issue that was to become critical for the future empire. Unlike Aristotle, who viewed non-Greeks as barbarians, the Macedonian Alexander was less prejudiced, and would come to rely on conquered Persians and other foreigners to play prominent roles governing his far-flung territory.

Alexander was a handsome youth with shoulder-length blond hair, prominent forehead, ruddy complexion and "a certain melting look in his eyes." Historical sources suggest Alexander was bisexual, an orientation that bore no stigma in his day. He had at least two male lovers—his childhood friend and fellow soldier Hephaestion, and the Persian eunuch Bagoas—and fathered a child with his Sogdian wife, Roxane, and perhaps one with his Persian mistress. Even so, he had an ambivalent attitude toward sex. "Sex and sleep alone make me conscious that I am mortal," he supposedly once remarked.

Raised to believe that he was descended from both the Greek heroes Achilles and Herakles, the young Alexander acquired a zealous reverence for the ancient Greek myths. He loved to recite passages from the plays of Euripides, and he slept with a dagger and a well-thumbed copy of the *Iliad* beneath his pillow during his campaigns.

In the year 336 B.C., as Philip entered an outdoor theater to preside over a wedding, he was fatally stabbed by a bodyguard named Pausanias. Although it was widely rumored that Olympias, recently rejected by the king in favor of a younger wife, colluded in the murder, Lane Fox says the idea that her son had a hand in the assassination is "a bit wild."

Nevertheless, Stone's film, playing with the son's possible Oedipal feelings for Olympias, keeps both of them on the hook. "Anybody who's a dramatist has to ask if Alexander and his mother had a role in Philip's death," the director counters with a conspiratorial grin. Unlike Oedipus, who did not know the man he killed was his father at the time of the murder, Alexander would have been fully aware of his crime's enormity.

Just 20 years old, Alexander seized the throne, summarily murdering or exiling a number of rivals. Within a year, he reasserted control over the recalcitrant cities and tribes that had frustrated Philip, expanding the boundaries of the Macedonian kingdom north to the Danube and west toward the Adriatic. When Thebes revolted, he slaughtered or sold into slavery some 30,000 citizens, then razed the city, except for temples and the house of the revered poet Pindar. After this example, Athens and the other Greek cities—with the stubborn exception of Sparta—pledged allegiance to the young king. Perhaps more important, they also promised him soldiers and financial support for an invasion of Persia.

In May 334 B.C., Alexander sailed his army three miles across the Hellespont (Dardanelles strait) in present-day Turkey, casting his spear into the sandy shore to dramatically claim all of Asia as his "spear-won prize," in the Roman historian Curtius' vivid first-century imagery.

After defeating an advance Persian force at the Granicus River 60 miles northeast of Troy and fighting all across Asia Minor, Alexander faced off against the Persian king Darius III at Issus in southern Turkey. Though sources disagree on the exact numbers, Alexander probably faced a larger force of Persians, across a narrow plain. Alexander's cavalry, backed by archers and by infantry wielding 16-foot-long pikes, smashed through the enemy in well-orchestrated charges. Alexander spurred Bucephalas headlong toward Darius, who spun his chariot around in retreat and ultimately made a successful getaway.

The conquest continued. Following a grinding, seven-month siege, Alexander captured the island fortress of Tyre, in present-day Lebanon; Egyptians, oppressed by the Persians, welcomed him as a liberator. Sailing down the Nile to the Mediterranean, the 24-year-old sovereign came across a former Persian fortress with a superb natural harbor that he chose as the site of his future Egyptian capital, the first of several Alexandrias he would establish as he swept east.

The young ruler still craved a clear-cut victory to lay claim to all of Persia. Darius, meanwhile, was conscripting a stupendous new army from the farthest reaches of his empire, gathering his forces in the Persian winter capital of Babylon. The Persian ruler (who hadn't taken Alexander seriously enough the first time they faced off) finally marched more than 200,000 men 275 miles north to the open plain at Gaugamela, where he deployed cavalry clad in chain mail, chariots equipped with scythe blades on their wheels, and mounted elephants.

With 47,000 men, Alexander was spectacularly outnumbered. When his senior generals advised him to attack at night to even the odds, he indignantly retorted, "I will not demean myself by stealing victory like a thief." The king slept late on the day of battle, coolly emerging with an all-or-nothing plan. He ordered one wing of his cavalry to charge Darius' far left flank, another to aim for the far right, leaving his own infantry vulnerable in the center. As Darius' mounted corps tore away in opposite directions to meet the Macedonian squadrons, Alexander spurred a wedge of riders straight into the heart of the Persian ranks, splitting them in two. The gamble worked. Within minutes, the battle turned into a debacle. The Persians sounded a retreat, and Darius again slipped away on horseback.

After Alexander occupied Babylon, he continued his triumphant march east to Persepolis, the ceremonial center of Persia. He marveled at the dazzling gilt, bronze and marble palace and the hundred-columned hall where kings reigned from a golden throne. Inside the treasury he seized 3,000 tons of gold and silver, among the richest hoards in history.

Alexander and his officers celebrated with a feast. The inebriated king grabbed a torch and set fire to the tapestries and beams of the massive palace. Other drunken revelers joined him, stoking the inferno to the accompaniment of flutes and singing. Within hours, Persia's hallowed shrine was a smoking ruin.

Darius ranged across the countryside in what is now northern Iran, trying to rebuild his devastated army. Alexander, in pursuit, caught up with him too late. Bessus, one of the monarch's own generals, had murdered Darius and proclaimed himself king. At about this time, Alexander was making a critical transformation, one that would later alienate his troops but lead to a dramatic cultural shift. Hoping to solidify control over his new territories, he adopted Persian dress and customs and invited former adversaries into his inner circle. To win the support of his new subjects, Alexander even ordered a royal burial in Persepolis for Darius. But "the sight of their young king parading in outlandish robes, and on intimate terms with the quacking, effeminate barbarian nobles he had so lately defeated, filled [his troops] with genuine disgust," Green writes in his biography *Alexander of Macedon, 356–323 B.C.*

When Alexander was informed that disgruntled soldiers were plotting to kill him, he arrested seven of the alleged conspirators, including Philotas, the son of Parmenio, a venerated general who had fought under both Philip and Alexander. Although the evidence against Philotas was weak, he and the others were stoned to death. Then, anticipating that Parmenio would seek revenge for his son's execution, Alexander had the 70-year-old commandant stabbed to death. The killings had a chilling effect on Alexander's men. "From now on, Alexander never trusted his troops," Green says. "The feeling was mutual."

But Alexander still thirsted for conquest. He led his unhappy men over the Hindu Kush, to capture Bessus and take control of his home province of Bactria in what is now northern Afghanistan. Crossing the 11,600-foot snow-bound passes in April, many of the soldiers suffered severe frostbite and snow blindness. Bessus and his Persian troops, caught off-guard by Alexander's risky offensive, retreated into Sogdiana (present-day Uzbekistan, Turkmenistan and Tajikistan). But Bessus' Sogdian allies, fearing Alexander's attack, handed him over. Alexander ordered Bessus' ears and nose cut off, then likely had him crucified.

In just five years, Alexander had toppled the mighty Persian Empire and expanded his empire eastward 2,500 miles. Yet he was far from content, and his control over his men was slipping. In the summer of 328 B.C., Alexander set up headquarters in Maracanda (now Samarkand in modern-day Uzbekistan). When he started boasting about his victories at yet another drunken banquet, Cleitus, a grizzled cavalry officer who had saved Alexander's life at the Granicus River, bluntly reminded him how much he owed his father and the Macedonian veterans. Incensed, Alexander accused Cleitus and other senior officers of cowardice. "Those who died defending you are the lucky ones," Cleitus roared back at him. "At least they never lived to see Macedonians thrashed with Median rods or kow-towing to Persians before they can have an audience with their own king!" Screaming that this was yet another plot against him, Alexander grabbed a spear and ran his beloved comrade through the chest, killing him instantly. Immediately, the king was possessed by remorse. Yanking the spear out of Cleitus' body, he tried to impale himself on it. After a few officers jerked it away from him, he shut himself up in his tent for days, grieving.

Eventually, Alexander rallied, prodding his multinational crew of Macedonian, Persian and Bactrian soldiers toward the next goal: India. En route, the 28-year-old became smitten with

Roxane, a princess captured in the siege of a Sogdian fortress and "the loveliest woman in Asia, after Darius's wife," according to Arrian, a second-century Greek biographer rarely given to exaggeration. Marrying for love in 327 B.C., the pragmatic Alexander also calculated that an alliance with a noble family from outer Persia would help legitimize his power.

Pushing farther east to the Hydaspes River (now the Jhelum River in Pakistan), the Macedonians faced off against the Indian king Porus at a crossing some 70 miles southeast of present-day Islamabad. Alexander's 50,000 troops vanquished a force of 35,000 soldiers and 200 mounted elephants, but his men proved no match for monsoon season. "It was pelting with rain, the men were terrified, there were snakes everywhere," says Lane Fox. "They were lost and did not feel they could go on any more."

Standing in front of the assembled ranks near the Hyphasis River, Coenus, a senior commander, did the unthinkable: he pleaded with Alexander to go home. Furious, the young king said that anyone who left would be considered a deserter, then stormed off to sulk in his tent for two days. But when Alexander's personal seer reported that the signs to continue east into India were unfavorable, the king used this excuse to save face and turn back to Macedonia. On hearing of Alexander's change of heart, the exhausted veterans erupted in cheers. Even in retreat, the contrarian Alexander scorned the known route home—back over the Hindu Kush to Babylon—in favor of leading his flotilla of 1,800 ships down the unfamiliar Jhelum, Chenab and Indus rivers to the Indian Ocean and hence west to the Persian Gulf.

It was far from smooth sailing. En route, hostile tribes put up fierce resistance—and were pitilessly exterminated. Cartledge views this trail of blood as one prolonged "fit of frustration at having been forced by his own troops to turn back." In July 325, nine months after setting sail, the Macedonians finally reached the Indian Ocean.

Still focused on building his empire, Alexander concocted an audacious scheme to revive ancient sea routes for transporting gold, spices, ivory and precious stones from India to the Middle East. The idea was that ships carrying food and supplies would sail up the coast of the Arabian Sea while Alexander led soldiers over a parallel inland route. The ships would drop off food for the army at prearranged intervals, while the soldiers in turn would supply the fleet with fresh water. If this land-sea relay made it to the Persian Gulf on a dry run, merchants could follow the same itinerary.

The scheme would prove to be one of Alexander's gravest mistakes, subjecting his men to what Lane Fox calls "the most hellish match that [he] could possibly have chosen." In the oppressive night—the only time the sprawling caravan could move—the temperature seldom dipped below 95 degrees. Worst of all, monsoon winds delayed the fleet after Alexander's departure; the navy and army never met up, forcing both to subsist on the limited food and water they had brought with them. Reportedly, by the end of the two-month march, 15,000 of Alexander's men, or nearly half of the corps accompanying him, had perished—more than all the men killed in battle. The fleet, in contrast, reached the Iranian coast almost intact.

Back in Kirman, Persia, Alexander did little to mend relations with his men. He executed 6 of 20 provincial governors, and deposed two more. Then, in what Cartledge describes as a "reign of terror," he executed 600 men from his own garrisons for rape and pillaging in his absence. At Susa, he commanded 90 of his officers to marry aristocratic Persian women to strengthen the political bonds between Macedonians and Persians.

Despite the growing tensions—and crises like the sudden death of his lover, the soldier Hephaestion—Alexander still "hunted, diced, played ball, joked and banqueted" with his men. At one of these banquets, Alexander downed his usual enormous quantity of wine, then collapsed with a fever. Twelve days later, on June 10, 323 B.C., he died, probably of malaria. Just before he expired, he was asked to name a successor. Alexander weakly answered that the empire should go "to the strongest," Arrian wrote. "I foresee a great funeral contest over me."

With Alexander gone, the empire was riven by dissent, with his commanders fighting over territory. Roxane and her son, Alexander IV, born six weeks after the king's death, were murdered by a distant relative when the boy was 12 or 13; so was the king's mother, Olympias. As Alexander's embalmed body was being transported to Macedonia in a magnificent chariot, Ptolemy hijacked it to Alexandria, where it would stay for six centuries. Lane Fox speculates that the coffin later disappeared, probably destroyed in riots in the third century A.D.

Although Alexander's empire splintered shortly after his death, Greek arts, science and culture continued to pervade Middle Eastern and Asian societies for centuries. In Egypt, Greek physicians taught the study of human anatomy. In Babylon, Greek physicists devised a technique to electroplate silver to copper. Greek city planning prevailed in the many towns the king had established and was widely adopted elsewhere. Greek myths and philosophy spread well beyond the former empire's borders.

Alexander's legacy has long been a matter of debate. Cleitarchus, a fourth-century B.C. historian from Alexandria, portrays the king as a cruel, paranoid alcoholic. Eratosthenes of Cyrene, a third-century B.C. scholar at the Alexandria library, suggests that Alexander's conquests opened the eyes of the Greeks to other civilizations. Plutarch ventures the opposite—that Alexander civilized Persians, Sogdians and others. Johannes Gustav Droysen, a 19th-century German historian, proposes that the Macedonian king wanted above all to unify the entire world. Yet the modern historian Brian Bosworth dismisses such idealism, comparing Alexander's Indian campaign to Cortez's genocidal war against the Aztecs and condemning the king as a cold-blooded imperialist.

Lane Fox says that "the fashion of the moment is to take a sour view of Alexander." But he adds: "You've still got to explain why so many people followed him with such devotion for so long."

"These days," says director Stone, a Vietnam veteran, "we have a strong antipathy for conquerors, but in Alexander's time, war was a way of life and soldiering a much more honorable profession."

As many historians conclude, it was his achievements as a commander on the field of battle that justify the name Alexander the Great. He was a military genius, and a hero to his men. He never asked them to do something he would not do himself, and he bore the wounds to prove it. He also shared his vast riches with his men. When he challenged his army to take the most difficult route, to do the impossible, they amazed themselves when they succeeded. At the Hyphasis River near Amritsar, when his soldiers pressured him to turn back, they may well have been too hasty. Alexander's promised land of India was nearly in their grasp.

Nowhere did Alexander articulate what was behind his all-consuming desire to master the world. To speculate that he was trying to surpass his father and win his mother's love, as some psychohistorians have done, is to take the easy way out. It may be, as Ptolemy wistfully concludes in the Stone film, that Alexander was blessed and cursed with an eternally unsatisfied longing, a pothos even he could not fathom. Perpetually racing the gods, his destiny remained exactly where it served him best—just out of reach.

Paris-based author RICHARD COVINGTON last wrote for *Smithsonian* about Cambodia's Angkor temples in February 2004.

From *Smithsonian*, November 2004, pp. 73–78, 80, 82. Copyright © 2004 by Richard Covington. Reprinted by permission of the author.

Etruscan Women
Dignified, Charming, Literate and Free

INGRID D. ROWLAND

Most travelers' tales from the ancient world have been told by men, so its not surprising that their yarns devote special attention to the local women they encounter. The most famous of all those ancient travelers, Homer's Odysseus, trooped off to Troy in pursuit of Helen of Sparta, lingering nine years on the Maltese island of Gozo with Calypso, touched down on the North African coast with the Lotus-Eaters, sailed past the Sirens of Sorrento en route to Circe's lair, popped out naked from behind a bush to approach Nausicaa of Corfu, and finally settled on the little island of Ithaca with his wife, Penelope—who still bests them all through her irresistible combination of integrity and intelligence.

Later sailors would have said, however, that Odysseus's 10-year itinerary left one huge gap: Homer makes only one reference to the Etruscans—the literate and sophisticated people who by the eighth century B.C.E. were inhabiting the region of central Italy bounded by the Arno and Tiber rivers and the Tyrrhenian Sea, a region corresponding to modern-day Tuscany. Moreover, in that one reference, Homer transforms the Etruscans into the seven-headed monster Scylla (her name means "the Bitch"), who snatches seven men from Odysseus's ship as it passes through the Straits of Messina.

The Athenian playwright Euripides, in his tragedy *Medea* (431 B.C.E.), was already claiming that Scylla stood in Homer's epic for the Etruscan pirates who jealously guarded access to the sea that still bears their name—the Greek word for "Etruscan" was "Tyrrhenian."

Perhaps only those monstrously fierce Etruscan pirates could have kept such an inveterate swain as Odysseus from working his charms on Etruscan women, those ravishing creatures who had already begun to captivate the Greeks of Homer's time. Perhaps we see something of their legendary allure in Circe, the witch of Monte Circeo (south of Rome), who serves Odysseus's men a potion that turns them into pigs before she hops happily into bed with the hero. Etruscan women's freedom of action, their appetite for wine and their loose morals were the talk of their Greek and, later, their Roman neighbors. In his *Histories,*

the fourth-century B.C.E. Greek historian Theopompus of Chios could hardly contain his leering fascination:

> Sharing wives is an established Etruscan custom. Etruscan women take particular care of their bodies and exercise often, sometimes along with the men, and sometimes by themselves. It is not a disgrace for them to be seen naked. They do not share their couches with their husbands but with the other men who happen to be present, and they propose toasts to anyone they choose. They are expert drinkers and very attractive.

Theopompus's account, which goes on to discuss public displays of affection, spouse-swapping and boy toys, is almost certainly exaggerated. The men and women who recline together in the painted banquet scenes from Tarquinian tombs, in a set of famous sarcophagi from Cerveteri (one in the Louvre and two in Rome's Villa Giulia Museum), and on sculpted relief decorations from buildings at Murlo and Acquarossa seem overwhelmingly to be married couples, whether they are divine or mortal. Their conviviality comes nowhere near Roman standards of probity—a Roman general was never supposed to laugh. But look at the banquet scenes from the tombs at Tarquinia, for example, and you will see nothing like the ribald parties held by the Greeks, with courtesans and Ganymedes; if anything, they resemble lively family outings in modem Tuscany.

The images of banquets begin as early as the sixth century B.C.E., the probable date of the Cerveteri sarcophagi and the architectural ornaments from Murlo and Acquarossa. Wealthy women, their pale skin set off by flushed cheeks and deep red lips, flaunt big earrings and close-fitting rounded caps much like those favored by their contemporaries along the Ionian coast of Asia Minor. Their finely woven dresses crinkle like Venetian silk scarves, and their soft red shoes, with flashy pointed toes, seem only natural on the ancestors of a Tuscan shoemaker named Cuccio Cucci. Their names, when we have them, are as sonorous as they are peculiar: Tanchvil, Larthia, Thania. Tanchvil—with its root *evil*, or "gift" must mean something like "Dorothy" (Greek for "God's gift").

One sixth-century B.C.E. Tanchvil entered Roman legend as Tanaquil, the resourceful wife of Lucumo, the fifth king of

Rome. As the Roman historian Livy tells the story, Lucumo, despite his thoroughly Etruscan name (*lauchme* means "chief"), was in fact the son of a Demaratus of Corinth, one of many Greek men who seem to have settled down along the shores of the Tynhenian Sea with an Etruscan wife. (The epitaph of another Etruscanized Greek, Larth Hipucrate, is still preserved in Lucumo's home town of Tarquinia.)

Tanaquil shares some characteristics with Homer's Circe: She has the gift of oracular vision, and she is a charmer of magical appeal. Her sage advice is what transforms Livy's Lucumo into a king. Upon ascending to the throne, Lucumo takes a new name, Tarquinius, and is later described as Priscus, meaning "The Early." Livy credits Tarquinius Priscus with most of the innovations that made Rome a real city—proper drainage, city planning, lavish temples, legal institutions—but he implicitly ascribes the king's authority to Tanaquil. Livy lived from 59 B.C.E. until 17 C.E., and his account of Tanaquil shows how consistently, half a millennium after Tanaquil and Tarquinius Priscus lived, the Romans continued to view Etruscan women as strong, influential participants in public as well as private life.

Not all the charms of Etruscan women were natural: A fifth-century B.C.E. tomb from Tarquinia shows dark-haired men reclining alongside wives as strikingly blonde as the angels in some 15th-century C.E. Tuscan paintings. Tuscan women of the Renaissance bleached their hair with a combination of sunlight and lemon juice. Etruscan women must have used much the same recipe. They perfumed themselves with scented oils, sold in tiny, exquisite Corinthian vases or glass vessels. They applied their cosmetics with ivory sticks and combed their hair with ivory combs, checking the results in the burnished golden glow of their bronze mirrors. The backs of many of these mirrors are incised with mythological scenes, often with written labels suggesting that Etruscan women were readers. These mirrors now provide important clues to Etruscan myth, Etruscan religion and some times even to the Etruscan language: One image of Leda and the swan is labeled "Lata" and "Tusna"—allowing the linguist Jaan Puhvel to add another word to an Etruscan vocabulary that still remains frustratingly small. Other mirrors simply show naked ladies with wings; thus the owners' charms are given mythological form.

The way the Etruscans—male and female—chose to memorialize themselves tells us much about the way they lived. The repertory of decorations on Etruscan ash urns from Chiusi and Volterra favors active scenes: battles, chariot races, hunting, whether the deceased is a man or a woman. Perhaps Etruscan men had the final say in the kinds of images they wanted associated with themselves and their wives. Or perhaps the unusual freedom Etruscan women enjoyed gave them a taste for action, in this way distinguishing them from their Greek and Roman counterparts.

The second-century B.C.E. sarcophagus of Larthia Seianti, from the Seianti family of Chiusi, was discovered in 1877 and now resides in the Florence Archaeological Museum. That of her relative Seianti Hanunia Tlesnasa, likewise discovered in the 19th century, traveled as far as the British Museum. (At the time, the city of Chiusi sold Etruscan antiquities without much concern for provenance, or even authenticity; in newspaper advertisements, the city encouraged buyers to order the kinds of artifacts they wanted!) Seianti Hanunia Tlesnasa's sarcophagus, however, was so authentic that it still contained the lady's mortal remains, which were recently analyzed by a team of curators and a forensic physician. Wealthy and well-connected as Seianti Hanunia Tlesnasa must have been, her life could not have been easy, it turns out. At the age of about 18, she was injured in what may have been a riding accident. The mishap crushed her pelvis and left her limping, and probably in constant pain. None the less, she lived into her 50s. (Medicine in Etruria was subject to all the drawbacks of an era before anesthesia and antibiotics, but the Etruscans did develop a sophisticated dentistry, which included bridges with prosthetic teeth.)

Both Larthia Seianti and Seianti Hanunia Tlesnasa recline on what could either be a banqueting couch or a bed; a sarcophagus of comparable size in the Chiusi museum shows another wealthy woman lying in bed with the covers up to her chin. More modest urns show the deceased wrapped in a blanket and curled up in a deep, comforting sleep. Quite a different picture of death, and of bereaved parenthood, is provided by an urn at Volterra, which has an extraordinary image of a skinny baby staring with huge eyes into the unknown, heart-breakingly lonely on its narrow blanket.

Two fourth-century B.C.E. Etruscan sarcophagi from Vulci, now side-by-side in the Museum of Fine Arts in Boston, show two couples from two generations of the same family reclining on their marriage-beds. The older pair, Larth Tetnies and Tanchvil Tarnai, wear the elaborate clothes in which most Etruscans dress up to face the afterlife, but Arnth and his wife, Visnai, despite their stylish Greek-inspired coiffures, lie daringly naked, looking deeply into each other's eyes for all eternity, as devoted, and with the same kind of attractive maturity, as Odysseus and Penelope.

Attractive maturity is less evident in an elderly, homely Etruscan couple from Volterra, stretched out on a banqueting couch, their wrinkled skin and piercingly shrewd expressions shown without compromise—though so, too, is the solidity of their bond to each other. In order to look into her husband's face while reclining beside him, the wife must twist her body around with all the agility of a contortionist. It is typical of Etruscan artistry to emphasize a powerful emotional tie at the expense of a strictly accurate depiction of physical reality. The director of Volterra's Guarnacci Museum, Gabriele Cateni, suggests that the couple may have commissioned this traditional Etruscan sarcophagus as late as the first century B.C.E., making it a touching document not only of two individuals but also of their entire culture, gradually disappearing under the steady pressure of Roman domination.

Conquest by the Romans eventually destroyed whatever was left of Etruscan literature, except for the ritual books whose use continued, remarkably, into the sixth century of the Common Era. It is doubly frustrating, therefore, to see how many of the little alabaster sarcophagi in which the Etruscans of Volterra buried their dead show women with wax writing tablets or folded linen books. What were they reading and writing? Pliny the Elder (23–79 C.E.) mentions an Etruscan writer of tragedies,

Volnius (whom the Etruscans themselves would have called Velnie), and we see ample evidence of the singers and dancers who must have helped to transmit the Greek and local myths we see depicted on temples, tombs, furniture, clothing, utensils and dishes. But most of what we know about Etruscan life is strictly material, as concrete as the spindles and loom weights from which Etruscan women produced their luxurious robes, the luxuries great and small for which Etruria was famous throughout the Mediterranean world.

How could the women of Etruria not have been the envy of their Greek and Roman counterparts? Look at Greek painted vases from the sixth century B.C.E., those colorful depictions of banquets and symposia, and the only women you will find are the prostitutes called *hetairai,* dancing and playing their pipes, posing no threat at all to the men gathered for an evening of heady intellectual debate. The banquet hall was certainly no place for a proper Athenian lady. Roman women led similarly restricted lives, sober and silent in the presence of men.

What a contrast, then, were the freedoms enjoyed by Etruscan women, who dined alongside Etruscan men, partaking of their wine without reservation. And in death, too, Etruscan women were not shortchanged, their burials rivaling those of their husbands, brothers and uncles, filled with great quantities of luxurious goods. The Larthias and Tanchvils and Thanias we encounter on sarcophagi and wall paintings were unusual in the ancient world. Powerful, dignified, elegant and aristocratic, they not only inhabited the world of men, they seem to have been every bit their equals.

Rome's Craftiest General
Scipio Africanus

JAMES LACEY

Publius Cornelius Scipio Africanus learned the art of war in the hardest and bloodiest of all forums—on the battlefield against Hannibal. As a 17-year-old, he followed his father, Roman consul Publius Cornelius Scipio, into Northern Italy on Rome's first engagement against the Carthaginian military genius at the Ticinus River. Though it would be the first of Rome's many defeats at Hannibal's hands, Scipio personally distinguished himself by charging a superior force of the Carthaginian cavalry to save his father's life. Over the next three years Scipio probably fought at both the Battles of Trebia and lake Trasimene, where Hannibal annihilated two more Roman armies, and was certainly present to witness Rome's greatest defeat at Cannae, where some 60,000 Romans perished in a single day's fighting.

At the end of that horrific day Scipio found himself amid a body of survivors who had cut their way through the Carthaginian center and regrouped a few miles away at Canusium. Hearing that a group of young Roman patricians was planning to desert, 20-year-old Scipio burst into their meeting place. One by one, he forced the waverers, at sword-point, to swear an oath never to desert Rome. After that he exacted a second oath that they would kill anyone else attempting to forsake the empire.

Scipio had performed exactly as expected of him. Facing defeat, a Roman leader was expected neither to die gloriously with his troops nor to consider surrender. Instead, he was to reconstitute whatever forces could be salvaged from the fiasco and ready them for the next effort. There was no shame in defeat, only in giving up.

On the other side, Hannibal was being handed a lesson in Roman perseverance—one that should have been absorbed by his father during the First Punic War. Despite suffering three successive routs at Hannibal's hands, Rome never considered surrender or a negotiated end to the Second Punic War. What's more amazing, though Hannibal's army continued to rampage through Italy for a dozen years and was to win several more major battles, Rome had the strategic wisdom to send many of its best legions to fight in other theaters. Roman legions' presence in Macedonia and Sicily, for instance, ensured that Hannibal was unable to draw upon those regions for supplies or reinforcements. It was from Spain that Hannibal drew the core of his strength, so Rome concentrated its major foreign push

there. If the legions could strip Spain away from Carthage, Hannibal would be cut off from the mines that financed his army and from his most reliable source of fresh troops.

Though Roman armies made steady progress in Spain for a half-dozen years after Cannae, the strategy ended abruptly in 211 BC when, on the eve of the Battle of the Upper Baetis, Rome's Spanish allies deserted and went over to the enemy. The now overwhelming Carthaginian force nearly wiped out the Roman army, commanded by Scipio's father. Both his father and uncle were killed. A remnant Roman force managed to hold out on a small patch of land in northeast Spain.

At this low ebb, the Roman senate called for a replacement to command the demoralized Roman force in Spain. As it was apart from the main theater facing Hannibal, and because Rome could not afford to send the Spanish legions much in the way of reinforcements, no senior Roman generals stepped forward. Finally, the senate called an assembly of the people to elect a proconsul for the "honor." As Livy relates, "They [the Roman voters] looked round at the countenances of their most eminent men . . . and muttered bitterly that their affairs were in so ruinous a state that no one dared take command in Spain." Spotting a unique opportunity, Scipio declared himself a candidate, though at 24 he was not officially old enough for the post. Age notwithstanding, he was unanimously elected.

Arriving in northern Spain the following year, Scipio learned of three Carthaginian armies operating in various regions, each of them larger than his own. Roman discipline and tactical ability still made it probable Scipio would defeat any single opposing force. But that could involve weeks of careful maneuvering, during which time his opponents would surely put aside their personal differences and join forces. So Scipio seized on the idea of striking at New Carthage, the main Punic base in Spain.

Defenses at New Carthage (modern-day Cartagena) were considered so strong that only a thousand Punic mercenaries had been left to guard the city The closest reinforcements were two weeks away. It was a plum for the picking, but only if Scipio could keep his intentions secret. As he spent the winter preparing his army, Scipio shared his plans with only one trusted subordinate, Laelius. When he launched his campaign in early spring, neither the army nor its senior commanders had any idea of his plans. By force-marching south 40 miles a day,

Scipio's 25,000 infantry and 2,500 cavalry arrived in less than a week to confront the city's stunned defenders. Simultaneously, Laelius arrived by sea with 35 Roman war galleys to blockade the port.

Just shy of the city walls, Scipio's army stopped and began digging a fortified camp. While the Romans dug, the Carthaginians manned the walls and hastily armed 2,000 citizens as reinforcements. New Carthage was a natural strongpoint, surrounded on three sides by water, but the defenders knew they needed time to prepare. To stall, they sallied out with 2,000 men to disrupt Roman preparations. Refusing to meet the Carthaginian onrush, Scipio instead withdrew his pickets to lure the defenders closer to his camp. His intention was to isolate the Carthaginians' best fighters far from the refuge of the city gates.

Scipio met the initial charge with his less experienced soldiers, but steadily fed in reserves to ensure there were fresh troops on the front line. Eventually, the consul sent the *Triarii* (battle-hardened men of the third line) into action. This proved too much for the Carthaginians, who broke in a rout. The Romans pursued and nearly forced the gates before they could be closed. Pressing the attack, the legionnaires began to scale the walls, but the defenders thwarted each attack. By midafternoon, Scipio ordered his exhausted troops back to camp to recoup.

The Carthaginians were at first elated, but as dusk arrived their joy turned to dismay when the legions advanced once again. It was time for Scipio's master-stroke: He had learned that the ebb tide reduced water levels in the lagoon north of the city, making it fordable. As his main force began its assault, the consul sent 500 chosen men to march across the lagoon and attack an undefended section of the wall. By then, the defenders were hard-pressed to hold off the frontal assault. The chosen 500 scaled the wall unnoticed and quickly made their way to the main gate just as the legionnaires outside began smashing away at it with heavy axes. Attacked from both front and rear, the defenders panicked, and New Carthage fell.

Just one week after launching his first military campaign, Scipio had upset the balance of power in Spain. He had deprived the Carthaginians of their main supply base, captured almost 20 war galleys and now held a large part of the Carthaginian treasury. Just as important, he recovered more than 300 noble hostages the Carthaginians had taken from Spain's most powerful tribes as a guarantee of good behavior. Despite the fact that many of these hostages had come from tribes that had betrayed his father, Scipio treated them honorably and allowed them to return home. That bit of wisdom, coupled with Scipio's proven ability to win, brought more Spanish allies into the Roman camp. Scipio used them, but was never so foolish as to trust them.

After consolidating his position at New Carthage, Scipio led his legions against the Carthaginian army under Hannibal's brother, Hasdrubal, winning a marginal victory at the Battle of Baecula in 208 BC. Either as a result of this battle or according to an earlier plan, Hasdrubal soon left Spain and marched his army into Italy to reinforce his brother. The Carthaginians arrived in Italy only to be destroyed by a Roman force led by the consul Nero. Hannibal learned his reinforcements had been wiped out when his brother's head was thrown over the wall of his camp.

Back in Spain, Scipio had only two armies to contend with, though by now they had combined forces. In 206 BC, with about 45,000 men—less than half of them well-disciplined legionnaires—Scipio marched against a Punic army nearly double that size, led by a different Hasdrubal and another of Hannibal's brothers, Mago. The armies met near Ilipa, north of Seville. For the next few days the opponents sized each other up. For each of these demonstrations, Scipio put his best troops, his two legions and Latin allies, in the center, while his Spanish allies held the flanks. To match the Romans, the Carthaginian commanders put their best African troops in the center and their own Spanish allies on the flank.

After several days of such preliminary moves, Scipio suddenly reversed his formation, putting a legion on each flank and the Spaniards in the center. Before Hasdrubal and Mago could adjust their own lines, the legions began to advance, while Scipio held his Spanish allies back. Instead of moving in the more typical line formation, Scipio advanced in columns, which allowed him to close the distance with the Carthaginians at an unheard-of speed. Then, at the last moment, the legions wheeled into line and smashed the Carthaginian flank. The Spaniards soon broke and ran for safety.

Throughout this decisive stage of the battle, Hasdrubal was unable to maneuver his center to help his flanks because Scipio's Spanish allies still menaced his front. Their flanks ultimately routed, the usually reliable African mercenaries in the center also ran for camp. That night, Hasdrubal's Spanish allies deserted. What was left of the Carthaginian army tried to escape in darkness during a storm, but was pummeled by Roman pursuers.

With Spain secured, Scipio returned to Rome. After a bitter political battle with jealous rivals, he secured permission to lead a Roman army into Africa and attack the base of Carthaginian power. Permission was only grudgingly granted, however, and the senate refused to allow him to recruit for the expedition, limiting his force to the two legions already in Sicily. But they couldn't prevent Scipio from enrolling eager volunteers. According to ancient historians, they came because "to fight under so brave and gallant a captain as Scipio was an adventure all good soldiers welcomed." That said, one suspects the promise of rich plunder was at least as much of a draw.

By allowing him to take Legions V and VI, the senate didn't think it was doing Scipio a service. These legions comprised survivors of Cannae. Following that rout, the defeated soldiers were sent to serve in exile—a degradation in direct contrast to the praise the senate bestowed on Cannae survivors of noble birth. These men keenly felt the stain of dishonor, and each year they petitioned the senate to allow them to return to Rome and prove their valor in battle against Hannibal. They were ignored.

Scipio understood such men and their desire for redemption. To him they were not simply the losers from Cannae. They were the men who by dim of sheer hard fighting had cut their way through an encircling army and re-formed to protect the Republic. He praised them and honored their service, and they in turn gave him utter devotion. Around this core of combat-hardened veterans Scipio spent a year training his volunteers and preparing the logistics required to support an invasion of Carthage's home territories.

In 204 BC Scipio's force sailed for North Africa and laid siege to the Carthaginian stronghold of Utica. The defenders held strong, their resistance buoyed by the promise of a large Carthaginian relief army. In time, Carthage did manage to assemble a large force, under the joint command of Hasdrubal and a local king, Syphax, who had previously pledged his support to Scipio. Despite overwhelming military superiority, however, Hasdrubal was reluctant to attack, perhaps recalling the drubbing he'd received at Ilipa.

Scipio took full advantage of the Carthaginian general's indecision to suggest peace talks, an offer that was eagerly accepted. Over the next several days, Roman emissaries, accompanied by their slaves, made their way to the two enemy camps. As the emissaries negotiated, the slaves—actually Roman centurions—roved around the camp, noting its layout and defensive works. To maintain the illusion these spies were actually slaves, several of them submitted to public whippings for having wandered off without permission.

Their familiarity with the enemy camp emboldened Scipio to conduct the most dangerous of operations—a nighttime assault on a fortified enemy position. The consul was about to find out whether his faith in the disgraced legions was misplaced. They didn't disappoint.

In a single night of brutality, Scipio's army massacred upwards of 40,000 of the enemy (twice their own number) and sent the rest into flight. Incredibly, Hasdrubal managed to raise another army in only a month and marched once again to engage Scipio. But no army so hastily raised and organized was a match for battle-disciplined legions, which made short work of this new army. Faced with these twin disasters and no army left in North Africa that could oppose Scipio, Carthage was forced to recall Hannibal from Italy. For all practical purposes, Rome had won the Second Punic War. But there was still one great battle left to be fought.

At Zama, in 202 BC, Scipio and Hannibal finally met on the field of battle. Each had about 40,000 men at his disposal, but—unlike at Cannae—this time the Romans had the better mounted force, thanks to King Masinissa, who swung his superb Numidian cavalry out of the Carthaginian orbit over to the Roman side. Scipio, like Hannibal, placed this cavalry on the flanks, and each organized his infantry in three lines. But Scipio also made a major tactical change to the standard Roman formation by separating his maniples, opening wide lanes through his lines.

After some initial skirmishing, Hannibal sent his 80 war elephants forward. But this was a different Roman army than the one he had faced at Cannae—tougher and more disciplined, led by men accustomed to Hannibal's tactics. Faced with the choice of smashing into the heavily armed legionnaires or running unimpeded through the gaps in their formations, most of the elephants took the path of least resistance and passed harmlessly through the Roman army. Others, frightened by the blasts of massed Roman trumpeters, ran down their own cavalry.

Noting the chaos, Laelius and Masinissa took the cavalry on each flank and charged the Carthaginian horsemen. These horsemen quickly retreated, with Roman and Numidian cavalry in close pursuit. As the cavalry departed, the legions crashed into the lead Carthaginian line, pressing the mercenaries hard until they turned to escape. But the second line refused to break formation, and as the Romans continued their advance, the Carthaginians began fighting each other. Ultimately, men in the second line also broke and ran for the rear, where they met a similar reception from the third line.

As the defeated first two lines skirted around the ends of Hannibal's final line, Scipio recalled his troops to within bow shot of the Carthaginians. Before them stood Hannibal's seasoned veterans, rested, unbowed and in numbers almost equal to his own. Scipio, rather than replace the exhausted legionnaires in his leading ranks, re-formed them into a tightly packed formation and moved the Triarii to each flank, intending to overlap the enemy line. In a testament to Roman discipline, the legions quickly negotiated these complex maneuvers in the face of an unbeaten enemy.

Given a short breather, the Romans came forward at a quickened pace, until at about 20 paces they let fly their throwing spears and drew their short swords. The advance became a rush as thousands of screaming Romans hurled themselves upon the Carthaginian line. For long minutes the issue remained in doubt, until at the peak of battle the Roman and Numidian cavalry returned to the battlefield and charged into the Carthaginian rear. With cavalry at the rear and the Triarii collapsing their flanks, Hannibal's veterans finally did the unthinkable—they broke.

Though Hannibal himself escaped, his army was lost and Carthaginian military power broken. Rome was now the uncontested master of the Western Mediterranean. Scipio's victories earned him tremendous popular support but also numerous enemies, envious of his popularity. Though he later accompanied his brother on a war of conquest in Asia Minor, he was never again to hold real power in Rome. Under constant legal attack, he ultimately went into a bitter retirement, dying at an early age.

How Rome treated its most victorious general was not lost on such future successful commanders as Marius, Sulla and Caesar. For them the overriding lesson of Scipio's fall from grace was that if you wanted to rule, you needed to return home with your legions.

For further reading, **JAMES LACEY** recommends: *Scipio Africanus: Greater Than Napoleon*, by B. H. Liddell Hart.

From *Military History*, July/August 2007, pp. 55–61. Copyright © 2007 by Weider History Group. Reprinted by permission.

UNIT 3

The Judeo-Christian Heritage

Unit Selections

14. **Did Captured ARK Afflict Philistines with E.D.?,** Aren M. Maeir
15. **Who Wrote the Dead Sea Scrolls?,** Andrew Lawler
16. **From Jesus to Christ,** Jon Meacham
17. **An Inconvenient Woman,** Jonathan Darman

Key Points to Consider

- Discuss the evidence for the author's thesis on *'opalim.*

- Why might the Essenes have written the Scrolls?

- Describe the traditions that shaped the Christian religion.

- Explain why there is a controversy surrounding Mary Magdalene?

Student Website

www.mhhe.com/cls

Internet References

Biblical Archaeological Review
   bib-arch.org
Institute for Christian Leadership/ICLnet
   www.iclnet.org
Newsweek
   www.newsweek.com
Selected Women's Studies Resources/Columbia University
   www.columbia.edu/cu/libraries/subjects/womenstudies
Smithsonian
   www.smithsonianmag.com

Western civilization developed out of the Greco-Roman world, but it is also indebted to the Judeo-Christian traditions. If Western civilization derives the concept of humanism and materialism, and philosophy, politics, art, literature, and science from the former, it derives its God and forms of worship from the latter. It is difficult to separate these traditions, for Judeo-Christian heritage comes to us through a Hellenistic filter.

On one hand, the history of the Jews seems similar to those of other small kingdoms of the Near East that were closely situated to powerful empires such as the Babylonians, Assyrians, and Persians. Yet, of all the ancient peoples, only the Jews had had a lasting influence. What appears to differentiate the Jews from all the rest, writes historian Crane Brinton, is "The will to persist, to be themselves, to be a people." The reappearance of Israel in the modern world, some 2,000 years after the Romans destroyed the Jewish client-state is remarkable.

The legacy of the Jews is a great one. It includes a rich literary tradition (see "Did Captured Ark Afflict Philistines with E.D.?") found in their sacred texts. They have also bequeathed to Western civilization their unique view of history; a linear and miraculous God, who intervenes in history to guide, reward, or punish his Chosen People. The Jewish religion also gave birth to the concept of morality found within the Ten Commandments, the moral wisdom of the prophets, and a messianic expectation, which inspired Christianity and other religions. Their monotheism and their god, Yahweh, formed the model for the Christian and Muslim ideas of God.

A brief comparison of Yahweh and the Greek god Zeus illustrates the originality of the Jewish conception. Both gods began as warrior deities of tribal cultures. But Zeus was chiefly concerned with Olympian affairs rather than human ones. Yahweh, on the other hand, was more purposeful and had few interests except for his people. And unlike Zeus, who was not the creator of the universe, Yahweh had created the universe and ordered the humans to rule over nature.

Certainly Christianity bears the stamp of Judaism. Jesus himself was a Jew. To his early followers, all of them Jews, he satisfied the prophetic messianic messages inherent in Judaism. The New Testament recounts the growth and spread of Christianity from an obscure Jewish sect in Palestine to a new religion with

© Ingram Publishing

great appeal (see "From Jesus to Christ") in the Roman world. Yet Jesus remains shrouded in mystery, for there is a lack of firsthand evidence. The Gospels, the greatest and most familiar sources, contain wide gaps in their accounts of his life. Nonetheless, they remain a profound record of early Christian faith.

As it separated from Judaism, Christianity took on a new dimension, including the promise of private salvation through participation in the sacraments. From the beginning, its theology reflected the teachings of St. Paul, who changed the focus from converting the Jews to spreading the faith among the Gentiles. Then, as it took hold in the Near East, Christianity absorbed some Hellenistic elements, Stoicism, Platonism, and the Roman pantheon. This prepared the way for a fusion of classical philosophy and Christianity. The personal God of the Jews and Christians became the abstract God of the Greek philosophers. Biblical texts were given symbolic meanings that might have confounded an earlier, simpler generation of Christians. The Christian view of sexuality, for instance, became fraught with multiple meanings and complexities (see "An Inconvenient Woman"). In effect, Christianity was no longer a Jewish sect; it had become Westernized. It would become a principal agent for the Westernization of much of the world.

Did Captured ARK Afflict Philistines with E.D.?

Aren M. Maeir

I've always been troubled by the Philistine hemorrhoids. The Hebrew word is 'opalim (עפלים). That was supposedly their affliction when they captured the Ark of the Covenant and placed it before a statue of their god Dagon.

The story is told about the Ark (sometimes called the Ark of God) when it was resting at Shiloh, cared for by Eli the priest, before it was ultimately brought to Jerusalem by King David. The Israelites had engaged their enemies the Philistines in battle at Ebenezer.[1] The battle went badly for the Israelites, and Eli's sons allowed the Ark to be brought from Shiloh to the battlefield at Ebenezer as a paladin in the hope that this would turn the tide of battle. Instead, the Philistines captured the Ark (1 Samuel 5–6).

The Philistines took the Ark to Ashdod and placed it before a statue of Dagon in the Philistine temple. The next day, the Philistines found Dagon toppled, lying on the ground. They set him back up, but the same thing happened the next day. The text goes on to tell us that "the hand of the Lord was heavy on the Ashdodites." The Lord afflicted them with "hemorrhoids" ('opalim).

The Philistines then took the Ark to Gath, another city of the Philistine pentapolis. This time the men of Gath were afflicted with "hemorrhoids."

Finally, the Philistines decided to send the Ark back to the Israelites. To mollify the Israelite God, the Philistines included five golden "hemorrhoids" (one for each city of the Philistine pentapolis) and five golden mice. (The text tells us that "hemorrhoids" and mice had been ravaging the land of the Philistines.)

These 'opalim have caused scholars lots of problems. The root of the word is 'pl (עפל), or Ophel, as in the acropolis [upper city] of ancient Jerusalem), which means "high" or "rise," hence a swelling.

But there is something strange, even a bit peculiar about 'opalim. Is it a vulgarity? Is it simply too intimate for use in a holy text? Or does it perhaps mean something entirely different?

The King James translation calls them "emerods." Modern translations, apparently a little embarrassed at hemorrhoids, often translate 'opalim as "tumors." To some scholars this suggests that the word isn't really referring to blood-rich rectal swellings, but to another kind of swelling, perhaps bubonic plague. Admittedly, in either event it is difficult to imagine what the golden hemorrhoids or tumors that the Philistines sent back with the Ark looked like.

The history of the Hebrew text also suggests that 'opalim is in some ways a strange or at least unusual word. Until about the tenth century C.E., Hebrew was written essentially without vowels (in modern Israel it still is). At that time a group of Hebrew textual scholars called Masoretes gathered in Tiberias and developed a series of superscripts and subscripts, called pointing, to indicate the proper vowels in the Hebrew text. Hence, the authoritative Hebrew text is referred to as the Masoretic Text, or simply MT. The Masoretes also included elaborate notes on the text, called the Masorah.

In these notes, the Masoretes indicated that some words *written* in the text were to be *read aloud* entirely differently. In their terms, they distinguished between the *ketib* (what is written) and the *qere* (what is read aloud). What is written is one thing, but what is read aloud in the synagogue may be entirely different.

Biblical passages containing the word 'opalim are still read aloud in synagogues on Sabbath in the annual cycle of Bible readings.[2] But 'opalim (מחרים) is one of those words that is not pronounced. The Hebrew word *tehorim* is substituted instead. That is the modern word for hemorrhoids; it appears nowhere in the Bible. It is the word for hemorrhoids used in polite society.

There is, however, another possibility. Based on recently recovered archaeological evidence, I believe that 'opalim refers not to hemorrhoids or tumors or the bubonic plague, but to the male sexual organ. The Philistines were afflicted in their *membra virile.*

In 604 B.C.E. the Babylonian monarch Nebuchadnezzar, who would soon destroy Jerusalem and the Israelite Temple, destroyed the Philistine city of Ashkelon. In this destruction level, archaeologist Lawrence Stager of Harvard University recovered seven small vial-shaped vessels called *situlae.* Based on comparative archaeological evidence, Stager concluded that these vessels were meant to represent uncircumcised, non-erect phalluses.[3] I agree with him.

The *situlae* were found in what was apparently a "cultic corner," along with other cult objects and a votive offering table. The *situlae* were apparently votives, much like the arms or legs that are often found in Egyptian and Greek (Aegean) cultic contexts.

The most prominent depiction on the Ashkelon *situlae* is of the Egyptian god Min, closely associated with male sexual potency. He is depicted on the *situlae* with an erect penis, which probably reflects the cure that the depositors of the votive *situlae* were seeking. Stager suggests that these *situlae* may have been filled with semen, milk or water symbolizing the life-giving force that the votive was intended to induce.

Stager's interpretation has been strengthened and, I believe, can now be elaborated based on the recent finds from Tell es-Safi/Gath.[4, 5]

In the 2004 excavation season at Tell es-Safi/Gath, we found two clay *situlae* in the shape of phalluses in a destruction level from the late ninth or early eighth century B.C.E. (This destruction was apparently the work of Hazael, king of Aram Damascus, as mentioned in 2 Kings 12:17.) Each of the *situlae* is hollow. Each is cylindrical with a bulbous-like thickening at the closed end. The identification of these vessels as *ithyphallii* (erect penises) has been confirmed by several urologists. Like the *situlae* from Ashkelon, they, too, were found in what appears to be a cult-related context.

In our 2007 excavation season at Tell es-Safi/Gath, we discovered an additional cultic context, also from the destruction level attributed to Hazael: an apparent cultic corner in a largely domestic building. In the "corner" we discovered a group of clearly cult-related objects, including a complete *kernos*[6] (and fragments of other ritual libation vessels), a zoomorphic vessel, various platters and seven additional phallic-shaped vessels. Interestingly, most of the vessels had holes that would have enabled them to be hung— apparently an ancient cultic mobile!

These phallic-shaped objects from Ashkelon and Gath are clear indications of the symbolic importance of the phallus in Philistine culture. While such depictions are relatively common in Egyptian and Greek (Aegean) religious iconography, they are very rare in Semitic religious iconography. The Philistines are, of course, widely believed to have originated in the Aegean area and arrived in Canaan via Egypt, and the phallus is known to be an attribute of various ancient Greek, Anatolian and Cypriot goddesses.

With this background, I suggest that the *'opalim* with which the Philistines were afflicted after they captured the Ark of the Covenant and placed it in the temple of Dagon involved penises rather than hemorrhoids. It is unclear precisely what the nature of the affliction of the Philistine *membra virile* was. Perhaps it was the failure to attain erection, the condition referred to today as E.D., or erectile dysfunction. Or perhaps it was some malady causing penile pain.

The root of *'opalim,* which means "a rise," suits the penile context as well as it does a hemorrhoid swelling. But it is far easier to visualize the Philistine offering, apparently to placate the Israelite God, as golden penises than golden hemorrhoids. Although we have much Philistine cultic material, nothing in it suggests the possibility of a visual reproduction of a hemorrhoid. Understanding *'opalim* as penises, on the other hand, has excellent parallels in the archaeological record.

The word *'opalim* is still very much a dirty word, inappropriate for use in the synagogue. But it would be quite appropriate (for reading), given the fact that the Biblical text is clearly making fun of the Philistines and their penile malady.

This coming summer we will be in the field again. Why don't you join us? Who knows—perhaps we will find some more *'opalim.*[7]

Notes

1. See Israel Finkelstein, "Shiloh Yields Some, but Not All, of Its Secrets," **BAR,** January/February 1986; Moshe Kochavi, with Aaron Demsky, "An Israelite Village from the Days of the Judges," **BAR,** September/October 1978.

2. For **BAR** articles on Ashkelon, see Patricia Smith and Lawrence E. Stager, "DNA Analysis Sheds New Light on Oldest Profession at Ashkelon," **BAR,** July/August 1997; Lawrence E. Stager, "The Fury of Babylon: Ashkelon and the Archaeology of Destruction;" **BAR,** January/February 1996; Lawrence E. Stager, "Eroticism and Infanticide at Ashkelon," **BAR,** July/August 1991; Lawrence E. Stager, "Why Were Hundreds of Dogs Buried at Ashkelon?" **BAR,** May/June 1991; Lawrence E. Stager, "When Canaanites and Philistines Ruled Ashkelon," **BAR,** March/April 1991.

3. See Carl S. Ehrlich and Aren M. Maeir, "Excavating Philistine Gath: Have We Found Goliath's Hometown?" **BAR,** November/December 2001.

4. A *kernos* is a hollow, ring-shaped vessel to which a number of cups or vases were attached. See "The Kibbutz Sasa *Kernos,"* **BAR,** June 1976.

5. In addition to the passages in the so-called Ark Narrative referred to above, the word also appears in Deuteronomy 28:27, but, again, is read aloud differently.

6. A. M. Maeir, "The Historical Background and Dating of Amos VI 2: An Archaeological Perspective from Tell es-Safi/Gath." *Vetus Testamentum* 54/3 (2004), pp. 319–34.

7. For more information about digging at Tell es-Safi/Gath, see "Digs 2008," **BAR,** January/February 2008, or visit www.findadig.com and www.dig-gath.org.

For additional details see **ARen M. Maeir,** "A New Interpretation of the Term 'opalim (Mylpe) in the Light of Recent Archaeological Finds from Philistia," *Journal for the Study of the Old Testament* 32, no. 1 (2007), p. 23.

Who Wrote the Dead Sea Scrolls?

Research at the ancient West Bank site of Qumran may help resolve the debate about the origins of the seminal religious documents and reshape our understanding of Judaism and Christianity.

ANDREW LAWLER

Israeli archaeologist Yuval Peleg halts his jeep where the Jagged Judean hills peter out into a jumble of boulders. Before us, across the flat-calm Dead Sea, the sun rises over the mountains of Jordan. The heat on this spring morning is already intense. There are no trees or grass, just a few crumbling stone walls. It is a scene of silent desolation—until, that is, tourists in hats and visors pour out of shiny buses.

They have come to this harsh and remote site in the West Bank, known as Qumran, because this is where the most important religious texts in the Western world were found in 1947. The Dead Sea Scrolls—comprising more than 800 documents made of animal skin, papyrus and even forged copper—deepened our understanding of the Bible and shed light on the histories of Judaism and Christianity. Among the texts are parts of every book of the Hebrew canon—what Christians call the Old Testament—except the book of Esther. The scrolls also contain a collection of previously unknown hymns, prayers, commentaries, mystical formulas and the earliest version of the Ten Commandments. Most were written between 200 B.C. and the period prior to the failed Jewish revolt to gain political and religious independence from Rome that lasted from A.D. 66 to 70—predating by 8 to 11 centuries the oldest previously known Hebrew text of the Jewish Bible.

Tour guides shepherding the tourists through the modest desert ruins speak of the scrolls' origin, a narrative that has been repeated almost since they were discovered more than 60 years ago. Qumran, the guides say, was home to a community of Jewish ascetics called the Essenes, who devoted their lives to writing and preserving sacred texts. They were hard at work by the time Jesus began preaching; ultimately they stored the scrolls in 11 caves before Romans destroyed their settlement in A.D. 68.

But hearing the dramatic recitation, Peleg, 40, rolls his eyes. "There is no connection to the Essenes at this site," he tells me as a hawk circles above in the warming air. He says the scrolls had nothing to do with the settlement. Evidence for a religious community here, he says, is unconvincing. He believes, rather, that Jews fleeing the Roman rampage hurriedly stuffed the documents into the Qumran caves for safekeeping. After digging at the site for ten years, he also believes that Qumran was originally a fort designed to protect a growing Jewish population from threats to the east. Later, it was converted into a pottery factory to serve nearby towns like Jericho, he says.

Other scholars describe Qumran variously as a manor house, a perfume manufacturing center and even a tannery. Despite decades of excavations and careful analysis, there is no consensus about who lived there—and, consequently, no consensus about who actually wrote the Dead Sea Scrolls.

"It's an enigmatic and confusing site," acknowledges Risa Levitt Kohn, who in 2007 curated an exhibit about the Dead Sea Scrolls in San Diego. She says the sheer breadth and age of the writings—during a period that intersects with the life of Jesus and the destruction of the Second Jewish Temple in Jerusalem—make Qumran "a powder keg" among normally placid scholars. Qumran has prompted bitter feuds and even a recent criminal investigation.

Nobody doubts the scrolls' authenticity, but the question of authorship has implications for understanding the history of both Judaism and Christianity. In 164 B.C., a group of Jewish dissidents, the Maccabees, overthrew the Seleucid Empire that then ruled Judea. The Maccabees established an independent kingdom and, in so doing, tossed out the priestly class that had controlled the temple in Jerusalem since the time of King Solomon. The turmoil led to the emergence of several rival sects, each one vying for dominance. If the Qumran texts were written by one such sect, the scrolls "help us to understand the forces that operated after the Maccabean Revolt and how various Jewish groups reacted to those forces," says New York University professor of Jewish and Hebraic studies Lawrence Schiffman in his book *Reclaiming the Dead Sea Scrolls*. "While some sects were accommodating themselves to the new order in various ways, the Dead Sea group decided it had to leave Jerusalem altogether in order to continue its unique way of life."

And if Qumran indeed housed religious ascetics who turned their backs on what they saw as Jerusalem's decadence, then the Essenes may well represent a previously unknown link between Judaism and Christianity. "John the Baptizer, Jesus' teacher, probably learned from the Qumran Essenes—though he was no Essene," says James Charlesworth, a scrolls scholar at Princeton Theological Seminary. Charlesworth adds that the scrolls "disclose the context of Jesus' life and message." Moreover, the beliefs and practices of the Qumran Essenes as described in the scrolls—vows of poverty, baptismal rituals and communal meals—mirror those of early Christians. As such, some see Qumran as the first Christian monastery, the cradle of an emerging faith.

But Peleg and others discount Qumran's role in the history of the two religions. Norman Golb, a University of Chicago professor of Jewish history (and an academic rival of Schiffman), believes that once Galilee fell during the Jewish revolt, Jerusalem's citizens knew that the conquest of their city was inevitable; they thus gathered up texts from libraries and personal collections and hid them throughout the Judean wilderness, including in the caves near the Dead Sea. If that's the case, then Qumran was likely a secular—not a spiritual—site, and the scrolls reflect not just the views of a single dissident group of proto-Christians, but a wider tapestry of Jewish thought. "Further determination of the individual concepts and practices described in the scrolls can be best achieved not by forcing them to fit into the single sectarian bed of Essenism," Golb argued in the journal *Biblical Archaeologist.*

One assumption that is now widely accepted is that the majority of the scrolls did not originate at Qumran. The earliest texts date to 300 B.C.—a century before Qumran even existed as a settlement—and the latest to a generation before the Romans destroyed the site in A.D. 68. A few scrolls are written in sophisticated Greek rather than a prosaic form of Aramaic or Hebrew that would be expected from a community of ascetics in the Judean desert. And why would such a community keep a list, etched in rare copper, of precious treasures of gold and silver—possibly from the Second Temple in Jerusalem—that had been secreted away? Nor does the word "Essene" appear in any of the scrolls.

Of course none of this rules out the possibility that Qumran was a religious community of scribes. Some scholars are not troubled that the Essenes are not explicitly mentioned in the scrolls, saying that the term for the sect is a foreign label. Schiffman believes they were a splinter group of priests known as the Sadducees. The notion that the scrolls are "a balanced collection of general Jewish texts" must be rejected, he writes in *Biblical Archaeologist.* "There is now too much evidence that the community that collected those scrolls emerged out of sectarian conflict and that [this] conflict sustained it throughout its existence." Ultimately, however, the question of who wrote the scrolls is more likely to be resolved by archaeologists scrutinizing Qumran's every physical remnant than by scholars poring over the texts.

The dead sea scrolls amazed scholars with their remarkable similarity to later versions. But there were also subtle differences. For instance, one scroll expands on the book of Genesis: in Chapter 12, when Abraham's wife Sarah is taken by the Pharaoh, the scroll depicts Sarah's beauty, describing her legs, face and hair. And in Chapter 13, when God commands Abraham to walk "through the land in the length," the scroll adds a first-person account by Abraham of his journey. The Jewish Bible, as accepted today, was the product of a lengthy evolution; the scrolls offered important new insights into the process by which the text was edited during its formation.

The scrolls also set forth a series of detailed regulations that challenge the religious laws practiced by the priests in Jerusalem and espoused by other Jewish sects such as the Pharisees. Consequently, scholars of Judaism consider the scrolls to be a missing link between the period when religious laws were passed down orally and the Rabbinic era, beginning circa A.D. 200, when they were systematically recorded—eventually leading to the legal commentaries that became the Talmud.

For Christians as well, the scrolls are a source of profound insight. Jesus is not mentioned in the texts, but as Florida International University scholar Erik Larson has noted, the scrolls have "helped us understand better in what ways Jesus' messages represented ideas that were current in the Judaism of his time and in what ways [they were] distinctive." One scroll, for example, mentions a messianic figure who is called both the "Son of God" and the "Son of the Most High." Many theologians had speculated that the phrase "Son of God" was adopted by early Christians after Jesus' crucifixion, in contrast to the pagan worship of the Roman emperors. But the appearance of the phrase in the scrolls indicates the term was already in use when Jesus was preaching his gospel.

Whoever hid the scrolls from the Romans did a superb job. The texts at Qumran remained undiscovered for nearly two millennia. A few 19th-century European travelers examined what they assumed was an ancient fortress of no particular interest. Then, near it in 1947, a goat strayed into a cave, a Bedouin shepherd flung a stone into the dark cavern and the resulting clink against a pot prompted him to investigate. He emerged with the first of what would be about 15,000 fragments of some 850 scrolls secreted in the many caves that pock the cliffs rising above the Dead Sea.

The 1948 Arab-Israeli War prevented a close examination of the Qumran ruins. But after a fragile peace set in, a bearded and bespectacled Dominican monk named Roland de Vaux started excavations of the site and nearby caves in 1951. His findings of spacious rooms, ritual baths and the remains of gardens stunned scholars and the public alike. He also unearthed scores of cylindrical jars, hundreds of ceramic plates and three inkwells in or near a room that he concluded had once contained high tables used by scribes.

Shortly before de Vaux began his work, a Polish scholar named Jozef Milik completed a translation of one scroll, "The Rule of the Community," which lays out a set of strict regulations reminiscent of those followed by a sect of Jews mentioned in A.D. 77 by the Roman historian Pliny the Elder. He called the sect members Essenes, and wrote that they lived along the western shore of the Dead Sea "without women and renouncing love entirely, without money, and having for company only the palm trees." Pliny's contemporary, historian Flavius Josephus, also mentions the Essenes in his account of the Jewish War: "Whereas these men shun the pleasures as vice, they consider self-control and not succumbing to the passions virtue." Based upon these references, de Vaux concluded that Qumran was an Essene community, complete with a refectory and a scriptorium—medieval terms for the places where monks dined and copied manuscripts.

Though he died in 1971 before publishing a comprehensive report, de Vaux's picture of Qumran as a religious community was widely accepted among his academic colleagues. (Much of his Qumran material remains locked up in private collections in Jerusalem and Paris, out of reach of most scholars.) By the 1980s, however, new data from other sites began casting doubt on his theory. "The old views have been outstripped by more recent discoveries," says Golb.

For example, we now know that Qumran was not the remote place it is today. Two millennia ago, there was a thriving commercial trade in the region; numerous settlements dotted the shore, while ships plied the sea. Springs and runoff from the steep hills were carefully engineered to provide water for drinking and agriculture, and date palms and plants produced valuable resins used in perfume. And while the heavily salinated sea lacked fish, it provided salt and bitumen, the substance used in ancient times to seal boats and mortar bricks. Far from being a lonely and distant community of religious nonconformists, Qumran was a valuable piece of real estate—a day's donkey ride to Jerusalem, a two-hour walk to Jericho and a stroll to docks and settlements along the sea.

And a closer look at de Vaux's Qumran findings raises questions about his picture of a community that disdained luxuries and even money. He uncovered more than 1,200 coins—nearly half of which were silver—as well as evidence of hewn stone columns, glass vessels, glass beads and other fine goods. Some of it likely comes from later Roman occupation, but Belgian husband-and-wife archaeologists Robert Donceel and Pauline Donceel-Voute believe that most of the accumulated wealth indicates that Qumran was an estate—perhaps owned by a rich Jerusalem patrician—that produced perfume. The massive fortified tower, they sag, was a common feature of villas during a conflict-prone era in Judea. And they note that Jericho and Ein Gedi (a settlement nearly 20 miles south of Qumran) were known throughout the Roman world as producers of the balsam resin used as a perfume base. In a cave near Qumran, Israeli researchers found in 1988 a small round bottle that, according to lab analyses, contained the remains of resin. De Vaux claimed that similar bottles found at Qumran were inkwells. But they might just as well have been vials of perfume.

Other theories abound. Some think Qumran was a modest trading center. British archaeologist David Stacey believes it was a tannery and that the jars found by de Vaux were for the collection of urine necessary for scouring skins. He argues that Qumran's location was ideal for a tannery—between potential markets like Jericho and Ein Gedi.

For his part, Peleg believes Qumran went through several distinct stages. As the morning heat mounts, he leads me up a steep ridge above the site, where a channel hewn into the rock brought water into the settlement. From our high perch, he points out the foundations of a massive tower that once commanded a fine view of the sea to the east toward today's Jordan. "Qumran was a military post around 100 B.C.," he says. "We are one day from Jerusalem, and it fortified the northeast shore of the Dead Sea." Other forts from this era are scattered among the rocky crags above the sea. This was a period when the Nabateans—the eastern rivals of Rome—threatened Judea. But Peleg says that once the Romans conquered the region, in 63 B.C., there was no further need for such bases. He believes out-of-work Judean soldiers and local families may have turned the military encampment to peaceful purposes, building a modest aqueduct that emptied into deep rectangular pools so that fine clay for making pots could settle. "Not every pool with steps is a ritual bath," he points out. He thinks the former soldiers built eight kilns to produce pottery for the markets of Ein

Gedi and Jericho, grew dates and possibly made perfume—until the Romans leveled the place during the Jewish insurrection.

But Peleg's view has won few adherents. "It's more interpretation than data," says Jodi Magness, an archaeologist at the University of North Carolina at Chapel Hill who shares de Vaux's view that the site was a religious community. She says that some archaeologists—by refusing to acknowledge evidence that residents of Qumran hid the scrolls—are inclined to leap to conclusions since their research relies solely on the ambiguous, physical remains at the site.

Even jurisdiction over Qumran is a source of contention. The site is located on the West Bank, where Palestinians and some Israeli archaeologists say that Peleg's excavations are illegal under international law.

The Qumran controversy took a bizarre turn last March, when Golb's son, Raphael, was arrested on charges of identity theft, criminal impersonation and aggravated harassment. In a statement, the New York District Attorney's office says that Raphael "engaged in a systematic scheme on the Internet, using dozens of Internet aliases, in order to influence and affect debate on the Dead Sea Scrolls, and in order to harass Dead Sea Scrolls scholars" who disputed his father's findings. The alleged target was Golb's old rival, Schiffman. For his part, Raphael Golb entered a plea of not guilty on July 8, 2009. The case has been adjourned until January 27.

About the only thing that the adversaries seem to agree on is that money is at the root of the problem. Popular books with new theories about Qumran sell, says Schiffman. Golb notes that the traditional view of Qumran is more likely to attract tourists to the site.

Some scholars seek a middle ground. Robert Cargill, an archaeologist at the University of California at Los Angeles, envisions Qumran as a fort that later sheltered a group producing not only scrolls but an income through tanning or pottery making. It was a settlement, he says, "that wanted to be self-reliant—the question is just how Jewish and just how devout they were."

Efforts at compromise have hardly quelled the conflicting theories. Perhaps, as French archaeologist Jean-Baptiste Humbert suggests, Qumran scholars are shaped by their personal experience as well as by their research. "One sees what one wants to see," says Humbert, whether it's a monastery, a fort, a tannery or a manor house.

But the debate matters little to the thousands of visitors who flock to the Holy Land. For them, Qumran remains the place where a modern-day miracle occurred—the unlikely discovery of sacred texts, saved from destruction to enlighten future generations about the word of God. As I climb into Peleg's jeep for the quick trip back to Jerusalem, new crowds of tourists are exiting the buses.

ANDREW LAWLER, who lives in rural Maine, wrote about the Iranian city of Isfahan in the April 2009 issue of SMITHSONIAN.

From *Smithsonian*, January 2010, pp. 46–51. Copyright © 2010 by Andrew Lawler. Reprinted by permission of the author.

From Jesus to Christ

How did a Jewish prophet come to be seen as the Christian savior? The epic story of the empty tomb, the early battles and the making of a great faith.

JON MEACHAM

The story, it seemed, was over. Convicted of sedition, condemned to death by crucifixion, nailed to a cross on a hill called Golgotha, Jesus of Nazareth had endured all that he could. According to Mark, the earliest Gospel, Jesus, suffering and approaching the end, repeated a verse of the 22nd Psalm, a passage familiar to first-century Jewish ears: "My God, my God, why have you forsaken me?" There was a final, wordless cry. And then silence.

Why have you forsaken me? From the Gospel accounts, it was a question for which Jesus' disciples had no ready answer. In the chaos of the arrest and Crucifixion, the early followers had scattered. They had expected victory, not defeat, in this Jerusalem spring. If Jesus were, as they believed, the Jewish Messiah, then his great achievement would be the inauguration of the Kingdom of God on earth, an age marked by the elimination of evil, the dispensation of justice, the restoration of Israel and the general resurrection of the dead.

Instead, on the Friday of this Passover, at just the moment they were looking for the arrival of a kind of heaven on earth, Jesus, far from leading the forces of light to triumph, died a criminal's death. Of his followers, only the women stayed as Jesus was taken from the cross, wrapped in a linen shroud and placed in a tomb carved out of the rock of a hillside. A stone sealed the grave and, according to Mark, just after the sun rose two days later, Mary Magdalene and two other women were on their way to anoint the corpse with spices. Their concerns were practical, ordinary: were they strong enough to move the stone aside? As they drew near, however, they saw that the tomb was already open. Puzzled, they went inside, and a young man in a white robe—not Jesus—sitting on the right side of the tomb said: "Do not be amazed; you seek Jesus of Nazareth, who was crucified. He has risen; he is not here, see the place where they laid him." Absorbing these words, the women, Mark says, "went out and fled from the tomb; for trembling and astonishment had come upon them; and they said nothing to any one, for they were afraid."

The cross on the Friday of this Passover, just as the disciples were expecting the arrival of heaven on earth, Jesus, far from leading the forces of light to triumph, died a criminal's death.

And so begins the story of Christianity—with confusion, not with clarity; with mystery, not with certainty. According to Luke's Gospel, the disciples at first treated the women's report of the empty tomb as "an idle tale, and . . . did not believe them"; the Gospel of John says that Jesus' followers "as yet . . . did not know . . . that he must rise from the dead."

For many churchgoers who fill the pews this Holy Week, re-enacting the Passion, contemplating the cross and celebrating the Resurrection, the faith may appear seamless and monumental, comfortably unchanging from age to age. In a new *Newsweek* Poll, 78 percent of Americans believe Jesus rose from the dead; 75 percent say that he was sent to Earth to absolve mankind of its sins. Eighty-one percent say they are Christians; they are part of what is now the world's largest faith, with 2 billion believers, or roughly 33 percent of the earth's population.

Yet the journey from Golgotha to Constantine, the fourth-century emperor whose conversion secured the supremacy of Christianity in the West, was anything but simple; the rise of the faith was, as the Duke of Wellington said of Waterloo, "the nearest-run thing you ever saw in your life." From the Passion to the Resurrection to the nature of salvation, the basic tenets of Christianity were in flux from generation to generation as believers struggled to understand the meaning of Jesus' mission.

Jesus is a name, Christ a title (in Hebrew, *Messias*, in Greek, *Christos*, meaning "anointed one"). Without the Resurrection, it is virtually impossible to imagine that the Jesus movement of the first decades of the first century would have long endured. A small band of devotees might have kept his name alive for a time, even insisting on his messianic identity by calling him Christ, but the group would have been just one of many sects in first-century Judaism, a world roiled and crushed by the cataclysmic war with Rome from 66 to 73, a conflict that resulted in the destruction of Jerusalem.

So how, exactly, did the Jesus of history, whom many in his own time saw as a failed prophet, come to be viewed by billions as the Christ of faith whom the Nicene Creed says is "the only-begotten Son of God . . . God of God, Light of Light, Very God of very God . . . by whom all things were made"? And why did Christianity succeed where so many other religious and spiritual movements failed?

The questions are nearly 2,000 years old, yet in this culturally divisive American moment, a time when believers feel besieged and skeptics think themselves surrounded, a reconstruction of Jesus' journey from Jewish prophet to Christian savior suggests that faith, like history, is nearly always more complicated than it seems. For the religious, the lesson is that those closest to Jesus accepted little blindly, and, in the words of Origen of Alexandria, an early church father, "It is far better to accept teachings with reason and wisdom than with mere faith." For the secular, the reminder that Christianity is the product of two millennia of creative intellectual thought and innovation, a blend of history and considered theological debate, should slow the occasional rush to dismiss the faithful as superstitious or simple.

The messenger Author of early documents, Paul says 'Christ died for our sins in accordance with the scriptures.'

As the sun set on the Friday of the execution, Jesus appeared to be a failure, his promises about the Kingdom of God little more than provocative but powerless rhetoric. No matter what Jesus may have said about sacrifice and resurrection during his lifetime, the disciples clearly did not expect Jesus to rise again. The women at the tomb were stunned; confronted with the risen Lord, Thomas initially refused to believe his eyes; and at the end of Matthew's Gospel, some disciples still "doubted."

Their skepticism is hardly surprising. Prevailing Jewish tradition did not suggest that God would restore Israel and inaugurate the Kingdom through a condemned man who went meekly to his death. Quite the opposite: the Messiah was to fight earthly battles to rescue Israel from its foes and, even if this militaristic Messiah were to fall heroically in the climactic war, the documents found at Qumran (popularly known as the Dead Sea Scrolls) suggest that another "priestly" Messiah would finish the affair by putting the

world to rights. Re-creating the expectations of first-century Jews, Paula Fredriksen, Aurelio Professor of Scripture at Boston University, notes: "Like the David esteemed by tradition, the Messiah will be someone in whom are combined the traits of courage, piety, military prowess, justice, wisdom and knowledge of the Torah. The Prince of Peace must first be a man of war: his duty is to inflict final defeat on the forces of evil." There was, in short, no Jewish expectation of a messiah whose death and resurrection would bring about the forgiveness of sins and offer believers eternal life.

Yet a sacrificial, atoning role is precisely the one the first followers of Jesus believed he had played in the world. In the earliest known writing in the New Testament, the apostle Paul writes that Jesus "gave himself for our sins to deliver us from the present evil age, according to the will of God the Father."

Where did this interpretation of Jesus' mission come from? Like the New Testament authors, conservative believers often argue that Jesus is the Christ "according to the Scriptures" of the Old Testament—that the Hebrew Bible does in fact envision a messianic sacrificial lamb who will redeem the sin of Adam. There is a general argument that all of Biblical history had led to the Crucifixion and Resurrection, and then there are what scholars call specific "prooftexts" (including Isaiah, Daniel, Jeremiah, Ezekiel, Hosea, among others) in which the early Christians found foreshadowings of Jesus' life and mission. Yet anyone reading the ancient Israelite texts outside the Christian tradition may not necessarily interpret them as prologue to the New Testament; the Biblical books have their own histories and tell their own stories. To think that Christianity negates God's covenant with Israel, meanwhile, is misguided and contrary to canonical apostolic teaching. God's choice of the Jewish people is eternal, Paul writes, no matter what: ". . . as regards election they are beloved for the sake of their forefathers . . . the gifts and the call of God are irrevocable."

Christianity does owe the basic elements of its creed to Jewish tradition: atoning sacrifice; a messiah; a general resurrection of the dead. Until Jesus, however, no one had ever, apparently, woven these threads together in the way the apostles did after the Resurrection. ("Messiah" appears fewer than 40 times in the Old Testament, and when it does, it refers to an earthly king, not an incarnate savior from sins.) The heart of the matter was, as Paul wrote in First Corinthians (circa 50): "For I delivered to you as of first importance what I also received, that Christ died for our sins in accordance with the scriptures, that he was buried, that he was raised on the third day . . . "

From the beginning, critics of Christianity have dismissed the Resurrection as a theological invention. As a matter of history, however, scholars agree that the two oldest pieces of New Testament tradition speak to Jesus' rising from the dead. First, the tomb in which Jesus' corpse was placed after his execution was empty; if it were not, then Christianity's opponents could have produced his bones. (Matthew also says the temple priests tried to bribe Roman guards at the tomb, saying, "Tell people, 'His disciples came by night and stole him away while we were asleep'"—implying the body was in fact gone.)

The source as a resurrected sacrificial lamb, Jesus redefined the Messiah's role, creating a new vision of salvation.

The second tradition is that the apostles, including Paul, believed the risen Jesus had appeared to them; writing in the first years after the Passion, Paul lists specific, living witnesses, presumably in order to encourage doubters to seek corroborating testimony. Paul seems quite clear about what the skeptical would find if they checked his story. Less clear is what we should make of the later, differing Gospel accounts of the discovery of the empty tomb and the appearances of the risen Jesus. Sometimes he appears as flesh and blood; at others, he can walk through walls. Sometimes he is instantly recognized; at others, even close followers fail to understand whom they are speaking with until Jesus identifies himself. Most likely the post-Resurrection stories represent different traditions within the nascent faith. The contrasting details do not help the Christian case on logical grounds, but the Gospel renderings do affirm that the tomb was empty, and that believers thought the resurrected Jesus had appeared to some of them for a time.

Written after Paul, the Gospels speak of sacrifice, redemption and resurrection. Yet we cannot responsibly skate around the Gospel reports that the disciples were initially mystified by the Resurrection. What explains the skeptical disciples' transformation from fear and wonder to clarity and conviction about the empty tomb and its significance in the history of salvation—that through his death and resurrection Jesus would redeem humankind?

Perhaps recollections of the words of Jesus himself. Though many scholars rightly raise compelling questions about the historical value of the portraits of Jesus in the Gospels, the apostles had to arrive at their definition of his messianic mission somehow, and it is possible that Jesus may have spoken of these things during his lifetime—words that came flooding back to his followers once the shock of his resurrection had sunk in. On historical grounds, then, Christianity appears less a fable than a faith derived in part from oral or written traditions dating from the time of Jesus' ministry and that of his disciples. "The Son of man is delivered into the hands of men, and they shall kill him; and after that . . . he shall rise the third day," Jesus says in Mark, who adds that the disciples at the time "understood not that saying, and were afraid to ask him."

That the apostles would have created such words and ideas out of thin air seems unlikely, for their story and their message strained credulity even then. Paul admitted the difficulty: ". . . we preach Christ crucified, a stumbling-block to Jews and folly to Gentiles." A king who died a criminal's death? An individual's resurrection from the dead? A human atoning sacrifice? "This is not something that the PR committee of the disciples would have put out," says Dr. R. Albert Mohler Jr., president of the Southern Baptist Theological Seminary in Louisville, Ky. "The very fact of the salvation message's complexity and uniqueness, I think, speaks to the credibility of the Gospels and of the entire New Testament."

Jesus' words at the last supper—that bread and wine represented his body and blood—now made more sense: he was, the early church argued, a sacrificial lamb in the tradition of ancient Israel. Turning to the old Scriptures, the apostles began to find what they decided were prophecies Jesus had fulfilled. Hitting upon the 53rd chapter of Isaiah, they interpreted the Crucifixion as a necessary portal to a yet more glorious day: ". . . he was wounded for our transgressions, he was bruised for our iniquities . . . and with his stripes we are healed." In the Book of Acts, Peter is able to preach a sermon in which Jesus is connected to passages from Isaiah, Joel and the Psalms.

The foes until Constantine's conversion, early Christians faced lions and, Tacitus said, 'were crucified and set on fire so that when darkness came they burned like torches in the night.'

Skepticism about Christianity was widespread and understandable. From a Jewish perspective, the first-century historian Josephus noted: "About this time there lived Jesus, a wise man. He worked surprising deeds and was a teacher . . . He won over many Jews and many of the Greeks . . . And the tribe of Christians, so called after him, has not disappeared to this day." In a separate reference, Josephus writes of "James the brother of the so-called Christ." A good Jew of the priestly caste, Josephus is not willing to grant Jesus the messianic title. In Athens, Stoic and Epicurean philosophers asked Paul to explain his message. "May we know what this new teaching is which you present?" they asked. "For you bring some strange things to our ears . . . " They heard him out, but the Resurrection was too much of a reach for them. In the second century, the anti-Christian critic Celsus called the Resurrection a "cock-and-bull story," and cast doubt on the eyewitness testimony: "While he was alive he did not help himself, but after death he rose again and showed the marks of his punishment and how his hands had been pierced. But who say this? A hysterical female, as you say, and perhaps some other one of those who were deluded by the same sorcery, who either dreamt in a certain state of mind and through wishful thinking had a hallucination due to some mistaken notion . . . or, which is more likely, wanted to impress others by telling this fantastic tale . . . "

But why invent this particular story unless there were some historical basis for it—either in the remembered words of Jesus or in the experience of the followers at the tomb and afterward? "Once a man has died, and the dust has soaked up his blood," says Aeschylus' Apollo, "there is no resurrection." Citing the quotation, N. T. Wright, the scholar and Anglican Bishop of Durham, notes that various ancients may have believed in the immortality of the soul and a kind of mythic life in the underworld, but the stories about Jesus had no direct parallel. And while Jews believed in a general resurrection as part of the Kingdom (Lazarus and others raised by Jesus were destined to die again in due course), Wright adds that "nowhere within Judaism, let alone paganism, is a sustained claim advanced that resurrection has actually happened to a particular individual."

The uniqueness—one could say oddity, or implausibility—of the story of Jesus' resurrection argues that the tradition is more likely historical than theological. Either from a "revelation" from the risen Jesus or from the reports of the earliest followers, Paul "received" a tradition that the resurrection was the hinge of history, the moment after which nothing would ever be the same. "If Christ has not been raised, then our preaching is in vain and your faith is in vain . . . " Paul writes. "Lo! I will tell you a mystery. We shall not all sleep, but we shall all be changed, in a moment, in the twinkling of an eye, at the last trumpet."

At this distance, such passages are stirring and have the glow of victory about them, but Jesus can be confounding, and he forced the early believers to become masters of theological improvisation. First the Kingdom failed to materialize at the time of the Passion, forcing the disciples—at least the male ones—into hiding. Next came the initially mystifying Resurrection. Then came . . . nothing. A central prophecy preached in Jesus' name, his Second Coming on "clouds of glory," failed to happen. "Truly, I say to you," Jesus tells his disciples in Mark, "there are some standing here who will not taste death before they see the kingdom of God come with power."

And yet, as the decades of the first century came and went, the world wore on. In writing the Gospels, and then in formulating church doctrine in the second, third and fourth centuries, Jesus' followers reacted to his failure to return by doing what they arguably did best, for by now they had a good bit of practice at it: they reinterpreted their theological views in light of their historical experience. If the kind of kingdom they had so long expected was not at hand, then Jesus' life, death and resurrection must have meant something different. The Christ they had looked for in the beginning was not the Christ they had come to know. His kingdom was not literally arriving, but he had, they came to believe, created something new: the church, the sacraments, the promise of salvation at the last day—whenever that might be. The shift of emphasis from the short to the long term was an essential achievement. Because they believed Jesus' resurrection had given them the keys to heaven, the hour of his coming mattered less, for God was worth the wait. Drawing on imagery in Isaiah, John the Divine evoked the ultimate glory in his Revelation: "And God shall wipe away all tears from their eyes; and there shall be no more death, neither sorrow, nor crying, neither shall there be any more pain: for the former things are passed away. And he that sat upon the throne said, Behold, I make all things new."

Not everyone saw the same visions. There were many different Christian groups at first, including Gnostic believers, some of whom, contrary to other apostolic traditions, thought Jesus was more divine than human. According to Yale historian Jaroslav Pelikan, Gnostic doctrine was noted for its "denial that the Savior was possessed of a material, fleshly body." Ignatius of Antioch, a second-century bishop, ferociously argued the opposite, writing that Jesus "was really born, and ate and drank, was really persecuted by Pontius Pilate, was really crucified and died . . . [and] really rose from the dead." Such a view had to be the case to track with the early understanding that, as Paul wrote, Jesus "was descended from David according to the flesh." Among the faithful, the notion that God would manifest himself in human form and subject himself to pain and death inspired martyrdom and suffering. Writing about Rome under Nero, Tacitus reported that Christians "were crucified or set on fire so that when darkness came they burned like torches in the night."

Still, the faith, intensely focused on Jesus, endured. "In Jesus Christ, Christianity gave men and women a new love, a very compelling story, and it meant becoming part of a rich, dense community," says Robert Louis Wilken, professor of the history of Christianity at the University of Virginia. In his book "The Rise of Christianity," the sociologist Rodney Stark calculates that the number of Christians rose from roughly 1,000 (or .0017 percent of the Roman Empire) in A.D. 40 to nearly 34 million in 350 (or 56.5 percent of the total population). Stark argues that once the early church "decided not to require converts to observe the [Jewish] Law, they created a religion free of ethnicity," a religion attractive not only to Gentiles but to the Jews of the wider Roman world. Christians also benefited from their own charity work. In an age of plagues, they took care of the sick; the apostate Emperor Julian hated the "Galileans" and their "support not only [for] their poor, but ours as well." Such mission work attracted converts, Stark says, as did the church's decision to value women. And by largely banning abortion and female infanticide, Christians increased the ranks of women who could in turn bear Christian children.

Numbers tell only part of the story. Whatever one thinks of Christianity, the history of Jesus gave birth to a new, lasting vision of the origins and destiny of human life, a vision drawn from the religion's deep roots in Judaism. Everyone is created in God's image; there is, as Paul said, "neither Jew nor Greek, there is neither slave nor free, there is neither male nor female; for you are all one in Christ Jesus"; all are equal, special, worthy. In the Christian world view, says the Roman Catholic theologian George Weigel, "we are not congealed stardust, an accidental byproduct of cosmic chemistry. We are not just something, we are someone." The promise at the heart of the faith: that God, as the fourth-century church father Athanasius said, "was made man that we might be made gods."

So many theological questions linger, and always will: Did Jesus understand his relationship to God the Father in the way Christians now do? Luke claims he did: "The Son of man must suffer many things, and be rejected . . ." Jesus says, "and be slain, and be raised the third day." Did he grasp his atoning role? John claims he did: "I am the living bread which came down from heaven; if any one eats of this bread, he will live for ever; and the bread which I shall give for the life of the world is my flesh." But how much of this is remembered history, and how much heartfelt but unhistorical theology? It is impossible to say. "How unsearchable are his judgments," Paul writes of the Lord, "and how inscrutable his ways!" And they will remain mysterious until believers, in Paul's words, come "face to face" with God.

In the meantime, we are left with an exhortation from a favorite text of Saint Augustine's, the 105th Psalm: "Seek the Lord, and his strength: seek his face evermore." As the search goes on for so many along so many different paths, Paul offers some reassuring words for the journey: "Be at peace among yourselves . . . encourage the faint-hearted, help the weak, be patient with them all. See that none of you repays evil for evil, but always seek to do good to one another and to all. Rejoice always, pray constantly, give thanks . . . hold fast what is good, abstain from every form of evil"—wise words for all of us, whatever our doubts, whatever our faith.

An Inconvenient Woman

She witnessed the resurrection, then vanished, leaving popes and painters and now 'The Da Vinci Code' to tell her story. In search of the real Mary Magdalene.

JONATHAN DARMAN

She was with him to the end, and beyond. As Jesus hangs in agony on the cross, his life ebbing, Mary Magdalene is there, beside his mother, Mary, watching. The Passion has been tumultuous and frightening, and crucifixion is slow, but still she stays. Finally the hour comes. "It is finished," Jesus says, and bows his head. His body is bound in linen, carried to a garden, buried in a tomb.

Before dawn on the day after the Sabbath, Mary Magdalene rises to anoint Christ's body and makes her way to the grave. It is empty. The Lord is gone; she is confused, and terrified. She races back to tell the others, returning with them so they can see for themselves. The male disciples come and go again, unsure what to think; Mary, paralyzed, stays in the garden, in tears.

Then comes a voice, and a question. "Woman, why are you weeping?" she hears from behind her. "Whom do you seek?" She turns and, thinking she sees the gardener, answers, "Sir, if you have carried him away, tell me where you have laid him, and I will take him away." Then, in a recognizable voice, Jesus

---

Women of Christ

Some were respected preachers. Many played more modest roles as hosts or servants. The women who followed Jesus:

Elizabeth

She was a relative of the Virgin Mary, wife of the priest Zacharias and a righteaus woman who, "barren" and already well into old age, gave birth to John the Baptist.

Woman by the Well

Though a sinner (she had five husbands), she was also one of the first to accept Jesus as the Messiah.

Tabitha

Tabitha, also known as Dorcas, was a model of Christian charity who is described as always doing good works for the poor particularly sewing clothes.

Susanna

She was both a follower of Jesus and a benefactor to him and his disciples, providing for them "of [her] substance" (Luke 8:3).

Lydia

After she and her household were converted by Paul, she opened her home as a ministry and allowed Christ's followers to gather there.

Junia

Highly respected by those who preached the Gospel, she was greeted by Paul as foremost among the apostles.

Phoebe

She is called a deaconess or minister of the church and is said to have helped many.

The Virgin Mary

Saint Catherine and Mary Magdalene, Mary was the mother of Christ. Later, in contrast with Mary Magdalene, she was an image of purity.

Martha

Lazarus' sister, she is best known for acting as a host to Christ and the disciples, serving them food whenever they came to her house.

Veronica

She isn't in the Gospels, but a popular legend says Christ's image appeared on the veil she used to wipe his face.

says, "Mary." Crying "Rabboni," she leaps up in joy to embrace her teacher.

"Do not touch me," Jesus says, distancing himself from her, "for I have not yet ascended to the Father; but go to my brethren and say to them, I am ascending to my Father and your Father, to my God and your God." Her words to the disciples are simple and few, yet transform the world: "I have seen the Lord."

I have seen the Lord: such is the story of the Resurrection, as told in the Gospel of John. With it begins the history of Christianity, and with it ends the New Testament history of Mary Magdalene. Peter and Paul form the new church, Stephen dies a martyr's death, John the Divine envisions the End Times. But Mary Magdalene—a critical figure in his earthly circle—is neither seen nor heard from again.

Yet the Magdalene—that part of her name derives from Magdala, her hometown—lives on in another tradition that can be found in an obscure second-century text. Dubbed "The Gospel of Mary," it depicts Mary as a leader of Jesus' followers in the days after his resurrection. Written by Christians some 90 years after Jesus' death, Mary's is a "Gnostic gospel"; the Gnostics, a significant force in the early years of Christianity, stressed salvation through study and self-knowledge rather than simply through faith. The text was lost for centuries until found in fragments by a collector in Cairo in 1896. In its telling, Jesus rises and vanishes after instructing his disciples to "preach the good news about the Realm." The exhortation makes them uneasy: Christ had died preaching that gospel. What was to save them from a similar fate?

Mary, however, is serene. "Do not weep and be depressed nor let your hearts be irresolute," she tells them. "For his grace will be with you and shelter you." Jesus, she says, has appeared to her in a vision where he gave her special knowledge of the soul's journey through mystical realms. She tells the men she will help them understand the true teachings of Christ: "What is hidden from you I shall reveal to you."

Her words seem to sting the others. Peter, "a wrathful man," takes particular offense. "Did he really speak with a woman in private, without our knowledge?" he asks. "Should we all turn and listen to her?" Mostly, he is jealous: "Did he prefer her to us?"

It is a question that is shaking Christianity after two millenniums. To many feminists and theological liberals, the Gospel of Mary suggests that the Magdalene, the first witness to the Resurrection, was the "apostle to the apostles," a figure with equal (or even favored) status to the men around Jesus—a woman so threatening that the apostles suppressed her role, and those of other women, in a bid to build a patriarchal hierarchy in the early church. To others, shaped by orthodoxy, Mary was an important player in the life and ministry of Jesus, but subordinate to the men who followed him. Now, thanks to Dan Brown's "The Da Vinci Code," read by some 60 million people and open in 3,735 movie theaters nationwide, Mary Magdalene has a new role: wife of Jesus and mother of his child, whom Mary, who purportedly escaped the Holy Land, raised after Jesus' death. According to the "Code"—which opened to tepid mainstream reviews but strong box office—the baby grew up to marry into a royal line in France—and descendants of Jesus

The Faces of Mary Magdalene

The Pope and the Prostitute Myth
The Sixth Century

In 591, Pope Gregory the Great, in need of a model of penance, claimed that Mary had worked as a prostitute: "She had coveted with earthly eyes, but now through penitence these are consumed with tears . . . She turned the mass of her crimes to virtues."

and Mary can be found in Europe to this day. In one particularly affecting but purely fanciful scene, one character argues that the figure at Jesus' right hand in Leonardo's "Last Supper" is not a male disciple but Mary Magdalene, and that if one recasts the painting by putting "Mary" on Jesus' left, they complete each other, male and female, a human whole—a married couple, joined together forever. It is cinematically intriguing, but like virtually all of Brown's novel and the movie, it is a fantasy, not fact, and, not for the first time, Mary Magdalene is a vehicle of fevered fiction.

The Gospel authors mention her only 13 times in the New Testament and only once outside the story of the resurrection.

From the beginning, the story of Mary Magdalene and Jesus has been the stuff of literature and legend, politics and theology, controversy and conflict. From age to age her changing image in the minds of believers and historians and artists has reflected the temper of the times—so much so that it is difficult to recover the historical Mary Magdalene from centuries of myth. Yet her history sheds light on essential questions, from the role of women in first-century Judaism to the nature of Jesus' ministry to the formation of early Christianity. Understanding her relationship with Jesus and with the religion that came to bear his name offers a window on the fluid nature of the faith, and of the tensions about sex and power that shape it still, in the third millennium since that morning at the empty tomb.

Mary was always an inconvenient woman. Although the Gospel authors can't avoid her— mentioning her 13 times in the New Testament—they offer few details of her life. This was perhaps no accident: women were considered untrustworthy in the Roman world, and the Gospels, eager to make new converts, probably did not wish to highlight the fact that a woman was a key witness to their story of the Resurrection—a story that was already difficult enough to explain. The New Testament Gospels "tell us a woman called Mary Magdalene was a follower of Jesus and played a role around the time of his betrayal and resurrection," says Elaine Pagels, a professor of early Christian history at Princeton. "But beyond that they tell us very little about what her role really was."

Scholars have picked apart the few hints the New Testament provides. Many have interpreted Luke's observation that Mary and other women around Jesus "ministered unto him of their substance" as evidence that they provided the financial support for Jesus' ministry. But where would this money have come from? A marriage contract? A divorce settlement? An inheritance? A job? The Gospels provide no direction, but a sign that women played an essential role in Jesus' life.

In the fourth century, fearing for their lives, the Gnostics buried their gospels, with their portrait of Mary Magdalene, in the sand.

Another vexing detail: Mary's name. Most New Testament women are identified by their relation to men (Mary the wife of Clopas, for example, is different from Mary the mother of James.) Yet the Magdalene is distinguished by her hometown, the port city of Magdala. No husband ever appears—an explanation, perhaps, for how she was able to travel freely with Jesus. Was she never married at all? "A freewoman who never married probably would have been exceedingly rare," says Ross Kraemer, a Brown University professor of religious studies. All the New Testament really tells us about Mary is that she entered Jesus' ministry as he preached throughout Galilee, that she had been possessed by seven demons but was no longer, and, of course, that she announced the Resurrection. We never learn her occupation, the color of her hair, if she was old or young, homely or beautiful.

Yet from the earliest hours of Christianity, there were other voices, too, those determined to present a fuller picture of the Magdalene. In several Gnostic Gospels, texts whose dissemination in the past 50 years has turned the study of Christian origins on its head, she is not the wallflower of the New Testament but rather a favored, perhaps favorite, follower of Christ. In the Gospel of Thomas, she and another woman, Salome, are one of six (not 12) true disciples of Jesus. In the Gnostic Dialogue of the Savior, she is referred to "as the woman who understood all things." Most compelling is the Gospel of Mary, not just for its portrait of the Magdalene as a strong, willful woman but also for its radical ideas about gender. While Mary is called the disciple "the Savior loved . . . more than all other women," she and Jesus see gender as irrelevant, something that will disappear in the path to the next life. "The text is arguing that the distinction between male and female is one of the body, which will dissolve," says Harvard historian Karen King. "The basis for leadership lies in spiritual development."

Why, then, did this woman, whom the New Testament tells us was Jesus' constant companion and whom the Gnostics claim was privileged above all others, disappear after the resurrection? If Mary were so important to Jesus, why is there no mention of her in Acts, or in the Epistles?

The noncanonical Gospels provide a troubling answer. In Gnostic texts, Mary is under constant attack, most often from

Legends of a French Saint
The 13th Century:

In 1275, Jacobus de Voragine, a Dominican monk, authored "The Golden Legend," which claimed Mary Magdalene had settled in France after the Resurrection. There, she preached the Gospel before retiring to a cave "in which place she had no comfort of running water, nor solace of trees, nor of herbs." The tale was among the most widely read of the Middle Ages.

Peter. "Tell Mary to leave us," he implores Jesus in the Gospel of Thomas, "for women are not worthy of life." Mary understands his threat. "I am afraid of Peter," she tells Jesus in the Gnostic Dialogue Pistis Sophia. "He threatens me and hates our race."

In her frightened voice, we can hear the beginnings of a rift that would determine Mary's future in the church. "You have one tradition where Peter plays a role of tremendous significance and Mary is on the margins," says Pagels, "while in another tradition Mary is the significant figure and Peter is suspect." And Peter's version is the one that comes down to us, which means it was his story, not hers, that carried the day.

The tension is not just a Gnostic aberration. For centuries the Resurrection sequence of the Gospel of John has vexed scholars. In John's version, Mary realizes the figure addressing her is Jesus and she reaches for him, but he holds her off, saying, "Do not touch me." Later that same day, however, Jesus appears to his male disciples and they recognize him instantly. He shows the men his hands, his sides, even breathes on them. Eight days later he appears to the Apostle Thomas, a doubter, and specifically asks to be touched so that Thomas will believe. "Reach hither thy finger and behold my hands," he says.

Mary's description of the risen Christ—unrecognizable, untouchable—is of a piece with the portrait of resurrection in the Gnostic texts. But in the New Testament, the men describe Jesus as a physical being in front of them, a body that lives, walks and breathes. In Luke, as the Lord invites the apostles to touch him, he points out, in case they missed it, that his physical resurrection makes him different from a ghost or an apparition. "Handle me and see me," he says, "for a spirit hath not hands and flesh."

The dispute—resurrection of flesh or of spirit?—would dominate the first three centuries of Christianity. Orthodox clerics worried that the Gnostic belief in resurrection as spiritual release would compromise their teaching that Christ physically suffered on the cross to atone for the sins of man. They called the Gnostics pagans and hedonists and spun wild tales to make them look profane. (The church writer Epiphanius, writing in the fourth century, claimed that Gnostics believed Jesus had forced Mary to watch him eat his own semen.) When the Roman Emperor Constantine converted to Christianity in the year 312, the orthodox won the power of the state, and the sword. Fearing that bishops enforcing the new orthodoxy would destroy the texts, monks tried to erase all evidence of the

Gnostic tradition. They buried the Gospels, with their powerful portrait of Mary Magdalene, in the sand.

The role played by women in the early church was also being erased. Jesus clearly had a rare empathy for women. Luke tells us that in addition to Mary, Jesus' Galilean ministry included an array of other women in prominent roles, including Susanna and Joanna, wife of Cuza. Luke also offers as a model of faith the story of Mary (a different Mary) who put aside concerns of keeping a household to listen attentively at the feet of Christ. Jesus' "last shall be first" message of salvation in the next life would certainly have been appealing to women who felt oppressed in this one. "Jesus was not a social reformer; he was focused on the apocalypse," says Bart Ehrman, professor of religious studies at the University of North Carolina and the author of "Peter, Paul and Mary Magdalene." "But his message would have been appealing to an egalitarian."

It wasn't long after Jesus' death, however, that male church leaders took steps to subordinate women. "As the church submits to Christ," Paul wrote to the Ephesians, "so wives should submit to their husbands." Yet Paul's letters also contain references to female missionaries throughout the empire. Among these women was Junia, whom Paul calls "outstanding among the apostles," and admits was in Christ "before I was." Christians in the first and second centuries came to believe in a trinity that included a holy spirit, filled with a decidedly feminine grace.

Yet as church teachings evolved, women took on a more sinister role: carriers of earthly sin. In the immediate aftermath of Jesus' death, his followers explained the resurrection as evidence that the apocalypse was at hand. But as the years passed and the kingdom of God did not come, church teachers needed a new theory of the Resurrection. By the second century, they had come to think of Jesus' time on the cross as the fulfillment of a Biblical cycle in the works since Eden. Jesus had died, the clerics now said, to rid the world of Adam's sin. But women, with their tie to sexual reproduction, were a problem, a reminder that the good work would not be done until Christ's return. Bishops barred women from the ordained ministry and accused them of spreading sin. "On account of [you] . . ." the prolific third-century author Tertullian wrote, addressing women, "even the son of God had to die."

It was only a matter of time before the Magdalene also came under attack. The moment arrived on an autumn Sunday in the year 591, in a sermon preached at the heart of the Catholic Church. Taking the pulpit at the Basilica San Clemente in Rome, Pope Gregory the Great offered a startling conclusion about the Magdalene: she had been a whore. Before she came to Christ, Gregory explained, Mary's sins were manifold: she had "coveted with Earthly eyes" and "displayed her hair to set off her face." Most scandalously, she had "used the unguent to perfume her flesh in forbidden acts." Looking out at his audience, a somber mass of monks, Gregory gave Mary a new identity that would shape her image for fourteen hundred years. "It is clear, brothers," he declared: she was a prostitute.

But it was not clear at all. Gregory's remarkable assertion was based on the idea that Mary was the unnamed "sinful woman" who anoints Jesus' feet in the seventh chapter of Luke—a conflation many contemporary scholars dismiss. Even if she were the sinful woman, there is no evidence in any Gospels that her sins were those of the flesh—in the first century, a woman could be considered "sinful" for talking to men other than her husband or going to the marketplace alone. Gregory created the prostitute, as if from thin air.

In England, Mary Magdalene was made the patron saint of lepers; in Florence, prostitutes and young men ran a race on her feast day.

The pope made his new Mary a reformed whore because he knew that the faithful needed a story of penance that was at once alluring and inspiring. The early Middle Ages were a time of tremendous social tumult—war and disease roiled nations and sent destitute women into the streets. Gregory's church needed a character from Jesus' circle who provided an answer to this misery, who proved that the path of Christ was an escape from the pressures of the sinful world. The mysterious Magdalene of the Resurrection story was peripheral enough to be reinvented. Finally, the church fathers were able to put the inconvenient woman to good use.

Christendom eagerly embraced its new saintly sinner. A Magdalene cult spread throughout Europe, from England where Mary was made the patron saint of lepers, to Florence where prostitutes and young men ran a race on her feast day. In Germany, the Penitent Sisters of the Blessed Magdalene took the lead in reforming wayward women; in Spain young men on stilts danced with Mary's icon in the streets.

The French were particularly enamored with the Magdalene— so enamored that, naturally, they made her French. In the 13th century, a Dominican monk published the Golden Legend, which claimed that after Jesus' death Mary had fled Jerusalem and ended up in southern Gaul. Her spirit, the story said, protected Frenchmen. There was no historical evidence to support this claim, only the imaginations of Provenal storytellers. Still, the legend persists. Dan Brown's claim that the Magdalene spent her final years in Provence has its roots in the tales of medieval France.

In the Renaissance, artists gloried in her versatility. The Virgin Mary was a difficult subject—how to make her compelling and controversial while still modest, graceful and chaste? The Magdalene knew no such restrictions, and the old masters

---

A Saint, a Sinner and a Superstar
The 20th Century

In 1971, Andrew Lloyd Webber's musical "Jesus Christ Superstar" introduced the world to a thoroughly modern Mary, powerful, pretty—and still a prostitute. In her signature song, "I Don't Know How to Love Him," she marveled at Jesus' effect on her: "He's just a man. And I've had so many men before, in very many ways, He's just one more."

With So Many Claims of Conspiracies and Cover-Ups in 'The Da Vinci Code,' It's Hard to Sort Out What's True. Here, We Do it for You: Fact or Fiction?

1. What is the Priory of Sion?
   Da Vinci Code: In 1099 a French king founded it to protect the truth about his bloodline and to pass that knowledge secretly to his heirs.
   What we know: The Priory was a small group created in 1956 by Pierre Plantard—once convicted of fraud—who fabricated its history.

2. What is Opus dei?
   Da Vinci Code: Opus Dei is a fringe branch of the church led by a corrupt bishop whose will is carried out by a self-flagellaring monk.
   What we know: It's a conservative set of mostly lay Roman Catholics, a minority of whom inflict minor pain on themselves daily. Most, however, lead devout—and average—lives.

3. Who is sitting to Jesus' right in the last supper?
   Da Vinci Code: The fair-faced figure at Jesus' side is none other than Mary Magdalene—a fact that has eluded critical eyes for centuries.
   What we know: Scholars agree overwhelningly that it's Saint John, and the notion that it's actually Mary Magdalene seems to have originated with 'The Da Vinci Code.'

4. Did Mary Magdalene flee to Gaul after the Crucifixion?
   Da Vinci Code: Fearing for her safety and that of her unborn baby, Mary Magdalene left the Holy Land for Gaul, now known as France.
   What we know: No written records exist that confirm this, though several legends abound. This one dates back to the early 11th century.

5. What is the Holy Grail?
   Da Vinci Code: Contrary to popular belief, the Grail was really Mary Magdalene or, more specifically, her womb, which held Christ's child.
   What we know: There are a number of myths, many of which identify it as the cup Christ used at the Last Supper to give wine to his disciples.

6. Who were the Knights Templar?
   Da Vinci Code: A military arm of the Priory, they were formed to retrieve a stash of hidden documents that held the truth about Christ's bloodline.
   What we know: The Templars were a monastic order of soldiers charged with protecting Christian pilgrims on their way to Jerusalem.

7. Did Constantine deliberately create a bible that emphasized christ's divinity?
   Da Vinci Code: To quell religious turmoil and unify the Roman Empire, Constantine had the Nicene Council compile a Bible that portrayed Jesus as more God than man.
   What we know: Constantine did not have a hand in making the Bible. The canon was basically set; only the council decided how to understand it.

8. What is the Gospel of Philip?
   Da Vinci Code: One of several noncanonical Gospels, it suggests that Jesus and Mary Magdalene were, in fact, married.
   What we know: It was part of the Nag Hammadi Library found in the 1950s. Experts, however, say any union it refers to is solely spiritual.

9. Did the church really downplay the role of women in early christianity to create a patriarchy?
   Da Vinci Code: To tip the scales in favor of men, the church began to demonize women, first labeling them witches to remove them from positions of power and later burning them by the thousands.
   What we know: Some women did play important roles in the early church. Whether the church defamed them to intentionally limit their role is subject to debate.

10. What is the Rose Line?
    Da Vinci Code: The Paris Rose Line served as the prime meridian for the entire globe. At the church of St-Sulpice, a marking in the floor indicates its course.
    What we know: The line, commonly known as the Paris Meridian, does run through Paris and even St-Sulpice, though the floor marking at the church doesn't quite match up.

11. What is the Origin of the Six-pointed Star?
    Da Vinci Code: It's implied that the star is a marriage of the pagan symbols for masculinity (the blade) and femininity (the vessel).
    What we know: The star is best known as the Star of David. But before it became a symbol of Judaism, it may have been used to signify a fusion of opposing forces.

12. Does the Rosslyn Chapel in Scotland really exist?
    Da Vinci Code: The chapel was built in 1466 by the Knights Templar and was at one point the resting place of Mary Magdalene's remains.
    What we know: The chapel exists, though it wasn't built by the Templars and became associated with them only in the 19th century. And Mary's bones were never there.

—Marc Bain

used her to explore the full range of femininity. In Titian she was buxom and bountiful; in Donatello she was haggard and ascetic. She was not, as "The Da Vinci Code" claims, the figure "with delicate folded hands, and the hint of a bosom" at Jesus' right in Leonardo's "Last Supper." Scholars have identified the figure as John the Evangelist: tender intimacy between two men was a possibility understood by Leonardo, if not by Dan Brown.

The gaps in the Gospel of Philip are maddening. Companion of whom? Loved her more than what? Kissed her where?

A Secret Bride to the King of Kings
The 21st Century

In 2003 "The Da Vinci Code" claimed that Jesus and Mary Magdalene were married and together conceived a child. Mary is the Holy Grail, the character Leigh Teabing explains: "When Grail legend speaks of 'the chalice that held the blood of Christ'—it speaks, in fact, of Mary Magdalene—the female womb that carried Jesus' royal blood line."

Even as other saints lost their luster in the modern era, the Magdalene remained a powerful force. When the Industrial Revolution upset gender roles and cities were plagued with prostitution and disease, preachers once again spoke her name from the pulpit, hoping to rein in the wayward world. Nineteenth-century artists from Wagner and Rilke to Rodin drew inspiration from her—or rather from Gregory's imagining of her. They explored her sexuality in new depth, even imagining her as erotically connected to Jesus.

The 20th century brought yet another new identity for Mary: feminist icon. Women's liberation brought a new generation of historians who argued that the Gnostic Gospels, together with the New Testament portrait of Mary as faithful witness, provided a better picture than Gregory's of who the Magdalene really was. Their outcry even managed to penetrate the Vatican's walls. In 1969, the church declared that, for the first time since Gregory's day, Mary should not be thought of as the sinful woman of Luke. In 1988, Pope John Paul II called Mary Magdalene "apostle to the apostles" in an official church document and noted that in Christians' "most arduous test of faith and fidelity," the Crucifixion, "the women proved stronger than the Apostles."

Yet Mary has continued to be defined by sex. In 1971, the musical "Jesus Christ Superstar" presented Mary as thoughtful, powerful and still a prostitute. The Magdalene of the era of free love and sexual liberty was so comfortable with her body she used it for power over men. "*He's just a man*," she sings in "Jesus Christ Superstar." "*And I've had so many men before, in very many ways, he's just one more*." Modern generations proved as adept as their forebears in adapting Mary to fit their needs. By the time "The Da Vinci Code" was published in 2003, the fires of feminism burned less brightly than they had in the "Superstar" days, and Mary was reinvented as the ideal working mother: protecting the mystery of faith by day, raising Jesus' child by night.

Indeed, for all its revolutionary claims, "The Da Vinci Code" is remarkably old-fashioned, making Mary important for her body more than her mind. In the movie, we see a stricken, shadowy Magdalene with swollen belly being spirited out of Jerusalem by a crowd of attendant men. But we never hear her voice. "The Da Vinci Code" seems to think that the secret tradition of Mary Magdalene speaks to the carnal. In reality, it tells of something far more subversive: the intellectual equality of the sexes. The current Magdalene cult still focuses on her sexuality even though no early Christian writings speak of her sexuality at all. "Why do we feel the need to re-sexualize Mary?" wonders Karen King, author of "The Gospel of Mary of Magdala." "We've gotten rid of the myth of the prostitute. Now there's this move to see her as wife and mother. Why isn't it adequate to see her as disciple and perhaps apostle?"

"The Da Vinci Code" especially misses the point about Mary when it makes its case that she was the bride of Christ. Both the novel and the film use as their evidence a gap-filled passage from the Gospel of Philip, a Gnostic Gospel of the second century. The passage reads as follows: "And the companion of the [gap] Mary Magdalene. [Gap] her more than [gap] the disciples [gap] kiss her [gap] on her [gap]." The gaps are maddening. Companion of whom? Loved her more than what? Kiss her where? But even if we fill in what seems to be the logical meaning—Jesus loved Mary more than the male apostles and kissed her on her mouth—the passage is less sensational than we might think. In the Gnostic tradition, kisses on the lips are not an erotic act but a chaste gesture meant to symbolize the passage of knowledge and spiritual truth. Elsewhere in the Gospel of Philip, Jesus also kisses his male disciples on the mouth. (If the makers of "The Da Vinci Code" wanted to interpret this act as erotic, they would no doubt be facing even more vehement protests from conventional Christians.) The passage is certainly significant, for it could imply that Jesus gave Mary special authority in his church. But "The Da Vinci Code" fails to make this point by mistaking the nature of Jesus' kiss.

Brown's mistake is understandable. Sex sells in our time, as it did in Gregory's, and probably Jesus', too. Mary remains a prisoner, a mistaken creature of sex. History may yet set her free. There are still undiscovered gospels sitting in unknown deserts or on unknown library shelves. Scholars say it is only a matter of time before some of them surface and upend our notions of Mary and Jesus once again.

Until then, she will remain a mystery. All we can really know about her is that she was always faithful to Jesus' message of love and hope, always willing to risk all for him, always open to the possibilities of grace—an example that transcends time and gender, a beacon in a modern-day fog of faction and fiction.

UNIT 4

Muslims and Byzantines

Unit Selections

18. **The Elusive Eastern Empire,** Dionysios Stathakopoulos
19. **The Lost Secret of Greek Fire,** Bruce Heydt
20. **Islam's First Terrorists,** Clive Foss
21. **Al-Kimiya Notes on Arabic Alchemy,** Gabriele Ferrario

Key Points to Consider

- What were some of the contributions of Byzantium to the world?

- Why was "Greek Fire" such a terrible weapon?

- Explain why the Kharijites were influential in Islamic history.

- Discuss what we owe to Islam in the realm of chemistry.

Student Website

www.mhhe.com/cls

Internet References

ByzNet: Byzantine Studies on the Net
www.thoughtline.com/byznet
Chemical Heritage Magazine
www.chemicalheritage.org/magazine
History Today
www.historytoday.com
Islam: A Global Civilization
www.templemount.org/islamiad.html
Military History
www.historynet.com/military-history

After the collapse of the Roman Empire in the west, three ethnic/religious entities emerged to fill the vacuum. Germanic kingdoms arose in central and western Europe. In the Balkans and Asia Minor, the eastern remnants of Rome evolved into the Byzantine Empire. The Near East, North Africa, and much of Spain fell under the control of the Arabs. Each area developed a unique civilization, based in each instance upon a distinctive form of religion—Roman Catholicism in most of Europe, Orthodox Christianity in the Byzantine sphere, and Islam in the Arab world. Each placed its unique stamp upon the classical tradition to which all three fell heir. The articles in this unit concentrate on the Byzantine and Muslim civilizations. The medieval culture of Europe is treated in the next unit.

Western perceptions of Islam and Arabic civilization have been clouded by ignorance and bias. To European observers during the medieval period, Islam seemed a misguided or heretical version of Christianity. In the wake of Arab conquests, Islam increasingly came to represent terror and devastation (see "Islam's First Terrorists"), a dangerous force loosed upon Christendom. Reacting out of fear and hostility, Christian authors were reluctant to acknowledge the learning and high culture of the Arabs.

Muslim commentators could be equally intolerant. Describing Europeans, one wrote: "They are most like beasts than like men. . . . Their temperaments are frigid, their humors raw, their bellies gross . . . they lack keenness of understanding . . . and are overcome by ignorance and apathy." The stereotypes formed in the early encounters between Christians and Muslims survived for generations. Centuries of hostility have tended to obscure the extent of cultural exchange between the Arab world and the West. Indeed, as historian William H. McNeil has observed, "Muslims have been written out of European history."

The lands of Islam encroached at too many places for the two cultures to remain mutually exclusive. In Western Europe Islam swept over Spain, crossed the Pyrenees, and penetrated France; in the central Mediterranean, it leaped form Tunis to Sicily and then into southern Italy; and in Eastern Europe, Islam broke into Asia Minor, the Balkans, and the Caucasus. In its expansion, early Islam was exposed to Jewish, Christian, and classical influences. History and geography determined that there would be much cross-fertilization of Islam and the West.

Yet there is no denying the originality and brilliance of Islamic civilization. The religion of Muhammad is unquestionably one of the world's most influential faiths. Additional evidence of Arab creativity can be found in the visual arts, particularly in the design and decoration of the great mosques. The Arabs also made significant contributions in philosophy, history, geography, science, and medicine (see "Al-Kimiya Notes on Arabic Alchemy").

The medieval West borrowed extensively from the Arabs. The magnificent centers of Islamic culture—Baghdad, Cairo, Cordoba, and Damascus outshone the cities of the West. Their

© Pixtal/age Fotostock

administration of Andalusia was a model of successful governance. Islamic scholars surpassed their Christian counterparts in astronomy, mathematics, and medicine—perhaps because the Arab world was more familiar than medieval Europe with the achievements of classical Greece. European scholars eventually regained access to the Greek heritage, at least partially, through translations from Arabic.

As for the Byzantine Empire, it was for nearly 1,000 years a Christian bulwark against Persians, Arabs, and Turks. Dionysios Stathakopoulos recounts the reasons for its success in "The Elusive Eastern Empire." It also made important cultural contributions. The beautiful mosaics and icons of Byzantine artists set the pattern for later visualizations of Christ in the West. Byzantine missionaries and statesmen spread Orthodox Christianity, with its unique tradition of Caesaropapism, to Russia, while Byzantine scholars and lawmakers preserved much of the classical heritage. Even hostile Islam was subject to a constant flow of ideas and traditions from the Byzantines.

The Elusive Eastern Empire

As the Royal Academy in London opens a major new exhibition on the artistic splendours of the Byzantine empire, Dionysios Stathakopoulos surveys its history from its foundation in 324 to its conquest in 1453.

DIONYSIOS STATHAKOPOULOS

The Byzantine empire means different things to different people. Some associate it with gold: the golden tesserae in the mosaics of Ravenna, the golden background in icons, the much coveted golden coins (besaunt as Wycliffe calls them), the golden-hued threads of Byzantine silks used to shroud Charlemagne. Others think of court intrigues, poisonings and scores of eunuchs. Most will think of Constantinople, which used to be Byzantium and is now Istanbul, and will possibly bring to mind the city's skyline with the huge dome of the Hagia Sophia. Little else perhaps exists in the collective imagination. All this is indeed evocative of Byzantium, but there is so much more to explore. The fascinating exhibition that has just opened at the Royal Academy is a unique chance to revisit familiar themes and be surprised by new discoveries.

To begin at the beginning is tricky. Did the empire begin when the emperor Constantine (r. 306–337) moved his capital from Rome to Constantinople in 324? When the city was consecrated by both pagan and Christian priests in May 330? Or did it begin in 395 when the two halves of the vast Roman empire were officially divided into East and West, or even later in the late 5th century when Rome was sacked, conquered and governed by the Goths, leaving Constantinople and the East as the sole heir of the empire? But, if its beginning is unclear, its demise is not: on May 29th, 1453, the armies of the Ottoman sultan Mehmed II entered the city and brought the existence of this state to an end after more than a millennium.

When Constantine moved his capital from Rome to the hitherto relatively obscure, though strategically placed, city of Byzantium and gave the city his name, it signalled a shift of interest towards the East, but perhaps little else initially. After the troubled third century a number of cities had functioned as imperial residences without necessarily challenging the idea of Rome as the centre: Trier, Split, Thessalonica, Nicomedia (modern Izmit). But with the advantage of hindsight we can see that this case was different: Constantinople was enlarged, decorated with famous statues and objects from the whole empire (some of which are still in place today), endowed with a Senate and its citizens given the traditional free bread handed out to Romans.

A number of the most important constituting traits of the Byzantine empire date back to this early era. The Byzantine state was, more or less from the beginning, a Christian Roman empire. After the edict of Milan in 313 ended the persecutions and made Christianity a tolerated religion, Constantine showed a marked (though not exclusive) preference for Christianity. He presided over the first ecumenical Council in Nicaea in 325 which defined the creed and dealt with heresies, thus setting the tone for the intimate relation between Church and state. This bond was made clear by a number of sacred buildings that Constantine erected, in his capital as well as in Palestine (both the Church of the Holy Sepulchre and the Church of the Nativity go back to this period), and by a number of relics of Christ and the Virgin that his mother, Helena, purchased in the Holy Land and sent back to Constantinople. Unlike Rome or Antioch, the new capital had not been graced by the presence of any apostle, but certainly entered Christian topography with the bonus of imperial patronage.

In the eleven hundred years that separate the first Constantine from the last emperor, another Constantine (the XI), the empire underwent many and significant changes. First came expansion. From the fourth to the early sixth centuries the East flourished: population boomed, cities proliferated and Constantinople itself grew to be the largest city in Europe with over 400,000 inhabitants. To support this growth its city walls were yet again enlarged in between 404 and 413, a triple system of inner wall, outer wall and moat that did not fail to protect it until the very end (large parts of which are still visible, albeit over-restored, today). The ecclesiastical head of the city, the patriarch of the new Rome, had risen to the second position in the hierarchy of the Church just below the old Rome, the result of political pressure that was to breed discontent between the two sees in the centuries to come. Together with Alexandria, Antioch and Jerusalem they formed the Pentarchy, the ultimate authority of the Church as decided by councils bringing together the senior clergy of the five sees.

While the city expanded, the empire underwent a transformation. In 395, Theodosius I (r. 347–95) divided the vast empire stretching from Britain to North Africa and from Spain to Mesopotamia and harassed by the Persians in the East and Germanic tribes in the North. A demarcation line running roughly from Belgrade to Libya turned, in the fifth century, into a true frontier. In the West, disaster: Huns and Goths overran the Roman world. In the East, Germanic officials were integrated into the government and occupied important positions in the state machinery up until the reign of the emperor Zeno (r. 474–91), when they were gradually excluded by his own people, the Isaurians from the mountains of Asia Minor. The Eastern Empire was an unbroken continuation of the Roman state, though with Greek as the dominant language. The West was now divided into several Germanic kingdoms who adopted Latin for their administration.

Enter Justinian (r. 527–565). The nephew and heir of a parvenu, an illiterate military man turned emperor (for Byzantium was for centuries a quite open society in which one could get ahead in life based on talent), he put an indelible mark on his era. In his time the empire sought to regain the lost territories in the West in a series of long wars. The Vandal kingdom in Africa was subdued in 533–34, but the reconquest of Italy took nearly twenty years until the final defeat and extinction of the Goths in 554. At the same time there was almost constant warfare with Persia, although imperial victories and territorial gains were not as decisive as in the West. But Justinian's lasting legacy stems from other contributions. Roman law, the backbone of the administration of such a vast empire, had already been collected and organized in the mid-fifth century. Justinian undertook a review of this massive material early in his reign between 529 and 534. The result was the huge (and hugely influential) *Corpus Iuris Civilis* which updated the previous Theodosian collection, weeding out all laws no longer deemed relevant, while adding all those passed since that date. It included legal writings of a more theoretical nature and pronouncements that spanned the period from Hadrian (r. 117–38) to Justinian. Ask any lawyer today and you are likely to hear superlatives about this colossal work that has been termed 'one of the most significant influences upon human society'. Justinian, naturally, continued to legislate and his new laws (the *Novels*) were issued for the first time in Greek. This was an acknowledgment of the developments that the empire had undergone since Constantine. It was now a state based on Roman law, Christian faith and Greek culture, one in which literacy was widespread and Homer's *Iliad* formed the basis of elementary education along with the equally popular book of Psalms.

Justinian was also a great builder. The single most iconic Byzantine building, the Hagia Sophia, is a product of his drive and vision. Completed in 537 after an earlier Theodosian church of the same name had been burned down during civil unrest in the city, the church dedicated to Holy Wisdom is still breathtaking today. The majestic dome with a diameter of about 32 metres gave the impression to contemporaries of being suspended from heaven. This feat of engineering was only surpassed in the fifteenth century by the dome of Santa Maria del Fiore (*Il Duomo*) in Florence. The original decoration of Hagia Sophia was not figurative: mosaics with geometrical patterns, deeply cut capitals with the monograms of the emperor and his infamous wife, Theodora, and the interplay of coloured marble on the walls and pavement—all were designed to reflect the light as it pierces the space from a multitude of windows. Justinian not only adorned his capital with new buildings; he erected or restored a great number of edifices throughout his vast empire. One of the most famous is the Monastery of Saint Catherine on Mount Sinai, still functioning today.

Justinian clearly saw himself as God's representative on earth. He strove for order and tolerated no dissent; it appears as if he was determined to align everyone to the divine plan for salvation, whether they wanted it or not. The academy in Athens was closed; the Olympic Games and the mysteries in Eleusis had long ceased; and it was probably around this time that the Parthenon in Athens was transformed into a Christian church. Justinian's unified vision of a Christian empire in a way mirrored a Mediterranean world unified by sea and land communications. This unification, however, allowed not only people and commodities to travel, but also germs. Bubonic plague broke out for the first time in pandemic form in 541 and ran its deadly course throughout the Mediterranean. It was to return in some eighteen waves until 750, causing a sharp demographic decline that was felt the strongest in coastal cities. Constantinople lost possibly as much as 20 per cent of its population in four months in the spring of 542.

At the end of Justinian's reign the empire began to collapse as a result of both demographic losses (from plague and long wars) and economic hardships brought about by these two factors and the cost of large-scale building. By the early seventh century much of the regained territory had been lost. The Lombards invaded Italy in 568 and seized the Po valley; the Visigoths regained the few Byzantine holdings in Spain in 624, while the eastern front collapsed under renewed Persian attacks. Moreover, a new force emerged in the Balkans: the Turkic Avars and the Slavs. From the 580s onwards the Slavs began their settlement of the Balkans, gradually taking almost the entire peninsula *de facto* out of Byzantine control for the next two centuries.

When Heraclius (r. 610–641) became emperor he raised great hopes that he could restore order and confidence in an empire that seemed in disarray. The Persians captured Syria, Egypt and Palestine between 613 and 619 and, in what must be seen as a calculated move of political warfare, they removed the True Cross of Christ from Jerusalem to their capital in Ctesiphon. Heraclius' counter-attack took years to prepare. It was almost brought to a halt before it produced any actual results when in 626, while the emperor was away, the Persians with the aid of Avars and Slavs besieged Constantinople. The city was saved, according to tradition, by a supernatural protector, the Virgin Mary, whose girdle had been in the city since the fourth century and who increasingly came to be regarded as Constantinople's patron saint. After this episode Heraclius took the war to Persia and ultimately defeated the Sassanian king in 628. In a highly significant gesture, he restored the True Cross to Jerusalem in 630.

Byzantium might have been victorious, but the wars that had lasted more than twenty years left both empires exhausted. The timing was perfect for the new emerging player in the Mediterranean, the Arabs. Their expansion began in the 630s. By the turn of the century the Byzantine Empire had irrevocably lost Egypt, Palestine, Syria and Northern Africa, while the Sassanid state had been overthrown. The Arab foray seemed unstoppable. It menaced Constantinople in 678 and again in 717–18, though failing both times to capture the city. The seventh century was a period of massive restructuring and reorganization as the Byzantine empire fought for its survival. The massive loss of territory—especially Egypt, the 'granary of the empire'—deprived the state of considerable human resources and commodities. From then on Byzantium concentrated on Asia Minor as an almost exclusive source for both. A large-scale reorganization of the army took place in that period, first in Asia Minor, spreading then to the entire empire. Territory was organized into administrative and military units, the *themata,* in which both civil and military powers were concentrated in the hands of one military commander. Soldiers were from then on recruited among the free peasant smallholders, who offered their military service in exchange for land that enjoyed certain privileges.

Disaster as a rule breeds the need for reform and in the Byzantine empire this was not only expressed in terms of administration. The movement of Iconoclasm (literally icon-breaking) has its roots in the traumatic experience of the seventh century. It does not need to concern us here when exactly it began—was the eruption of the volcano at Thera/Santorini in 726 an omen suggesting divine wrath? Surely the Arabic juggernaut must have seemed reason enough for this divine displeasure. And the Arabs did forbid figurative art. A sober look at this development would look like this: from the early-to-mid-eighth century Byzantine emperors had religious images removed and later destroyed. Their main motive must have been to counteract the excessive veneration of images which came close to idolatry—surely this could have been a reason why the infidels were winning and God's chosen people were being chastised by one defeat after another. Persecution of those opposing these measures, mainly monks, varied, but some of the most fervent supporters of icons were executed. Iconoclasm was reversed by an empress: the widowed Irene (r. 780–802), acting as a regent for her young son, summoned a council in 787 (the seventh and last ecumenical one) in Nicaea, which condemned it and restored the veneration of images, while in the process destroying pretty much all that their adversaries had ever written and thus making it very difficult for us to view the events in a balanced way.

Iconoclasm coincided with the successes of Constantine V (r. 741–775) in both Asia Minor and the Balkans. However, after Irene, the empire suffered a series of setbacks that led to a second phase of Iconoclasm that began in 815 and ended in 843. Again, an empress acting as regent, Theodora (r. 842–55), restored the images in what is still today celebrated as the 'Triumph of Orthodoxy'. At the end of Iconoclasm, Christian art had prevailed and became an essential aspect of worship.

On Christmas Day 800 during the reign of Irene as empress, the coronation of Charlemagne, ruler of a western empire controlling France, the Rhineland and Northern Italy, in Rome gave the world a second Roman emperor. Despite the fact that Charlemagne's state did not enjoy a long life, the ideological antagonism from the West would become a recurrent phenomenon in the centuries to come.

After 843 the empire began a period of revival that lasted for two centuries and marked a long phase of territorial expansion, political and cultural radiance over its neighbours and a flourishing of education and the arts. Gradually, imperial authority was restored in the Balkans and parts of Syria and Asia Minor were reconquered. In what is perhaps the most enduring consequence of Byzantine policy, a number of Slavic states embraced Christianity coming from Constantinople (not without fierce competition with Rome). Byzantine missionaries developed the first Slavic alphabet and the newly converted were allowed to use it in their services. These were the early steps in creating what was termed a 'Byzantine Commonwealth'.

With the state expanding and the economy growing, a cultural revival developed as well. It was marked by an effort at collecting and systematizing knowledge by compiling vast encyclopaedias with the most varied contents: ancient epigrams, lives of saints, dictionaries, medical and veterinary texts, practical agricultural wisdom and military treatises, as well as thematically organized volumes on embassies or hunting. The central figure in this revival (perhaps more as a result of imperial propaganda than of actual contribution) was the learned emperor Constantine VII (944–959) under whose auspices a number of works were created dealing with the imperial ceremonies, the administrative division of the empire and a secret manual of governance addressed to his son. This revival of learning was a direct result of the important scholars produced by the fostering of education from the ninth century. Classical Antiquity, no longer carrying the negative connotation of paganism, was studied and copied.

Classical Antiquity, no longer carrying the negative connotation of paganism, was studied and copied

The economic and political stimulus behind the revival, however, fuelled some rather untoward trends as well. The military aristocracy gained more and more power, and, in its quest for more land, started to encroach on the villages and their free peasants, potentially stripping the state of tax revenues and the army of its manpower. The emperors legislated against this and civil wars ensued. It took as resolute an emperor as Basil II (r. 976–1025) to crush those military clans, but his victory was short-lived. Following the general and growing disarray that ensued after his death, the aristocracy made a decisive comeback in the person of Alexius I Comnenus (r. 1081–1118). When he took over the reins of the empire he faced a very different political situation from that which had existed less than half a century before him. The Seljuk Turks had started conquering Asia Minor, the empire's heartland. Moreover, the Normans had taken over large parts of Italy and then attacked the empire in the Balkans, while Venice, aided by commercial privileges accorded to it by Byzantium, was branching out in the eastern Mediterranean. Finally, the papacy's zeal for reform was changing it into a formidable power able to stand above secular rulers. Certainly the schism between Rome and Constantinople that had occurred in 1054 was not a positive development, although it was hardly surprising given the troubled history of antagonism between the two sees.

The crusades should also be seen in this context of Western expansion. Under the first three Comnenian emperors (roughly until 1180) Byzantium managed to escape the onslaught of the crusaders largely unscathed (and even partially to use them to its advantage in Syria and Asia Minor). Towards the close of the twelfth century the relationship with the West deteriorated. The tragic endpoint of this process was the capture and looting of Constantinople by the French and Venetian armies of the Fourth Crusade in 1204.

The fragmentation of the once centralized empire was a blow from which it never fully recovered. Constantinople itself was governed by the Latins for some sixty years, and a number of Latin and Greek states of varying size and importance were established in Greece and Asia Minor. From this period onwards, the interaction with the West became the dominant theme in Byzantine affairs. Both cultures came much closer to each other and a true exchange took place—not always favoured by the Byzantines. After 1204 a great number of artefacts of the highest quality wandered to the West, but not many of them have survived until today (for example, the relics from Constantinople that were housed in the Sainte Chapelle in Paris were destroyed in the 1789 Revolution).

In 1261 Constantinople was recaptured and a new dynasty, the Palaeologoi, gained power and held on to it for the last two centuries of the empire's existence. But 'empire' was now hardly the right designation for this state. From the very beginning it was engaged in a fight for survival against foreign forces and internal frictions. A civil war that began in 1341 functioned as a watershed for the fate of the state. Until that time the empire had weathered its problems with difficulty, but still preserved

an international importance. It is unfortunate that the civil war ended only a few months before the outbreak of the Black Death in 1347. There was no time for recovery, with both Ottoman Turks and Serbs expanding at the empire's expense. The last century saw the empire in constant decline, although some Byzantines profited from the decentralization of power and the massive influx of Italian merchant capital into the Levant. In the face of danger, opposing factions emerged dynamically. On the one side were people who looked to the West for help; there were conversions to Catholicism and for the first time after many centuries the translation and study of works in Latin. Ending the Schism was seen by those pro-Western advocates as the only solution. Many of the emperors pursued this policy right to the very end, when John VIII (r. 1425–1448) took part at the Council of Ferrara-Florence in 1438–39. But the movement of knowledge functioned the other way around as well; Greek scholars travelled to Italy, taught Greek to enthusiastic audiences and brought with them manuscripts containing texts long forgotten in the West—Plato, above all. There, these texts were translated into Latin and certainly made an important contribution to humanism and gave impetus to the Renaissance. Yet there was a different Byzantine reaction at the same time, inward-looking amidst the imminent disaster. This was focused on tradition and Orthodoxy; it rejected union with the Roman church and feared that the Latins would undermine their Byzantine identity. The gap would not be bridged. Perhaps not surprisingly, the Palaeologan period saw a remarkable flourishing of literature and art, both in response to Western impulses and in keeping with Byzantine traditions. Ancient texts were studied, meticulously edited and commented on by large numbers of intellectuals who enjoyed patronage. Brilliant monuments of the period survive, such as the church of the Chora Monastery and the Virgin Pammakaristos in Constantinople.

As the state became weaker, the church was swiftly becoming the only reliable institution. 'A church we have, an emperor we don't,' claimed Basil I, the prince of Moscow, only to be strongly rebuked by the patriarch: 'It is impossible for Christians to have a church and no empire.' Yet this is what happened after 1453 when the young Mehmed II accomplished what a number of his predecessors had failed, the capture of Constantinople, the City (Greek: *polis*) *par excellence* and the colloquial phrase *eis tin polin* (to the city) became then the name of Istanbul.

The Lost Secret of Greek Fire

To this day, nobody is quite sure of the exact formula for the Dark Ages' most terrifying 'weapon of mass destruction.'

BRUCE HEYDT

"If you will make a flying fire which rises above and burns what it encounters, take one part colophonium, that is Greek resin, two parts of native sulphur, and three parts of saltpeter. Rub all small and then rub it with one of linseed oil or laurel oil till it is taken up and becomes like a paste. Put this in a long bronze tube and kindle it and blow into the tube, when it goes to wherever you turn the tube and destroys and burns up everything it meets."

—Albertus Magnus, c. AD 1250

The rise of Islam at the beginning of the 7th century presaged centuries of conflict with the Byzantine Empire. The jihad, or holy war, led by the military commanders of the new faith toppled one outlying city and province after another. In 634 Caliph Omar attacked Syria. Emperor Heraclius' Byzantine army suffered defeat at Ajnadain in the same year. Damascus fell in 635, followed in rapid succession by Jerusalem and Antioch. The last remnants of Syria capitulated in 636.

Heraclius' woes outlived him, and his successor, Constans II, inherited them. The Muslim advance continued across Asia Minor and into Africa. Cyrenaica, Tripoli, Armenia, Cyprus and Rhodes had all fallen to Islam by 654. Encouraged by their unbroken string of victories in the name of Allah, the Arab caliphs turned their attention to the very heart of the Byzantine Empire, Constantinople.

The Byzantine historian Theophanes recorded in his *Chronographia* that in the fourth year of Constantine IV's reign: "[The] deniers of Christ equipped a great fleet, and after they had sailed past Cilicia, Mohammed, son of Abdelas, wintered at Smyrna, while Kaisos wintered at Cilicia and Lycia. . . . The emir Khalid was also sent to assist them insomuch as he was a competent and bold warrior. The aforesaid Constantine, on being informed of so great an expedition of God's enemies

against Constantinople, built large biremes bearing cauldrons of fire and *dromones* equipped with siphons and ordered them to be stationed at the Proclianesian harbor of [Constantinople]."

Constantine IV is not remembered as one of the great military strategists of the ancient world. Nor was the empire itself renowned for the sort of martial prowess that its antecedent, Rome, had earned in the preceding centuries; it depended more upon diplomacy than weaponry to keep potential enemies from its gates. So when the Arab commander Yazid approached the imperial capital in 671, he must have been supremely confident of the outcome.

Theophanes' chronicle for the following year's campaign provides few details, yet it is clear that the Arabs met unexpectedly stiff resistance: "In this year the aforesaid fleet of God's enemies set sail and came to anchor in the region of Thrace, between the western point of the Hebdomon, that is the Magnaura, as it is called, and the eastern promontory, named Kyklobion. Every day there was a military engagement from morning until evening, between the outworks of the Golden Gate and the Kyklobion, with thrust and counter-thrust."

Two factors worked in the Byzantines' favor. First, while the "Greek" armies were not noted for their offensive prowess, they had become masterful at holding well prepared defenses. Constantinople was a formidable citadel. In addition, it was the adopted home of a refugee from the overrun city of Heliopolis in Syria, an architect named Kallinikos. It was not Kallinikos' skill as an architect, though, that made him valuable to Constantine, but rather the extraordinary volatile properties of the formula he is credited with inventing for a liquid that the Byzantines themselves called "artificial fire" and the Western Crusaders of a later century dubbed more famously "Greek fire."

Descriptions of Greek fire in the historical records of the Byzantines—and of their enemies against whom it was used—are tantalizingly brief and imprecise. A few of its characteristics, however, are more or less universally agreed upon. Incendiary weapons of various sorts had been used in warfare before, but none with the frightening effectiveness of Greek fire. It proved especially useful for the defenders of the port city of Constantinople, whose most worrisome threat was the Arab fleet, since the liquid burned even on water. The only things that would extinguish it, according to the Byzantines, were vinegar and urine. What's more, the flammable liquid would cling to any surface, so that it would indeed, as 13th-century philosopher Albertus Magnus wrote, burn up everything it met.

According to Byzantine historians, it burned up the Arab fleet, or at least a good portion of it, compelling the survivors to flee. When the would-be conquerors returned in 718, fire literally rained down on them once again, with the same results. Not surprisingly, the Byzantines took pains to make sure that the secret of their artificial fire stayed secret. A letter written by Emperor Constantine VII to his son in the middle of the 10th century reveals the awe in which the Byzantines themselves held Greek fire, and their obsession with having a monopoly on the weapon: "[Greek fire] was revealed and taught by God through an angel to the great and holy Constantine, the first Christian emperor, and concerning this. . .he received great charges from the same angel, as we are assured by the faithful witness of our fathers and grandfathers, that it should be manufactured among the Christians only and in the city ruled by them, and nowhere else at all, nor should it be sent or taught to any other nation whatsoever."

Greek fire, Constantine VII declared, 'was revealed by God,' to be 'manufactured among the Christians only.'

Whether those in the know really believed in their supreme weapon's divine origins is doubtful. More likely, the story was circulated in order to enhance the mystique surrounding it, and to reinforce the fear of divine wrath against any Byzantine commander unpatriotic enough to consider enhancing his personal fortune by selling the secret. But lest anyone doubt God's readiness to punish such traitors, Constantine VII reminded his heir: "He who should dare give of this fire to another nation should neither be called a Christian, nor be held worthy of any rank or office; and if he should be the holder of any such, he should be expelled therefrom and be anathematized and made an example for ever and ever, whether he were an emperor, or patriarch, or any other man whatever, either ruler or subject, who should seek to transgress this commandment. And [Constantine] adjured all who had the zeal and fear of God to be prompt and to make away with him who attempted to do this, as a common enemy and a transgressor of this great commandment, and to dismiss him to a death most hateful and cruel."

As a result of the secrecy imposed upon the manufacture and use of Greek fire, historians today are nearly as mystified by the exact nature of the weapon as Yazid's mariners were terrified by it. The weapon embodied two secrets: the composition of the combustible mixture, and the means of projecting the stream of fire toward the enemy. A number of accounts, each dating from several centuries after Yazid's defeat, provide some tantalizing but generally unreliable testimony as to how the liquid was made. Anna Comnena, daughter of the 12th-century Emperor Alexius I, wrote in her biography of her father: "This fire they made by the following arts. From the pine and certain such evergreen trees inflammable resin is collected. This is rubbed with sulphur and put into tubes of reed, and is blown by men using it with violent and continuous breath."

The description is clearly incomplete at best, and probably reflects the sad reality that by Anna's day the secret had already been long since lost and even the Byzantines were reduced to guessing. The best that modern researchers have been able to confirm is that "the formula was surely based on naphtha, perhaps with resin added as a thickener. Quicklime may have been added to make it burn in water, though not to ignite it, and saltpeter may have been added to produce an explosive effect, but neither of these components was necessary."

Greek fire was not the first incendiary weapon by any means, and the Arabs themselves had similar flammable agents in their own arsenals. But something set Greek fire apart and earned it legendary status. Exactly what this distinctive element was remains part of the mystery. A clue may be found in the fact that the ancient accounts nearly always speak of it as a naval weapon. The only reference to its being employed against land forces appears to be the result of confusion on the part of the chronicler, who seems to have mixed up the accounts of two different battles.

The use of Greek fire exclusively at sea suggests that its uniqueness consisted in its ability to burn on water and the amazing difficulty of extinguishing it. When other incendiary weapons would have to score a direct hit to have any effect, Greek fire could probably set the surface of the sea ablaze over a wide area. Even if it did not succeed in destroying wooden ships outright, a few "rounds" of Greek fire would likely have been sufficient to close narrow straits like the Bosporus for hours on end. Interestingly, Theophanes' account of Yazid's defeat does not explicitly credit Greek fire with destroying any Arab ships. It says only that the Arabs withdrew after an unsuccessful siege in which the Byzantines had employed Greek fire, and that the Arab fleet was "sunk by God" on the return voyage. Theophanes goes on to say: "And in the spring they set out and, in similar fashion, made war on sea against the Christians. After doing the same for seven years and being put to shame with the help of God and His Mother; having, furthermore, lost a multitude of warriors and had a great many wounded, they turned back with much sorrow. And as this fleet (which was to be sunk by God) put out to sea, it was overtaken by a wintry storm and the squalls of a hurricane in the area of Syllaion. It was dashed to pieces and perished entirely."

The traditional view is that Greek fire obliterated many of the Arab vessels, but it could be that the secret weapon simply kept the enemy ships at bay until dwindling supplies and sickness and fatigue among the Arab crews made their retreat necessary. The "multitude" of casualties Theophanes wrote of might just as well have been inflicted by archers, upon whom the Byzantine military heavily relied.

In spite of all the Byzantine precautions, their enemies did finally get their hands on Greek fire. In the same letter written by Constantine VII to his son, in which he described the punishment merited by anyone rash enough to divulge the secret, the emperor admitted, "It happened once, as wickedness will still find room, that one of our military governors, who had been most heavily bribed by certain infidels, handed over some of this fire to them. . . ." As his account ends with the unfortunate traitor being consumed by fire from heaven, it may be nothing more than another fabrication intended to strike fear into the heart of anyone who might have been tempted to accept a bribe. Even so, in 814 the Bulgars did manage to capture a large stock of Greek fire but were unable to figure out how to use it. Apparently, the incendiary liquid was not a simple weapon; employing it effectively required a good deal of technical skill. That technical knowledge comprised the second part of the Byzantine secret.

The incendiary liquid was not a simple weapon; employing it effectively required a good deal of technical skill.

A manuscript kept in the Vatican contains an image that documents the apparatus used to deliver the fire against an enemy, at least in very general terms, far more concretely than any record of the formula itself. The image shows a small boat crewed by three oarsmen. In the bow,

two additional men operate a device that seems to consist of a large flared tube from which a cloud of fire issues forth to envelop an enemy vessel.

That depiction is reinforced by a written description attributed to either Emperor Leo III or Leo VI: "The front part of the ship had a bronze tube so arranged that the prepared fire could be projected forward to left or right and also made to fall from above. This tube was mounted on a false floor above the deck on which the specialist troops were accommodated and so raised above the attacking forces assembled in the prow. The fire was thrown either on the enemy's ships or in the faces of the attacking troops."

The statement that Greek fire was "thrown" at the enemy has led to the assumption that a variant form of the weapon, similar to a hand grenade or what is today called a Molotov cocktail, was also used. But in context the Byzantines seem to have intended "throwing" the fire to be understood in the same sense as that of a modern-day flamethrower.

The purpose of these spigots, or "siphons" as the Byzantines themselves called them, is readily apparent. Not so obvious is the method employed to pressurize the liquid in the tube. Surely, this, too, comprised a vital element of the secret and explains why the Bulgars failed to make use of their captured stock of the substance. Suppositions as to how it was done postulate that the volatile concoction was stored in tanks below deck, where it was heated prior to discharge. If so, it must have been a delicate operation requiring quite a bit of nerve. Such a volatile concoction would not take kindly to being heated in a sealed container. Another chronicler states that compressed air was used to force the fire from the mouth of the siphons.

Whatever the exact method, it seems certain that a specialized vessel, or at least a substantially modified warship, was needed to project the file onto an enemy ship. The equipment involved in creating the necessary pressure is probably another reason that Greek fire was used primarily, if not exclusively, as a naval weapon. The hold of a warship might be fit for storing and pressurizing large quantities of liquid fire, but it is harder to imagine how the technology could have been incorporated into an effective and portable platform for land combat. (One Byzantine source, on the other hand, does recommend its use by the garrisons of fixed defenses to protect themselves against siege towers.)

Both the formula for the liquid and the means of delivering it, then, seem to have been closely guarded technological innovations. But the most mysterious aspect of this ancient weapon has to be why the Byzantines didn't make greater use of it. Throughout the centuries following the rout of the Arab fleet, the defenders of a Byzantine Empire that was in decline and beset by frequent attacks seem to have employed Greek fire on only a handful of occasions. As technical historian Alex Roland has noted, "During the years when Byzantium had a supposed monopoly on the ultimate naval weapon system of the medieval world, it suffered repeated and often disastrous naval reverses all over the Mediterranean Sea." As an example, he points out that during four successive attacks against Constantinople in the late 9th and early 10th centuries, the Russians encountered Greek fire only once.

Several likely reasons suggest themselves for this very limited use. The first stems from the Byzantines' obvious obsession with secrecy. The more the Byzantines used their super weapon, the more they risked a fire ship being captured and reverse engineered by an enemy. "Greeks" were probably more willing to lose battles and even fleets than their precious secret.

Practical aspects are also likely to have limited the weapon's usefulness. Though no contemporary account explicitly confirms it, Greek fire seems to have been much more effective in defense than on the attack. As mentioned before, the Byzantine fire ships used defensively could probably lay down a wall of flames that would stop an oncoming fleet dead in its tracks, but on the attack, they would have had to mix with the enemy fleet, leaving themselves vulnerable to counterattacks from the rear. In such a case, a clever enemy commander would have made sure to keep the wind at his back so that the fire would tend to blow back into the attackers' faces. In fact, the technology of the day cannot have provided any sure safeguards against accidents, and Greek fire may have been as frightening to the Byzantine sailors as to their opponents. While there is no mention in the records of a Byzantine ship immolating itself, this end seems inevitable given a frequent enough use of the weapon.

To those reasons for the limited deployment of Greek fire must be added a third and truly remarkable certainty. At some point between the 8th and 13th centuries, the Byzantines themselves lost the secret. The explanation for this extraordinary blunder—akin to the United States forgetting how to build an atomic bomb after World War II—lies in the same obsession with secrecy that kept the weapon out of the hands of Byzantium's enemies. According to tradition, only two families in Byzantium were privy, to the full knowledge of how to make and use Greek fire—the emperor's and that of Kallinikos' descendants, the Lamptoses. There is even a legend that an underground tunnel connected the royal palace with Constantinople's main arsenal at Manganes, where the

mixture would most likely have been made. Certainly a few chemists, shipwrights and engineers, at least, would be required to know enough to create the liquid, fire ships and siphons. But restricting the knowledge to each one's own narrow, specialized component of the entire system would have ensured that only two individuals in each generation would know the full process involved in creating and deploying Greek fire. The chemists would have been capable of delivering the liquid to the engineers, but would have had no idea how to heat and pressurize it without blowing themselves into oblivion. The engineers would have had no idea how to build the naval platform necessary to stove and deliver the liquid fire at sea. And commanders would have no authority to make or employ Greek fire at their own discretion, but could only use what the emperor supplied them. Judging from the number of military coups throughout Byzantine history, this seems to have been a wise precaution.

The dangers of this strict secrecy are as obvious as the advantages. In a very stable and peaceful society, it might have worked well, but a stable and peaceful society would have had no need to keep such a secret. In fact, Byzantium was neither stable nor peaceful, and while the tight security surrounding the weapon ensured that it would not be revealed to the empire's enemies, it also ensured that it would sooner or later be lost to the Byzantines themselves.

In addition to foreign invaders, the Byzantine emperors had plenty to worry about at home, and relatively few of them lived to a ripe old age. The traditional reference to the secret's being known to "the emperor's family" does not mean a single, unbroken line of descent from father to son. The royal family changed frequently, as disputed successions and coups deposed one line after another. Between 685 and 717, a dizzying series of coups deposed a succession of rulers. First General Leontius of Hellas took the throne. He was supplanted by a fleet commander named Tiberius, who was in turn ousted by the Armenian General Philippikos. Within two years, another coup deposed Philippikos in favor of a civilian, Artemius, who was then chased out by troops loyal to Theodosius III. Theodosius held onto power for less than two years before being supplanted by the Anatolian Leo III, who finally brought some degree of stability to Byzantine politics.

Roland postulates that during one of those coups, the usurpers too hastily put the sole guardians of the secret to death, and thus sent the knowledge of Greek fire to the grave with them. It is indeed hard to imagine that anyone close enough to the emperor to be trusted with the greatest state secret of all would escape the inevitable purges when a rival took the throne by force.

It is intriguing to consider what might have been the fate of the Byzantine Empire had the secret of Greek fire not been lost. Effective as the weapon seems to have been under ideal circumstances, however, it would be hard to imagine its having any decisive effect on history. As a defensive weapon system, it would not have helped Byzantium to recover the Western empire that had collapsed following the sack of Rome.

As a naval weapon, it would not have helped the empire to hold those lands that they did reclaim.

As for its own defense, Byzantium held out against the Arab onslaught for several centuries, even without the benefit of true Greek fire. Ultimately and ironically, Constantinople's end came first at the hands of its erstwhile Western allies, the Crusaders. In 1204 knights of the Fourth Crusade, hoping to establish a kingdom of their own, achieved what centuries of Islamic campaigns had not—the destruction of the city. Against this brand of treachery, Greek fire would have been of no use.

In 1261 remnants of the Byzantine Empire under Michael VIII recaptured the city, but the rapidly sinking fortunes of the Byzantines were irreversible. A new enemy, the Ottoman Turks, drove the final stake into the empire's heart in 1453. It was here, at the very end, that Greek fire might have served, if nothing else, to delay the inevitable defeat for a short while.

Although it is impossible to say exactly when the secret was lost, it was surely long gone by this time. The Byzantines did employ an incendiary weapon of similar nature against the Turks, which is often referred to as Greek fire. Most likely, however, this weapon was a poor substitute, the result of a gallant but futile effort to reinvent the decisive weapon of the 7th century. Or perhaps the Turks, knowing full well the stories of the legendary ancient fire, simply assumed that any incendiary weapon the Byzantines used must be Greek fire.

Was Greek fire ever really as potent a weapon as legends and sketchy historical accounts depict? Or was its effectiveness due mostly to the terror it provoked in Byzantium's enemies? Barring the unexpected discovery of its recipe in some still hidden archive, only the ghosts of Constantinople can say.

BRUCE HEYDT, a former editor of *British Heritage* Magazine, is a freelance author who publishes on a variety of historical topics and eras. For further reading, try *Greek Fire, Poison Arrows and Scorpion Bombs: Biological and Chemical Warfare in the Ancient World,* by Adrienne Mayor.

Islam's First Terrorists

CLIVE FOSS

Before dawn on the seventeenth day of the holy month of Ramadan in the year 40 of the Hegira (January 24th, An 661), the Caliph AH entered the great mosque of Kufa to prepare for the day's prayers. A conspirator lurking in the shadows sprang at him and plunged a poisoned sword into his head. The Caliph died later the same day. He was the third of the Prophet's four successors to be assassinated, but the first to fall victim to religion. The murderer, who was soon caught, was part of a conspiracy to kill all the leaders of the Islamic community: Ali himself, Muawiya, governor of Syria, and Amribn al-As, governor of Egypt. It only succeeded in the case of Caliph Ali.

The plotters belonged to a new sect, the Kharijites, who had only come into existence four years previously. When the Caliph Othman had been assassinated in 656, Ali, who was the Prophet's cousin and son-in-law, was recognized in Medina as the new head of the Islamic community—but not by everyone. He soon faced the opposition of Muawiya, who demanded revenge for the murder of his cousin Othman (both were members of the powerful Umayyad family that was to found the first dynasty of Islam after Ali's death). War soon followed. The course of its only armed conflict, the battle of Siffin in 657, was indecisive but apparently going against the Syrians, when they raised the Koran on their lances and brought the fighting to a stand-still, demanding instead arbitration by the authority of the sacred text. AH agreed, but the result of his agreement turned out to be fatal.

One party of Ali's followers, numbering some 12,000, refused to accept the idea of arbitration by humans, on the grounds that only God could decide. They proclaimed la hukma illa li-llah, 'judgment belongs to God alone', and withdrew from the field. Although Ali managed to persuade them to return peacefully to his base of Kufa in Iraq, resentment took a more serious turn when the results of the arbitration, which was unfavourable to Ali, were announced in 658. A hard core of intransigents, joined by supporters from Basra, then left Kufa, elected their own caliph or spiritual leader, and took a stand in central Iraq. They became known as the 'withdrawers' (Arabic khariji, pl. khawarij from kharaja 'withdraw'). On their way, they murdered Muslims who did not support their uncompromising position, considering them worse than infidels. Ali's army attacked the rebels in July, killed their leader and destroyed the majority of their forces. However, this marked not the end but the beginning of a movement that was to cause turmoil in the Islamic world for centuries.

Ever since the death of the Prophet in AD 632, the Islamic community had faced a serious, and as it turned out insoluble, problem: who was to be their head? Muhammad himself had revealed a religion that provided a new basis for forming a community and a nascent state. When he emigrated from Mecca to Medina in 622, he became head of both state and religion, creating a position that had to be filled. No one of course could be another prophet, but Islam needed a Commander of the Faithful who would lead it in prayer, war and government. There was no idea of separating religion from statecraft. The Prophet's first two successors had been his close associates, and the third, Othman, had been chosen by a council, but he represented the old ruling classes of Mecca who had opposed the Prophet in the beginning and only converted to Islam at the last moment.

The civil war that broke out between the Umayyad Muawiya and Ali reflected two irreconcilable points of view: should a powerful family lead Islam, or should it be in the hands of the Prophet's relatives and descendants? Muawiya's followers came to be called the Sunnis (those who follow the example, sunna, of the Prophet), while the champions of AH were the Shi'ites (from shi'at Ali, the party of Ali). Long after the Umayyads were gone from the scene, the difference remained to inspire a sectarianism that became perpetual and often hostile. The Kharijites had their own point of view on this question.

After Ali's assassination, the remnants of the Kharijites began to organize, choosing leaders who usually took the caliph's title amir almu'minin, 'Commander of the Faithful'. Their radical doctrines attracted a large following, especially in Iraq. They were egalitarians who tolerated non-Muslims and looked favourably on converts, whom many of the pure Arabs regarded with disdain. Islam had begun in a purely Arab milieu but the great conquests of the generation after the prophet had incorporated vast populations of foreigners, principally Syrians, Egyptians, and Persians, into its realm. How to deal with them? The new state left them alone as a subject population paying taxes, but as foreigners began to convert to Islam, questions arose about their status. The Arabs accepted the new converts as 'clients', which usually implied an inferior position in society and limited rights.

The Kharijites believed in the absolute equality of all believers, maintaining that any Muslim who followed the precepts of the Koran, even if he were an Abyssinian slave, was qualified to head the community. Any leader who deviated from the true faith, though, or indulged in corruption or tyranny, had to be removed. This was against the normal Islamic doctrine that rulers, however bad, had to be obeyed unless they ordered the sacred law to be violated. Kharijiles rejected any principle of heredity or supremacy based on ethnic, tribal or family origin. This meant they spurned equally the claims of the Quraysh (Muhammad's own tribe) and of the Umayyads. Their views, reflecting an ancient tribal system based on consensus, were far more democratic than any prevailing in the greater Muslim community. Consequently, the Kharijites became a focus for discontented elements and those opposed to any form of established authority. They attracted the young, the obscure and many ex-slaves and converts.

The Kharijites had a particular idea of who was a Muslim. Strictly following the Koranic injunction to 'command the good and forbid the evil', they were uncompromising puritans for whom a Muslim was defined not only by his faith but his practice. Anyone who deviated from what the Kharijites considered the path of righteousness was an apostate, worse than an infidel and deserving any punishment. The more extreme were prepared to sacrifice their lives for their faith, and to kill any Muslims they considered as sinners or heretical, even with their wives and children. They recognized only the first two caliphs, Abu Bakr and Omar, and proclaimed their own leaders as heads of the entire Muslim community. By so doing, they implied that all others who claimed supremacy were illegitimate.

Opposition to Caliph Ali was easily transferred to his successor Muawiya (r.660–80), against whom the Kharijites continually rebelled in Basra, Kufa and the surrounding regions; sixteen outbreaks are recorded during his reign. They usually formed small bands adopting guerrilla tactics, striking suddenly and unexpectedly at cities and towns, then retiring to the safety of the marshes around Basra or the hill country east of the Tigris. Muawiya's governors in Iraq reacted with ferocity, killing thousands, driving them from Kufa altogether, and restoring stability. As a result, many Kharijites in Basra went underground, maintaining their beliefs in secret and creating a new stream of Kharijite development.

When Yazid, Muawiya's son and chosen successor, died suddenly in 683, he was succeeded by a young son who only lasted a few weeks. Supreme power lay open to be claimed. Abd Allah ibn Zubayr was proclaimed caliph in Arabia, but he had to face the opposition of the Umayyads in Syria, led by their caliph Abd al-Malik (r.685–705). The ensuing decade of civil war gave the Kharijites the opportunity to rise up in a series of devastating revolts. The main centres were in Arabia, Iraq, and northern Mesopotamia. In 683, two leading Kharijites, Nafi ibn al-Azraq and Najda ibn Amir went to Mecca to join ibn Zubayr, at the time when Umayyad forces were besieging the city. They soon realized, however, that ibn Zubayr was far from sharing their point of view, so they departed in hostility and returned to Basra—where the two leaders themselves fell out and came to head two separate movements.

In 684, one group of Kharijites left Mecca to settle in north central Arabia. Najda ibn Amir joined them and was chosen as their caliph. He rapidly took over a vast region including Bahrain, the Yemen and Hadramawt. Everywhere he went, he appointed governors and collected taxes, becoming a serious rival to Ibn Zubayr, whose control of Arabia was fatally weakened. Consequently, the pilgrimage to Mecca of 687 featured no fewer than four prospective leaders of the Islamic umma (community) and their followers: ibn Zubayr, the Umayyad Abd al-Malik, ibn al-Hanifiyya (a son of Ali) and Najda ibn Amir. The Kharijites were claiming equal authority with the two rival caliphs.

By this time, Najda had sent one of his followers, Atiyya ibn al-Aswad, to subjugate Oman. Although temporarily successful there, he soon broke with Najda and moved his base to eastern Iran, which he dominated during the 690s.

Najda's success, however spectacular, did not last long, for reasons typical of the Kharijites. Followers even stricter than he revolted in 691 and chose a new leader, who gained Bedouin support. But the next year the Kharijites of Arabia were crushed by a combined force from Kufa and Basra. The followers of Najda survived in obscurity, but with a real peculiarity: unlike other Islamic communities, they did not believe in a powerful leader. Their secular head was chosen by the whole community, with a mandate that could be revoked at any time; rule was basically by consensus. Nor did they need an imam, or religious leader, for all Najdis were equally qualified so long as they knew and followed the precepts of the Koran. No free man was to be subject to another, in what has been described by historian Patricia Crone as the 'most radical affirmation of intellectual and political freedom in the formative centuries of Islam'. Such a doctrine, though suitable to a small homogenous community, was never conducive to the formation of a powerful state.

Meanwhile, Nafi ibn al-Azraq, who had returned from Mecca to Basra, he started a revolt in the spring of 684. His followers, known as Azraqites, assassinated the governor and seized the city. They publicly announced the policy that identified them as the most extremist and violent wing of the Kharijites: that all Muslims—even other Kharijites—who disagreed with their strict interpretation of doctrine and practice were worse than unbelievers and worthy of immediate death. They held Basra until ibn Zubayr's forces drove them into southwestern Iran where they were defeated and Nafi' ibn al-Azraq killed in January 685. From there, the surviving Azraqites spread far to the east, making use of the excellent horses, weapons and chain-mail that they stripped from Iran. In 687, they descended once more into the heart of Iraq, attacking and devastating al-Mada' in, the ancient Sasanian capital. They slaughtered women and children of the opposing parties, and were even accused of ripping open pregnant women. When an army approached from Kufa, however, they again withdrew to Iran (for they were always too few to face a regular army), where their leader was killed. In 688 or 689, the Azraqites chose a new caliph, Qatari ibn al-Fujaa, who was to be their most formidable champion.

Qatari used loot and taxes from southern Iran to increase the forces which he led toward Iraq, facing and often defeating the militias of the local governors for four years. By now, however, the wider civil war was at an end and Abd al-Malik firmly in charge of the vast Islamic realm. In 694, his ferocious governor of Iraq, al-Hajjaj, moved against the Azraqites, pushing them back and securing the country with a series of fortified camps.

Although Qatari gained some victories in surprise night attacks, he had to abandon central Iran by 697 and retreat into the southeast, where he successfully held out for eighteen months. His power finally succumbed not to the caliphal army but to the typical Kharijite penchant for disunion. When his forces split over a quarrel about the murder of a fellow Kharijite, Qatari was doomed. Al-Hajjaj sent a Syrian army against Qatari who had stirred the resentment of the local population by his rigid collection of the poll-tax on non-Muslims; he was caught in an ambush, and killed in 698 or 699. His head was sent to the Caliph in Damascus, visible witness of the defeat of this ferocious enemy. His followers were soon mopped up and the threat from the Azraqites finally brought to an end. By this lime, terrorism had made the Kharijites deeply unpopular with mainstream Islam. In 686, a Shi'ite described them as 'the worst religion amongst us' and three years later a Kharijite who proclaimed la hukma illa l-illah during the pilgrimage in Mecca was killed on the spot by the people.

The last great Kharijite uprising of this period began in 695 in northern Mesopotamia, when the Sufris rose in revolt. These were the moderate Kharijites who (unlike the extremist Azraqites) regarded other Muslims not as infidels to be killed but as misguided people with whom it might be possible to compromise. Their revolt was provoked by the persecutions of al-Hajjaj, who had no tolerance for any kind of Kharijite. After their forces were defeated by al-Hajjaj, the Sufris resorted to guerrilla tactics.

Their leader Shabib ibn Yazid al-Shaybani gained stunning success in Iraq thanks to the swift and unexpected moves of his small forces and the help he received from the local Christians. Victory followed victory, culminating in 696, when Shabib entered Kufa in al-Hajjaj's absence, banged an iron bar against the door of his palace, attacked the mosque and killed the people he found praying there. He then withdrew into the mountains where he was joined by many who opposed the harsh regime of al-Hajjaj. When he came down again into the plain, Shabib not only defeated the armies sent against him but even seized the city of al-Madain. Al-Hajjaj, who was occupied at the same time with the struggle against the Azraqites, finally called on 'Abd al-Malik who sent him a force of battle-trained Syrian troops. This army forced Shabib to retreat to Iran, where he drowned in a river late in 097 having terrorized Iraq for more than a year.

Al-Hajjaj had worked so thoroughly that the Caliphate enjoyed a half-century of respite from serious Kharijite troubles. When Umayyad power began to break up in the mid-eighth century, however, revolts spread, two of them led by Kharijites who enjoyed spectacular if momentary success in Mesopotamia and Arabia. In both cases, the religious element became merged with the revolutionary, and the Kharijites found themselves at the head of considerable armed forces. These revolts were the products of the two moderate Kharijite sects, the Sufris and the

Ibadis. The Sufris had survived in Mesopotamia, and the Ibadis were the real quietists, who believed in peaceful accommodation with other Muslims, among whom they were willing to live, concealing their true beliefs.

The greatest Sufri outbreak began in 744. Under the leadership of the religious scholar Dahhak ibn Qays al-Shaybani, the Sufris moved from Mosul against the Arab bases in Iraq, reinforced by thousands of armed followers from Kurdistan and the north, where their doctrine had taken root. Dahhak commanded the largest force Kharijites had ever put into the field. In April 745 he took Kufa and appointed his own governor, then besieged the main military base of Wasit whose governor, to universal astonishment, pledged allegiance to him. The next year, Dahhak returned to Mosul and raised a huge force from the local inhabitants. By now, though, the Umayyad Caliph Marwan II (r.744–50) had subdued his opponents in Syria and could turn his attention to Dahhak, whom he defeated and killed late in 746. Although Sufris continuously rebelled through the ninth century, they were never again a major threat to the central government.

The future belonged to the Ibadis, who had lived peacefully in the Muslim community, enjoying friendly relations even with al-Hajjaj. After the death of Abd al-Malik in 705, however, al-Hajjaj began to persecute them, driving many into exile in Oman and arresting others. Among these was the scholar and (as it turned out) great organizer Abu Ubayda Muslim, who became leader of the Ibadis of Basra when he was freed in 714. Not willing to risk the adventurous Azraqite policy of withdrawing to build an army outside Basra, he raised money from rich sympathizers and used it to create a network of missionaries who would spread the sect and preach revolution at the same time.

His ideal was to establish bases for revolts that would destroy the Umayyad caliphate and lead to a universal Ibadi state. Secretly trained teams spread through the Islamic world and enjoyed great success. One team reached Arabia, where they helped the rebel Abd Allah ibn Yahya to organize a regime, thus founding the first Ibadi state in 746. Abd Allah soon look of all southern Arabia. He set up a regular administration incorporating many officials of the previous regimes, and proclaimed that Kharijites and other Muslims could live at peace. Many Kharijites from other regions came to join his movement. His forces participated in the pilgrimage of that year, and even seized the holy cities of Mecca and Medina. However, his threat to the heartland of the caliphate provoked a strong response: Marwan II sent a tough Syrian army that reestablished Umayyad control by the end of 748.

Another centre of successful missionary activity was North Africa, where the Ibadis took root in the eighth century and spread to the Berbers, making great headway among tribes who were hostile to Arab rule. After a bitter conflict with the local Sufris, the Ibadis established their own Rustamid dynasty (776–909) whose domain stretched from Algeria to Tripolitania, with much of southern Tunisia. Imams, or religious leaders, ruled this state which was noted for its tolerance—Christians rose to high positions—and its network of merchants who spread the Ibadi doctrine far and wide in North Africa and south of the

Sahara. True to their principle of equality, the Ibadis chose leaders who were not Arabs. The Rustamids eventually succumbed to the dynamic Shi'ite Fatimids (who later conquered Egypt), ending any hope of setting up an Ibadi imamate in the Maghreb, though sporadic revolts sometimes managed to occupy small territories into the late tenth century.

Although Abd Allah's regime in Arabia was extinguished, his followers had great success in Oman, where in 793 they established an independent state that became the headquarters of the Ibadi movement. They chose their leaders by a complex electoral system, rejecting the demands of heredity. Although subdued by the Abbasids in 893, the Ibadis retained real local control and regained independence as the central caliphate declined. From Oman, they spread their doctrine to East Africa, where it still flourishes.

The modern Ibadis of Oman, East Africa and the Maghreb have evolved far from the violence and hostility of their Khanjite forebears. Instead of regarding Muslims of other sects as unbelievers worthy of death, they consider them as ungrateful to God and to be kept at arm's length. That means avoiding friendship but not association with them. Ibadis and others can pray in the same mosques. The Ibadis are generally regarded as peaceful members of the community, and far from fanatical. They have substantial differences with other Muslims, however: they condemn the memory of the caliphs Othman, Ali and Muawiya and believe that there is no possibility of redemption from eternal punishment in hell for those who deserve it. Like the early Kharijites, they follow a democratic principle in choosing their leader who is named by the community elders according to his morals, religion and leadership ability. Their imam, Ahmad ibn Said (r.1754–83) united all Oman under his religious leadership, founding the currently ruling Bu Sa'id dynasty, though its rulers now claim secular leadership only. In the late nineteenth century, the tribes of the interior broke with those of the coast, establishing a ruler whom they call Imam of the Muslims; they remained independent until the 1950s, forming the last purely Kharijite state. The sultanate that the Omanis established in Zanzibar in 1832 also became a major seat of Ibadi doctrine and learning, though its rulers did not claim to be imams.

The Kharijites, then, have a history almost as long as that of Islam itself. They erupted on the scene spectacularly in the late seventh century, and caused widespread chaos during the Arab civil wars of the late seventh and mid-eighth century. They flourished in times of instability, attracting large followings and undermining existing rulers. In some instances, they set up regular states, with a caliph and an army that controlled a territory from which they collected taxes. This was the case of Najda ibn Amir in Arabia and Qatari in the east. Qatari and Atiyya ibn al-Aswad even struck coins, a sure symbol of claimed sovereignty, as did Dahhak in Mesopotamia and some of the ephemeral states of North Africa. But none of these states lasted; they could exploit turmoil and civil war, but their harsh, demanding extremism was of limited appeal in times of peace. Their very democracy undermined strong leadership, while their fanaticism often led to splits within the community, with factions continually breaking away or rising in revolt if their leader failed to maintain the high standards the community demanded. An even more extreme potential leader was usually lying in wait. The extremists attracted all kinds of followers, especially from non-Arab Muslims, but never appealed to an entire class of the population, and so never managed to take root in a region. Only the Ibadis, who learned to bide their time and to compromise, lasted into the present. Terrorism and extremism failed; the future belonged to those who could adapt and cooperate.

For Further Reading

Julius Wellhausen, *The Religio-Potitical Factions in Early Islam* (North Holland, 1975); Abd al-Ameer Dixon, *The Umayyad Caliphate* (S. Illinois University Press. 1971); Michael Morony, *Iraq after the Muslim Conquest.* (Princeton, 1984); Patricia Crone, *God's Rule: Government and Islam* (Columbia University Press, 2004).

CLIVE FOSS is Professor of History at Georgetown University in Washington DC.

Al-Kimiya Notes on Arabic Alchemy

GABRIELE FERRARIO PhD

According to the 10th-century scholar Ibn Al-Nadim, the philosopher Muhammad ibn Zakariya Al-Razi (9th century) claimed that "the study of philosophy could not be considered complete, and a learned man could not be called a philosopher, until he has succeeded in producing the alchemical transmutation." For many years Western scholars ignored Al-Razi's praise for alchemy, seeing alchemy instead as a pseudoscience, false in its purposes and fundamentally wrong in its methods, closer to magic and superstition than to the "enlightened" sciences. Only in recent years have pioneering studies conducted by historians of science, phitologists, and historians of the book demonstrated the importance of alchemical practices and discoveries in creating the foundations of modern chemistry. A new generation of scholarship is revealing not only the extent to which early modern chemistry was based on alchemical practice but also the depth to which European alchemists relied on Arabic sources. Yet scholars are only beginning to scratch the surface of Arabic alchemy: a general history based on direct sources still has to be written, and an enormous number of Arabic alchemical manuscripts remain unread and unedited—sometimes not even cataloged—in Middle Eastern and European libraries. This brief survey is offered in hopes of giving *Chemical Heritage's* readers a glimpse into this fascinating yet largely unexplored world.

In the 7th century the Arabs started a process of territorial expansion that quickly brought them empire and influence ranging from India to Andalusia. Fruitful contacts with ancient cultural traditions were a natural consequence of this territorial expansion, and Arabic culture proved ready to absorb and reinterpret much of the technical and theoretical innovations of previous civilizations. This was certainly the case with respect to alchemy, which had been practiced and studied in ancient Greece and Hellenistic Egypt. The Arabs arrived in Egypt to find a substantial alchemical tradition; early written documents testify that Egyptian alchemists had developed advanced practical knowledge in the fields of pharmacology and metal, stone, and glass working. The first translations of alchemical treatises from Greek and Coptic sources into Arabic were reportedly commissioned by Khalid ibn Yazid, who died around the beginning of the 8th century. By the second part of that century Arabic knowledge of alchemy was already far enough advanced to produce the *Corpus Jabirianum*— an impressively large body of alchemical works attributed to Jabir ibn Hayyan. The

Corpus, together with the alchemical works of Al-Razi, marks the creative peak of Arabic alchemy.

As is typical in the chain of transmission of ancient knowledge, the origins of alchemy are steeped in legend, and the links of this chain are either mythical or real authorities in the fields of ancient science and philosophy. The doctrines on which Arabic alchemy relied derived from the multicultural milieu of Hellenistic Egypt and included a mixture of local, Hebrew, Christian, Gnostic, ancient Greek, Indian, and Mesopotamian influences.

The presence of the Arabic definite article *al* in *alchemy* is a clear indication of the Arabic roots of the word. Hypotheses about the etymology of the Arabic term *al-kimiya* hint at the possible sources for early alchemical knowledge in the Arab world. One of the most plausible hypotheses traces the origin of the word back to the Egyptian word *kam-it* or *kem-it,* which indicated the color black and, by extension, the land of Egypt, known as the Black Land. Another hypothesis links *kimiya* to a Syriac transliteration of the Greek word *khumeia* or *khemeia,* meaning the art of melting metals and of producing alloys.

A third interesting but far-fetched etymology suggests that the word *al-kimiya* derives from the Hebrew *kim Yah,* meaning "divine science." The idea of a connection between the origins of alchemical knowledge and the Jews was widespread among medieval Arabic alchemists, who saw in this etymology a possible confirmation of their belief. These alchemists tended to attribute the mythical origins of alchemy alternately to the angels who rose against God, to the patriarch Enoch, to king Solomon, or to other biblical characters who taught humankind the secrets of minerals and metals. This interpretive strategy dignified the origins of alchemy and attributed alchemical books pseudepigraphically to authorities of the past, providing a safe mechanism for spreading alchemical knowledge, which could otherwise be persecuted for its proximity to magic.

In contrast with the modern term *alchemy,* the word *al-kimiya* lacks abstract meaning. Rather than designating the complex of practical and theoretical knowledge we now refer to as alchemy, it was used to describe the substance through which base metals could be transmuted into noble ones. In Arabic alchemical books *al-kimiya* tended to be a synonym of *al-iksir* (elixir) and was frequently used with the more general meaning of a "medium for obtaining something." Expressions like *kimiya al-sa'ada* (the way of obtaining happiness), *kimiya al-ghana* (the way of obtaining richness), and *kimiya al-qulub* (the way of touching hearts) testify to the broad meaning of this word. What we now call alchemy was called by other words: *san'at al-kimiya* or *san'at al-iksir* (the art or production of the elixir), *ilm al-sina'a* (the knowledge of the art or production), *al-hikma* (the wisdom), *al-'amal al-a'zam* (the great work), or simply *al-sana'a*. Arabic alchemists called themselves *kimawi, kimi, kimiya'i, san'awi,* or *iksiri*.

The contribution of Arabic alchemists to the history of alchemy is profound. They excelled in the field of practical laboratory experience and offered the first descriptions of some of the substances still used in modern chemistry. Muriatic (hydrochloric) acid, sulfuric acid, and nitric acid are discoveries of Arabic alchemists, as are soda *(al-natrun)* and potassium *(al-qali)*. The words used in Arabic alchemical books have left a deep mark on the language of chemistry: besides the word *alchemy* itself, we see Arabic influence in *alcohol (al-kohl), elixir (al-iksir),* and *alembic (al-inbiq)*. Moreover, Arabic alchemists perfected the process of distillation, equipping their distilling apparatuses with thermometers in order to better regulate the heating during alchemical operations. Finally, the discovery of the solvent later known as *aqua regia*—a mixture of citric and muriatic acids—is reported to be one of their most important contributions to later alchemy and chemistry.

> **The contribution of Arabic alchemists to the history of alchemy is deep: they excelled in the field of practical laboratory experience and offered the first descriptions of some of the substances still used in modern chemistry.**

Arabic books on alchemy stimulated theoretical reflections on the power and the limits of humans to change matter. Moreover, we have the Arabic alchemical tradition to thank for transmitting the legacy of the ancient and Hellenistic worlds to the Latin West.

Theoretical Assumptions

The alchemical authorities most often quoted as sources in Arabic alchemical texts were Greek philosophers, such as Pythagoras, Archelaus, Socrates, and Plato. During the Middle Ages, Aristotle himself was considered the authentic author of the fourth book of *Meteorologica,* which deals extensively with the physical interactions of earthly phenomena, and of one letter on alchemy addressed to his pupil Alexander the Great. Arabic language sources also quoted Hermes, the supposed repository of the knowledge God gave to man before the Deluge and to whom legend attributes the famous *Tabula smaragdina* (Emerald Tablet); Agathodaimon; Ostanes, the Persian magician; Mary the Jewess (probably 3rd century), for whom the

bain-marie (akin to a double boiler) is named; and Zosimus of Panopolis (3rd–4th centuries), believed to be the author of an alchemical encyclopedia in 28 books. Indeed, Zosimus is said to have introduced religious and mystical elements into the alchemical discourse: his books meld Egyptian magic, Greek philosophy, Neoplatonism, Babylonian astrology, Christian theology, pagan mythology, and doctrines of Hebrew origin in a highly symbolic writing full of allusions to the interior transformations of the alchemist's soul.

Arabic alchemists largely worked from an Aristotelian theory of the formation of matter in which the four elementary qualities (heat, coldness, dryness, and moisture) generate first-degree compounds (hot, cold, dry, and moist), which, in turn, combine in pairs, acquire matter, and generate the four elements: hot + dry + matter = fire; hot + moist + matter = air; cold + moist + matter = water; cold + dry + matter = earth. Everything on earth consists of varying proportions of these four elements. A particularly clear explanation of how alchemists made sense of Aristotelian theory can be found in the pseudo-Avicennian treatise *De Anima in arte alchimiae* (Basel, 1572), an alchemical work probably of Arabic origins that survives only in Latin translation. According to this treatise, every existing body is a compound of the four elements: if a body is defined as cold and dry, this means that the qualities of coldness and dryness predominate, while heat and moisture occur in minor proportions and thus remain concealed. An external cause—either natural or artificial—could generate a change in the structure of the body, rebalancing the natural proportion of its external and internal qualities, thereby changing its appearance. The alchemist in his laboratory seeks to artificially overturn the balance of qualities in the body he is trying to transmute by adding or removing heat, coldness, dryness, or moisture.

Arabic natural philosophy similarly accepted the classical theory of the formation of minerals in mines. This explanation held that two different movements take place in the depths of caves as the caverns are heated by the sun: particles of water (cold and moist) rise to the surface and generate vapors *(bukhar)* when they make contact with air (hot and moist); particles of earth (cold and dry), however, rise to the surface and generate fumes *(duhan)*. The meeting of vapors and fumes creates quicksilver, if the vapors predominate, or sulfur, if the fumes predominate. Gold is generated when quicksilver and sulfur are pure and in a balanced proportion, and the soil and astral conditions are positive. Imperfections in any of these conditions create metals of progressively lesser value. An impressive description of the formation of metals in caves can be read in Epistle 19, on mineralogy, of the *Rasa'il Ikhwan al-safa'* (Epistles of the Brethrens of Purity), a 10th-century encyclopedia of science, religion, and ethics attributed to a group of philosophers influenced by Neoplatonism and Pythagorism.

The alchemist's goal, to be achieved through study and practical expertise in the laboratory, was to reproduce these natural processes in a shorter period or to interfere somehow with the natural processes to produce "natural accidents." The alchemist's knowledge was, therefore, often compared to the

The Roy G. Neville Historical Chemical Library houses several early modern translations of original or pseudepigraphic treatises by Arabic scholars.
Alchemy in the Library

Jabir ibn Hayyan (8th century) is purported to be the author (under his Latin name Geber) of an enormous number of alchemical works that have survived only in medieval Latin translations. The Neville collection holdings feature several of these gems of early printing, including *De Alchimia Libri Tres* (Strasbourg, 1531), *Summa Perfectionis magisterii* (Venice, 1542), *Alchemiae* (Bern, 1545), and *Chimia, sive, Traditio summae perfectionis* . . . (Leiden,1668).

Ibn Sina (11th century), universally known by his Latin name, Avicenna, was one of the most influential scholars of the Middle Ages and was considered to be a leading authority in medicine and philosophy. Avicenna is said to be the author of five books on alchemy, some portions of which are represented in compilations in the Neville collection. *De Anima in arte alchemiae,* known only in its Latin translation, is one of several works included in *Avicenne perhypatetici philosophi* (Venice, 1508). The treatise entitled *congelazione et conglutinatione lapidum,* originally written as part of his medical masterpiece *Kitab al-Shifa,* deals with minerals and their generation in caves and is reproduced in Latin in *Ginaeceum chimicum* (Leiden, 1679) alongside works on mineralogy by Geber, Georg Horn, Giovanni Bracesco, Trevisansus, and others. Other volumes in the Neville collection that include translations of Avicenna's work are Roger Bacon's *De arte chymiae scripta* (Frankfurt, 1603); *Artis chemicae principes, Avicenna atque Geber* (Basil 1572); and Werner Rolfinck's *Liber de purgantibus vegetabilibus* (Vienna. 1667).

Arabic-language scholars' impact was felt on the Iberian Peninsula long before Arabic works were translated into Latin. Al-Zahrawi (10th century), who is said to have been active as a doctor and a physician in Córdoba, is known to be the author of the *Tasrif.* This treatise deals with the principles of medicine, pharmacology, and surgery, and the symptoms and the treatments of over 300 illnesses. The *Tasrif* appeared in Latin as early as the 12th century; portions appear in *Opera de medicamentorum purgantium delectu, castigatione, et usu* (Venice, 1581), a compilation attributed to Pseudo-Mesuë. This volume also includes selections attributed to Ibn Wafid (11th century), an Andalusian physician and pharmacologist who also wrote on agriculture. Little is known about his life: among the seven treatises traditionally attributed to him, only four medical books on simple remedies are still extant.

A'ma Al-Tutili (12th century), a poet who lived in Spain, is mostly known for his skills in the *muwashshah,* a kind of panegyric poem that contains verses in classical Arabic, Andalusian-Arabic dialect, and Spanish. Less elegant but perhaps more practical were his writings on mineral waters, such as *Tratado de las aquas medicinales de Salam–Bir* (Madrid, 1761).

As alchemy began to appear in European books of secrets, authors frequently invoked ancient and Arabic authorities as predecessors of their work. A fine example of an author attempting to establish an intellectual patrimony is Roger Bacon's (13th century) *The Mirror of Alchimy* (London, 1597), which accompanies Bacon's "excellent discourse of the admirable force and efficacie of art and nature," with material supposedly written by Hermes Trismegistus, Hortulanus, and the 7th-century Arabic philosopher Khalid ibn Yazid.

creative power of God (for instance, in the 10th-century treatise *Rutbat al-hakim,* by Al-Majriti) and represented the highest level of knowledge attainable by humans. Yet Arabic alchemists were, for the most part, able to harmonize alchemical doctrines with Islam. The belief in a pure and absolute version of monotheism led Islamic theology to assume the existence of a single creator: according to classical Islamic philosophy, God is the creator of everything that exists and is the direct cause of every action that takes place in the sublunary world. Since only God can create a change—a *fasl (differentia specifica,* substantial difference)—alchemy, with its aim of changing the internal nature of metals and stones, could have been considered religiously unacceptable. In the 12th century, however, the alchemist Al-Tughra'i proposed an intriguing solution: since nothing can be created unless God wants it to be so, the alchemist simply prepares matter to receive the *fasl* God will bestow.

Perhaps because of alchemy's association with divine knowledge, Arabic alchemical treatises persistently appeal to secrecy: alchemists should avoid the transmission of recipes to greedy people whose main aim is to obtain riches rather than wisdom. As would their European followers several centuries later, Arabic alchemists used rhetorical tricks to conceal the secrets of the art from the uninitiated. In the introductory essay to his translation of the first 10 books of Jabir ibn Hayyan's *Kitab al-sab'in* (The Book of the Seventy), Pierre Lory underlines the author's habit of "scattering knowledge" *(tabdid al-'ilm)* by intentionally presenting alchemical procedures out of order so that only the initiated could understand how to read the text. Alchemical authors used a highly enigmatic language, marked by abundant metaphors and technical and allusive terminology, to describe their processes and ingredients. Like the Hellenistic alchemists before them, the Arabic alchemists referred to a metal by the name of the planet that was thought to exert influence over it, so that recipes included Moon for silver, Mercury for quicksilver, Venus for copper, Sun for gold, Mars for iron, Jupiter for tin, and Saturn for lead. Modern readers must bear in mind that even when the names of the alchemical ingredients appear identical to those used in modern chemistry, they rarely designate the same substance.

Arabic Alchemists

Our knowledge of Arabic alchemists has been largely mediated through the voices of their Latin translators, whose works are more likely to have survived to the present day. Scholarly research in this field is still in the preliminary stages, and every new discovery, every new edition of a manuscript, can lead to substantial changes in our perception of the history of Arabic alchemy. Even so, two philosophers have emerged as leading figures.

Jabir ibn Hayyan was born in Tus (in present-day Iran) in 721/2. Besides his Islamic studies, he was well educated in mathematics and science. After settling in the city of Kufa, he became the court alchemist of the Abbasid caliph Harun Al-Rashid (786–809) and was reportedly a close friend of the sixth imam, Ja'far Al-Sadiq. He probably died in 803. Given the enormous number of alchemical books that have been attributed to him (more than 300) and the fact that the word *jabir* can mean "the one who rectifies things," some scholars have suggested that the *Corpus Jabirianum* should be seen as the work of a group of anonymous alchemists. Some of the most famous books traditionally attributed to Jabir include *Mi'a wa-ithna 'ashara kitaban* (The One Hundred and Twelve Books), which explains how to produce the elixir from vegetables and animals and was supposedly based on Ja'far Al-Sadiq's teachings; *Kitab al-sab'in* (The Book of the Seventy), a rich source for studying the operations and the equipment of medieval Arabic alchemy; *Kutub al-tashih* (The Books on Rectification), a survey of the progress of earlier alchemists; and *Kitab al-mizan* (The Book of the Balance), in which Jabir clearly outlines the double aim of his alchemical practice as both the transmutation of bodies in the laboratory and the transformation of his own soul. Jabir's importance is not limited to the history of Arabic alchemy: numerous translations of his works appeared in Latin, and an abundant pseudo-Jabirian literature was transmitted under the name of Geber.

Muhammad ibn Zakariya Al-Razi was born around 864 in the city of Rayy (in present-day Iran). A versatile mind, he was well learned in mathematics, astronomy, astrology, music, and medicine. In this last field Latin translations of his works— together with Avicenna's *Canon*—became the basis of the *cursus studiorum* for European students of medicine. Tradition holds that he lost his sight as a consequence of one of his alchemical experiments, but in spite of his blindness he was appointed head of the Baghdad hospital, where he remained in charge until his death in 925. His most important and influential alchemical book is the *Sirr al-Asrar* (the Latin *Secretum secretorum,* Secret of Secrets), in which he explains alchemical operations in detail and describes the equipment and ingredients needed in a medieval alchemical laboratory in a plain and clear style.

Historians of science would do well to look to the works of Al-Razi rather than Jabir's highly complex and symbolic *Corpus* for evidence on how to reconstruct a medieval alchemical laboratory. Al-Razi mentions two groups of instruments: those used for melting metals and those used for preparing other substances. In the first group he lists the furnace (*kur*), bellows (*minfakh*), crucible (*bawtaqa*), double crucible (*but bar but,* known as *botus barbatus* to Latin alchemists), spoon (*mighrafa*), tweezers (*masik*), scissors (*miqta'*), hammer (*mukassir*), and file (*mibrad*). In the second group we find the cucurbit (*qar'*), alembic with evacuation tube (*anbiq dhu khatm*), receiving matrass (*qabila*), blind alembic (*al-anibiq al-a'ma*), vessel for liquids (*qadah*), cauldron (*marjal* or *tanjir*), and oven (*al-tannur*), as well as a cylindrical pot used for heating the matrass (*mustawqid*), different kinds of vessels (*qarura*), funnels, sieves, filters, and so on. Al-Razi's clear descriptions of operations have made it possible to identify some of the alchemical procedures referred to in Arabic texts: *tadbir* is the word used in general for defining the treatment of bodies; *sahq* indicates grinding, decomposing, and the production of amalgams; *hall* or *tahlil* is solution; *iqama* is the procedure for solidifying; *sabk* is the fusion of metals; and *taqtir* means distillation and filtering.

As with the works attributed to Geber, many of the books attributed to Al-Razi— or the Latin author Rhazes—are pseudepi-graphical. Given Al-Razi's wide fame and the general medieval trend to fake the attribution of alchemical books, this should not come as a surprise.

The Legacy of Arabic Alchemy

Today no one doubts that Latin alchemy is mainly based on Arabic heritage. Before the first infiltrations of Arabic alchemical texts, the Latin West knew only a few translations of Greek books of recipes, largely out of context. The history of the influence of Arabic alchemy in the West faces some major problems directly connected with its sources: not all the Latin translations from Arabic are cataloged or identified, their handwritten tradition is scarcely known, and translators' names are rarely specified.

Translations of complete Arabic alchemical treatises started to appear with regularity in the first half of the 12th century. Robert of Chester, Hugo of Santalla, Arnold of Villanove, Albert the Great, Gerard of Cremona, and Raymond of Marseille dedicated their efforts to the translation of Arabic alchemical treatises by Jabir, Al-Razi, and other known or anonymous Arabic alchemists. By the first decades of the 13th century, Arabic-language alchemical knowledge seems to have been completely absorbed by Latin authors who started to produce original works on alchemy strongly influenced by what they could read in previous translations. Alchemical passages in the works of Albert the Great, Roger Bacon, Michael Scot, and Hermann of Caryntia testify to the degree of assimilation of Arabic-language alchemical doctrines in the West. It was only in the Renaissance that Latin authors, in search of closer contacts with the ancients, started to recreate a line of tradition that reached back directly to the Greeks, skipping over the Islamic world altogether.

For Further Reading

Anawati, Georges C. "L'alchimie arabe." In *Histoire des sciences arabes,* edited by R. Rashed, vol. 3, 111–141. Paris: Seuil, 1997.

Carusi, Paola. "*Meteorologica IV* e alchimia islamica, Qualità ed elementi a confronto." In *Aristoteles Chemicus. II IV Libro dei Meteorologica nella tradizione antica e medievale,* edited by C. Viano, 81–97. Sankt Augustin, Germany: Academia, 2002.

Holmyard, Eric John. *The Arabic Works of Jabir ibn Hayyan.* Paris: Geuthner, 1928.

Jabir ibn Hayyan. *Dix traités d'alchimie. Les dix premiers traités du Livre des Soixantedix,* edited and translated by Pierre Lory. Paris: Sindbad, 1983.

Nasr, Seyyed Hossein. *Science and Civilization in Islam.* 2d ed. Lahore, Pakistan: Suhail Academy, 1983.

Stapleton, Henry Ernest, et al. "Chemistry in Iraq and Persia in the 10th Century A.D." *Memoirs of the Asiatic Society of Bengal* 8 (1927), 317–418.

GABRIELE FERRARIO recently obtained a PhD in Oriental studies at Ca'Foscari University in Venice. He is currently Frances A. Yates Fellow at the Warburg Institute (London) and has been awarded a Neville Fellowship at CHF for early 2008.

From *Chemical Heritage,* Fall 2007, pp. 32–37. Copyright © 2007 by Chemical Heritage. Reprinted by permission.

UNIT 5

The Medieval Period

Unit Selections

22. **The Church in the Middle Ages,** Marius Ostrowski
23. **What Did Medieval Schools Do for Us?,** Nicholas Orme
24. **1215 and All That,** James Lacey
25. **The Fourth Crusade and the Sack of Constantinople,** Jonathan Phillips
26. **Monsoons, Mude and Gold,** Paul Lunde
27. **How a Mysterious Disease Laid Low Europe's Masses,** Charles L. Mee Jr.

Key Points to Consider

- Why was the Church so important in Europe during the Middle Ages?

- Discuss the changes that occurred in education during the Middle Ages.

- Explain why the barons and King John were all foolish.

- Explain why the Fourth Crusade was so devastating to the Byzantine Empire.

- Determine what made Venice the most prosperous city in Europe during the Middle Ages.

- Describe the effects of the "Black Death" on medieval civilization.

Student Website
www.mhhe.com/cls

Internet References

EuroDocs: Primary Historical Documents from Western Europe
http://eudocs.lib.byu.edu
Feudalism
www.fidnet.com/~weid/feudalism.htm
The Labyrinth: Resources for Medieval Studies
www.georgetown.edu/labyrinth/
History Review
historytoday.com/archive/history-review
History Today
historytoday.com
Military History
historynet.com/military-history
Saudi Aramco World
saudiaramcoworld.com
Smithsonian
smithsonian.com
The World of the Vikings
www.worldofthevikings.com

In the aftermath of barbarian invasions, Western civilization faced several important challenges: to assimilate Roman and Germanic people and cultures, to reconcile Christian and Pagan views, and to create new social, political, and economic institutions to fill the vacuum left by the fall of the Roman order—in sum, to shape a new unity out of the chaos and diversity of the post-Roman world. The next millennium (550–1500) saw the rise and demise of a distinctive phase of Western experience—medieval civilization.

Medieval culture expressed a uniquely coherent view of life and the world. In theory, medieval society provided a well ordered and satisfying life. The Church looked after people's souls, the nobility maintained civil order, and a devoted peasantry performed the work of the world. Ideally, as historian Crane Brinton explains, "a beautifully ordered nexus or rights and duties bound each man to each, from the swineherd to emperor and pope."

Of course, medieval society, like our own, fell short of its ideal. Feudal barons warred among themselves. Often the clergy was ignorant and corrupt. Peasants were not always content and passive. And medieval civilization had other shortcomings too. During much of the Middle Ages, there was little interest in nature and how it worked. While experimentation and observation were not unknown, science (or "natural philosophy") was subordinate to theology, which generally attracted the best minds of the day. An economy based on agriculture and a society based on inherited status had little use for innovation. Aspects of Medieval society are treated in the articles such as "The Church in the Middle Ages", and "What Did Medieval Schools Do For Us?," while "The Fourth Crusade and the Sack of Constantinople" explores facets of medieval warfare.

All this is not to suggest that the medieval period was static and sterile. Crusaders, pilgrims, and merchants enlarged Europe's view of the world. And there were noteworthy mechanical innovations: the horse collar, which enabled beasts of burden to pull heavier loads; the stirrup, which altered mounted combat; mechanical clocks, which made possible more exact measurement of time; the compass, which brought the age of exploration closer; and the papermaking process that made feasible the print revolution, which in turn played a key role in the Reformation and the Scientific Revolution. And the commercial encounter between the two faiths produced cross-cultural influences that contributed to fundamental economic, military, and political changes in the West as seen in "Monsoons, *Mude* and Gold."

The medieval order broke down in the fourteenth and fifteenth centuries. Plague, wars, and famines produced a demographic catastrophe that severely strained the economic and political systems. Charles Mee's article, "How a Mysterious Disease Laid Low Europe's Masses," explains how the Black

© Royalty-Free/CORBIS

Death affected many aspects of medieval life. During this period, social discontent took the form of peasant uprisings and urban revolts. Dynastic and fiscal problems destabilized England and France. The Great Schism and the new heresies divided the Church. Emerging capitalism gradually undermined an economy based on land. Yet, these crises generated the creative forces that later gave birth to the Renaissance and the modern era. The nation-state, the urban way of life, and the class structure, and other aspects of modern life existed in embryonic forms in the Middle Ages. It was in medieval Europe that the West prepared itself for its modern role as "chief disturber and principal upsetter of other people's way."

The Church in the Middle Ages

Marius Ostrowski explains why the Church was so dominant in the Middle ages, but also sees traces of a growing secularism.

MARIUS OSTROWSKI

This year there were 99 entries, many of very high quality. Exceptionally, the Committee has awarded the Prize to a Lower Sixth candidate: Marius Ostrowski of Eton College, whose essay is published below. A second award was made to Beatrice Ramsay of the Perse School for Girls, Cambridge, who submitted an essay on the State of Catholicism in pre-Reformation Norfolk.

The thousand-year span of the medieval era, which coincided in essence with the period of the church's greatest power and status, was framed by the collapse of two once-mighty civilisations. At its start in AD 476, the Western Roman Empire, the superpower of the ancient world, cracked under the multiple strains of military, social and economic turmoil, and at its end the shrinking Byzantine Empire was finally obliterated by the Ottomans in 1453.

Sources of Survival

The church's compact organisation and resilience, shaped by strict doctrine and severe persecution, enabled it to survive even the momentous collapse of the civilisation which had raised it to prominence. Its versatile structure allowed it to run Western Europe in the absence of a successor to the outgoing Roman administration and to negotiate a mutually profitable alliance with the replacement Frankish administration when it finally emerged. Moreover, the church's close political involvement under the Franks brought it to such a height of power and influence that it survived the grand decline of the Carolingian empire to remain one of the most potent players of the European scene.

A mixture of luck and adept diplomacy allowed it to maintain this dominance in the Carolingian empire's three successive states—France, Germany and Italy—to such an extent that few Western rulers could hope to resist the church's power. Its unprecedented ability to galvanise large numbers of Westerners into mass warfare even gave it the means to launch repeated attacks against other major religions around the Mediterranean, until the Reformation signalled the end of the church's ideological unity. On the cultural front, similarly, it was the church that kept alive the spark of Western civilisation until its own philosophical limitations forced the burgeoning culture to extend into the secular mainstream.

Western and Eastern Empires

The decline of the Western Roman Empire, and the resultant rise of the church, was set in motion by the appearance of the Huns in Eastern Europe in the 370s. As the Huns gradually advanced into Western Europe, the inhabitant people were forced to settle within the borders of the Roman Empire, beginning with the Visigoths in 378. They had set a precedent for the other displaced barbarian peoples, who poured across the Rhine after 406 and began to occupy the lands of the Western Empire, eventually ousting Roman power completely. Bombarded by incessant waves of marauding invaders, weakened by a long line of corrupt and ineffectual Emperors, denied Eastern military support, and lacking a dependable army to defend its territory, the Western Empire bowed to the inevitable and finally disappeared in 476.

The Eastern Roman Empire under Theodosius' successors was largely spared the difficulties of the West, in part because the vast sums of money diverted to the development of the East by previous emperors, as well as the wealth generated by copious natural resources, meant that urban culture was better established there. The East's better defences, coupled with an effective administrative and fiscal organisation, enabled successive rulers to stave off the threat of barbarian invasion, and thus maintain Roman civilisation for another millennium. In comparison with the stable East, therefore, the crippled West would have seemed a much more inviting prospect to the barbarian invaders.

Role of the Church

The disintegration of the Roman administration produced a sociopolitical vacuum which the less sophisticated barbarian cultures could not fill. The only firmly established organisational body with the hierarchy and infrastructure to take over the reins of authority in the West was the Christian church, to which local governance in the old Roman provinces/religious dioceses soon defaulted. In the absence of a stable secular ruler, care of the Christian communities in the old imperial lands reverted to the religious leaders, the bishops.

Thus is was that the bishops added to their ecclesiastical roles the responsibilities that would previously have belonged to the regional imperial governors. They were no longer merely local religious figureheads but also rulers and commanders, with legal and military powers. As the Roman garrisons were disbanded or recalled to Italy, the local church authorities had to ensure the survival of their community, either by dealing diplomatically with the barbarians or by organising a militia to replace the outgoing soldiers.

The crucial difference from the imperial model, where the bishops looked after the spiritual welfare of their community while the day-to-day running was in the hands of the imperial delegates, was that the bishops were not ultimately answerable to an overall leader in the same way that their predecessors had been to the emperor. The most obvious result was that, while religion was still run on a centralised basis, secular administration became increasingly localised, a process which was aided by the tribal divisions of the new barbarian leaders and which set a precedent both for the later feudality of medieval France and the rise of the city-states in 12th-century Italy.

By the 650s, the period of transition from Roman to barbarian rule was complete: political control of Western Europe on a 'national' scale had passed from Roman officials to the rulers of the new Germanic kingdoms. The military and political weakness of the other Germanic states, however, gave the Frankish kingdom of northern Gaul the opportunity to 'plug the gap' and thus greatly expand its control over Western Europe.

The Franks

Among the first to achieve both internal unity and some sense of continuity with their Roman predecessors were the Franks. The immediate safety of the Frankish kingdom secured, the ruling elite converted to Christianity in 496, not to the Arian heresy practised by other Gothic kings but to Trinitarian Catholicism, which prevailed among the population of the Western dioceses. This was a bold move, not least because many of the Franks themselves still adhered either to Arian or pagan beliefs. For Frankish development as a whole, however, it proved not only beneficial but crucial, as the adoption of their subjects' religious beliefs cemented the bond between the Gallo-Roman population and their Germanic overlords. Moreover, this religious connection between secular and ecclesiastical rulers enabled the start of a real assimilation between the two administrative systems.

For the Frankish rulers, the link with the existing religious hierarchy enabled them to adopt the church's infrastructure and organisation, inherited from the Romans, thus establishing a connection with the imperial past. Also, good relations with the church gave the Merovingian kings the chance to tap into its vast wealth, as well as ensuring them its staunch support in the case of civil strife. For the church, the emergence of a line of powerful, religiously-alike secular rulers not only allowed it

to hand over to royal delegates the more onerous tasks of lay administration, but also gave its leaders their first close involvement with high-level international politics.

This alliance between the Franks and the Catholic church continued with mutually beneficial consequences past the end of the Merovingian dynasty into the mass expansion of the Carolingian period, by the end of which the Franks had conquered all of what remained of Christian Western Europe (Gaul, Germany and northern Italy). The Carolingians successfully combined elements of Roman tradition (Roman *gubernatores,* local officials, becoming Frankish *ministeriales*), their own Germanic culture and the church to create a new continental superpower that strove to imitate, if not replace, the empire their predecessors had helped destroy. In this sense, Charlemagne's coronation as *imperator Romanorum* by Pope Leo III in 800 was fully justified. Just as the inherent church infrastructure throughout Western Europe had facilitated the Frankish takeover of regional control, so the spread of the Franks' dominions had sealed Catholicism's dominance within Christian Europe, as well as turning the church into one of Europe's most politically influential institutions.

It was a sign of just how powerful the church had become by the 9th century that it managed to survive the disintegration and collapse of the Carolingian empire. After 840, the mighty empire was split into West, Middle and East Francia by the Frankish tradition of partible inheritance, coupled with one-off civil strife, first in the Treaty of Verdun of 843 and then the Partition of Meersen in 870, by which West and East Francia divided Lotharingia between them, forming the first recognisable outlines of France, Italy and Germany. The three parts of the old Carolingian empire fell back onto their individual concerns and agendas, and thus drifted ever further apart. The one uniting factor between them remained their common adherence to Catholic Christianity. Though the old empire fragmented, the church remained just as dominant and politically active as before.

Though the old empire fragmented, the church remained just as dominant and politically active as before.

National Churches?

Although the international nature of the Catholic church's hierarchy sustained links between the French, German and Italian churches, political divisions allowed the three churches to develop independently.

In France, the weakness of the Capetian monarchy until the 12th century, coupled with the emergence of a dense feudalistic geopolitical landscape created by the practice of partible inheritance, resulted in the church's taking a more passive political stance. Instead, it chose to emphasise its religious role by advocating and sponsoring pilgrimages and later crusades, at which the Abbey of Cluny particularly excelled.

In Germany, the evolution of Frankish rule into a strong elected monarchy, with a small group of elector-princes in charge of vast tracts of land, was balanced by the church's close political involvement. Not only did the German church take charge of the Christianisation of the pagans beyond the border marches, but it also became directly drawn into the monarch's territorial ambitions. Similarly, the Italian church, which through the imperial claims of the German monarchy had fallen almost completely under the German church's jurisdiction, attempted to assert its authority not only over the imperial legates but also over the emerging Italian city-states, which constantly fought to shrug off both imperial and papal subjugation.

Whatever the individual national situations, however, it becomes clear that from the 10th century onwards the real power of the medieval church lay in its ability to 'make or break' the reigns or ambitions of any contemporary ruler. Only a handful of rulers of the time were able to resist the church with any measure of success. Some tried and failed. Henry IV of Germany attempted to control the Gregorian Papacy regarding the appointment of church officials in the 'Investiture contest' in the late 11th century and early 12th centuries, but he failed utterly, suffered excommunication, was embroiled in endless church-fomented civil wars against the great princes and bishops, and finally suffered the humiliation of public penance. Instead of subjecting the church to imperial authority, Henry had confirmed its role as an independent player in the political system of the Holy Roman Empire.

> **From the 10th century onwards the real power of the medieval church lay in its ability to 'make or break' the reigns or ambitions of any contemporary ruler.**

Of the few who succeeded, Frederick I Barbarossa stands out prominently. Most monarchs, however, in particular the French, chose the safe route of co-operating with the French church and the Papacy, an attitude which paid dividends. Its evasion of an investiture contest, and its subsequent strengthening of royal ties with the prominent abbeys, enabled the French monarchy to take on successfully the Angevin and Holy Roman empires.

The Crusades and Religious Warfare

Religious warfare *per se* had never been seen in Europe before the medieval era, and even in the Middle East, where conflict between Turks, Arabs and Byzantines had been ongoing since the 6th century, the idea of superimposing a religious theme on essentially border warfare had not yet emerged. However, the rise of Christian pilgrimage to places of religious significance by the 10th century anticipated the notion of 'holy war'. The first mention of religious campaigns is made in the early 11th century with reference to the church's call for military assistance from European knights against Spanish Muslims to protect Christian pilgrims to the shrine at Santiago de Compostella, an assistance which quickly evolved into religion-inspired warfare and even the start of the Spanish *Reconquista*. Thus the idea of 'armed pilgrimage', which Pope Urban II preached at Clermont after Alexius I of Byzantium's appeal for Western military help against the Seljuqs, was not entirely new, even though its use in the context of Western involvement in Eastern politics was unprecedented.

It is yet another sign of how important the church was that the Western response in the five years after Urban's appeal numbered upwards of 120,000 soldiers. Although many of these would have been drawn to the Crusades by hopes of plunder and conquest, a significant percentage would have taken part out of pure religious zeal. Previous secular appeals from Byzantium had produced maybe 400 mercenaries at best, but when the plea was channelled through the Pope and phrased in moral and personal religious terminology, the difference in response was staggering. Therein lay another of the church's great powers and achievements, one which no secular ruler could hope to emulate: the ability to sway large sections of the Christian population of Western Europe into concerted action for a single cause.

While 'religious warfare' truly came into its own in the medieval period, with Christian *peregrinations* and Muslim *jihad*, the notion of using religion to justify non-religious military conflict was not a product of the medieval period—combatants in previous eras had instinctively referred to 'higher powers' to raise both their morale and the 'moral worth' of their cause. In the Middle Ages, however, the involvement of the church in lay warfare rose to new heights, partly on account of the sheer amount of internecine strike that took place. It was now, for example, that the first chronicled references to patron saints and national heroes began to appear, a product, no doubt, of the Christian fervour and chivalric ideals that gripped Christendom at this time.

On a more practical note, it became increasingly common for European rulers to invoke God and the various saints in their non-religious wars, a practice to which involvement in the Crusades may well have accustomed them. In the Hundred Years' War, for instance, both sides routinely claimed that God favoured their cause. Rampantly biased chroniclers would describe in lurid and gory detail how 'the wrath of God put fear into the hearts of the enemy', and how piously the victors thanked God for his support. Understandably, when any side fared particularly badly, they would play down the religious part of their claims, blaming instead their leaders' inefficiency for their misfortune.

Interestingly, however, whereas Western sources for major conflicts within Europe nearly always contain a large spread of chroniclers' opinions, generally with several sources on each side, records for conflicts between Christians and other non-Western cultures are much more one-sided and patchy. These sources almost exclusively mention Christian successes and victories, whether against European pagans or the Muslims of Spain or the Holy Land. This may be due to the chroniclers' selective attitude towards the events they were recording—after all, many of the Christian military expeditions outside Western Europe often assumed the mantle of religious warfare.

As a result, while in inter-Christian conflict it seemed obvious that the winning side had curried God's favour and the losers incurred his wrath, Christian campaigns against non-Christians presented a major problem. Surely, the chroniclers reasoned, the Christians ought to be guaranteed God's favour. Therefore, if the Christians were successful, God had been on their side as expected. But if the Christians were unsuccessful, God must have actively prevented their victory, and, as He could not possibly have favoured unbelievers over Christians, they must have done something to anger Him. The losing leaders were thus the worst possible role models and should be eradicated from history as far as possible, as was the case with the leaders of the two less unsuccessful waves of the first Crusade, evidence of whom survives only in non-Western sources. Other Christian failures may well have been whitewashed out of history by Christian chroniclers.

Christian failures may well have been whitewashed out of history by Christian chroniclers.

The Church and Culture

The church's other major contribution to medieval European history lay in the evolution of Western art and education.

During the transition from imperial to barbarian rule after the 4th century, the old Roman executive and public buildings fell into disuse. Consequently, Christian communities' focal points moved from the Roman forum to the Christian monasteries, which became the new centres of education throughout Western Europe. As the secular rulers, the usual patrons of the arts, tussled for supremacy until the 9th century, churches and their adherent monasteries often proved the only sanctuaries where works of art and culture were preserved from ignorant destruction.

Over the centuries, the church presided over Western culture's gradual recovery in the development of new artistic and architectural styles, the evolution of the Western musical tradition, the flourishing of literature, and even some scientific innovation. Although advances in the later Middle Ages increasingly began to take place independently of ecclesiastical supervision, the importance of the church in 'kick-starting' European cultural progress is undisputed.

In art and architecture, the first main style to emerge was the Pre-Romanesque, which combined the Mediterranean crafts evident in Early Christian artwork with the Germanic influences of Migration Period art, manifesting itself especially in the illuminated manuscripts at the Carolingian and Ottonian Renaissances. Its successor, the Romanesque, harked back to the architecture of ancient Rome with the forms and material used, and reestablished Monumental stone sculpture in Western Europe. Finally, the Gothic style imbued buildings with a more narrative character, including figurine sculpture, stained-glass windows and the typical pointed arches. All three styles were well represented in religious and secular art and architecture.

In music, the church unified the extant European chant traditions into Gregorian chant, around whose melodies later monks developed 'organum' (early polyphony). At the same time, clerical authors imbued Roman theatrical forms with spiritual themes, creating 'liturgical dramas'; and 'goliards', itinerant ecclesiastics, acted as the precursors to the unattached poet-musicians of later centuries. The Notre-Dame school of polyphony developed 'ars antiqua', the introduction of rhythmic notation into Western music. Finally, 'ars nova', the export of church polyphony to secular music, laid the foundations for all later advances in Western music.

The dominance of Latin as the ecclesiastical *lingua franca*, and the church's role as the primary source of education, meant that much medieval literature not only avoided the national vernaculars but also tended to focus on religious themes. As monastic culture and learning began to percolate into the secular world, however, an increasing number of non-religious works began to appear: analyses and chronicles, epic poetry, courtly romances, travel literature and moral allegories. As with other art forms, medieval literature, though initially very much a part of ecclesiastical culture, moved increasingly into the secular domain.

Finally, meaningful progress in science was seriously hampered before the 11th century by the rigidity of Christian philosophy and the incomplete availability of ancient texts for reference. Western science was rescued from utter stagnation by contact and exchange with Byzantine and Arab scholars, who gave the West access to meticulously preserved classical texts and the knowledge of the Middle East. This, together with the inauguration of the first universities as independent centres of learning, created a new group of thinkers who, by the 1300s, had made anticipatory moves towards the church-science conflict of the Renaissance by challenging the 'accepted wisdom' of Biblical doctrine. Even so, the West still lagged behind the Muslim world, whose Islamic authorities encouraged every form of research.

Conclusion

The church's fate was inextricably bound with that of Europe throughout the medieval period, and even beyond. Its vital role in shaping the course and development of our history, as well as its day-to-day importance in the lives of Western Christians, is undeniable. With Christian power in the East finally ousted by Islam in 1453, the religious-military love affair that Western Europe had conducted with the Christian lands of the East lost focus and catalyst, bringing to an end one of the main political driving-forces of the Middle Ages. For the best part of another century, however, the fundamental ideological ties that brought together Western politics, religion, warfare and culture endured relatively unchanged, until the indulgence controversy in 1517 that produced Martin Luther's 95 Theses, split the Christian church and paved the way for the religious wars that characterised early modern Europe.

Where the church in its unwavering unity had been the Christian world's mainstay, it now became the author of its greatest period of instability and discontent. The moral questions raised by reformers and reactionaries remained unresolved, with the religious practices of entire countries decided by the haphazard outcomes of war, and even single battles.

We have seen the same issues of religious intolerance torment us again and again, down to the ongoing 'war on terror'. Perhaps, therefore, it is not just medieval history but all of human civilisation that is the history of the church, or rather of religion and its effects on us, even in our increasingly agnostic modern age. Maybe the lessons from the Middle Ages, as yet unlearnt, will return to haunt us in due course.

Further Reading

Geoffrey Barraclough, *Origins of Modern Germany* (1947)

Georges Duby, *L'Histoire de France* (1987)

A.J. Marks and G.I.F. Tingay, *The Romans* (1990)

H.E. Mayer and John Gillingham, *The Crusades* (2nd edition, 1988)

John Julius Norwich, *A Short History of Byzantium* (1989–95)

Steven Runciman, *A History of the Crusades* (1951–54)

W.L. Warren, *King John* (1978)

From *History Review,* December 2006, pp. 21–25. Copyright © 2006 by History Today, Ltd. Reprinted by permission.

What Did Medieval Schools Do for Us?

Nicholas Orme

There are few worse insults than 'medieval', or safer ones, because those who might be offended are no longer with us! Where education is concerned, independent schools, old school buildings, unfashionable subjects like the classics, or strict regimes, can all be dismissed as 'medieval' without imagining what medieval schools might have been like. If anyone does imagine them, it is probably as few in numbers, poorly equipped, with unimaginative teaching, and pupils kept in order by vigorous corporal punishment—altogether different from what good modern schooling should be.

The history of schools in England begins a long way back, probably soon after the Romans came in AD 43. The Romans used reading and writing for a wide range of purposes, and many signs of these survive today. There are milestones and tombstones carved with inscriptions, and words stamped onto pottery and tiles. There are the wooden tablets from Vindolanda near Hadrian's Wall containing letters and inventories, and the metal plates with prayers and curses found in the waters of Bath. These writings were in Latin, and if you wished to learn to read or write in Roman Britain, you did so in that language.

Little is known of how schools functioned in Britain. In the Roman empire as a whole, however, it was common to find elementary teachers of reading in towns, and the major cities supported more learned schoolmasters who would teach grammar and rhetoric (how to write and speak Latin correctly and read the best classical authors). While only the noblest and wealthiest in Britain would have studied these subjects, mostly boys at that, many others must have learnt to read and write at a basic level since the bits of Latin that have survived on everyday objects are often crudely spelt and expressed.

When Roman control in Britain evaporated soon after AD 400, the western half of the country reverted to rule by native British kings. The eastern half became infiltrated by Anglo-Saxons, who established kingdoms of their own. One might have expected Latin literacy to have dried up also. It did not—any more than literacy in English or French disappeared when colonialism ended in Africa. By AD 400 Britain was becoming Christian, and Christianity is a religion of books and writings: the Bible, prayer-books, letters, laws, and non-Christian Latin scholarly works. British Christians–clergy and the more important laity–needed to go on learning Latin to read or write it. As soon as the Anglo-Saxons were converted to Christianity, which happened after 597, they followed this path as well.

There were, however, two big educational changes in the post-Roman era. One was a change in where schooling took place. By 400 the towns in Britain were in decline. They no longer contained enough literate people to support schoolmasters teaching the public. The centres of literacy in Britain moved from the towns to monasteries, and it was monks who now provided schooling, primarily for boys and youths intending to be monks but not invariably so. It was to be a long time before free-standing teachers appeared again in the towns of what by then would be England.

The other change involved how schooling was done. In Roman times, when a good deal of Latin was spoken even in Britain, you went to school to learn the Latin alphabet, but after that you could pick up much of your knowledge of Latin from Latin speakers around you. The advanced teachers of grammar and rhetoric assumed that you had a basic knowledge of Latin already, and sought to polish and improve it.

After 400, when there were far fewer Latin speakers in Britain, learning it informally became difficult. One solution was to learn the Latin alphabet but to use it to write in your local language, and from about the fifth or sixth century this was done in Welsh and Irish, and later on (by the seventh century) in English. But although these languages were suitable for composing poetry and local laws and customs, you still needed Latin to access religious and learned writings and to communicate with people in France and Italy.

The Romans had hardly thought how to teach Latin to non-Latinists. Roman grammars, the most popular of which was by Donatus who lived in the mid-fourth century, were rather like Fowler's English Usage. They took it for granted that you knew basic Latin, and told you how to write it correctly. This wasn't good enough for non-Latinists. Latin is a complicated language. There are five major types of nouns and four major types of verbs, and unlike English nouns and verbs they have many 'paradigms' or forms, depending on the roles they play in a sentence.

So, in the post-Roman period, Irish, British, and eventually Anglo-Saxon teachers, compiled new grammars, based on those of the Romans, but expanded to help learners who knew no Latin already and whose own language worked in different ways. These teachers developed an important tool of education: the foreign-language grammar. The texts they produced are the direct ancestor of the ones that we use for learning French,

German, or any other language, which expect their readers to have difficulties with an unfamiliar language and take them into it by gentle stages.

Along with Latin grammars came Latin word-lists, eventually with English translations, and Latin dialogues imagining scenes of everyday life and helping you to converse about them. These works too anticipated modern phrase-books and foreign language readers. At first the books that taught you Latin were in Latin themselves. But in the 990s a monk named Ælfric, teaching at Cerne Abbey in Dorset, produced the first-known Latin textbook in English, and this was widely used in England up to and even beyond the Norman Conquest.

For most of the 'Anglo-Saxon period', then, from the seventh century to the mid-eleventh, schooling shared much in common with schooling today. It set out to give you access to all knowledge, which at that time required reading and studying Latin. Increasingly, from about the ninth century onwards, there was knowledge available in English too, and having learnt the Latin alphabet you could use your literacy to access English as well as Latin.

The Anglo-Saxons were also modern in that their schooling was, in principle, suitable for anyone. Although it took place chiefly in monasteries of monks or nuns, or later on in minsters (churches staffed by more worldly clergy), it soon attracted boys and even girls who did not intend to become clergy (or did not end up in that life). The Venerable Bede makes it clear that the great northern bishops of the seventh century like Aidan of Lindisfarne and Wilfrid of York had lay youths in their households, as well as young clerics, who were learning the scriptures and even going on to careers as warriors.

Some of the Anglo-Saxon kings of Bede's day were literate in Latin. He tells us that Aldfrith of Northumbria was 'most learned in the scriptures' and was given a book on the holy places in Palestine by the abbot of Iona. Bede also reports a story about a warrior in Mercia, who died between 704 and 709 after seeing a vision of angels and demons. They showed him books in which his good and bad deeds had been written, and in each case he was given the book 'to read' and did so.

Women's education is less clear. They certainly learnt to read basic Latin in the nunneries, in the sense of being able to pronounce the Latin of the services, and by the time of King Alfred (871–99) lay noblewomen were learning to read. Alfred's daughter Ælfthryth is said to have learnt the Latin psalter and to have read books in English, especially poetry. Edith, the daughter of Earl Godwine and wife of Edward the Confessor, who spent part of her childhood with the nuns of Wilton Abbey in the 1030s and 40s, was later credited with having known music, grammar, and languages, which she had presumably learnt in the abbey.

By the time of the Norman Conquest there were dozens of places in England where schooling could be had. They included monasteries, cathedrals and minsters, and possibly some royal and noble households like Alfred's. Before 1066, however, schools are not recorded as independent bodies. Schooling was an activity within some other body, and teaching was a task rather than a vocation. The teacher, when not in the class, was a monk, a nun, or a cleric, not a professional instructor.

By 1100 this situation was changing. In the 1070s, soon after the Norman Conquest, we start to hear of schools as distinct institutions and, in the twelfth century, of school teaching as a distinct occupation. How far these changes were due to the Normans is hard to say. They were reformers who may have tried to make schools more effective, but other forces were tending to separate schooling from church institutions.

One was the revival of towns. Once again, as in Roman times, there were sizeable settlements of people who needed and practised literary skills: clergy, merchants, and administrators. It was becoming feasible again for a teacher to make a living from charging fees to boys from the neighbourhood. Another factor was to be found in the Church reforms of the twelfth century, by which the monasteries and many of the minsters became stricter and more enclosed in their way of life. It was less easy for them to admit children and youths to their premises and provide a cleric to teach them. The increasing demand for education, in itself, dictated that it needed a teacher's full-time attention.

As a result, during the twelfth century, schools in England began to achieve two other features that we take for granted as modern. First of all, many schools moved out of churches and acquired separate identities. They occupied their own buildings, usually in a street accessible to the public. Their schoolmasters became full-time teachers, rather than doing the job along with religious duties. Monks stopped teaching schoolboys, and teachers from now on were either laymen or chaplains akin to parish clergy.

Secondly, there was an explosion in the number of schools. We can't easily say how many there were in England and Wales before the nineteenth century, because no one kept lists and they tend to be recorded only by chance. Currently we know of free-standing schools in about forty places during the twelfth century, seventy-five in the thirteenth, and two or three hundred by the fourteenth and fifteenth. There would have been many more than we know of, and new ones emerge in records all the time.

They occur from Norham on the Scottish border to western Cornwall where Cornish was spoken, and from Haverfordwest to Ipswich. There were other schools in Scotland and Ireland. By the thirteenth century it seems likely that all cities and market towns had them, and we hear of them even in villages like Awre in Gloucestershire, Kinoulton in Nottinghamshire, and Rudham in Norfolk. The schools in the larger towns were relatively grand organizations with impressive buildings, graduate teachers, book collections, and a good record of continuity. Others were small private ventures that came and went, possibly leaving places without a school for a time.

Some schools, known by contemporaries as song or reading schools, concentrated on elementary education. They took in boys from about the age of five. You started by learning the Latin alphabet from a small tablet held in the hand or from a small prayer-book, known as a primer. Once you could pronounce the letters, you learnt how to read Latin words from basic prayers. 'The Paternoster' (Lord's Prayer), 'Ave Maria' (Hail Mary), and 'Apostles' Creed' were commonly used for this purpose. Then you went on to read psalms, again in Latin, and learnt how to chant them in plainsong.

Up to this point you did not know what the words meant. Chaucer's 'Prioress's Tale' describes two small boys in a song school, one of whom confesses that he cannot translate what he is singing because 'I learn song, I know but little grammar'. Grammar—understanding how Latin worked and what it meant—came next, for those between the ages of seven and ten. Sometimes you left the song school at this stage for a specialized grammar school, but in small towns schoolmasters often taught the whole range of learning in a single school.

In the grammar school, where you stayed for four or more years depending on your career ambitions, you learnt—as you had done in Anglo-Saxon times—how Latin worked grammatically and how to write and to speak it. You wrote your notes and exercises on tablets that could be wiped, and after 1400 you did so on paper, which became cheap at about that time. Some pupils' paper notebooks still survive. To improve your style, and to teach you knowledge and wisdom, you read Latin poetry. Two popular school authors were Cato, who wrote wise advice in couplets, and Theodulus, whose poem gave a brief guide to classical mythology and compared it with some of the main historical episodes in the Bible.

The school year started in September and occupied three terms, ending in about June. This familiar arrangement goes back as early as we know, to the thirteenth century, reflecting the custom of taking holidays in June and then concentrating on getting in the harvest during August. The school day mirrored the working day, starting at day-break and ending in the late afternoon, with a break for breakfast and a long interval of an hour or so for midday dinner. In school the master presided from a large chair, and the pupils sat around the edge of the room on benches. The master did not move about but sat like a king or the lord of the manor, and called out boys for questioning or punishment as necessary.

If you stayed there long enough, you left school with a thorough knowledge of Latin and an ability to read, write, and speak it, and to understand other people speaking it. This was essential for going to university, where lectures and books would be entirely in Latin. Most schoolboys did not go to university, however, and became gentlemen, merchants, parish clergy, or secretarial clerks. For them it was sufficient to know enough Latin to read documents and financial accounts, or to do fairly simple writing in the language. Practical studies, like arithmetic, accountancy, and law were not taught in grammar schools. You learnt them 'on the job' or, if necessary, went to a specialist teacher after leaving school.

This was the infrastructure that produced the great shift in English culture that Professor Michael Clanchy has called the change 'from memory to written record'. In the time of William the Conqueror and even Henry II, a dispute about land, for example, would be decided on the evidence of what witnesses could remember about the ownership. By the reign of Henry III (1216–72), in the mid-thirteenth century, the parties were likely to produce written documents–charters–to establish their claims. Even the serfs of Peterborough Abbey acquired and disposed of bits of land with charters by this date, and the charters were kept as evidence.

By about 1250 English society was not yet totally literate. Many people, perhaps most, were still illiterate. But it was literate in a collective sense. Nearly everyone was dependent on writings to some extent and could access these through other people, if not personally. The schools trained the people who wrote and read these records and not only records, of course, but church service-books, private prayer books, letters, accounts, and works of literature.

Not enough of the growing literate population could cope with Latin. Many boys continued to learn it in school, but other boys and many girls, once they could read, soon deviated to reading in English or, up to the fifteenth century, French. By 1400 schoolmasters were once again producing Latin textbooks in English as Ælfric had done. This was a recognition that their pupils were reading English more easily than they were Latin.

In 1382 William Wykeham founded Winchester College–the first school to be a fully-endowed and self-governing institution. It provided education, board, and lodging for seventy scholars. Previous schools had been largely (though not totally) dependent on charging fees. Winchester offered teaching free of charge, but it was not available to everyone. The scholarships at the college were reserved for the founder's family, the sons of tenants on the college estates, and boys who lived in the counties where the estates were situated.

Wykeham laid down that the scholars must have no private income greater than £3 6s. 8d. per annum. In practice (perhaps on the grounds that boys or youths have no real income of their own) the places soon came to be taken by the sons of gentry, merchants, or wealthy yeomen farmers who had some connection with the college or influence in it. In consequence Wykeham's foundation was the ancestor of modern public schools rather than of state schools today.

But Winchester was also an unusually large and rich foundation, untypical of its period and for a long time matched only by Henry VI's imitation of it, Eton College founded in 1440. The model for free schools in the later Middle Ages was not Winchester but a more modest foundation contemporary with it, situated in a small Cotswold town: the grammar school of Wotton-under-Edge.

Wotton School was founded in 1384 by Katherine Lady Berkeley, a wealthy baron's widow. She planned it on a modest scale with an endowment to pay for the salary of a single schoolmaster teaching grammar without charge to anyone who came to the school. No arrangement was made for boarding, and the pupils were drawn from the town and its neighbourhood. In these respects Wotton was more like a modern state school than was Winchester.

Many free grammar schools like Wotton were founded during the fifteenth century and, indeed, down to the nineteenth century when state education arose. Though called 'grammar schools', they often taught reading as well as Latin and gathered in boys at any age for any part of the process. Most of them were day schools, catering for the local community. Perhaps inevitably they came, like Winchester, to be taken over by the local elites. People already literate and wealthy had a better understanding of the value of schooling, and could better afford the extra charges that even free schooling entails, like decent clothes, books and payments for school activities. There is nothing new in middle-class parents seeking out the best available schools for their children!

Girls' education, even in 1500, was less formal. The new free grammar schools were for their brothers. Girls who learnt to read did so chiefly at home from literate mothers, siblings, or clergy, or at the top of society from nuns. Their studies did not reach so high as those of boys. They learnt Latin in the sense of pronouncing it correctly and being able to do so at sight from a prayer-book, but rarely learnt the grammar of Latin to unlock the meaning. They did not spend hours in class writing exercises, and so their handwriting skills were less developed.

Nevertheless, there were plenty of literate women at the level of the nobility, the gentry, and the merchant class—women able to read fluently in French or English. And, in a shy and unobtrusive way, the first schools for girls and the first schoolmistresses were making their appearance. So unobtrusive was this development that no one commented on it.

In 1335 there is a casual reference to a certain Margaret Skolmaystres in Oxford. A similar woman, Matilda Maresflete, occurs in Boston in 1404 with her occupation given in Latin (magistra scolarum), and two others, E. Scolemaysteresse and Elizabeth Scolemaystres, turn up in London in 1408 and 1441 respectively. A fifth women with a similar title, Agnes 'teacher of girls' (doctrix puellarum), is recorded in London before 1449.

Nothing is known about them but their names point to the likelihood that they taught reading at home to girls or small boys. Yet the fact that four of them were called 'school mistress' shows that people were familiar enough with women teachers to develop a standard term to describe them. This suggests that such teachers were common, yet so lowly that nobody tried to regulate or record them. Even for girls, education was beginning to move out of the home to a school and to a specialized teacher.

If we stop the history of education in 1500, when, roughly speaking, we cease to talk of the Middle Ages, the achievements of medieval school founders, schoolteachers and pupils turns out to have been impressive. They were anything but 'medieval' in the modern dismissive term. They were modern in being free-standing, self-governing institutions. They were extremely common all over the country. They had recognizable fulltime schoolmasters and mistresses.

Education was free in some places. It had some of the same aims that it does today. It gave children knowledge of the world of learning and the skills to navigate in that world. It used sophisticated methods, like the Latin textbook written for a non-Latinist in his own language. It tried to empathize with pupils through humour and references to everyday life. That is not to deny that schools were smaller in buildings and pupil numbers than most modern ones, and that books were scarcer (though not absent). They also used corporal punishment in a way that we would find unacceptable, but one that was taken for granted down to the twentieth century, both in home life and in the judicial system.

Our understanding of schooling is that you start it at about four or five and follow it until you are about eighteen. The school year falls into three terms, divided by Christmas and Easter holidays, with a long holiday in the summer. You start by learning to read and go on to more complicated studies. The teacher tries to gain your interest, rather than just communicating facts. You get an education that is not narrowly vocational, but fits you for a wide range of careers.

None of these is a modern invention. They all developed in the schools of the Middle Ages, and we have kept them because they work. They are what medieval schools did for us.

For Further Reading

N. Orme, Medieval Schools (Yale UP, 2006) and Medieval Children (Yale UP, 2001). Anglo-Saxon education: P. Riché, Education and Culture in the Barbarian West, Sixth through Eighth Centuries (University of South Carolina Press, 1976); M. Lapidge, Anglo-Latin Literature 900-1066 and Anglo-Latin Literature 600-899 (Hambledon Press, 1993 and 1996). History of the study of Latin: Vivien Law, The History of Linguistics in Europe from Plato to 1600 (Cambridge UP, 2003). History of literacy: M.T. Clanchy, From Memory to Written Record: England 1066-1307, 2nd ed. (Blackwell, 1993).

NICHOLAS ORME is Professor of History at the University of Exeter. His new book Medieval Schools was published by Yale University Press in May, price £25.

This article first appeared in *History Today*, June 2006, pp. 10–17. Copyright © 2006 by History Today, Ltd. Reprinted by permission.

1215 and All That

In the Bitter 13th century struggle between King John and the upstart English Barons, The Magna Carta was far from The Last Word.

JAMES LACEY

Vengeance has been called the true sport of kings, and few monarchs have taken it as seriously as England's King John. While not nearly the warrior his older brother Richard the Lionheart had been, John proved himself more than adept at exacting revenge for injuries real and imagined.

Among the former were insults hurled at the monarch by the same barons who in June 1215 had forced their sovereign to sign one of history's great documents, the Magna Carta, which limited John's royal powers and protected the barons' privileges as freemen. John's signature would have ended the long-standing strife between king and barons, had either side possessed the good sense to make some small measure of accommodation toward the other. Unfortunately, that is not the way of over-proud men. No sooner was the "Great Charter" signed than the barons turned to drink and, in their drunkenness, loudly proclaimed John a "disgrace," "a worthless man and a king contemptible to his people," "a slave" and "the scum of the people," according to 13th century English chronicler Roger of Wendover.

Upon hearing of these insults, John flew into an impressive rage, "gnashing his teeth, scowling with his eyes, and gnawing at the limbs of trees." Once he calmed down, he shifted his energies to the business of vengeance. And serious business it would be.

John's first concern was to ensure the safety of what he still possessed. He sent royal writs to the mercenaries guarding his castles, ordering them to secretly provision their strongholds and prepare for war. He then snuck off to the Isle of Wight, accompanied by the seven nobles who remained faithful to him. There, John gathered forces for a campaign that would break the power of England's barons.

For two months, John busied himself with amassing funds and buying the loyalty of the southern ports' garrisons. Even as he tackled these tasks, his emissaries were making their way to Rome to seek papal support, while his military commanders were dispatched to France to gather a mercenary army. In

the first of these tasks, John's cause was greatly assisted by his having ended a long conflict with Pope Innocent III two years before. As part of the deal he made with Innocent, John agreed to become the pope's vassal, thereby transforming Innocent from bitterest foe to closest ally. That process also made England a part of Innocent's papal holdings.

So when Innocent learned of the baron's revolt and the Magna Carta, he saw the latter as a challenge to his papal prerogatives and reportedly exclaimed, "Are the barons of England removing from the throne a king who is under the protection of the apostolic see? By St. Peter, we cannot pass over this insult without punishing it!" He then condemned and forever annulled what he called the "shaming and demeaning document," and composed a letter to the barons, ordering them to desist from their revolt or face excommunication. Soon after, when John refused to meet the barons for a peace conference, England's bishops, whose sympathies lay with the barons, used the exact wording of the papal bull to excommunicate all "disturbers of the peace." As the barons saw themselves as peacemakers and the king as the true disturber of the peace, the dreaded papal anathema and excommunication had little immediate effect.

With the pope's blessing in hand and a formidable mercenary army now at his back, John was ready to march by late September 1215. The barons, on the other hand, had spent the months since the signing of the Magna Carta waiting in London in a state of indolence. Not until John's war plans became obvious did they rouse themselves to action and besiege the royal strongholds at Oxford and Northampton. In early October, the barons advanced into Kent to engage the king, who was in Canterbury at the head of a small reconnoitering force. Realizing he was only a few miles from the full might of the barons' army, John beat a hasty retreat to Dover, where his mercenaries awaited their orders. Ironically, the barons—upon hearing a rumor that the king was advancing from Canterbury—withdrew despite their superior numbers.

To delay King John's advance while they concentrated their force for a decisive battle, the rebellious barons convinced Reginald of Cornhill, then securing Rochester Castle for

Archbishop of Canterbury Stephen Langton, to turn over the fortress to them. One of England's most formidable fortresses, Rochester stood athwart the route from Dover to London. Whoever held it would dominate most of Kent and control London's communications to the south and the sea.

The site of a timber fortification since Roman times, Rochester took form as a castle proper when the Normans built stone walls in the late 11th century. Henry I presented the castle to Archbishop of Canterbury William de Corbeil in 1127 and charged him with building its great keep, a formidable tower within the castle.

By the 13th century, Rochester Castle was considered virtually impregnable. Attackers faced three lines of defense; the walls around the town of Rochester itself, then the castle's solid curtain walls and, finally, the formidable keep, with six levels and four towers. By any measure, taking the castle by force was a daunting challenge. Ironically, just before the Barons' War, John had improved the castle's defenses, an act he surely regretted now that he faced the task of storming the very walls he had reinforced.

To hold Rochester Castle against John's attack, the barons picked a force of 140 knights led by veteran warrior William d'Aubigny. When d'Aubigny and his men arrived in Rochester, they expected to find the fortress well stocked and ready for war but instead found it completely unprepared to withstand a siege. Many of the knights thought to abandon the mission but were held to their duty by the exhortations of d'Aubigny, who simultaneously shamed them and appealed to their martial vigor. In a burst of activity, the small band of warriors stockpiled all available supplies within the town. But within three days of their arrival, John and his army appeared at the walls of Rochester.

And what an army it had become. Joined by knights from Poitou and Gascony loyal to the House of Anjou (which ruled much of northern France) and to John, by opportunistic warriors who coveted the lands of England's barons and by battalions of mercenary crossbowmen who, in the words of Roger of Wendover, "thirsted for nothing more than human blood," the royal army was so immense that one contemporary chronicler asserted, "All who beheld it were struck with fear and dismay." Once he learned that d'Aubigny and his followers had occupied Rochester, John ordered his murderous throng to attack.

'Once he learned that d'Aubigny and his followers had occupied Rochester, John ordered his murderous throng to attack'

For the townspeople manning Rochester's walls, the sight of John's fearsome professionals was too much, and they fled the battlements. John's knights burst through the town gates and in a short, vicious fight pushed d'Aubigny's troops across the castle drawbridge and into the stronghold. If some chroniclers are to be believed, the defenders fought only to cut their way through John's men and beat a hasty retreat to London. But they failed miserably and were now trapped within the keep, facing one of the greatest castle breakers of the Middle Ages.

Despite recent attempts to rehabilitate his reputation, neither history nor literature speak well of King John. Most historians have agreed with English medievalist William Stubbs, who in 1875 labeled John "the very worst of all our kings . . . a faithless son, a treacherous brother . . . polluted with every crime . . . false to every obligation. . . . In the whole view, there is no redeeming trait." Indeed, the monarch gained the nickname "John Softsword" after losing Normandy to the French, supposedly because he would not leave the bed of his young bride.

In truth, Normandy and the rest of the Angevin Empire's once extensive possessions in France could not have resisted the resurgent power of the French monarchy. Even Richard the Lionheart, against whom John's supposed military failings are often measured, was hard-pressed to hold what his father, Henry II, had gained. Still, it was John who lost an empire, and with it his military reputation.

In reality, John had an enviable war record: In 1202, for example, the king marched his army 80 miles in 48 hours to rescue his aging mother, Eleanor of Aquitaine, who was besieged in Mirabeau Castle. He routed the unsuspecting besiegers, freed his mother and captured almost all of the enemy nobles. John was equally effective at assaulting strongholds, as he proved in 1206 when he took the supposedly impregnable fortress of Montauban. In short, few of John's contemporaries would have underestimated him as a combat commander. Indeed, throughout 1215 the barons showed a marked reluctance to face the king in battle.

For some historians, John's failures resulted from his inability to win a peace: He could not resist kicking his opponents when they were down, thus his many enemies never forgave him for his slights and insults and pounced at any opportunity for revenge. No matter how many armies John defeated or how many castles he broke, his arrogance, inability to compromise and maladroit diplomatic efforts ensured he would have more enemies and fewer allies.

The barons in London seemed paralyzed with consternation at John's rapid response to their seizure of Rochester. They had sworn to rush to d'Aubigny's aid, were he attacked, but two weeks passed before they took any action. On October 26, Robert Fitzwalter led 700 knights to lift the siege. They had only reached Dartford—less than 20 miles from London—when they learned John was marching to confront them. Contemptuous chroniclers noted that although Fitzwalter's warriors faced little more than a mild south wind, they retreated to London to amuse themselves with gambling, drinking and "practicing all other vices."

Rochester Castle

Built on the site of Roman-era timber fortifications, the castle first took shape when the Normans built stone walls sometime in the late 11th century. Continuously enlarged and strengthened over two centuries, the riverside fortress was considered virtually impregnable by the time of the 1215 siege. Attackers faced three lines of defense—the walls around Rochester town itself, the castle's solid curtain walls and, finally, the keep.

1. Three **towers**, each a self-contained strongpoint, guarded the eastern approach.
2. With six levels and four towers, the **keep** was an immensely strong defensive position and defenders' last redoubt.
3. A second gatehouse controlled access to the **inner bailey**, which was ringed by its own walls.
4. Battlements atop the stout **main gate** enabled defenders to cover the base of the curtain wall.
5. The perimeter ditch forced attackers to advance uphill under fire to reach the base of the wall.
6. Attackers who breached the curtain wall had to cross the **outer bailey**, open ground subject to fire from all sides.
7. Several feet thick and crenellated on top the **curtain wall** was a daunting outer defense.
8. The **northwest bastion** anchored the castle's riverside defenses.

Forefather of Our Country

William d'Aubigny's deliverance from the gibbet in 1215 would, 500 years later, have a profound effect on the course of American history. When d'Aubigny died in 1236, he was succeeded by his son, also named William. William, in turn, died in 1247, leaving only daughters. One of them, Isabel, married Robert de Ros. Their marriage produced a direct line of descent to George Washington, who thus numbered among his ancestors one of the 25 barons chosen as guarantors of the Magna Carta.

On the first day of his siege of Rochester, an emboldened John set up his headquarters on nearby Boley Hill and ordered the erection of five great siege engines. He also ordered the destruction of the bridge over the Medway River, isolating the castle from any support from London. Finally, John sent orders for every smith in Canterbury to work nonstop making pickaxes and send them immediately to Rochester.

Day and night, John pressed his attack on the castle. As his siege engines rained large stones upon the defenders, the king's archers and crossbowmen maintained an unceasing barrage of missiles. Through it all, John ordered continual assaults on the walls. D'Aubigny and his men repulsed every attack with courageous determination. Despairing of ever receiving the king's mercy and "endeavoring to delay their own destruction," they "made no small slaughter amongst their assailants," according to Roger of Wendover's account of the siege. For several weeks, d'Aubigny's exhausted band of men "hurled stone for stone and weapon for weapon from the walls and ramparts upon the enemy."

Ultimately, however, John's forces breached the castle walls, either with the siege engines or by mining. "The soldiers of the king now rushed to the breach in the wall," wrote Roger of Wendover, "and by constant fierce assaults, they forced the besieged to abandon the castle, although not without great loss on their own side." The defenders then fell back into the castle keep, pressed by John's men. Some attackers managed to force their way into the keep, but D'Aubigny's fierce counterattack

slew many of the king's men and "compelled the rest to quit." By this time, hunger—an enemy as deadly as King John's army—was taking its toll on the defenders. They had been living on the rotting meat of their slaughtered warhorses for a week. Now even that was gone.

But John did not have the patience to let starvation do his work. He set his miners to work undercutting the foundations of the keep. On November 25, the miners reported they had tunneled beneath the 13-foot-thick stone walls, bracing the passages with wooden supports. John then sent a royal writ to Hubert de Burgh, his chief minister, ordering him to "send to us with all speed by day and night 40 of the fattest pigs of the sort least good for eating to bring fire beneath the tower," according to the Barnwell chronicler. The miners used the pig fat to fire the tunnel supports. (Today, a monument at Rochester memorializes the 40 pigs that made the ultimate sacrifice for the king.)

The subterranean blaze brought the intended result, collapsing the southeast corner of the keep, and John's soldiers swarmed into the breach. D'Aubigny led a countercharge and pushed the king's men to retreat, but fresh assaults followed one upon the other, and John's men were at last able to force back the defenders. Even then, a quirk in the keep's construction brought d'Aubigny's men temporary respite: A wall bisecting the keep restricted the assault force to one half of the stronghold, while the defenders took refuge behind a wall as stout as those the miners had spent weeks undermining.

By then, though, starvation was doing King John's work for him. Perhaps still hoping for succor from the barons holed up in London, d'Aubigny decided on a desperate move: He ordered that all men unfit due to hunger or wounds be expelled from the castle. But if d'Aubigny was counting on the king's mercy, he had misjudged his adversary's temper. Incensed by the continuing resistance, John ordered the hands and feet of many of the outcasts cut off. His food gone, d'Aubigny held a council of his knights. Despite what John had done to their expelled brethren, they voted to surrender, deciding it would, in Roger of Wendover's words, "be a disgrace to them to die of hunger when they could not be conquered in battle."

On November 30, two months into the siege, the surviving defenders marched out of the castle. Considering the delay the castle's resistance had imposed on his plans, the number of his troops slain and the cost of the siege, John found it hard to contain his fury. He ordered gallows prepared and swore he would hang every captive. In the end, he allowed himself—however reluctantly—to be dissuaded by one his loyal knights, Savaric de Mauleon, who told John, "My lord king, our war is not yet over, therefore you ought carefully to consider how the fortunes of war may turn; for if you now order us to hang these men, the barons, our enemies, will perhaps by a like event take me or other nobles of your army and, following your example, hang us; therefore, do not let this happen, for in such a case, no one will fight in your cause."

John contented himself with imprisoning the leading knights and handing over the men at arms to his soldiers for ransom. The only defenders hanged were the mercenary crossbowmen, whom John's men generally despised for the carnage they had caused.

With Rochester Castle and his line of communication to the port of Dover now secure, King John unleashed a revenge-driven campaign of terror intended to bring the barons to their knees. Considering London too well fortified to be taken in a winter siege that might wreck his own army, John marched on Northampton. As Roger of Wendover related:

[John,] spreading his troops a broad, burnt the houses and buildings of the barons, robbing them of their goods and cattle, and thus destroying everything that came in his way, he presented a miserable spectacle to all who beheld it. And if the day did not satisfy the malice of the king for the destruction of property, he ordered his incendiaries to set fire to the hedges and towns on his march, that he might refresh his sight with the damage done to his enemies and by robbery might support the wicked agents of his iniquity.

As John expanded his depredations, the despondent barons, in 1216, invited Prince Louis, son of King Philip II of France, to bring an army to England and claim the throne. Louis accepted the offer and landed in England on May 21, 1216. Within a week he was in London, receiving the homage of the barons. John, distrusting the loyalty of his own French mercenaries in battle against their prince, retreated west as a reinvigorated baronial army took the offensive. The tides of war had turned against the despised monarch when he succumbed to dysentery in October 1216.

For further reading, James Lacey recommends: John Lackland, *by Kate Norgate, and* Flowers of History, *by Roger of Wendover.*

The Fourth Crusade and the Sack of Constantinople

JONATHAN PHILLIPS

The capture of Constantinople by the armies of the Fourth Crusade was one of the most remarkable episodes in medieval history. One of their number wrote, 'No history could ever relate marvels greater than those as far as the fortunes of war are concerned'. On April 12th, 1204, an army of perhaps 20,000 men and a fleet of about 200 ships crewed by Venetian sailors and warriors, broke in and began to loot the greatest metropolis in the Christian world. Constantinople's mighty walls had resisted numerous onslaughts as the Avars, Persians and Arabs had tried to assail its defences over the centuries. Yet always 'the queen of cities', as the Byzantines described their capital, had survived. What had brought the crusaders to attack their fellow Christians and how did they manage to succeed? The crusaders understood their success as a manifestation of God's will. One commented, 'There can be no doubt that the hand of the Lord guided all of these events'.

There was a history of difficulties between the two parties, dating from the 1054 Schism between the Catholic and Orthodox churches. This concerned matters of doctrine, religious practice and papal authority and gave an added sharpness to future disputes. The advent of the crusades in 1095 brought further tensions often created by large and sometimes ill-disciplined armies passing through the Byzantine Empire en route to the Holy Land. Greek purges of the Venetian (1171) and western (1182) communities in Constantinople added to this record of troubles.

Relations between Byzantium and the West at this time were often characterised as a clash of cultures. The Greeks viewed themselves as civilised superiors to the barbaric and violent westerners; the people of Europe regarded the Byzantines as unwarlike, effeminate and duplicitous. In the fullest sense, of course, these stereotypes were inaccurate: the Latin West produced thinkers of the calibre of Anselm of Bec and St Bernard of Clairvaux; magnificent buildings such as the 531-feet long abbey of Cluny testify to practical and artisitic qualities as well. Equally, brutality was not exclusive to the westerners; the Byzantines were capable of extraordinary unpleasantness. The death of Emperor Andronicus I Comnenus in 1185 bears witness to this. With one eye gouged out, his teeth pulled out and his right hand severed, he was paraded through the streets of Constantinople, pelted with excrement before being hung upside down, having his genitals hacked off and finally killed by sword thrusts into his mouth and between his buttocks.

Nonetheless, however unsubtle or partial these respective viewpoints were, they can cast some light on the events of 1203-4 because, though other issues were involved, one key factor was the contrast between the westerners' military power and the Greeks' lack of fighting ability.

By the start of the thirteenth century the chivalric culture gripped the knightly classes of northern Europe. The intensive internecine warfare of the early twelfth century had become subsumed under an all-encompassing code of conduct that fell under the banner of chivalry. This included notions of honour and service, the patronage of *chansons de geste,* ideas of courtly love and, most pertinently to the crusades, the popularity of tournaments.

At the time of the Fourth Crusade, tournaments were not yet orderly contests between two individuals facing each other across the lists in front of ordered ranks of spectators. Rather, they were fast-moving, brutal struggles, sometimes involving hundreds of men. Contests ranged over many acres of lands with the 'arena' designated by particular fortresses or villages. Spectators were confined to the safety of castle walls to watch the fighting. On the herald's signal, two teams would charge each other; the thundering of hooves and the shouts of men were followed by a terrible impact as the combatants began with a lance charge. Then, hand-to-hand fighting broke out and victory was usually achieved by the side that preserved best order. The idea was to capture opponents, rather than to kill or harm them, although in such a heated atmosphere accidents were frequent. In 1186, for example, Richard the Lionheart's younger brother, Geoffrey of Brittany—a man famed for his fighting prowess— perished at a tournament. In spite of the dangers, many knights took part in a circuit of such events across northern Europe. The co-ordination of groups of knights and the violent ebb and flow of a tournament provided by far the most realistic preparation for actual warfare that could be imagined. Alongside the military aspect of these gatherings there were also splendid feasts. Castles might be specially decked out in bright banners, minstrels and entertainers hired and long evenings spent celebrating the deeds of warriors past—some of whom included the heroes of the First Crusade.

Churchmen viewed tournaments in a darker light because, alongside the promotion of violence, they appeared to encourage the vices of pride, envy, gluttony and lust. Prohibitions of such occasions were largely in vain, however, because by the time of the Fourth Crusade they had become an integral part of the knightly culture of the West. Ironically, among the leading patrons were the nobility of Champagne and Flanders—the two areas most associated with the crusades at this time. The counts of Flanders had been on crusades to the Holy Land in 1099, 1108, 1139, 1147, 1157, 1164, 1177 and 1191—an unequalled commitment to the cause of Christ.

When Pope Innocent III (1198–1216) launched recruitment for the Fourth Crusade he was unable to enlist the kings of the West; Richard I was killed in 1199, King John was too preoccupied fighting Philip II Augustus of France, and the German empire was the subject of a bitter succession dispute. It fell to the leading noble families of northern Europe to take the cross, including Count Baldwin of Flanders, his brother-in-law Count Thibaut of Champagne, Count Hugh of St Pol and Count Louis of Blois. Alongside the extensive crusading traditions in these men's blood, a number of them—such as Louis of Blois—had taken part in the Third Crusade (1189–92). The most important addition to their number was the northern Italian, Marquis Boniface of Montferrat, another veteran of the tournament scene and member of a family that had been twice married into the ruling dynasty of Jerusalem over recent decades. The men at the core of the Fourth Crusade, therefore, were tough, highly experienced fighters.

In tandem with this formidable force came the Venetian fleet. The northern Europeans had decided that the most effective way to regain Jerusalem was through the conquest of Egypt. The Nile delta would provide the financial and strategic strength for a long-term tenure of the Holy Land, but to capture it would require a huge naval force. The crusaders approached the acknowledged master mariners of the day and contracted the Venetians to supply a fleet. In the autumn of 1202, around 200 ships, adorned with brightly coloured pennants, set sail. As the crusaders sang hymns to fortify themselves ('Come Holy Ghost, our souls inspire and lighten with celestial fire') an eyewitness wrote of 'the finest thing to see that has ever been since the beginning of the world.'

These ships represented the most advanced naval technology of the day and were crewed by expert sailors, accompanied by many Venetian warriors who had also taken the cross. While the Venetians were among the leading commercial powers of the time they were, as was the entire Latin West intensely religious and had been involved in earlier crusades. On this occasion they were led by the remarkable Doge Enrico Dandolo, who was probably in his early nineties, and had been blind since the 1170s. One of the most charismatic leaders of any military campaign, the doge was commended by his allies as 'a maxi who is prudent, discreet and skilled in hard decision-making'.

A combination of the powerful knights of northern Europe and the excellent Venetian navy formed a potent threat. Yet the forces of Christian Europe had only a patchy military record and could be defeated for a variety of reasons, some self-inflicted and others a reflection of their opponents' strengths.

The overriding difficulties that faced the Fourth Crusaders in particular were a lack of men and money. In April 1201, the leaders made a contract with the Venetians to transport to the Holy Land and provision 33,500 men for a year, in exchange for 85,000 silver marks. The Venetians would also take part as an equal crusading party. By the summer of 1202, however, only around one-third of the provisional number of crusaders had reached Venice and these men could not hope to find the sum of money outstanding. To forestall the payment Doge Dandolo suggested an attack on the port of Zara (now Zadar in Croatia), a settlement that, until recently, had been under his control. There was, however, a serious problem with this idea: Zara was a Catholic city and its new overlord, King Emico of Hungary, was also signed with the cross. Emico was, therefore, under the protection of the papacy and to take Zara would be to invite almost certain excommunication. Some of the crusaders could not stomach the idea of fighting their fellow Christians and left to seek other ways to travel to the Holy Land, but the remainder—who argued that, without the help of the Venetians, the expedition would collapse immediately—stayed to capture the city, taking it on November 24th, 1202. Innocent III was furious and issued a bull of excommunication, although this was soon withdrawn from the French crusaders after a penitent delegation persuaded him that the liberation of the Holy Land was best served by such a move. The Venetians, however, saw the Zarans as rebels and refused to apologise. Their excommunication remained in place, although the crusade leaders suppressed it for fear of' inciting further discontent.

In early 1203, another ingredient was added to the mix. Envoys from Prince Alexius Angelos, a claimant to the Byzantine imperial title, arrived in the crusaders' camp at Zara. Well aware of the westerners' lack of men and money he made a persuasive offer: if they helped to reinstate him in Constantinople he would pay them 200,000 marks, give them all the supplies they needed and provide an army of 10,000 men. He would also place the Greek Orthodox Church under the authority of the papacy. But once again, the prospect of turning their weapons against their Christian brothers appalled many of the crusaders and another body of men chose to leave. Those who remained were convinced that joining with the Prince presented the most effective way of achieving the means to their goal.

Prince Alexius had assured the westerners that he would be welcomed back by his people. Unfortunately, these hopes were unfounded and by June 1203 it was evident to all in the crusader army that they would have to fight to get him re-instated. The mere sight of' Constantinople's massive walls put fear into their hearts; they had 'never imagined there could be so fine a place in the world', yet 'there was indeed no man so brave and daring that his flesh did not shudder at the sight'. What hope did such a small force have against the mighty Byzantine Empire?

In fact, by the early thirteenth century, the Byzantine world was in a fragile condition, corroded by two decades of internal feuding. The death of Emperor Manuel Comnenus (1143–80), presaged a series of regencies, usurpations and coups. Between 1180 and 1204 no fewer than fifty-eight rebellions or uprisings took place across the empire. Prince Alexius's father, Isaac Angelos (1185–95), had come to power by such means, but was deposed and blinded by his brother, Alexius III. Coupled with this chaos in leadership, external and internal forces had also imposed serious pressure on the Greeks. In 1176 the Seljuks of Asia Minor had heavily defeated a large Byzantine army at the Battle of Myriocephalum. In 1185, the Sicilians had sacked Thessalonica, the empire's second city. Five years later, an alliance with Saladin brought the Greeks into conflict with the huge crusading army of Emperor Frederick Barbarossa of Germany (1152–90) and the Byzantines were swiftly pushed to one side. With the decline in central authority the provinces sought advantage too. In 1184, Cyprus broke away, the following year the Bulgarians revolted, and in 1188 the city of Philadelphia in Asia Minor seceded.

Amid such chronic instability, it is not surprising that the Byzantines' military strength declined, most alarmingly in the navy. In 1169, the Greeks had sent a splendid fleet of 150 ships to help the Crusader States fight the Egyptians. By the time of the Fourth Crusade, however, Niketas Choniates, an eyewitness, observed that only twenty half-rotten vessels could be mustered to face the invaders. The Greeks' land forces, were not so feeble. At their core was the Varangian Guard, an elite unit made up of foreign mercenaries (often Scandinavians) armed with fearsome double-headed axes. Furthermore, the sheer size of Constantinople's population gave the Byzantines numerical superiority.

In July 1203 the crusaders staged an amphibious landing. Capturing the suburb of Galata, they broke through into the harbour of the Golden Horn and took a section of the sea walls. The Venetian mariners were able to brush aside Greek opposition and use their skills to adapt their vessels to take siege towers, bringing the ships up to the sea walls to disgorge safely the armed men necessary to continue the assault.

In contrast, the Greek resistance was patchy and usually relied on the presence of contingents of the Varangian Guard. There was a glaring difference between the two forces in quality of leadership. When Dandolo sensed that his men were making insufficient progress during the assault he threatened dire punishment for any that shirked the fight and demanded that the sailors land him on the shore. The crew obeyed and propelled his vermilion vessel forwards; Dandolo on the prow, the winged lion on the banner of St Mark flying before him. As the doge calculated, the other Venetians were shamed by the old man's bravery in landing—they could not abandon their venerable leader. Instead they rushed to join him. This sudden onslaught had the desired effect and the Venetians took a length of the walls.

Dandolo's boldness contrasts with the actions of Emperor Alexius III later the same day. Realising that he needed to make some kind of response he led his men onto the plains outside the land walls to confront the crusader knights. As line after line of Greek troops strode out of the city the sheer size of the Byzantine army daunted Geoffrey of Ville-hardouin: 'you would have thought that the whole world was there assembled'. Another witness believed that the Greeks had seventeen divisions of men compared to the crusaders' seven, but the westerners' mounted men, who probably numbered around 1,000, took the initiative and advanced. The Byzantine army seemed to cover the plain, flanked to one side by the walls of Constantinople which were also crammed with troops. As the Greeks moved forwards too, the westerners seemed briefly on the verge of losing formation—one group wanted to keep going and, in chivalric fashion, viewed the pause proposed by the others as a loss of honour. Fortunately, the moment passed and the battle line held: the crusaders waited for the onslaught, yet, incredibly, it never came. The Emperor ordered a retreat back into the city and the bemused and relieved westerners watched their opponents march away. Whatever tactical reasons lay behind this move, psychologically it appeared to all as a devastating admission of defeat. The crusaders wrote that 'astounded at our steadfastness (given our small number), he ignominiously turned his reins and retreated'; the Byzantine writer Niketas Choniates wrote that Alexius 'returned to the city in utter disgrace'. That same night the emperor fled into exile and the following day the crusaders and Prince Alexius entered the city in triumph.

Ten months later, the crusaders had to break into the city a second time. In the interim, their hopes of receiving the support promised by the Prince (now Emperor Alexius IV) had evaporated. The Byzantines resented his 'barbarian' allies and suspected the Venetians of being motivated by a desire to secure commercial privileges. When Alexius IV started pressurising his people for the money he owed the crusaders, they began to turn against him; equally, the westerners were increasingly angry at the Emperor's failure to fulfil his side of the bargain. Eventually, Alexius IV's position became untenable and he was murdered by the virulently anti-western noble known as Murtzuphlus, a name that denoted his huge eyebrows that joined together on his forehead. Murtzuphlus intensified aggression towards the crusaders and they began to struggle to find sufficient food supplies.

Thus, by March 1204, the westerners were camped outside a deeply hostile city, thousands of miles from home, with only limited provisions and facing increasingly frequent assaults from a man who had murdered their ally, the rightful ruler of Byzantium. Their position desperate, they felt compelled to attack Constantinople, and justified in doing so. As the crusade progressed, Pope Innocent III had issued edicts forbidding attacks on Christian lands, but by this stage the churchmen in the crusader army argued that they had sufficient cause to fight the 'heretics'. The longstanding effects of the schism were brought to bear and the Byzantines were described as 'the enemies of God' in a sermon delivered to the troops. In opposing the crusade they might also be seen to be hampering God's work, which was another reason to incur divine disapproval.

On April 9th, 1204, therefore, the crusaders launched an attack on the sea walls along the Golden Horn. Once again their ships were topped with huge and unwieldy siege towers. Some bore walkways, made from ships' yard-arms 110 feet long, lashed high on the masts, 95 feet above deck. Handrails and fire-resistant coverings of hide were added to protect those inside as they prepared to try to get a foothold on the walls.

This time, however, the Byzantines were well prepared. Murtzuphlus had ordered enormous wooden constructions, some six or seven storeys high according to contemporaries, to be erected on top of the existing walls to prevent the crusaders from gaining access. The crusaders began their assault, but the

Greeks stood firm and they were forced to withdraw. Murtzuphlus and his people were jubilant; they mocked and jeered at their enemies and some dropped their trousers and exposed their backsides in contempt.

The crusaders were despondent. Their expedition, which had set out in such splendour almost two years previously, appeared to be foundering on the shores of the Bosphorus. They would either face death or imprisonment at the hands of the Greeks, be forced to return home in disgrace, or else struggle on to the Levant where, penniless and tired, they could hope to achieve little. The leadership steeled the men for one final effort, and on April 12th, another attack was launched.

All through the morning the battle raged and it seemed as if the Byzantines were poised to gain the upper hand again. Then, just after midday, the crusaders received a crucial stroke of good luck: the wind began to blow from the north and their ships, which had been unable to reach the walls along the Golden Horn, were able to move up close. Two of the largest vessels, the *Paradise* and the *Lady Pilgrim,* had been tied together to create a larger fighting platform and the great siege equipment reached out to embrace one of Constantinople's towers.

The first man across, a Venetian, was killed, but the second, Andrew of Dureboise, managed to survive and enable a tower to be taken. Further along, Aleaumes of Clari squeezed through a small hole created in the walls and fought off enough Greeks to allow his comrades to follow him in. This astonishing feat was the trigger to the collapse of Byzantine resistance and the crusaders began to pour into the city. The toughness acquired on the tournament fields of Europe, the shared bond of their long expedition and the skills of the Venetian sailors enabled them to exploit the favourable elements and to capture the city.

That same night Murtzuphlus fled. Over the next few days the westerners began to put the city to the sword. Many of its citizens were slaughtered and women of all ages were raped as the crusaders ruthlessly despoiled the metropolis. The great cathedral of the Hagia Sophia was stripped of its priceless relics and the hundreds of churches and palaces of Constantinople were pillaged.

To the crusaders, God had approved their actions by granting them victory and many returned home proudly bearing precious relics. At first, Pope Innocent III was delighted but, as news of the atrocities became clear, he changed his view and began to express anger and disgust at the westerners' actions. He accused one senior noble of 'turning away from the purity of your vow when you took up arms not against Saracens but Christians . . . preferring earthly wealth to celestial treasures'.

On May 16th, 1204, as the crusaders gathered in the Hagia Sophia to acclaim Baldwin, Count of Flanders, the first Latin Emperor of Constantinople, some may have reflected how fate had conspired to bring them to the Bosphorus. An expedition of warriors sworn to liberate the Holy Land had created a new outpost of the Catholic Church, yet it was at the expense of fellow-Christians. In pursuing their attempts to sustain the crusade to the Holy Land, they had become tragically sidetracked. Until the murder of Alexius IV their hopes might have been realised, but after this they were trapped. Ironically, in the long run, the need to support the new Latin Empire of Constantinople against Byzantine counter attacks proved a drain on the crusading resources of the West, and by 1261 Constantinople was again in Greek hands. Yet it was the unleashing of the tensions generated through arduous months camped outside Constantinople, coupled with longstanding problems between Byzantium and the West, that was to leave a legacy of ill-feeling. To the Greeks, the barbarians of Europe had lived up to their reputation.

JONATHAN PHILLIPS is Senior Lecturer in History at Royal Holloway, University of London.

This article first appeared in *History Today*, May 2004, pp. 21–28. Copyright © 2004 by History Today, Ltd. Reprinted by permission.

Monsoons, Mude and Gold

The "global economy" of the Middle Ages was created by linking the Indian Ocean trading networks with those of the Mediterranean Sea and its African and European hinterlands. By the eighth century, Spain and the African shores of the Mediterranean were part of the expanding empire that Muslims called *dar al-islam* ("the house of Islam") and had commercial links, both maritime and overland, with Egypt and Syria. Between the years 800 and 1000, the Mediterranean was dominated by Muslim shipping.

PAUL LUNDE

The Fatimid Dynasty arose in what is now Tunisia in the early 10th century. Their subsequent invasion of Egypt gave them control of the most important port of the eastern Mediterranean: Alexandria. This famous port linked the new Fatimid capital of Cairo, founded in 969, to the whole Mediterranean world via the Nile. With the conquest of Egypt, the Fatimids made a concerted drive to shift the economic center of the Islamic world from Baghdad, capital of their political rivals, the Abbasids, to Cairo. They revived the Red Sea as the principal conduit of maritime trade with the Indian Ocean, restoring that route to the role it had played in Ptolemaic and Roman times.

It was during the Fatimid period (909–1171) that the European economy began to recover from the barbarian invasions that had put an end to the Roman Empire.

European courts began to demand the goods that the Indian Ocean trading networks supplied to Alexandria and Constantinople. These products, together with ceramics, textiles and sugar from Egypt and Syria, reached European markets almost exclusively through the Italian maritime republics of Amalfi, Pisa, Genoa and Venice. By the 15th century, Venice had eclipsed its competitors and established a virtual monopoly of the eastern trade, leaving Genoa to concentrate on trade with Spain, North Africa and the Black Sea.

Synchronized to the clock-like regularity of the monsoon winds in the Indian Ocean was the equally regular sailing of the Venetian convoys, the *mude,* which set out toward the end of August and made their way slowly through the Adriatic and the Aegean to Cyprus and Alexandria, timing their arrival there to coincide with the availability of monsoon-borne goods from the East, and returned to Venice 11 months later. The economies of northern Europe were similarly linked—indirectly, like a train of interlocking gears—to the Indian Ocean monsoon: From Venice, after the return of the mude, spices and textiles traveled overland and by internal waterways to the trade fairs of northern Europe. (Another set of gears driven by the monsoon linked the Indian Ocean economies with China.)

In 1204, Venice led the Crusader conquest of Constantinople. A few years later, a commercial treaty with the Mamluk sultan, ruler of Egypt and Syria, gave the Venetians a virtual monopoly of trade at Alexandria, Tripoli and Beirut. Toward the middle of the 14th century, the number of mude was doubled.

Until the ninth century, Venice had been part of the Byzantine Empire, and it never lost its half-oriental quality. Just as the physical city seems to float magically on the surface of the lagoon, belonging neither to land nor sea, Venice did not seem to fully belong to the European world in which it was tenuously anchored. Here was a city devoted entirely to trade, with the full apparatus of money, banks, credit and letters of exchange—all uncanny mysteries to most of northern Europe. The Venetian capacity to transform humble products like salt, grain and cloth into gold was to outsiders a kind of alchemy.

The famous Venetian Arsenal, immortalized by Dante in Canto XXI of the *Inferno,* was the largest industrial site in Europe. Galleys were built and fitted out on an assembly-line basis that seemed little short of miraculous to visitors. Pero Tafur, a Castilian nobleman who visited the city in 1438, was astonished to see 10 galleys readied for sea, fully crewed, provisioned and armed, in three hours flat.

He was equally astonished to find Spanish fruit for sale in Venice as fresh and cheap as at home. The markets were full of goods from Syria too, he wrote, and even from India, "since the Venetians navigate all over the world." But the Venetians of course did not sail to India: The spices and textiles in Venice had come from Alexandria, shipped there from India and points east via Aden and Jiddah.

The Venetians' commercial dream, which the Portuguese would inherit, was to break the Muslim monopoly of the Indian Ocean trade.

Roman Gold, Persian Silver

Cosmas Indicopleustes ("Cosmas the Traveler to India"), who wrote soon after AD 547, tells the story of a Roman merchant from Egypt named Sopatro who met the Persian ambassador at the court of one of the kings of Sri Lanka. "Which of your kings is the richest and most powerful?" asked the king. "Ours is the most powerful, magnificent and rich," answered the Persian ambassador. "And you, Roman, what do you have to say to that?" asked the king. Sopatro answered, "If you want the truth, you have both kings right here. Look at each and see for yourself which is the most brilliant and powerful." "What do you mean: I have both kings before me?" asked the king. "You have both their coins," answered Sopatro. "You have the *nomisma* of one and the *drachma* of the other. Look at both and know the truth." The king ordered both coins to be brought. The Egyptian nomisma was of pure gold, splendid and beautiful; the Persian drachma was of silver and, to tell the truth, could not compare with the gold piece. The king, after looking carefully at both sides of each coin, praised the nomisma and said, "In truth, the Romans are splendid, powerful and wise."

Venice had long dreamed of breaking the Muslim monopoly of the Indian Ocean trade. A hundred years before Pero Tafur's visit, the Venetian traveler Marin Sanuto put forward a plan to outflank Egypt and seize control of the Indian Ocean trade by launching ships in the Red Sea and the Arabian Gulf. Although impractical, his plan nevertheless reveals the overweening confidence and ambition of the Venetian Republic.

As a maritime republic dedicated to international trade, Venice was an anomaly in a feudal Europe that measured wealth by land, not money. In 1423, as the Doge Tommaso Mocenigo lay dying, he wrote in his last testament: "If you heed my advice, you will find yourselves masters of the gold of the Christians; the whole world will fear and revere you." He was stating the obvious: Venice functioned on gold. It was gold that bought their cargoes, gold that supplied their city with grain, gold that built their ships. Sooner or later, the gold of northern Europe and Africa found its way to Venice.

The Venetian gold ducat, first issued in 1282, was of exceptional purity and was eagerly sought throughout Europe and the East. The year before Mocenigo died, the Arab chronicler al-Fasi could write: "In our time the Venetian ducat has invaded the major cities of the world: Cairo, the whole of Syria, the Hijaz and Yemen, to the point that it has become the most commonly used currency." The ducat undoubtedly voyaged to India long before the Portuguese.

"Gold equals fear plus respect" is a peculiarly Venetian equation. In the feudal world, fear and respect were attributes of kingship. The power of the ruler was derived from his lands and the number of men he could mount. Venice, which had neither king nor lands, made do instead with the king of metals, to which the traditional fear and respect were transferred.

In the Islamic world, gold and silver currency had been issued since 691, when the first dinar was struck at Damascus.

Both the coin and the word derived from the Byzantine *denarion,* just as the Islamic silver coin, the *dirham,* was based on the Byzantine drachme. Gold dinar and silver dirham together formed the bimetallic monetary system that Muslim writers referred to as *al-naqdayn,* "the two coins."

In the Islamic world, gold was a tool. Mocenigo's equation, in which fear and respect could be had for gold, would have sounded blasphemous to Muslims, for whom it is God alone who commands fear and respect. Muslims believed that gold and silver must circulate, and this circulation, called *rawaj,* was a social and religious duty. Hoarding gold and silver was forbidden by the Qur'an: "Those who store up gold and silver and do not spend them in the way of God, tell them of a painful chastisement!" The cosmographer al-Qawini, writing only a decade or so after the minting of the first florin, says:

Gold is the noblest of the blessings of Almighty God upon his servants, for it is the foundation of the affairs of this world and brings order to the affairs of mankind. . . . With silver and gold coins, everything can be bought and sold. They must circulate, unlike other forms of wealth, for it is not desirable for anyone to accumulate silver and gold. . . . Anyone who stores them up destroys the wisdom created by God, just as if one imprisoned the qadi of a town and prevented him from carrying out his duties toward the people."

On the eve of the Islamic conquests in the early seventh century, however, there was a large and powerful state in which gold, the regulator of the affairs of men, was imprisoned. This was Sasanian Persia. Luxury goods from India, Southeast Asia and China passed through Sasanian hands on their way to Byzantium, but the gold the Byzantines paid for them never returned. The Sasanians themselves only circulated silver.

The Arab conquest of Persia thus released huge quantities of gold into the world economy, first in the form of booty, then in the form of taxes levied in gold. Still more gold was obtained from the church treasuries in conquered Byzantine territories and from taxes levied on the non-Muslim population. And astounding quantities were obtained from the systematic looting of pharaonic tombs in Egypt, a practice that went on for more than a millennium.

The release of this flood of gold was comparable to the release of the Aztec and Inca gold hoards at the hands of the Spanish conquistadors eight centuries later. Just as the incredible wealth of Mexico and Peru quickly evaporated and forced the Spaniards to look for new sources of precious metals, so the supplies of "old" gold in the victorious Muslim empire soon needed to be supplemented.

By the 14th century, Africa was supplying as much as two-thirds of the world's gold.

There were a number of sources: Russia, Central Asia beyond the Oxus River, Afghanistan, western Arabia (the Hijaz) and the famous Egyptian mines of Wadi 'Allaqi south of Aswan. But by far the richest were in Africa south of the Sahara, the area the Arabs called *bilad alsudan,* "the land of

How the Monsoon Works

The word "monsoon" comes from the Arabic *mawsim,* meaning "season." In Arabic, *mawsim* refers to the period of time in which ships could safely depart from port, as in *mawsim 'adani,* "the season of Aden." Collectively, these times were called *mawasim al-asfar,* "sailing seasons." The regular periods of northeast and southwest winds that we call the monsoon are called by the Arabs *rih al-azyab* and *rih al-kaws,* respectively.

While there are monsoon systems that affect parts of North America, Central America and northern Australia, the largest is found in the area of the Earth's largest landmass: the Indian subcontinent and eastern Asia. Generally speaking, monsoon systems are powered by the seasonal warming and cooling of very large continental air masses, and depend on the fact that temperatures over land change faster than temperatures over oceans.

From the spring equinox through summer, warming air over southern Asia rises, drawing in toward land the relatively cooler and more humid ocean air. This creates southwest winds heavy with moisture. As the ocean air warms and rises in turn, the moisture condenses, resulting in the torrential monsoon rains.

From the fall equinox through winter, the system reverses as relatively warmer ocean air rises, drawing after it the relatively cooler dry air above the land. This creates northeast winds with cool, sunny and dry weather.

From mid-March, traders knew, the prevailing wind blew from the southwest, and the last ships left Yemen eastbound for India by mid-September, so they could complete their voyage before the northeast monsoon began. Westbound, the first ships left western India for Yemen on October 16, arriving—if all went well—a mere 18 days later. If departure and arrival dates were carefully enough calculated, the turnaround times could be very short.

Each sailing season was divided into two major periods, one at the beginning, called *awwal al-zaman,* "first of the season," and one at the end, called *akhir al-zaman,* "last of the season." Each offered an advantage: The convoys that left during the first of the season found the readiest markets, and those that left at the last had the shortest turnaround time.

Of the two monsoons, the southwest was the more dangerous. In June and July, heavy swells and the famous torrential rains closed the ports of western India. The northeast monsoon, on the other hand, beginning in August in western India, meant clear sailing with steady winds and few squalls. Because it arose on the mainland, it carried little or no rain, and could be sailed with ease throughout its season.

Overland contact between the North African coast and sub-Saharan Africa probably dates back to the days of the Phoenicians. The introduction of the camel to North Africa in Roman times made regular trade across the Sahara economically viable, but it was not until the foundation in 747 of the caravan city of Sijilmasa, in southern Morocco, that the gold trade with the south came to be organized on a regular basis.

This was cheap gold. The lands south of the Sahara had no salt, and men suffering from salt deficiency were willing to trade gold for an equal weight of salt. The resulting trans-Saharan trade led to the rise of powerful African kingdoms in the south.

One of the largest was the Mandingo kingdom of Mali, whose rulers seem to have become Muslims sometime during the first quarter of the 12th century. At its height, the kingdom stretched from the Atlantic to the upper Niger. The arrival of the Mandingo ruler Mansa Musa in Cairo in 1324, on his way to Makkah to perform the pilgrimage, caused a sensation. He crossed the Sahara accompanied by thousands of followers and 100 camel-loads of gold attended by 500 slaves—each bearing a golden staff weighing nearly three kilograms (6 lb). Mansa Musa spent so lavishly in the markets of Cairo that the price of gold fell and took years to recover. Stories of his fabled wealth reached Europe.

African gold attracted merchants from Portugal, Spain, Majorca, France and Italy, all of whom had traded with North African ports since the 10th century. In the 12th, the Genoese sailed through the Strait of Gibraltar and began trading with the towns on the Atlantic coast of Morocco. In 1253, the year after the first gold coins were struck in Genoa and Florence, they established a trading station farther south in Safi, where they perhaps first learned of the gold-producing lands south of the Sahara.

These European merchants funneled African gold into the rapidly monetizing European economy. Just as in Roman times, both silver and gold then flowed eastward to pay for imported luxuries, ultimately reaching India and China.

The gold that flowed to India never returned. It was hoarded, in the form of temple treasure or jewelry, rather than circulated. Just as Sasanian Persia had been, India was the graveyard of gold.

It was just the opposite in China. Gold held no monetary value to the Chinese, and China always exchanged gold for silver at an advantageous rate, thus draining silver from the world economy. Although it did not serve as currency—the standard currency was copper "cash"—China absorbed vast quantities of silver, which was used as bullion for major payments. And because China paid for her imports with silks and ceramics, silver rarely left the Chinese empire, except as the result of invasion from the western steppes and, in the late 18th century, British insistence that China should pay for opium with silver. Just as India was the graveyard of gold, China was the graveyard of silver.

In fact it has been estimated that between a third and a half of all the silver produced in Mexico and Peru found its way to China. Between 1531 and 1660, the fabulous mines of Zacatecas and Potosí officially sent 16,887 tons of silver to Spain; unofficially, that figure should probably be doubled to include

the Blacks." Alluvial gold was found along the upper reaches of the Senegal and Niger rivers, and along the Guinea coast. These areas, together with gold-bearing regions in southeastern Africa near Sofala, were so productive that by the 14th century Africa was supplying as much as two-thirds of the world's gold.

contraband and private exports. Although small by modern standards—world silver production reached 16,117 metric tons in 2004 alone—it was a huge amount for the pre-modern world economy to absorb. A great deal of it went to India too: The coins of the Mughal rulers of India were minted from New World silver. In the late 16th and 17th centuries, the Spanish piece of eight, prototype of the dollar, circulated throughout Asia, finally ending its journey in the Celestial Kingdom. The piece of eight, containing 25.5 grams (about ¾ oz) of pure silver, had become the first global currency, used in all of the New World, Europe and Asia.

This flow of precious metals from West to East is a constant of pre-modern world history. From classical times until the late 18th century, the West had a trade deficit with the East. The imbalance was caused by the failure of European products and manufactured goods, with a few exceptions, to find buyers in the East. Sir Thomas Roe, ambassador to the Mughal court in the 17th century, was chagrined to discover that Indian craftsmen took no more than a day to reproduce the fine gifts, including paintings, that he had brought to the emperor. European merchants who wanted the textiles, ceramics, metalwork, dyestuffs and spices of the Islamic world generally had to pay cash.

The Mediterranean trading network, led by the commercial republics of Italy, was thus driven to a constant search for new supplies of silver and gold. It was this search that led to the Portuguese exploratory expeditions down the west coast of Africa in the 15th century, journeys that culminated in 1498 in Vasco da Gama's discovery of the sea route to India. It was the search for gold that led Columbus to seek an Atlantic route to Japan and China, lands he mistakenly believed to be rich in gold. It is one of the ironies of history that instead he discovered a new world, richer in precious metals than the old.

Gold is incorruptible, a metaphor for purity and eternal life. It seemed logical to the men of the Middle Ages that this purest of metals should abound in, or near, the Earthly Paradise, which scripture placed in the East, where the sun rose.

Four rivers flowed from the Earthly Paradise and one of them was the Nile. Then what easier way to reach the Earthly Paradise than to follow the Nile to its source? Rumors of a great river in sub-Saharan Africa had circulated since antiquity, and it was logical to suppose that this must be the Nile. As the Portuguese explorers moved down the western African coast, they identified each of the great rivers they encountered—the Senegal, the Niger and the Congo—in turn with the Nile, eagerly questioning local people about the lands where each river arose.

These geographical misconceptions were extraordinarily fruitful. Without them, it is doubtful the Portuguese would ever have begun the punishing series of expeditions around Africa that finally led to the sea route to India. The myth of the Earthly Paradise had a powerful political dimension as well. It was widely believed in Europe that somewhere near the Earthly Paradise lay the realm of a Christian monarch named Prester John. When the legend first arose in the 12th century, his kingdom was located in Asia, and is so marked on some maps.

Closer acquaintance with Asia, the result of the travels of men like Marco Polo and William of Rubruck, did not put an end to the legend of Prester John. Instead, his realm was displaced to lesser-known lands, first to India, then to Africa. Pilgrims had learned from Ethiopian priests in Jerusalem of the Christian kingdom of Ethiopia, and in 1481 a mission from Ethiopia somehow found its way to Lisbon. Not long afterward the Portuguese King João II dispatched an expedition up the Senegal River, which he identified with the Nile, searching for the land of Prester John. This was not the first such expedition. When the Venetian explorer Ca' da Mosto reached the Cape Verde Islands in 1456, sailing under Portuguese auspices, he had reported that he had heard that the realm of Prester John lay 300 leagues into the African interior. How hearts must have leapt in Lisbon! All that was needed was to make contact with Prester John and his army, and the Islamic world would be outflanked and the Muslim monopoly of the eastern trade at last broken.

That gold would abound in the Earthly Paradise, and that the mythical king Prester John would help the Europeans discover it—if only he could be found—were entirely rational ideas of the time.

Legend, politics and economics were intimately intertwined. In 1487, the same year Bartolomeu Dias set off on his epoch-making voyage around the Cape, King João sent the Arabic-speaking Pero de Covilhã overland to search for the kingdom of Prester John. He visited Makkah, gathered information on trade in the Indian Ocean, sailed down the East African coast as far south as Sofala and eventually made his way to Ethiopia. He had found the land of Prester John, but, sadly, it was not the Earthly Paradise. This disappointment was palliated by a single fact which he reported back to Portugal by messenger before his 30-year captivity in Ethiopia: It was possible to reach India by sailing around Africa. He could only have learned a geographical fact of such overwhelming importance from Indian Ocean sailors, probably in Sofala. His report reached the Portuguese court and confirmed Dias's discovery. And incidentally, it showed that the true shape of Africa was known to the Arabs before Vasco da Gama's voyage.

Men had speculated on the true shape and extent of Africa since the days of Herodotus in the fifth century BC, and though Herodotus himself is the source of two accounts of the circumnavigation of Africa, later Greek writers uniformly dismissed both as fantasy. They followed Aristotle and Ptolemy, who believed that Africa was joined to Asia somewhere east of India, making the Indian Ocean a landlocked sea like the Mediterranean. This view, with some modifications, became geographical orthodoxy for medieval scholars in both Europe and the Islamic world.

Toward the end of the 13th century, advances in shipbuilding and navigation nourished Europeans' curiosity about what lay beyond the Pillars of Hercules. The round ship, adopted from Atlantic shipbuilders, and the compass, introduced by the Arabs from China, made Atlantic voyages possible. In 1291, two brothers from Genoa, Ugolino and Vadino Vivaldi,

Barter and the Monetary Frontier

On the west coast of Africa, the coastal settlements of the Portuguese, beginning in 1455 with São Jorge da Mina, traded for gold from the remote interior, where tribes mined it and exchanged it by barter for salt, cloth and trinkets. On the east coast of Africa, the gold was bought in the interior by intermediaries, also through barter, and then brought to the Arab merchants at the port of Sofala. In both places, it was rumored that the tribesmen who dug the gold from the ground were cannibals. The same stories were told throughout the Indonesian archipelago. Barter and reputed cannibalism apparently marked the limits of the Mediterranean–Indian Ocean monetary economy. Even peoples who lay beyond the linguistic and monetary boundaries of the expanding world economy were its silent partners. These frontiers between monetary and non-monetary economies coincided with the shifting boundaries between the known and the unknown, both geographical and cultural.

passed through the Pillars of Hercules and voyaged south down the West African coast, *"volentes ire in Levante ad partes Indiarum"* ("desiring to go east, to the regions of India"). It was the first recorded attempt to circumnavigate Africa since antiquity. This single phrase from the chronicle recording their voyage could serve as the motto for the history of European maritime expansion.

The Vivaldi brothers vanished at sea. What is remarkable about their voyage is that they thought they could reach India by sailing around Africa. Why did they think this was possible?

One of the few Muslim scientists to challenge geographical orthodoxy was al-Biruni, who wrote in the later 10th century. This great scientist, in one work, stated quite categorically that no one could sail the sea south of Sofala on Africa's east coast, and that no one foolish enough to try had ever returned. Yet in another work, meditating on a story he had read in al-Mas'udi of the discovery in the Mediterranean of a carved plank from an Indian Ocean vessel, al-Biruni concluded that it could only have come there by drifting around Africa—and indeed a sketch map in one of his works clearly shows Africa as a peninsula.

A similar story occurs in the accounts of the Roman geographer Strabo, so both the Arabic and the classical sources contain two diametrically opposed views of the shape of Africa. In the "non-Ptolemaic" tradition, found in the earliest Arab geographers, the ocean surrounded the world, and hence the Atlantic and the Indian Ocean were one and the same body of water. The Ptolemaic tradition had the eastern shore of Africa joined to China.

There was an almost uncrossable divide between the theories of the geographers and the practical experience of the seamen who sailed the Indian Ocean. It only began to be bridged in the 15th century, when the Arab navigator Ahmad ibn Majid codified the experience of a lifetime navigating the Indian Ocean and the lower reaches of the Red Sea in a series of remarkable

works. In one of these, the *Kitab al-Fawa'id fi Usul 'Ilm al-Bahr wa' l-Qawa'id (The Book of Useful Information on the Principles and Rules of Navigation),* written about 1490, he describes the possibility of circumnavigating Africa from east to west as if it were common knowledge.

Ibn Majid names the major East African ports from Mogadishu to Sofala and then says, "When you reach Sofala you pass the island of Madagascar on your left, separated from the coast on your right. There the land turns to the northwest, where the regions of darkness begin. . . . Then you come to the coast of the Maghrib, which begins at Masa. . . . When you have passed Masa, you come to Safi. . . . Now you have reached the Moroccan coast. You then enter the Strait of Ceuta, the entrance to the Mediterranean." The route is described in a clockwise direction, showing the writer's Indian Ocean orientation. It is clear that toward the end of the 15th century, outside conventional learned circles, new information about the true shape of Africa was beginning to circulate.

Two far-off events at the beginning of the 15th century had profound repercussions in the Indian Ocean: the Portuguese capture in 1415 of Ceuta, on the Moroccan coast opposite Gibraltar, and the death in 1405 of the Central Asian conqueror Tamerlane (Timur). Ceuta was the port from which the Muslim invasion of Spain had been launched in 711; its capture marked the beginning of the Portuguese push around Africa that culminated in the discovery of the sea route to India.

Azurara, the official chronicler of the capture of Ceuta, painted a glowing picture of the town, which he called "the key to the whole Mediterranean Sea." The city astonished the Portuguese soldiers, who were amazed at its fine houses, the gold, silver and jewels in the markets and the cosmopolitan population. They saw men "from Ethiopia, Alexandria, Syria, Barbary, Assyria . . . as well as those from the Orient who lived on the other side of the Euphrates River, and from the Indies." Azurara clearly states that one of the motives of the expedition was to seize control of the African gold trade: Forty years later, with the establishment of the fortress of São Jorge da Mina on the Guinea coast, 25 to 35 percent of the gold that had formerly made its way across the Sahara to North African markets and to Mamluk Egypt now passed into the hands of the Portuguese instead.

"Desiring to go east, to the regions of India," the Genoese Vivaldi brothers made the first recorded European attempt to circumnavigate Africa in 1291. They vanished.

In Asia in the late 1300's, the armies of Tamerlane, a descendant of Genghis Khan, swept over Iran, Iraq and Syria. The major cities of the Islamic heartlands were destroyed with great loss of life. To the east, Delhi was sacked in 1398, and China was spared only by Tamerlane's death. The overland Silk Roads from China to the West were disrupted as the cities they had linked were destroyed. Concerned at the disruption of their overland export trade and anxious to explore maritime alternatives, the Chinese in 1402 sent an embassy to the newly founded city of Malacca, in what is today Malaysia, a port that would grow to be the linchpin of trade between the Indian Ocean and the Pacific. In 1405, the year Tamerlane died, the Ming emperor of China dispatched the first of seven great argosies to the Indian Ocean under the admiral Zheng He.

At the same time that the vast Chinese fleets crossed and recrossed the Indian Ocean, Muslim sultanates began to appear in Malaysia, Indonesia and the Philippines. Ahmad ibn Majid composed his navigational works and, in the West, European ships sailed into the Atlantic. The simultaneity of this sudden burst of maritime activity is fascinating. The Orient was reaching out to the Occident at the very time the Occident was "desiring to go east, to the regions of India."

How a Mysterious Disease Laid Low Europe's Masses

In the 1300s, a third of the population died of plague brought by fleas, shocking the medieval world to its foundations.

CHARLES L. MEE JR.

In all likelihood, a flea riding on the hide of a black rat entered the Italian port of Messina in 1347, perhaps down a hawser tying a ship up at the dock. The flea had a gut full of the bacillus *Yersinia pestis*. The flea itself was hardly bigger than the letter "o" on this page, but it could carry several hundred thousand bacilli in its intestine.

Scholars today cannot identify with certainty which species of flea (or rat) carried the plague. One candidate among the fleas is *Xenopsylla cheopis,* which looks like a deeply bent, bearded old man with six legs. It is slender and bristly, with almost no neck and no waist, so that it can slip easily through the forest of hair in which it lives. It is outfitted with a daggerlike proboscis for piercing the skin and sucking the blood of its host. And it is cunningly equipped to secrete a substance that prevents coagulation of the host's blood. Although *X. cheopis* can go for weeks without feeding, it will eat every day if it can, taking its blood warm.

One rat on which fleas feed, the black rat *(Rattus rattus),* also known as the house rat, roof rat or ship rat, is active mainly at night. A rat can fall 50 feet and land on its feet with no injury. It can scale a brick wall or climb up the inside of a pipe only an inch and a half in diameter. It can jump a distance of two feet straight up and four horizontally, and squeeze through a hole the size of a quarter. Black rats have been found still swimming days after their ship has sunk at sea.

A rat can gnaw its way through almost anything—paper, wood, bone, mortar, half-inch sheet metal. It gnaws constantly. Indeed, it *must* gnaw constantly. Its incisors grow four to five inches a year: if it were to stop gnawing, its lower incisors would eventually grow—as sometimes happens when a rat loses an opposing tooth—until the incisors push up into the rat's brain, killing it. It prefers grain, if possible, but also eats fish, eggs, fowl and meat—lambs, piglets and the flesh of helpless infants or adults. If nothing else is available, a rat will eat manure and drink urine.

Rats prefer to move no more than a hundred feet from their nests. But in severe drought or famine, rats can begin to move en masse for great distances, bringing with them any infections they happen to have picked up, infections that may be killing them but not killing them more rapidly than they breed.

Rats and mice harbor a number of infections that may cause diseases in human beings. A black rat can even tolerate a moderate amount of the ferocious *Yersinia pestis* bacillus in its system without noticeable ill effects. But bacilli breed even more extravagantly than fleas or rats, often in the millions. When a bacillus finally invades the rat's pulmonary or nervous system, it causes a horrible, often convulsive, death, passing on a lethal dose to the bloodsucking fleas that ride on the rat's hide.

The Ultimate Bacillus Breeder

When an afflicted rat dies, its body cools, so that the flea, highly sensitive to changes in temperature, will find another host. The flea can, if need be, survive for weeks at a time without a rat host. It can take refuge anywhere, even in an abandoned rat's nest or a bale of cloth. A dying rat may liberate scores of rat fleas. More than that, a flea's intestine happens to provide ideal breeding conditions for the bacillus, which will eventually multiply so prodigiously as finally to block the gut of the flea entirely. Unable to feed or digest blood, the flea desperately seeks another host. But now, as it sucks blood, it spits some out at the same time. Each time the flea stops sucking for a moment, it is capable of pumping thousands of virulent bacilli back into its host. Thus bacilli are passed from rat to flea to rat, contained, ordinarily, within a closed community.

For millions of years, there has been a reservoir of *Yersinia pestis* living as a permanently settled parasite—passed back and forth among fleas and rodents in warm, moist nests—in the wild rodent colonies of China, India, the southern part of the Soviet Union and the western United States. Probably there will always be such reservoirs—ready to be stirred up by sudden climatic change or ecological disaster. Even last year, four authentic cases of bubonic plague were confirmed in New Mexico and Arizona. Limited outbreaks and some fatalities have occurred in the United States for years, in fact, but the disease doesn't spread, partly for reasons we don't understand, partly because patients can now be treated with antibiotics.

And at least from biblical times on, there have been sporadic allusions to plagues, as well as carefully recorded outbreaks. The emperor Justinian's Constantinople, for instance, capital of the Roman empire in the East, was ravaged by plague in 541 and 542, felling perhaps 40 percent of the city's population. But none of the biblical or Roman plagues seemed so emblematic of horror and devastation as the Black Death that struck Europe in 1347. Rumors of fearful pestilence in China and throughout the East had reached Europe by 1346. "India was depopulated," reported one chronicler, "Tartary, Mesopotamia, Syria, Armenia, were covered with dead bodies; the Kurds fled in vain to the mountains. In Caramania and Caesarea none were left alive."

Untold millions would die in China and the rest of the East before the plague subsided again. By September of 1345, the *Yersinia pestis* bacillus, probably carried by rats, reached the Crimea, on the northern coast of the Black Sea, where Italian merchants had a good number of trading colonies.

From the shores of the Black Sea, the bacillus seems to have entered a number of Italian ports. The most famous account has to do with a ship that docked in the Sicilian port of Messina in 1347. According to an Italian chronicler named Gabriele de Mussis, Christian merchants from Genoa and local Muslim residents in the town of Caffa on the Black Sea got into an argument; a serious fight ensued between the merchants and a local army led by a Tartar lord. In the course of an attack on the Christians, the Tartars were stricken by plague. From sheer spitefulness, their leader loaded his catapults with dead bodies and hurled them at the Christian enemy, in hopes of spreading disease among them. Infected with the plague, the Genoese sailed back to Italy, docking first at Messina.

Although de Mussis, who never traveled to the Crimea, may be a less-than-reliable source, his underlying assumption seems sound. The plague did spread along established trade routes. (Most likely, though, the pestilence in Caffa resulted from an infected population of local rats, not from the corpses lobbed over the besieged city's walls.)

In any case, given enough dying rats and enough engorged and frantic fleas, it will not be long before the fleas, in their search for new hosts, leap to a human being. When a rat flea senses the presence of an alternate host, it can jump very quickly and as much as 150 times its length. The average for such jumps is about six inches horizontally and four inches straight up in the air. Once on human skin, the flea will not travel far before it begins to feed.

The first symptoms of bubonic plague often appear within several days: headache and a general feeling of weakness, followed by aches and chills in the upper leg and groin, a white coating on the tongue, rapid pulse, slurred speech, confusion, fatigue, apathy and a staggering gait. A blackish pustule usually will form at the point of the fleabite. By the third day, the lymph nodes begin to swell. Because the bite is commonly in the leg, it is the lymph nodes of the groin that swell, which is how the disease got its name. The Greek word for "groin" is *boubon*—thus, bubonic plague. The swelling will be tender, perhaps as large as an egg. The heart begins to flutter rapidly as it tries to pump blood through swollen, suffocating tissues. Subcutaneous hemorrhaging occurs, causing purplish blotches on the skin. The victim's nervous system begins to collapse, causing dreadful pain and bizarre neurological disorders, from which the "Dance of Death" rituals that accompanied the plague may have taken their inspiration. By the fourth or fifth day, wild anxiety and terror overtake the sufferer—and then a sense of resignation, as the skin blackens and the rictus of death settles on the body.

In 1347, when the plague struck in Messina, townspeople realized that it must have come from the sick and dying crews of the ships at their dock. They turned on the sailors and drove them back out to sea—eventually to spread the plague in other ports. Messina panicked. People ran out into the fields and vineyards and neighboring villages, taking the rat fleas with them.

When the citizens of Messina, already ill or just becoming ill, reached the city of Catania, 55 miles to the south, they were at first taken in and given beds in the hospital. But as the plague began to infect Catania, the townspeople there cordoned off their town and refused—too late—to admit any outsiders. The sick, turning black, stumbling and delirious, were objects more of disgust than of pity; everything about them gave off a terrible stench, it was said, their "sweat, excrement, spittle, breath, so foetid as to be overpowering; urine turbid, thick, black or red. . . ."

Wherever the plague appeared, the suddenness of death was terrifying. Today, even with hand-me-down memories of the great influenza epidemic of 1918 (SMITHSONIAN, January 1989) and the advent of AIDS, it is hard to grasp the strain that the plague put on the physical and spiritual fabric of society. People went to bed perfectly healthy and were found dead in the morning. Priests and doctors who came to minister to the sick, so the wild stories ran, would contract the plague with a single touch and die sooner than the person they had come to help. In his preface to *The Decameron,* a collection of stories told while the plague was raging, Boccaccio reports that he saw two pigs rooting around in the clothes of a man who had just died, and after a few minutes of snuffling, the pigs began to run wildly around and around, then fell dead.

"Tedious were it to recount," Boccaccio thereafter laments, "brother was forsaken by brother, nephew by uncle, brother by sister and, oftentimes, husband by wife; nay what is more and scarcely to be believed, fathers and mothers were found to abandon their own children, untended, unvisited, to their fate, as if they had been strangers. . . ."

In Florence, everyone grew so frightened of the bodies stacked up in the streets that some men, called *becchini,* put themselves out for hire to fetch and carry the dead to mass graves. Having in this way stepped over the boundary into the land of the dead, and no doubt feeling doomed themselves, the *becchini* became an abandoned, brutal lot. Many roamed the streets, forcing their way into private homes and threatening to carry people away if they were not paid off in money or sexual favors.

Visiting Men with Pestilence

Some people, shut up in their houses with the doors barred, would scratch a sign of the cross on the front door, sometimes with the inscription "Lord have mercy on us." In one place, two lovers were supposed to have bathed in urine every morning for protection. People hovered over latrines, breathing in the stench. Others swallowed pus from the boils of plague victims. In Avignon, Pope Clement was said to have sat for weeks between two roaring fires.

The plague spread from Sicily all up and down the Atlantic coast, and from the port cities of Venice, Genoa and Pisa as well as Marseilles, London and Bristol. A multitude of men and women, as Boccaccio writes, "negligent of all but themselves . . . migrated to the country, as if God, in visiting men with this pestilence in requital of their iniquities, would not pursue them with His wrath wherever they might be. . . ."

Some who were not yet ill but felt doomed indulged in debauchery. Others, seeking protection in lives of moderation, banded together in communities to live a separate and secluded life, walking abroad with flowers to their noses "to ward off the stench and, perhaps, the evil airs that afflicted them."

It was from a time of plague, some scholars speculate, that the nursery rhyme "Ring Around the Rosy" derives: the rose-colored "ring" being an early sign that a blotch was about to appear on the skin; "a pocket full of posies" being a device to ward off stench and (it was hoped) the attendant infection; "ashes, ashes" being a reference to "ashes to ashes, dust to dust" or perhaps to the sneezing "a-choo, a-choo" that afflicted those in whom the infection had invaded the lungs—ending, inevitably, in "all fall down."

In Pistoia, the city council enacted nine pages of regulations to keep the plague out—no Pistoian was allowed to leave town to visit any place where the plague was raging; if a citizen did visit a plague-infested area he was not allowed back in the city; no linen or woolen goods were allowed to be imported; no corpses could be brought home from outside the city; attendance at funerals was strictly limited to immediate family. None of these regulations helped.

In Siena, dogs dragged bodies from the shallow graves and left them half-devoured in the streets. Merchants closed their shops. The wool industry was shut down. Clergymen ceased administering last rites. On June 2, 1348, all the civil courts were recessed by the city council. Because so many of the laborers had died, construction of the nave for a great cathedral came to a halt. Work was never resumed: only the smaller cathedral we know today was completed.

In Venice, it was said that 600 were dying every day. In Florence, perhaps half the population died. By the time the plague swept through, as much as one-third of Italy's population had succumbed.

In Milan, when the plague struck, all the occupants of any victim's house, whether sick or well, were walled up inside

together and left to die. Such draconian measures seemed to have been partially successful—mortality rates were lower in Milan than in other cities.

Medieval medicine was at a loss to explain all this, or to do anything about it. Although clinical observation did play some role in medical education, an extensive reliance on ancient and inadequate texts prevailed. Surgeons usually had a good deal of clinical experience but were considered mainly to be skilled craftsmen, not men of real learning, and their experience was not much incorporated into the body of medical knowledge. In 1300, Pope Boniface VIII had published a bull specifically inveighing against the mutilation of corpses. It was designed to cut down on the sale of miscellaneous bones as holy relics, but one of the effects was to discourage dissection.

Physicians, priests and others had theories about the cause of the plague. Earthquakes that released poisonous fumes, for instance. Severe changes in the Earth's temperature creating southerly winds that brought the plague. The notion that the plague was somehow the result of a corruption of the air was widely believed. It was this idea that led people to avoid foul odors by holding flowers to their noses or to try to drive out the infectious foul odors by inhaling the alternate foul odors of a latrine. Some thought that the plague came from the raining down of frogs, toads and reptiles. Some physicians believed one could catch the plague from "lust with old women."

Most Christians believed the cause of the plague was God's wrath at sinful Man.

Both the pope and the king of France sent urgent requests for help to the medical faculty at the University of Paris, then one of the most distinguished medical groups in the Western world. The faculty responded that the plague was the result of a conjunction of the planets Saturn, Mars and Jupiter at 1 P.M. on March 20, 1345, an event that caused the corruption of the surrounding atmosphere.

Ultimately, of course, most Christians believed the cause of the plague was God's wrath at sinful Man. And in those terms, to be sure, the best preventives were prayer, the wearing of crosses and participation in other religious activities. In Orvieto, the town fathers added 50 new religious observances to the municipal calendar. Even so, within five months of the appearance of the plague, Orvieto lost every second person in the town.

There was also some agreement about preventive measures one might take to avoid the wrath of God. Flight was best: away from lowlands, marshy areas, stagnant waters, southern exposures and coastal areas, toward high, dry, cool, mountainous places. It was thought wise to stay indoors all day, to stay cool and to cover any windows that admitted bright sunlight. In addition to keeping flowers nearby, one might burn such aromatic woods as juniper and ash.

The retreat to the mountains, where the density of the rat population was not as great as in urban areas, and where the weather was inimical to rats and fleas, was probably a good idea—as well as perhaps proof, of a kind, of the value of empirical observation. But any useful notion was always mixed in with such wild ideas that it got lost in a flurry of desperate (and often contrary) stratagems. One should avoid bathing because that opened the pores to attack from the corrupt atmosphere, but one should wash face and feet, and sprinkle them with rose water and vinegar. In the morning, one might eat a couple of figs with rue and filberts. One expert advised eating ten-year-old treacle mixed with several dozen items, including chopped-up snake. Rhubarb was recommended, too, along with onions, leeks and garlic. The best spices were myrrh, saffron and pepper, to be taken late in the day. Meat should be roasted, not boiled. Eggs should not be eaten hard-boiled. A certain Gentile di Foligno commended lettuce; the faculty of medicine at the University of Paris advised against it. Desserts were forbidden. One should not sleep during the day. One should sleep first on the right side, then on the left. Exercise was to be avoided because it introduced more air into the body; if one needed to move, one ought to move slowly.

By the fall of 1348, the plague began to abate. But then, just as hopes were rising that it had passed, the plague broke out again in the spring and summer of 1349 in different parts of Europe. This recurrence seemed to prove that the warm weather, and people bathing in warm weather, caused the pores of the skin to open and admit the corrupted air. In other respects, however, the plague remained inexplicable. Why did some people get it and recover, while other seemed not to have got it at all—or at least showed none of its symptoms—yet died suddenly anyway? Some people died in four or five days, others died at once. Some seemed to have contracted the plague from a friend or relative who had it, others had never been near a sick person. The sheer unpredictability of it was terrifying.

In fact, though no one would know for several centuries, there were three different forms of the plague, which ran three different courses. The first was simple bubonic plague, transmitted from rat to person by the bite of the rat flea. The second and likely most common form was pneumonic, which occurred when the bacillus invaded the lungs. After a two- or three-day incubation period, anyone with pneumonic plague would have a severe, bloody cough; the sputum cast into the air would contain *Yersinia pestis.* Transmitted through the air from person to person, pneumonic plague was fatal in 95 to 100 percent of all cases.

The third form of the plague was septocemic, and its precise etiology is not entirely understood even yet. In essence, however, it appears that in cases of septocemic plague the bacillus entered the bloodstream, perhaps at the moment of the fleabite. A rash formed and death occurred within a day, or even within hours, before any swellings appeared. Septocemic plague always turned out to be fatal.

Some people did imagine that the disease might be coming from some animal, and they killed dogs and cats—though never rats. But fleas were so much a part of everyday life that no one seems to have given them a second thought. Upright citizens also killed gravediggers, strangers from other countries, gypsies, drunks, beggars, cripples, lepers and Jews. The first persecution of the Jews seems to have taken place in the South of France in the spring of 1348. That September, at Chillon on Lake Geneva, a group of Jews were accused of poisoning the wells. They were tortured and they confessed, and their confessions were sent to neighboring towns. In Basel all the Jews were locked inside wooden buildings and burned alive. In November, Jews were burned in Solothurn, Zofingen and Stuttgart. Through the winter and into early spring they were burned in Landsberg, Burren, Memmingen, Lindau, Freiburg, Ulm, Speyer, Gotha, Eisenach, Dresden, Worms, Baden and Erfurt. Sixteen thousand were murdered in Strasbourg. In other cities Jews were walled up inside their houses to starve to death. That the Jews were also dying of the plague was not taken as proof that they were not causing it.

Very rarely does a single event change history itself. Yet an event of the magnitude of the Black Death could not fail to have an enormous impact.

On the highways and byways, meanwhile, congregations of flagellants wandered about, whipping themselves twice a day and once during the night for weeks at a time. As they went on their way they attracted hordes of followers and helped spread the plague even farther abroad.

The recurrence of the plague after people thought the worst was over may have been the most devastating development of all. In short, Europe was swept not only by a bacillus but also by a widespread psychic breakdown—by abject terror, panic, rage, vengefulness, cringing remorse, selfishness, hysteria, and above all, by an overwhelming sense of utter powerlessness in the face of an inescapable horror.

After a decade's respite, just as Europeans began to recover their feeling of well-being, the plague struck again in 1361, and again in 1369, and at least once in each decade down to the end of the century. Why the plague faded away is still a mystery that, in the short run, apparently had little to do with improvements in medicine or cleanliness and more to do with some adjustment of equilibrium among the population of rats and fleas. In any case, as agents for Pope Clement estimated in 1351, perhaps 24 million people had died in the first onslaught of the plague; perhaps as many as another 20 million died by the end of the century—in all, it is estimated, one-third of the total population of Europe.

Very rarely does a single event change history by itself. Yet an event of the magnitude of the Black Death could not fail to have had an enormous impact. Ironically, some of the changes brought by the plague were for the good. Not surprisingly, medicine changed—since medicine had so signally failed to be of any help in the hour of greatest need for it. First of all, a great many doctors died—and some simply ran away. "It has pleased God," wrote one Venetian-born physician, "by this terrible mortality to leave our native place so destitute of upright and capable doctors that it may be said not one has been left." By 1349, at the University of Padua there were vacancies in every single chair of medicine and surgery. All this, of course, created room for new people with new ideas. Ordinary people began wanting to get their hands on medical guides and to take command of their own health. And gradually more medical texts began to appear in the vernacular instead of in Latin.

An Old Order Was Besieged

Because of the death of so many people, the relationship between agricultural supply and demand changed radically, too. Agricultural prices dropped precipitously, endangering the fortunes and power of the aristocracy, whose wealth and dominance were based on land. At the same time, because of the deaths of so many people, wages rose dramatically, giving laborers some chance of improving their own conditions of employment. Increasing numbers of people had more money to buy what could be called luxury goods, which affected the nature of business and trade, and even of private well-being. As old relationships, usages and laws broke down, expanding secular concerns and intensifying the struggle between faith and reason, there was a rise in religious, social and political unrest. Religious reformer John Wycliffe, in England, and John Huss, in Bohemia, were among many leaders of sects that challenged church behavior and church doctrine all over Europe. Such complaints eventually led to the Protestant Reformation, and the assertion that Man stood in direct relation to God, without need to benefit from intercession by layers of clergy.

Indeed, the entire structure of feudal society, which had been under stress for many years, was undermined by the plague. The three orders of feudalism—clergy, nobility and peasantry—had been challenged for more than a century by the rise of the urban bourgeoisie, and by the enormous, slow changes in productivity and in the cultivation of arable land. But the plague, ravaging the weakened feudal system from so many diverse and unpredictable quarters, tore it apart.

By far the greatest change in Western civilization that the plague helped hasten was a change of mind. Once the immediate traumas of death, terror and flight had passed through a stricken town, the common lingering emotion was that of fear of God. The subsequent surge of religious fervor in art was in many ways nightmarish. Though medieval religion had dealt with death and dying, and naturally with sin and retribution, it was only after the Black Death that painters so wholeheartedly gave themselves over to pictures brimming with rotting corpses, corpses being consumed by snakes and toads, swooping birds of prey appearing with terrible suddenness, cripples gazing on the figure of death with longing for deliverance, open graves filled with blackened, worm-eaten bodies, devils slashing the faces and bodies of the damned.

Well before the plague struck Europe, the role of the Catholic Church in Western Europe had been changing. The Papacy had grown more secular in its concerns, vying with princes for wealth and power even while attempts at reform were increasing. "God gave us the Papacy," Pope Leo X declared. "Let us enjoy it." The church had suffered a series of damaging losses in the late 1200s—culminating in 1309 when the Papacy moved from Rome to Avignon. But then, the Black Death dealt the church a further blow, for along with renewed fear and the need for new religious zeal came the opposite feeling, that the church itself had failed. Historical changes rarely occur suddenly. The first indications of change from a powerful catalyst usually seem to be mere curiosities, exceptions or aberrations from the prevailing worldview. Only after a time, after the exceptions have accumulated and seem to cohere, do they take on the nature of a historical movement. And only when the exceptions have come to dominate, do they begin to seem typical of the civilization as a whole (and the vestiges of the old civilization to seem like curiosities). This, in any case, is how the great change of mind occurred that defines the modern Western world. While the Black Death alone did not cause these changes, the upheaval it brought about did help set the stage for the new world of Renaissance Europe and the Reformation.

As the Black Death waned in Europe, the power of religion waned with it, leaving behind a population that was gradually but certainly turning its attention to the physical realm in which it lived, to materialism and worldliness, to the terrible power of the world itself, and to the wonder of how it works.

From *Smithsonian*, February 1990, pp. 67–74, 76, 78. Copyright © 1990 by Charles L. Mee Jr.. Reprinted by permission of the author.

UNIT 6

Renaissance and Reformation

Unit Selections

28. **Joan of Arc,** Kelly DeVries
29. **Christian Humanism: From Renaissance to Reformation,** Lucy Wooding
30. **The Luther Legacy,** Derek Wilson
31. **Explaining John Calvin,** William J. Bouwsma
32. **Who Was Henry VIII and When Did It All Go Wrong?,** Suzannah Lipscomb
33. **Women in War,** John A. Lynn

Key Points to Consider

• Discuss how Joan of Arc was helpful to French Nationalism.

• How did "Humanism" differ from "Christian Humanism?"

• What ideas do we find in Martin Luther's writings?

• Discuss why our opinion of John Calvin as a cold and inflexible moralist is a mistaken view.

• Describe the various aspects of Henry VIII's personality and explain why he is one of the most famous Tudor monarchs.

• Discuss why women were important in wars during the16th century.

Student Website

www.mhhe.com/cls

Internet References

1492: An Ongoing Voyage/Library of Congress
http://lcweb.loc.gov/exhibits/1492

Burckhardt: Civilization of the Renaissance in Italy
www.idbsu.edu/courses/hy309/docs/burckhardt/burckhardt.html

Elizabethan England
www.springfield.k12.il.us/schools/springfield/eliz/
elizabethanengland.html

History Net
www.historynet.com

The Mayflower Web Pages
www.mayflowerhistory.com

Sir Francis Drake
www.mcn.org/2/oseeler/drake.htm

Society for Economic Anthropology Homepage
http://sea.org.ohio-state.edu

History Today
historytoday.com

History Review
Historytoday.com/archive/history-review

Military History
historynet.com/military-history

The Wilson Quarterly
wilsonquarterly.com

The departure from medieval patterns of life was first evident in the Italian Renaissance. There, the growth of capital and the development of distinctly urban economic and social organizations promoted a new culture. This culture, which spread to other parts of Europe, was dominated by townsmen whose tastes, abilities, and interests differed from those of medieval clergy and feudal nobility.

The emerging culture was limited to a minority—generally those who were wealthy. But even in an increasingly materialistic culture, it was not enough just to be wealthy. It was necessary to patronize the arts, literature, and learning, and to demonstrate some skill in a/any profession. The ideal Renaissance man, as Robert Lopez observes (in *The Three Ages of the Italian Renaissance,* University of Virginia Press, 1970), "came from a good old family, improved upon his status through his own efforts, and justified his status by his own intellectual accomplishments."

The new ideal owed much to the classical tradition. Renaissance man, wising to break out of the otherworldly spirituality of the Middle Ages, turned back to the secular naturalism of the ancient world. Indeed, the Renaissance was, among other things, a heroic age of scholarship that restored classical learning to a place of honor. It was classical humanism in particular that became the vogue. And in the new spirit of individualism, humanism was transformed.

Civic humanism was another Renaissance modification of the classical heritage. It involved a new philosophy of political engagement, a reinterpretation of political history from the vantage point of contemporary politics, and the recognition that men would not simply imitate the ancients but would also rival them. Renaissance art and architecture reflected the new society and its attitudes. Successful businessmen were as likely as saints to be subjects of portraits. Equestrian statues of warriors and statesmen glorified current heroes while evoking memories of ancient Rome. Renaissance painters rediscovered nature, which generally had been ignored by medieval artists, often depicting it as an earthly paradise—the appropriate setting for humanity in its new image. And in contrast to the great medieval cathedrals, which glorified God, the Renaissance structure focused on humanity.

Some of these developments in art and architecture indicate the changes in the role of Christianity and the influence of the Church, which no longer determined the goals of Western civilization as they had during the medieval period. Increasingly, civil authorities and their symbols competed with churchmen and

their icons, while Machiavelli and other writers provided a secular rationale for a new political order. Nonetheless, most Europeans, including many humanists retained a deep and abiding religious faith (see "Christian Humanism: from Renaissance to Reformation").

The Reformation, with its theological disputes and wars, is a powerful reminder that secular concerns had not entirely replaced religious ones, especially in northern Europe. The great issues that divided Protestants and Catholics—the balance between individual piety and the Church's authority, the true means of salvation—were essentially medieval in character. Indeed, in their perceptions of humanity, their preoccupation with salvation and damnation, and their attacks upon the Church's conduct of its affairs, Martin Luther, John Calvin, Ulrich Zwingli, and other Protestant leaders echoed the views of medieval reformers. These Protestant reforms are treated in the articles, "The Luther Legacy," and "Explaining John Calvin,"

Taken together, then, the Renaissance and the Reformation constituted a new compound of traditional elements—classical and medieval, secular and religious—along with elements of modernity. The era was a time of transition, or as Lynn D. White describes it, "This was a time of torrential flux, or fearful doubt, making the transition from the relative certainties of the Middle Ages to the new certainties of the eighteenth and nineteenth centuries."

Joan of Arc

Forget the gauzy Hollywood saint—she was an inspired battlefield leader.

KELLY DEVRIES

The most famous woman writer of the Middle Ages, Christine de Pisan, wrote her last treatise about the most famous woman in the Middle Ages, Joan of Arc. De Pisang Ditié de Jehanne d'Arc was a paean to the French military leader whose victories were turning the tide of the Hundred Years' War and would lead to the crowning of Charles VII on July 17, 1429. Her account is also a contemporary recognition that Joan's mission was not an act of heresy but had come from God, just as Joan had declared.

Addressing herself to the English and Burgundians then fighting against Joan, de Pisan poses the questions they were afraid to have answered:

Oh, all you blind people, can you not detect God's hand in this? If you cannot, you are truly stupid, for how else could the Maid who strikes you all down dead have been sent to us? And you do not have sufficient strength! Do you want to fight against God?

Christine de Pisan was well positioned to ask those questions. She had lived through the military resurgence of France at the end of the 14th century, and she had witnessed its many defeats at the hands of Henry V since 1415: Harfleur, Agincourt, Caen and Rouen. Ultimately, nearly all of northern France had fallen into his hands. She had watched her former patron, John the Fearless, duke of Burgundy (head of a faction of French nobles that had wrested control of the throne from King Charles VI, whose madness had rendered him unable to rule), lead the conquering English king into Paris and then into a marriage with Catherine of Valois, Charles' daughter. For his part in this intrigue, John was later assassinated by men under the command of Catherine's brother, Charles, the disinherited Dauphin—the very man Joan would crown king. And, following Henry's early death in 1422, de Pisan had also seen the English armies push French forces across the Loire River, far to the south of Paris. Indeed, by 1429

and the advent of Joan of Arc, the English occupied some two-thirds of France, their Burgundian allies controlling even more.

The 1415 Battle of Agincourt had been a resounding English victory. An estimated 6,000 Englishmen defeated a force that may have numbered more than 25,000 (although, one authority on that battle, Anne Curry, has recently suggested closer numbers: 7,000 English against 12,000 French). French losses, especially among knights and nobles, had been high. The French had been not only militarily defeated, but also profoundly demoralized. After Agincourt, French resistance to their conquerors was light and ineffective. Fearing other embarrassing and costly losses, les armées grew cautious and avoided open confrontations. Leadership problems, recruitment woes and logistical troubles multiplied on the French side, while the smaller English army, under the dynamic leadership of Henry V, went on to conquer Normandy, Brittany, Le Maine and Île-de-France with unprecedented speed during between 1415 and 1422. The English had also capitalized on a civil war that raged throughout France, dividing the kingdom and making allies of the Burgundians, led after 1419 by Duke Philip the Good.

Such setbacks prompted many French towns to surrender to the English and Burgundians without even being attacked. They sought to avoid any punishment that might follow a failed defense. Often, the English didn't even assign garrisons to the surrendered towns, enabling them to disperse their limited forces and cover even more threatened territory.

But through these years of setbacks, pockets of French resistance did hold out, largely unsupported by the Dauphin or his generals. The successful defenses at Mont-Saint-Michel, Tournai, Vaucouleurs and Orléans gave hope to many French patriots who thought the occupiers of their lands were vulnerable to a concerted, aggressive military effort. Such leaders as Jean, duc d'Alençon;

Robert de Baudricourt; Étienne de Vignolles, dit La Hire; Louis de Culen; and Jean Poton de Xaintrailles, not to mention many anonymous French soldiers, believed that the English could be defeated, but that the French needed inspiring leadership. The Dauphin had certainly not provided any such thing. Nor was he likely to, as his favorites, Georges de la Trémoille and Archbishop Renault de Chartres, were counseling him to proceed with caution against the English and Burgundians. That the spark of inspiration for more aggressive military action was to arise in the person of a peasant female was probably not anticipated by any of those willing French warriors. However, when Joan of Arc appeared, they felt her confidence and determination and soon followed her with a fervent loyalty few soldiers in history have given their leaders. Joan responded by leading them to victory.

Joan's approach to military action was simple. In this regard, some of her detractors are correct: Joan did not appear to possess the kind of strategic or tactical cleverness in campaign and battlefield maneuvers that would have impressed classical theorists like Xenophon or Frontinus. But because she believed God had sent her on a mission to save France, and had even provided her with a means of fulfilling that mission by arranging for the Dauphin to give her leadership within the French army (Joan was never appointed as the leader of the French army, only one of several leaders), her strategy and tactics reflected her belief that she could do nothing wrong, and that direct and aggressive action was the means to victory. Joan's convictions further meant that anyone who died in her army, while doing God's bidding, was a martyr for a righteous cause, destined for heaven.

Joan best demonstrated effective leadership in her relief of the Siege of Orleans, although her pre-Orléans history had forecast her battlefield successes. Indeed, her confidence in confronting Robert de Baudricourt at Vaucouleurs, the Dauphin at Chinon, the ecclesiastical leaders in Chinon, the officials in Poitiers and, finally, Charles' mother-in-law, Yolande d'Aragon, queen of Sicily, in Poitiers, brought her prominence and a devoted following even before she reached the French camps at Orléans. Her early reputation also elicited animosity from the other French leaders she encountered upon her arrival at the besieged Loire holdout. But who could blame them? Sending a peasant girl to assist them in their struggles to relieve the English siege of Orléans—regardless of whether she had received this mission directly from God—was an indictment of their military leadership.

Joan would have none of such negative attitudes; she had neither the time nor the patience for their hurt feelings. She was anxious only to engage the enemy. At their first meeting, on April 29, 1429, the following exchange occurred (later recalled in a deposition by Jean, the Bastard of Orleans, commander of the French armies at Orléans):

> Then Joan spoke to him those words which follow: "Are you the Bastard of Orleans?" He answered her: "Yes, I am so and I rejoice at your coming." Then said she to him: "Did you give counsel that I should come here, to this side of the river, and that I should go not straight there where Talbot [Lord John Talbot, head of the English army] and the English are?" [Joan had been led around the English army.] He answered that he and others, wiser on this matter, had given this counsel, believing that they were doing the best and surest. Then Joan said to him, "In the name of God, the counsel of our Lord God is surer and wiser than yours. You thought to deceive me, but it is you who are deceived, for I am bringing you better help than ever came from any soldier or any city, because it is the help of the King of Heaven. It does not come through love for me, but from God himself, who, on the petition of Saint Louis and Saint Charlemagne, has had pity on the town of Orleans and has refused to suffer the enemy to have [this] city."

Jean was not used to enduring such a direct affront to his authority. But then, neither was he prepared to attack the English. In fact, there is evidence he intended to pull away from the town, in effect surrendering it to the English force of some 5,000, then led by the Earl of Suffolk. Joan took that intention as an insult to herself, to the people of Orleans and to God. She also had difficulty understanding why the Bastard would do this, as the English did not even have sufficient troops on hand to surround Orléans. Instead, they had manned only four strongholds, or "boulevards," along the east side of town, one on an island in the Loire River farther east, one more to the north, and another on the road from Orleans to Jargeau. Each held few English troops. Indeed, in coming to Orleans, Joan and her relatively large retinue had passed one English stronghold, the Boulevard of Saint-Loup, without notice. (Joan and a few Orléanais would later capture that same boulevard with ease.) The English had more soldiers on the south bank of the Loire, most of them concentrated at Les Tourelles, the fortification beside the single bridge into Orléans, and in the adjacent Boulevard Augustin, amid the ruins of an Augustinian monastery. The bridge no longer spanned the river, having been destroyed by the Orléanais at the beginning of the siege the previous October, but it remained the defensive hub for the English. To relieve the siege, the French would have to concentrate their efforts on that fortification.

Perhaps this is what frightened the Bastard of Orléans. A boulevard was one of the most daunting fortifications of the later Middle Ages, despite being constructed simply out of earth and wood. Defended by soldiers with gunpowder weapons, however, it could hold out seemingly forever against almost any size force. Most military leaders, unwilling to sacrifice a large number of their men in attacking such a position, simply left the boulevards alone. Complicating matters, the English troops at Les Tourelles could directly support the Boulevard Augustin. It was also rumored that an English force led by the capable Sir John Fastolf was approaching Orleans.

Joan's reaction to the Bastard's withdrawal plans was to be expected. After discovering he had left her out of leadership councils that addressed how to handle Fastolf's arrival, she again rebuked, even threatened, the French leader. Joan's squire, Jean d'Aulon, later recalled her words: "Bastard, Bastard, in the name of God I command you that as soon as you hear of Fastolf's coming, you will let me know. For if he gets through without my knowing it, I swear to you that I will have your head cut off." The count "answered that he did not doubt that, and that he would certainly let her know."

Once firmly established within the French military leadership ranks, Joan devised a plan to relieve the siege before the arrival of the English reinforcements. It was simple and direct: She herself would lead an assault on the Boulevard Augustin. The Bastard and the other French leaders quickly agreed with her plan. They had little choice and after all could only profit from the position in which she had placed herself: If she succeeded, they would share in her victory. If she failed, they could blame her for the incautious attack.

The only potential flaw in Joan's plan was the high number of French casualties likely to result from an attack against such a strong position defended by well-armed men. Fortified by her belief in God's will and presence, Joan didn't seem concerned. Nor were the French soldiers, for they had been drawn to her patriotism and shared her spiritual zeal. It was almost as if they believed they couldn't die in this struggle, and that if they did, they would gain otherwise unattainable salvation.

Many apparently did gain that salvation on May 7, 1429. The bloodiest encounter of the Hundred Years' War since the battle of Agincourt is described in the contemporary Journal du siège d'Orléans:

Early in the morning on the day after, which was Saturday, the 7th day of May, the French attacked Les Tourelles and the boulevard while the English were attempting to fortify it. And there was a spectacular assault, during which there were performed many great feats of arms, both in the attack and in the defense, because the English had a large number of strong soldiers and had strengthened skillfully all of the defensible places. And also they fought well, notwithstanding that the French scaled the different places adeptly and attacked the angles at the highest of the strong and sturdy fortifications, so that they seemed by this to be immortal. But the English repulsed them from many places and attacked with artillery both high and low, both with cannons and other weapons, such as axes, lances, pole-arms, lead hammers and other personal arms, so that they killed and wounded many Frenchmen.

Despite being wounded herself, Joan persisted in the assault. Delivering a fiery speech "in the name of God," she urged her men forward, claiming that the English "were not a stronger force" than they she promised "to touch the staff of her standard on the boulevard." Her troops responded with shouts and a renewed charge forward. Les Tourelles soon fell. The English defenders fled, and Joan—now bearing her well-earned nickname, the "Maid of Orleans"—entered the city at the head of her victorious army. She had made believers out of those who had doubted her.

Similar direct assaults against other English-held Loire Valley towns brought similar results. Despite Fastolf's attempt to reinforce Jargeau with troops and gunpowder weapons, it fell on June 12. Beaugency succumbed just five days later after an intense bombardment by French guns of the 12th century castle where English troops had holed up. "The English were able to put up only a small amount of resistance," wrote Jean Chartier, a 15th century French monk and historian. That same night the English abandoned the town of Meung-sur-Loire, slipping away under cover of darkness.

English military leaders were not accustomed to such defeats, and Talbot and Fastolf were determined to turn things around. They met the French in battle outside the town of Patay on June 18, 1429. The French were again victorious. Talbot was captured, while Fastolf barely escaped and retreated to Paris. Joan was present, although how much of a role she took in the battle is disputed.

In less than a month, Joan of Arc had relieved the siege of Orléans, retaken the towns of Jargeau, Meung-sur-Loire and Beaugency and participated in the major French victory at Patay. And a month later, on July 17, 1429, when the Dauphin was crowned King Charles VII of France at Reims, Joan was by his side. All along their route to Reims, towns that had earlier willingly subjugated themselves to English rule—Auxerre, Châlons, Troyes and even Reims itself—welcomed "liberation" by the Maid.

Paris, however, remained in enemy hands, and thus Joan undertook a new mission: She would recapture the French capital, then under the control of a sizable

Anglo-Burgundian army led by John, duke of Bedford, commander of all English troops in occupied France. Again, Joan did not shrink from this challenge. Before the year was out, she conducted minor bloodless skirmishes with the duke of Bedford's force, then attacked and captured the Parisian suburb of Saint-Denis, the basilica of which held the bones of many earlier French kings. The French saw its capture as divine endorsement of their attempts to win back their kingdom.

But when Joan's forces attacked Paris on September 8, it did not fall. "The assault was difficult and long," wrote Percival de Cagny, who rode under the standard of Alençon and later chronicled the conflict, "and it was a marvel how much noise was made by the cannons and couleuvrines, which fired at those outside the walls at such a rate and in such a quantity as to be without number." Still, Cagny insists, because of the Maid's presence with the army and by the grace of God, "no man was wounded or killed." (A more credible eyewitness is French artist Clément de Fauquembergue, who says the guns killed and wounded many French soldiers.) During the fighting, Joan was wounded in the thigh by a crossbow bolt.

Joan cannot be blamed for the failure to retake Paris, declared the Journal du siège d'Orléans: "She wished to attack such a strong town and so well stocked with men and artillery simply because it was the city of Paris." The anonymous author of the journal was undoubtedly accurate in his assessment of the military situation at Paris. But his was not the opinion that prevailed at Charles VII's court: Joan had failed, and her failure cast doubt on the divinity of her mission. It also cast doubt on the tactical methods she had used to gain her Loire victories and assault Paris.

Over the objections of many French military leaders, Charles sought the overly cautious advice of La Trémoille and Chartres. They urged deliberation, to avoid bringing the Burgundians more actively into the fray. They even suggested that the king return to the English some of the towns captured by Joan. This the king refused, but La Trémoille and Chartres did persuade Charles to disband his coronation army and to send Joan—once she had recovered from her wound—to a less significant theater of operations, against a band of mercenaries led by Perrinet Gressart, along the southern Loire River. There she was able to capture the town of Saint-Pierre-le-Moutier by direct assault, despite being woefully undersupplied. But she failed to take heavily fortified La Charitésur-Loire. The reason for her failure at La Charité is suggested in a letter Joan had written on Nov. 9, 1429, to the townspeople of nearby Riom at the outset of the siege:

Because of the "great quantities of gunpowder, arrows and other equipment of war expended before the said town [Saint-Pierre-le-Moutier], and because the lords who are in this town and I are so poorly provided to besiege La Charité, where we are going presently, I beseech you, that as you love the good and honor of the king and also those others here, that you would instantly send help for this siege, of gunpowder, saltpeter, sulphur, arrows, heavy crossbows and other equipment of war. And do this so that, for lack of the said powder and other equipment of war, the situation will not be prolonged, and that you will not be said to be neglectful or rejecting.

Petitions that winter from her friends at court, including the king's mother-in-law, returned Joan to more pressing military engagements the following spring. She answered by skirmishing with English troops at Senlis, Crépy-en-Valois and Melun. But again her leadership was less than successful in these engagements. Although Joan and her contemporaries considered them victories, they failed to move the English from any of their occupied territory. But her persistence was enough to further irritate the duke of Bedford and to drag Philip the Good, duke of Burgundy, into the fray.

In April 1430, the Burgundians, urged on by the English, attacked the French-controlled town of Compiègne, forcing Joan to move her troops there to thwart a Burgundian occupation. Defense had never been a part of Joan's strategy, and fighting from behind protective walls was certainly not her military style. She frequently sortied out against the attacking Burgundian troops. On May 23, 1430, leading one of these sorties out of Compiègne, Joan got separated from the main body of her force and was captured by the Burgundians, who eventually ransomed her to the English. Some historians believe she was betrayed by Guillaume de Flavy, the garrison commander at Compiègne, but later trial testimony indicates otherwise:

She crossed over the bridge and through the French boulevard and went with a company of soldiers manning those sections against the lord of Luxembourg's men [Jean de Luxembourg was one of the Burgundian leaders at Compiègne], whom she drove back twice, all the way to the Burgundian camp, and a third time halfway back. And then the English who were there cut her and her men off, coming between her and the boulevard, and so her men retreated from her. And retreating into the fields on her flank, in the direction of Picardy, near the: boulevard, she was captured.

Joan of Arc was burned to death as a heretic in the marketplace of Rouen a little over a year later, on May 30, 1431.

It would be a satisfying end to the story of Joan of Arc if one could say she was the direct cause of the end of the Hundred Years' War and the expulsion of England from most of France. But that war did not end for 23 years after her capture. So if Joan did not directly end the Hundred Years' War, why is she so celebrated? No doubt the character of her trial and execution have much to do with her celebrity. But Joan's renown stems from her military ability, her skill at leading men in battle against great odds and at the risk of death.

Not long after Joan's death, French military leaders began to adopt tactics similar to hers. Her policy of direct engagement and frontal assault was costly, but it ultimately proved more effective than any other military tactic in wresting the English from France. And possibly, as other French generals started to use her tactics, they too began to believe that, should their soldiers die in battle, they might join the Maid who inspired them, the later-to-be Saint Joan of Arc.

For further reading, **KELLY DEVRIES** recommends his book, *Joan of Arc: A Military Leader,* as well as *Joan of Arc: La Pucelle,* edited by Craig Taylor

Christian Humanism: From Renaissance to Reformation

Lucy Wooding introduces a highly significant, but often much misunderstood, cultural force.

LUCY WOODING

"Immortal God, what a world I see dawning! Why can I not grow young again?" This was written in 1517 by Desiderius Erasmus, the most famous of all Christian humanists. He was surveying the European culture he knew so well and was full of hope for the future. By tragic irony, even as he wrote these words, a small storm was brewing in the remote university town of Wittenberg, which would in time obstruct and obscure everything Erasmus valued most. Even more confusingly, both Erasmus and Luther could be described as Christian humanists, sharing the excitement about the Bible which so characterised the age, using their scholarship to uncover the beliefs and devotions of the early church, using their skills as teachers and writers to reform and inspire the world around them. Yet less than ten years later they were bitterly divided, with Erasmus lamenting the 'disaster' that Luther had brought upon them all.

So what was Christian Humanism? It hovers in the background of all our discussions of Renaissance and Reformation; it is applied to many great figures, from Erasmus and Luther to such ill-assorted individuals as Thomas More, Huldrych Zwingli, Reginald Pole or even Elizabeth I. It is immediately clear that the chief proponents of Christian humanism were often incapable of agreeing with one another, and sometimes became fiercely opposed. Can the label of 'Christian humanist' be of any value to the historian today?

The first thing we need to wrestle with is the problem of definitions. 'Christian humanism' was itself a form of a wider movement we call 'humanism', which might broadly be described as the intellectual aspect of the Renaissance, another historical movement which evades easy categorisation. At this point it is easy to feel discouraged, but it is important to persevere, because humanism was a movement of extraordinary richness, inventiveness, ideological commitment and literary beauty, worth studying for its own sake, but also for its important intellectual legacy. We might locate its heyday in the fifteenth and sixteenth centuries, but its influence was to shape the literature, thought, art, architecture and music of every subsequent century until our own. Furthermore, humanists wrestled with problems of conflicting cultures, religious division, the encounter between Christianity and Islam, poverty, disease, war and political corruption. These are all issues with relevance to the modern world, and the works of the humanists still speak with startling immediacy and moral force to our own contemporary problems.

Humanism was a movement of extraordinary richness, inventiveness, ideological commitment and literary beauty, worth studying for its own sake, but also for its important intellectual legacy.

The Renaissance and the 'Golden Age' of Humanism

The Renaissance was, broadly speaking, a movement of cultural revival which sought to rediscover and redeploy the languages, learning and artistic achievements of the classical world. It used to be claimed as the 'dawn of modernity', with humanism seen as a set of convictions concerning the dignity of man; the beginnings of that individualism which would one day find expression in the Enlightenment. These grand claims are now seen as deeply misleading. The Renaissance was not a new dawn after the darkness and ignorance of the 'Middle Ages', but a gradual development with a huge intellectual debt to the medieval past. We also now understand how distinct Renaissance ideas were from the ideas of the Enlightenment, or from modern attitudes. We have largely stopped trying to find our own ideas and attitudes in the past, and started looking at the work of the humanists in its own context; still an astonishing achievement, but coloured less by individualism and the beginnings of secularism than by the particular political, religious and cultural currents of the fifteenth and sixteenth centuries.

> **The Renaissance was not a new dawn after the darkness and ignorance of the 'Middle Ages', but a gradual development with a huge intellectual debt to the medieval past.**

The idea of the Renaissance as an age of gold after an age of darkness was actually a tale spun by the humanists themselves, and makes the important point that this was a very self-conscious movement, which shaped its own reputation. In 1492 the Italian humanist Marsilio Ficino claimed glory for his native city of Florence, when he wrote that 'this century, like a golden age, has restored to light the liberal arts, which were almost extinct: grammar, poetry, rhetoric, painting, sculpture, architecture, music . . . and all this in Florence.' In 1575 the French humanist Loys le Roy wrote how 'we here in the West have in the last two hundred years recovered the excellence of good letters and brought back the study of the disciplines after they had long remained as if extinguished. The sustained industry of many learned men has led to such success that today this our age can be compared to the most learned times that ever were. For we now see the languages restored, and not only the deeds and writings of the ancients brought back to light, but also many fine things newly discovered.'

Some of the grander claims about humanism, therefore, were self-promotion, and need to be treated with care. Yet some historians, reacting against the old-fashioned view of the Renaissance as the dawn of modernity and humanism as the discovery of individualism, have gone too far

in the other direction and become overly cautious about their definitions. For them 'humanism' is little more than a type of educational programme based upon classical Greek and Latin authors, and a 'humanist', strictly defined, a university teacher within such a programme, called at the time *studia humanitatis*. But this approach not only excludes such important figures as Erasmus, More and Montaigne, it fails to appreciate the excitement of the movement, its grandiose ambitions, and its often impressive achievements. For humanists not only sought to go back *ad fontes*—to the original founts of knowledge—they also sought to redesign their own world with the knowledge and inspiration derived from the classical past. Just as artists and architects began to copy the techniques and derive ideas from classical statues, temples and paintings, so humanists looked back to the political thought of Cicero, the histories of Livy, the moral philosophy of Seneca or Plutarch, the ethics of Aristotle and the stories of Homer.

Christian Humanism

If this was humanism, how should we understand 'Christian humanism'? It used to be thought that this was a clearly distinct offshoot of the main Renaissance movement, rooted in Northern Europe, detached from Italian preoccupations, less 'modern' because more religious, and in large part a prelude to Protestantism. This is unhelpful, not least because it suggests that Christian humanists were an oddly old-fashioned splinter group from the mainstream of Renaissance ideas. In fact, humanism nearly always had a Christian dimension, and it was the pure republican types, or the mavericks like Machiavelli, who were the exception, not the rule. The Spanish humanist Juan Luis Vives wrote about education: 'as for what books should be read . . . there are some on which everyone is agreed, as the Gospels of the Lord, the Acts of the Apostles and the Epistles, the historical and moral books of the Old Testament, Cyprian, Jerome, Augustine, Ambrose, Chrysostom, Hilary, Gregory, Boethius, Fulgentius, Tertullian, Plato, Cicero, Seneca and other such authors.' This is a characteristic example of how the Bible—also a classical text—and early church fathers were placed alongside Plato, Cicero, Boethius and the rest. Someone like Thomas More was at home in the world of classical antiquity, translating the Greek satirist Lucian or writing *Utopia,* which was modelled on Plato's *Republic.* Yet More was also famous for his piety, insisting that his children study the church fathers, discussing church reform with Erasmus, ultimately dying for his faith.

Christian humanism makes the point that we have misunderstood the Renaissance if we see it in terms of a pagan revival, a straightforward championing of the abilities of man. In any Renaissance art gallery, the motifs remain predominantly Christian, and most Renaissance thinkers continued to work within a Christian context. But Christian humanists were not afraid to pose a vigorous challenge to the religious assumptions of the time, particularly where they saw hypocrisy and corruption. Although as individuals they were shaped by their local circumstances, a key feature of the movement was its internationalism. This was maintained in various ways: through the travelling of scholars around Europe; through copious correspondence, which was intended for circulation to third parties and often published; through the use of the printing press, whose spread throughout Europe mirrored and facilitated the spread of humanist concerns. Most of all, the international aspect of Christian humanism was encouraged by the humanists' use of a single common language—they all spoke and wrote Latin fluently, which facilitated the kind of intellectual exchange which the modern world, hampered by language differences, still struggles to attain.

It is important here to issue a warning. Christian humanism was a highly diverse movement. It contained individuals as distinct as the German Cornelius Agrippa who studied the occult and the Kabbala; the Italian noblemen Pico della Mirandola who befriended Savonarola and some of whose religious ideas were condemned for heresy; the Spaniard Juan de Valdes who was the centre of an evangelical Catholic circle in Italy or the Englishman John Fisher who combined humanist learning with a renowned piety, died a Cardinal and in due course became a saint. Christian humanism could manifest itself at the most basic level as little more than a style of writing, full of classical, biblical and patristic allusions and quotations. Even a thorough humanist education could not be guaranteed to produce the same results: Mary I and Elizabeth I were both given the best humanist education of which English scholars were capable, and they were both exceptionally learned, but still had very different religious convictions. Yet Christian humanism was more than just a form of religious education; there were enough shared aims and ideals for us to see it as movement which comprised ideology, not just techniques for instruction. This ideology of Christian renewal was channelled in different ways, often with very different consequences, but it sprang from the same sources of inspiration.

Education

At the heart of Christian humanism was a fervent desire for education. In part this meant education for the humanists themselves, many of whom studied at a succession of universities all over Europe. But they also sought to educate society at large. Erasmus wrote to a friend that 'to be a schoolmaster is an office second in importance to a king. Do you think it a mean task to take your fellow-citizens in their earliest years, to instil into them from the beginning sound learning and Christ himself, and to return them to your country as so many honourable upright men?' Yet if Christian humanists sought to reconfigure their world, they planned to do so from the top down. Erasmus might write dreamily of a time when the ploughman would 'sing texts of the Scripture at his plough, and . . . the weaver . . . hum them to the tune of his shuttle', but works like *The Education of a Christian Prince* targeted those at the apex of the social pyramid. Humanists sought the company—and the patronage—of Popes, archbishops and princes, nobility and gentry, and tried to encourage their patrons to implement programmes of reform based on the recommendations of their scholarly advisors. Meanwhile these influential individuals courted the humanists in their turn, anxious to be perceived as educated and enlightened Renaissance princes, or as nobles or churchmen of scholarly renown.

Erasmus wrote to a friend that 'to be a schoolmaster is an office second in importance to a king.'

Christian humanism was thus to set a pattern for the education of the ruling classes which would long endure. The starting point was the study of ancient languages. Rabelais had Pantagruel's father exhort him to become 'a perfect master of languages. First of Greek, as Quintilian advises; secondly, of Latin; and then of Hebrew, on account of the Holy Scriptures; also of Chaldean and Arabic, for the same reason; and I would have you model your Greek style on Plato's and your Latin on that of Cicero.' This—pruned of the satire—was essentially the humanist model. Even women were included in this, although it was royal and aristocratic women, or the daughters of men like Thomas More, who most immediately benefited. That Elizabeth I was fluent in Latin and Greek, as well as French and Italian, was a testimony to the humanist programme of study she had followed.

Rediscovering the Bible

Above all else, the study of ancient languages enabled Christian humanists to read the Bible with new-found accuracy and enthusiasm. On one level, the biblical revival was a practical matter. To read the Old Testament required an understanding of Hebrew; to read the New Testament required Greek, which also enabled the reading of the Septuagint, the ancient translation of the Old Testament into Greek from the 3rd and 2nd centuries BC. New universities, or university colleges, were therefore established which emphasised the learning of these ancient languages, from the University of Alcala founded 1499 to Corpus Christi College in Oxford, founded 1517, or the 'Collegium Trilingue' in Louvain, also founded 1517, where three lecturers were 'to read and expound publicly to all comers both Christian and other moral and approved authors, in the three languages, that is in Latin, Greek and Hebrew.'

Latin was still a living language, and the main form of communication among humanists, who latinised their own names to indicate their intellectual status. Greek was something new, and to study Greek, or patronise the study of Greek, was to mark yourself out as a cutting-edge thinker, dedicated to the pursuit of truth. It gave access not just to the Bible, but to the Greek fathers who had written in the centuries immediately after Christ. Erasmus translated the works of the Greek fathers St John Chrysostom, St Ireneus and St Basil among others. Most importantly of all, in 1516 he published a new translation of the New Testament in Greek and Latin. This *Novum Instrumentum* caused a storm of excitement, and in many cases, of protest from those who challenged his right to question the usual Latin text, commonly called the Vulgate. He was accused of trying to undermine the church. In his own defence, Erasmus pointed out that the text had been approved by his bishop, and accepted by Pope Leo X to whom it was dedicated. His was only one of several attempts to achieve a flawless edition of the Bible. The Complutensian or 'Polyglot' Bible, produced at the university of Alcala, set texts in different languages side by side for purposes of comparison. In the Old Testament the Latin text of the Vulgate was given between the Hebrew and the Greek of the Septuagint, with an Aramaic text and its Latin translation added at the bottom of the page for the first five books, or Pentateuch. The New Testament had Greek and Latin Vulgate texts placed side by side. This great work took from 1502 to 1517, the year in which Martin Luther began to cause a stir. It could be argued that everything Luther had to say about the importance of reading the Bible, and paying attention to the literal meaning of the text, had already been anticipated by the work of the Christian humanists.

Humanists were not merely interested in points of grammar and translation. Their study of Greek and Hebrew, their rediscovery of the Bible, were all undertaken for a reason, namely the revival of Christianity. It was a moral revolution that Christian humanists intended; a revolution to be achieved by learning. And although it began with the educated, it was a revolution which was to extend in time to all. Erasmus wrote 'I disagree very much with those who are unwilling that Holy Scripture, translated into the vulgar tongue, be read by the uneducated, as if Christ taught such intricate doctrines that they could scarcely be understood by very few theologians, or as if the strength of the Christian religion consisted in men's ignorance of it.'

The Road to Protestantism

Equipped with a knowledge of the ancient tongues, and thus with an understanding of the Bible and the early church fathers, humanists were poised to renew Christian society. The conclusions they drew could be radical, on the one hand exhorting the laity to lives of uncompromising religious commitment, on the other telling princes to embrace pacifism. Erasmus's *Handbook of the Christian Soldier* portrayed the Christian life as a spiritual struggle, aiming at a state of being where 'we shall be high-minded in Christ, of abundant charity, strong and constant in good or bad fortune, closing our eyes to petty things, striving towards higher things, full of enthusiasm, full of knowledge.' In order to achieve this, many forms of ignorance, superstition and corruption had to be put aside. Erasmus and his like vigorously attacked the wealth and indolence of many of the clergy, the moral laxity of many monks, the stupidity of popular religious traditions, the pomposity and obscurantism of theologians. *In Praise of Folly,* for example, attacked those ignorant clergy, who 'believe it's the highest form of piety to be so uneducated that they can't even read. Then when they bray like donkeys in church, repeating by rote the psalms they haven't understood, they imagine they are charming the ears of their heavenly audience with infinite delight.' Satire was the humanist weapon, gleefully and skilfully deployed. Popes, prelates, monks, nuns and the credulous laity were all mocked in turn.

Satire was the humanist weapon, gleefully and skilfully deployed.

We tend to see Christian humanism as only a prelude to Protestantism, but in 1517 Erasmus was a scholar of international repute and Luther was an unknown friar in an obscure German town. We might do better to see humanism as the bigger movement, with far wider concerns, from which the theologians who would later be termed Protestants became a small break away group. Humanism, however, was a movement of intellectuals and scholars, who sought to change the world through the enlightened application of humanist ideals by intelligent and educated heads of state. Protestantism worked in much more crude and efficient ways, mobilising popular opinion, deploying cheap print and propaganda, whipping up antagonism and protest. Erasmus had at first given cautious encouragement to Luther, but warned him that 'one gets further by courtesy and moderation than by clamour. That was how Christ brought the world under his sway.' As the Lutheran movement gathered momentum, however, Erasmus began to deplore the violence involved. 'What was the point of a savage torrent of invective directed against men whom it was unwise to treat like that if he wished to make them better, and impious if he did it to provoke them and set the whole world by the ears?'

We might do better to see humanism as the bigger movement, with far wider concerns, from which the theologians who would later be termed Protestants became a small breakaway group

The Reformation as it unfolded in Europe after 1517 used humanist ideas about the Bible, about the defeat of ignorance and superstition, about moral renewal and pious reform. It also relied heavily on the scholarly achievement of the humanists—their language skills, their editions of the Bible and the church fathers, their attacks upon popular ignorance, monastic corruption and scholastic obscurantism. But it was a world away from its aims of regeneration through education, cultural exchange and influence upon the elites. Erasmus in 1527 wrote to Martin Bucer, and gave an explanation of why he had not become a Protestant. 'If I could have been convinced that this movement came from God I would have enlisted long ago', he wrote. But he was alarmed at the human cost of the movement, particularly 'the constant in-fighting between the leaders', and said 'if you were what you brag of being, they would have set an example of godly and patient conduct which would have made the Gospel widely acceptable.' And with ominous clear-sightedness, Erasmus wrote 'I foresee a violent and bloody century should those who are angry get their strength back, as they surely will.'

Christian humanism and early Protestantism shared many characteristics. But it could be argued that it was the humanist vision which had the greater breadth, where Protestantism was to lose itself in precise definition of doctrine and the subsequent violent defence of those doctrines. Christian humanism could be put to many uses, many of them of only localised importance. It was deployed in Spain in the service of the wider aims of Ferdinand and Isabella; in Switzerland it served to underpin political dissatisfaction, facilitating the emergence of Swiss national identity, and the Swiss reformation; in England it was used to construct Henry VIII's case for the Royal Supremacy, and a reformation which attacked abuse and superstition but equally rejected Protestantism. Yet Christian humanism never lost its international dimension, reinforced by the exchange of scholars and books as well as the exchange of ideas. It continued to uphold a vision of educated and civilised exchange, of the pursuit of learning, of biblical and patristic renewal, of new standards of lay piety, of the rejection of obscurantism and ignorance. These ideals remained a key part of early modern culture, the foundations of education, a formative influence in a range of different disciplines. Yet in the area where the humanists had most wanted to make a difference, conflict raged. The Bible became a familiar part of early modern vernacular culture, and a source of pious inspiration as they had wished; but it also became a battle-ground, its meaning fiercely contested between different religious groups. Still the older movement, although challenged, was never eclipsed. Despite the confessional divide which resulted from the Reformation, Christian humanism, as both an educational and an ideological force, refused to go away.

Issues to Debate

- What were the key features of the Renaissance?
- Should we see Christian humanism as a coherent ideological movement?
- What was the relationship between Christian humanism and Protestantism?

DR LUCY WOODING is lecturer in early modern history at King's College London. She has recently published a biography of Henry VIII.

From *History Review*, September 2009, pp. 13–18. Copyright © 2009 by History Today, Ltd. Reprinted by permission.

The Luther Legacy

Derek Wilson

Over the centuries Luther (1483–1546) has been variously identified as an advocate of absolute monarchy, democracy, individual freedom, intellectual repression, nationalism, internationalism, spirituality and secularism. The fact that so many later 'movers and shakers' have claimed the monk of Wittenberg as a progenitor of their own convictions is testimony to the stature of the man. Indeed, it would be difficult to identify any other individual who, without wielding political power or leading armies, more decisively changed the course of history. Even our supposedly post-Christian age cannot write him out of the record. Yet, we have to resist the temptation to recreate him in our own image. He was a religious figure; his battles were fought over theological issues that may seem to us obscure but whose implications touched every area of life, individual and corporate.

Jakob Burckhardt was essentially right in identifying the Reformation as an escape from discipline. For centuries the Church had held the monopoly of propaganda: its murals, stained glass, the polychromed paraphernalia of shrines and altars, the pastoral and educational activities of the clergy, all spoke of the awesome need for people to prepare for the world to come. That meant availing themselves of the prescribed means of grace entrusted to their spiritual superiors. The clergy held the keys to eternal bliss or torment. Any who did air doubts or proclaim a rival programme were heretics and were dealt with severely. The only spiritual authority emanated from Rome. Luther, however, insisted that there was another, higher, source of authority: the word of God written in the Bible. In his preaching and teaching—but above all in his public confrontations with spiritual and temporal leaders—he gave people permission to doubt everything the Catholic hierarchy taught; to judge it for themselves against the testimony of the Bible.

Any attempt to assess Luther's impact must begin with his redefining of the individual. His spiritual journey was an intensely personal one. In 1505 he forsook the legal career for which he had been destined and entered the Augustinian monastery at Erfurt, in order to save his own immortal soul. He was following the path of self-denial and holiness as prescribed by the Church for centuries. For at least eight years he gave it his best shot. He failed to find the consolation he sought because, as well as a sensitive conscience, he was blessed with a sharp, logical mind. He could see the flaw in the system of penitence that the Church preached: if contrition and abnegation were practised in the interests of self-preservation then they were selfish, hence sinful. His was not the first earnest soul to find itself on the treadmill of sin, confession, absolution, doubt, confession. It was a terrifying, never-ending predicament. Ever-present was the 'doom' image of Christ separating the sheep and the goats and consigning the latter to the torments of hell. Famously, Luther discovered in Paul's Epistle to the Romans (Romans 1.17) the sword to sever the Gordian knot: 'the righteousness (justice) of God is revealed from faith to faith. . . the just man will live by faith'. Like countless Christians before and since, he experienced an ecstasy of release.

He might have left it there and, as a good monk, preached justification by faith alone as a truth that could somehow be made to fit with the Church's traditional penitential system. But it could not. The maze of scholastic theology seemed to prevent access to the great central truth which he had discovered. His relentless logic persuaded him to suggest, in the 95 Theses by which he publicly challenged the Church in 1517, that the practice of selling indulgences—by which the buyers could secure remission from the penalties of sin in the next world—was a matter for urgent theological debate. When the papal regime refused to grant this debate, the real problem began. Luther defied the Pope, the Inquisition and the corps of Catholic theologians. Called before the Imperial Diet by the Emperor Charles V at Worms in April 1521, Luther refused to recant insisting, 'my conscience is captive to the word of God . . . Unless I am convinced by Scripture *and reason* [my emphasis], I will not recant'.

It is scarcely possible to exaggerate what those words implied. Luther was not just challenging the accumulated teaching of the Church; he was saying that any man or woman possessed of the open Bible could be his or her own theologian. If God had provided the Bible as a lamp to the believer's path, then as many people as possible should be encouraged to read it. So he translated it into German, and had his translation printed (New Testament, 1522, Old Testament, 1534). Within a few years hundreds of untrained lay people were writing devotional and polemical books and pamphlets. Gone was the assumption that people only needed those skills that enabled them to perform their God-given calling in a hierarchical society. Learning was now something to be valued for its own sake. In 1524, Luther wrote to the municipal authorities throughout Germany urging them to establish elementary schools for all children, including girls. The response was not dramatic but by 1580 half the parishes in Electoral Saxony had schools for boys and 10 per cent had made similar provision for girls. As the American historian Steven Ozment has suggested, 'It is not too much to call the early Protestant movement the first Western enlightenment'.

Luther replaced the authority of the Church with that of the Bible. But it was always the Bible *and reason.* With the plain text in his hand everyone could work out his own salvation and no longer needed the ministrations of an intermediary priesthood. This had far-reaching consequences. If truth is the exclusive preserve of a priestly caste, any system built on this foundation will be autocratic. But, if truth is to be found in a book which anyone can read, then authority can be challenged with divine sanction. The way lies open for the development of alternative polities, even democracy. To be sure, Luther himself drew back from the more revolutionary implications of the open Bible. He did not personally initiate debates on such issues as how to establish a godly commonwealth, whether tyrants might be deposed or the balancing of crown and parliament. But his courageous stand against the Pope and the Holy Roman Emperor, the political embodiments of traditional authority, fired the imagination and stiffened the resolve of more radical spirits throughout western Christendom.

Yet Luther never set out to challenge the establishment. That marks him out from most other religious reformers of his day. Wycliffe, Savonarola, Hus and other rebels and charismatic preachers usually had begun from a starting point of popular grievances—oppression, corruption, extortion. Many clothed their message in gaudy apocalyptic language, claiming they had been sent to cleanse the world in preparation for the Second Coming. Not so Luther. He wanted to restore the Church to its New Testament purity. In that desire he was at one with a large swathe of public opinion, including humanist scholars, kings and even the Emperor. There was a clamour for a general council of the Church to initiate reform. It was only when successive popes refused to concede anything which might weaken the power of Rome, that Luther concluded that the papacy must be the Antichrist, subverting the Christian community from within.

In terms of secular politics, an anachronistic but perhaps appropriate label for him is 'right-wing reactionary'. The political theory he found in the New Testament was that God ordained kings to maintain order and that all subjects (including clergy) were to render due obedience to them. It followed that secular rulers were charged with the reformation of the churches in their domains. He therefore advocated such measures as the ending of ecclesiastical jurisdiction in matters matrimonial and the restoration of ex-monastic property to lay ownership.

Luther had an abhorrence of anarchy. He shared the fear of rebellion and chaos that lay close to the surface of medieval life, but for him public disorder was a particularly sensitive issue because politico-religious upheaval in Germany gave his enemies a stick to beat him with. This explains why he reacted so violently to the Peasants' War of 1524–25, a widespread popular rising against secular princes by ordinary people some of whom drew socially radical conclusions from Luther's teaching. By

doing so Luther forfeited the support of most of the populace. His notorious invocation of the German nobility to 'smite, slay and stab' any rebel, just as 'one might kill a mad dog' gave rise to the accusation that he was in the pocket of the princes, a taunt that was in large measure justified. Having already enlisted the aid of the German warlords to protect him from the Church and the Emperor, Luther could not prevent his movement becoming hijacked by these men of power, who banded together in 1530 to form the Schmalkaldic League. Over and again Luther warned them not to wage war against the Emperor. If they did, they would have 'no good conscience before God, no legal ground before the Empire, and no honour before the world. This would be dreadful and terrifying.' (1528) But few people were listening. The new Protestant establishment had taken what it wanted from Luther and his politically non-confrontational agenda seemed to them hopelessly out of touch.

This raises the question of whether Luther should be seen as an apostle of absolutism. Some later autocrats certainly claimed him as a founding father. It is no coincidence that memorial statues of the reformer were erected in Worms and Wittenberg during the nineteenth century, a time of German empire-building; nor that Hitler, scrabbling around for anything that would justify his manifesto, claimed Luther as a fellow-traveller in *Mein Kampf.* But what would the man who had set his face against militarism in the service of the Protestant state have had to say to pickelhaubed soldiers who, in 1914, marched to the front singing his own hymn, *Ein feste Burg?* This same 'apostle of absolutism' was also lauded by the German philosopher Johann Fichte in 1793 as the 'patron saint of freedom' who 'broke humanity's chain' and whose shade raised his hand in benediction over Frenchmen overthrowing the *ancién regime.*

Luther was certainly a German patriot. A basic element in his opposition to Rome was his loathing of 'effete Italians'. He shared the resentment of many of his countrymen at benefices and senior clerical appointments held by absentee shepherds who cared not a whit for their flocks and who creamed off Church revenues to finance a luxurious transalpine lifestyle. When Pope Julius II (1503–13) initiated an indulgence to pay for the building of his new basilica of St Peter's in Rome (1506), it was always going to be unpopular in the German states and his successor Leo X (1513–21) waited four years after Julius's death in 1513 before dispatching his agents thither. When Luther expressed his opposition to the project in the 95 Theses, he was echoing a complaint heard in every *bierhaus* and marketplace.

This resentment expressed itself in official protest at the highest level. At the very Diet of Worms where Luther was examined and condemned by the Emperor, the German estates also presented a catalogue of 102 'oppressive burdens and abuses imposed upon . . . the German Empire by the Holy See of Rome'. But a fissure had already appeared two years earlier in 1519 when the Austrian-born Holy Roman Emperor Maximilian I had been succeeded by the Spanish-born Charles V, giving Germany's political leaders another foreign entity against which to define themselves.

In the early sixteenth century the 'Holy Roman Empire of the German Nation', which was described in 1667 as 'a body that conforms to no rule and resembles a monster', was a hotchpotch of electoral, princely and ecclesiastical states and free cities that possessed only the vaguest of yearnings for a cultural identity. But the Reformation set its scholars, artists and historians on a quest for what marked the heirs of Charlemagne as a people distinct from others. Luther himself made one massive contribution to this. Between 1520 and 1546 he was personally responsible for a third of all the vernacular publications that emerged from German print-shops. He wrote in a vigorous vernacular which could be, by turns vulgar and poetic. His greatest achievement was the German Bible (published in 1534), which did more than anything else to merge regional identities. Scarcely less influential were the catechisms Luther wrote for his 'dear German people', which gave them shared versions of the Creed and the Lord's Prayer.

If 1517 and 1521 are important dates in the life of Luther, 1525 is just as significant. In the midst of the Peasants' War and at a time when he was engaged in a theological contest with Erasmus, Luther astonished all his friends and distressed some of them: he got married. When asked why he was taking this step at the age of almost forty-three, he explained that since he had been advising monks and nuns who had left the cloister to espouse matrimony he should set an example. It may have been nearer the truth that the lady made the running. Katharina von Bora was a strong-willed and determined woman, a Catholic nun seventeen years his junior whom Luther helped escape from a convent. The event divided Luther's mature life into two equal halves: it was twenty years since he had entered the cloister and he had just over twenty years left to enjoy family life. But he did not retire into humdrum domesticity. His new status was as much a demonstration of biblical truth as his opposition to indulgences had been. It declared that virginity and celibacy were not superior vocations. It exalted the nuclear family as the essential building block of society. It emphasized the importance of the home for the nurturing of children in the Christian way and for the exercise of hospitality. It involved him in that little world of intimate relationships with its joys and griefs where lay people actually spent their lives. In short, the Luther family which grew up in the old Augustinian convent at Wittenberg became the model Protestant paternalistic *ménage,* a microcosm of the Church, where the head of the household was its bishop, gathering his children and servants around him for daily prayers and leading them to the church building for worship on Sundays. Over the years scores of university students lodged with the Luthers and it is thanks to some of them that we have the celebrated *Table Talk,* a collection of *obiter dicta* on all manner of subjects with which the great man regaled his guests at meal times.

Since the end of the Holy Roman Empire in 1806, Germany has endured successive identity crises that have impacted disastrously on the rest of Europe. The old north-south divide was resolved by Bismarck's Prussification of the new empire but resulted in a nationalist euphoria which the Iron Chancellor was powerless to control. So too the disasters of 1914–18 and 1939–45, which we can now see as a single conflict at the end of which Germany was once more divided, this time between east and west. The achievement of nationhood has cost Germany and her neighbours dear. It is inevitable that partisans of a greater reich have wanted to enlist to their cause one of the greatest and most patriotic of Germans. At the turn of the twentieth century Lutheran leaders had to choose whether or not to support expansionist policies. Those who did so, such as the members of the German-Christian party, unhesitatingly used their founder's name to persuade the electorate that the triumph of the master race was written into the marrow of the German people and that Luther had set the nation on its inevitable course by his defiance of foreign interference. Thus the Luther-to-Hitler myth was born. But the reformer was never a nationalist in the modern sense of the word. He was, above all, a pastor. Many of his convictions were expressed in books and pamphlets written to help people who consulted him about their problems. Thus, for example, when a mercenary soldier came to him with a troubled conscience the result was another pamphlet (1526): *Whether Soldiers, Too, Can Be Saved.* Although he lived to a good age, Luther worked himself to death. It is characteristic of the man that he hastened his end by travelling through atrocious weather to sort out a dispute between a landlord and his neighbours.

Luther, then, touched life at every level—the individual, the family, the church, the state—and he did so not as a dry-as-dust philosopher but as a flesh-and-blood, fallible human being, agonising about the important issues which faced all his contemporaries. He was a theologian who lived his theology.

He put the Bible at the centre of everything and, as well as applying it to every problem of prince and peasant, he tried to live it himself. Indeed, no one more than Martin Luther resembles the flawed hero of which the sacred text affords so many examples. If we do not, now, find him *simpatico* it is probably because we cannot share his biblical world view.

For Further Reading

Jacob Burckhardt, *Judgements on History and Historians,* (Eng. Trs, 1958); Steven Ozment, *The Reformation in the Cities,* (1975) *Luther's Works* (Eng. Trs, 55 vols, 1955–1986); R.H. Fife, *The Revolt of Martin Luther* (1957); H.A. Oberman, *Luther, Man Between God and the Devil* (Eng trs, 1989); M. Brecht, *Martin Luther,* 3 vols (Eng. Trs, 1985–93).

DEREK WILSON'S *Out of the Storm: The Life and Legacy of Martin Luther* is published this month by Hutchinson.

Explaining John Calvin

WILLIAM J. BOUWSMA

John Calvin (1509–64) has been credited, or blamed, for much that defines the modern Western world: capitalism and the work ethic, individualism and utilitarianism, modern science, and, at least among some devout Christians, a lingering suspicion of earthly pleasures. During [a] recent American presidential campaign, the two candidates appealed to "values" that recall the teachings of the 16th-century churchman, indicating that what William Pitt once said of England—"We have a Calvinist creed"—still may hold partly true for the United States. But the legend of the joyless tyrant of Geneva obscures both the real man, a humanist as much as a religious reformer, and the subtlety of his thought. Here his biographer discusses both.

Our image of John Calvin is largely the creation of austere Protestant churchmen who lived during the 17th century, the century following that of the great reformer's life. The image is most accurately evoked by the huge icon of Calvin, familiar to many a tourist, that stands behind the University of Geneva. There looms Calvin, twice as large as life, stylized beyond recognition, stony, rigid, immobile, and—except for his slightly abstracted disapproval of whatever we might imagine him to be contemplating—impassive.

Happily, the historical record provides good evidence for a Calvin very different from the figure invoked by his 17th-century followers. This Calvin is very much a man of the 16th century, a time of religious strife and social upheaval. His life and work reflect the ambiguities, contradictions, and agonies of that troubled time. Sixteenth-century thinkers, especially in Northern Europe, were still grappling with the rich but incoherent legacy of the Renaissance, and their characteristic intellectual constructions were less successful in reconciling its contradictory impulses than in balancing among them. This is why it has proved so difficult to pigeonhole such figures as Erasmus and Machiavelli or Montaigne and Shakespeare, and why they continue to stimulate reflection. Calvin, who can be quoted on both sides of most questions, belongs in this great company.

Born in 1509 in Noyon, Calvin was brought up to be a devout French Catholic. Indeed, his father, a lay administrator in the service of the local bishop, sent him to the University of Paris in 1523 to study for the priesthood. Later he decided that young John should be a lawyer. Accordingly, from 1528 to 1533, Calvin studied law. During these years he was also exposed to the evangelical humanism of Erasmus and Jacques Lefèvre d'Étaples that nourished the radical student movement of the time. The students called for salvation by grace rather than by good works and ceremonies—a position fully compatible with Catholic orthodoxy—as the foundation for a general reform of church and society on the model of antiquity.

To accomplish this end, the radical students advocated a return to the Bible, studied in its original languages. Calvin himself studied Greek and Hebrew as well as Latin, the "three languages" of ancient Christian discourse. His growing interest in the classics led, moreover, to his first publication, a moralizing commentary on Seneca's essay on clemency.

Late in 1533, the French government of Francis I became less tolerant of the Paris student radicals, whom it saw as a threat to the peace. After helping to prepare a statement of the theological implications of the movement in a public address delivered by Nicolas Cop, rector of the University, Calvin found it prudent to leave Paris. Eventually he made his way to Basel, a Protestant town tolerant of religious variety.

Up to this point, there is little evidence of Calvin's "conversion" to Protestantism. Before Basel, of course, he had been fully aware of the challenge Martin Luther posed to the Catholic Church. The 95 Theses that the German reformer posted in Wittenberg in 1517 attacked what Luther believed were corruptions of true Christianity and, by implication, the authors of those errors, the Renaissance popes. Luther, above all, rejected the idea of salvation through indulgences or the sacrament of penance. Excommunicated by Pope Leo X, he encouraged the formation of non-Roman churches.

In Basel, Calvin found himself drawing closer to Luther. Probably in part to clarify his own beliefs, he began to write, first a preface to his cousin Pierre Olivétan's French translation of the Bible, and then what became the first edition of the *Institutes,* his masterwork, which in its successive revisions became the single most important statement of Protestant belief. Although he did not substantially change his views thereafter, he elaborated them in later editions, published in both Latin and French, in which he also replied to his critics; the final versions appeared in 1559 and 1560.

The 1536 *Institutes* had brought him some renown among Protestant leaders, among them Guillaume Farel. A French Reformer struggling to plant Protestantism in Geneva, Farel persuaded Calvin to settle there in late 1536. The Reformation was in trouble in Geneva. Indeed, the limited enthusiasm of Geneva for Protestantism—and for religious and moral reform—continued almost until Calvin's death. The resistance was all the more serious because the town council in Geneva, as in other Protestant towns in Switzerland and southern Germany, exercised ultimate control over the church and the ministers.

The main issue was the right of excommunication, which the ministers regarded as essential to their authority but which the town council refused to concede. The uncompromising attitudes of Calvin and Farel finally resulted in their expulsion from Geneva in May of 1538.

C alvin found refuge for the next three years in Protestant Strasbourg, where he was pastor of a church for French-speaking refugees. Here he married Idelette de Bure, a widow in his congregation. Theirs proved to be an extremely warm relationship, although none of their children survived infancy.

During his Strasbourg years, Calvin learned much about church administration from Martin Bucer, chief pastor there. Attending European religious conferences, he soon became a major figure in the international Protestant movement.

Meanwhile, without strong leadership, the Protestant revolution in Geneva foundered. In September of 1541, Calvin was invited back, and there he remained until his death in 1564. He was now in a stronger position. In November the town council enacted his *Ecclesiastical Ordinances,* which provided for the religious education of the townspeople, especially children, and instituted his conception of church order. It established four groups of church officers and a "consistory" of pastors and elders to bring every aspect of Genevan life under the precepts of God's law.

The activities of the consistory gave substance to the legend of Geneva as a joyless theocracy, intolerant of looseness or pleasure. Under Calvin's leadership, it undertook a range of disciplinary actions covering everything from the abolition of Catholic "superstition" to the enforcement of sexual morality, the regulation of taverns, and measures against dancing, gambling, and swearing. These "Calvinist" measures were resented by many townsfolk, as was the arrival of increasing numbers of French Protestant refugees.

The resulting tensions, as well as the persecution of Calvin's followers in France, help to explain the trial and burning of one of Calvin's leading opponents, Michael Servetus. Calvin felt the need to show that his zeal for orthodoxy was no less than that of his foes. The confrontation between Calvin and his enemies in Geneva was finally resolved in May of 1555, when Calvin's opponents overreached themselves and the tide turned in his favor. His position in Geneva was henceforth reasonably secure.

But Calvin was no less occupied. He had to watch the European scene and keep his Protestant allies united. At the same time, Calvin never stopped promoting his kind of Protestantism. He welcomed the religious refugees who poured into Geneva, especially during the 1550s, from France, but also from England and Scotland, from Italy, Germany, and the Netherlands, and even from Eastern Europe. He trained many of them as ministers, sent them back to their homelands, and then supported them with letters of encouragement and advice. Geneva thus became the center of an international movement and a model for churches elsewhere. John Knox, the Calvinist leader of Scotland, described Geneva as "the most perfect school of Christ that ever was on the Earth since the days of the Apostles." So while Lutheranism was confined to parts of Germany and Scandinavia, Calvinism spread into Britain, the English-speaking colonies of North America, and many parts of Europe.

A cademic efforts to explain the appeal of Calvinism in terms of social class have had only limited success. In France, his theology was attractive mainly to a minority among the nobility and the urban upper classes, but in Germany it found adherents among both townsmen and princes. In England and the Netherlands, it made converts in every social group. Calvinism's appeal lay in its ability to explain disorders of the age afflicting all classes and in the remedies and comfort it provided, as much by its activism as by its doctrine. Both depended on the personality, preoccupations, and talents of Calvin himself.

Unlike Martin Luther, Calvin was a reticent man. He rarely expressed himself in the first person singular. This reticence has contributed to his reputation as cold and unapproachable. Those who knew him, however, noted his talent for friendship as well as his hot temper. The intensity of his grief on the death of his wife in 1549 revealed a large capacity for feeling, as did his empathetic reading of many passages in Scripture.

In fact, the impersonality of Calvin's teachings concealed an anxiety, unusually intense even in an anxious age. He saw anxiety everywhere, in himself, in the narratives of the Bible, and in his contemporaries. This feeling found expression in two of his favorite images for spiritual discomfort: the abyss and the labyrinth. The abyss represented all the nameless terrors of disorientation and the absence of familiar boundaries. The labyrinth expressed the anxiety of entrapment: in religious terms, the inability of human beings alienated from God to escape from the imprisonment of self-concern.

One side of Calvin sought to relieve his terror of the abyss with cultural constructions and patterns of control that might help him recover his sense of direction. This side of Calvin was attracted to classical philosophy, which nevertheless conjured up for him fears of entrapment in a labyrinth. Escape from this, however, exposed him to terrible uncertainties and, once again, to the horrors of the abyss. Calvin's ideas thus tended to oscillate between those of freedom and order. His problem was to strike a balance between the two.

He did so primarily with the resources of Renaissance humanism, applying its philological approach to recover a biblical understanding of Christianity. But humanism was not only, or even fundamentally, a scholarly movement. Its scholarship was instrumental to the recovery of the communicative skills of classical rhetoric. Humanists such as Lorenzo Valla and Erasmus held that an effective rhetoric would appeal to a deeper level of the personality than would a mere rational demonstration. By moving the heart, Christian rhetoric would stimulate human beings to the active reform of both themselves and the world.

Theological system-building, Calvin believed, was futile and inappropriate. He faulted the medieval Scholastic theologians for relying more on human reason than on the Bible, which spoke uniquely to the heart. The teachings of Thomas Aquinas, and like-minded theologians, appealed only to the intellect, and so were lifeless and irrelevant to a world in desperate need.

As a humanist, Calvin was a *biblical* theologian, prepared to follow Scripture even when it surpassed the limits of human understanding. And its message, for him, could not be presented as a set of timeless abstractions; it had to be adapted to the understanding of contemporaries according to the rhetorical principle of decorum—i.e. suitability to time, place, and audience.

Calvin shared with earlier humanists an essentially biblical conception of the human personality, not as a hierarchy of faculties ruled by reason but as a mysterious unity. This concept made the feelings and will even more important aspects of the personality than the intellect, and it also gave the body new dignity.

Indeed, Calvin largely rejected the traditional belief in hierarchy as the general principle of all order. For it he substituted the practical (rather than the metaphysical) principle of *utility*. This position found expression in his preference, among the possible forms of government, for republics. It also undermined, for him, the traditional subordination of women to men. Calvin's Geneva accordingly insisted on a single standard of sexual morality—a radical departure from custom.

Calvin's utilitarianism was also reflected in deep reservations about the capacity of human beings to attain anything but practical knowledge. The notion that they can know anything absolutely, as God knows it, so to speak, seemed to him deeply presumptuous. This helps to explain his reliance on the Bible: Human beings have access to the saving truths of religion only insofar as God has revealed them in Scripture. But revealed truth, for Calvin, was not revealed to satisfy human curiosity; it too was limited to meeting the most urgent and practical needs, above all for individual salvation. This practicality also reflects a basic conviction of Renaissance thinkers: the superiority of an active life to one of contemplation. Calvin's conviction that every occupation in society is a "calling" on the part of God himself sanctified this conception.

But Calvin was not only a Renaissance humanist. The culture of 16th-century Europe was peculiarly eclectic. Like other thinkers of his time, Calvin had inherited a set of quite contrary tendencies that he uneasily combined with his humanism. Thus, even as he emphasized the heart, Calvin continued to conceive of the human personality as a hierarchy of faculties ruled by reason; from time to time he tried uneasily, with little success, to reconcile the two conceptions. This is why he sometimes emphasized the importance of rational control over the passions—an emphasis that has been reassuring to conservatives.

Calvin's theology has often been seen as little more than a systematization of the more creative insights of Luther. He followed Luther, indeed, on many points: on original sin, on Scripture, on the absolute dependence of human beings on divine grace, and on justification by faith alone. Other differences between Calvin and Luther are largely matters of emphasis. His understanding of predestination, contrary to a general impression, was virtually identical to Luther's; it was not of central importance to his theology. He believed that it meant that the salvation of believers by a loving God was absolutely certain.

In major respects, however, Calvin departed from Luther. In some ways he was more radical, but most of his differences suggest that he was closer to Catholicism than Luther, as in his insistence on the importance of the historical church. He was also more traditional in his belief in the authority of clergy over laity, perhaps as a result of his difficulties with the Geneva town council. Even more significant, especially for Calvinism as a historical force, was Calvin's attitude toward the everyday world. Luther had regarded this world and its institutions as incorrigible, and was prepared to leave them to the devil. But for Calvin this world, created by God, still belonged to Him; it remained potentially His kingdom; and every Christian was obliged to devote his life to make it so in reality by reforming and bringing it under God's law.

Calvin's thought was less a theology to be comprehended by the mind than a set of principles for the Christian life: in short, spirituality. He was more concerned with the experience and application of Christianity than with mere reflection about it. His true successors were Calvinist pastors rather than Calvinist theologians. Significantly, in addition to devoting much of his energy to the training of other pastors, Calvin was himself a pastor. He preached regularly: some 4,000 sermons in the 13 years after his return to Geneva.

Calvin's spirituality begins with the conviction that we do not so much "know" God as "experience" him indirectly, through his mighty acts and works in the world, as we experience but can hardly be said to know thunder, one of Calvin's favorite metaphors for religious experience. Calvin also believed that human beings can understand something of what God is like in the love of a father for his children, but also—surprisingly in one often identified with patriarchy—in the love of a mother. He denounced those who represented God as dreadful; God for him is "mild, kind, gentle, and compassionate."

Nevertheless, in spite of this attention to God's love for mankind, Calvin gave particular emphasis to God's power because it was this that finally made his love effective in the work of redemption from sin. God, for Calvin, represented supremely all the ways in which human beings experience power: as energy, as warmth, as vitality, and, so, as life itself.

Sin, by contrast, is manifested precisely in the negation of every kind of power and ultimately of the life force given by God. Sin *deadens* and, above all, deadens the feelings. Saving grace, then, must be conceived as the transfusion of God's power—his warmth, passion, strength, vitality—to human beings. It was also essential to Calvin's spirituality, and a reflection of his realism, that this "transfusion" be not instantaneous but gradual.

Calvin's traditional metaphor for the good Christian life implied activity: "Our life is like a journey," he asserted, but "it is not God's will that we should march along casually as we please, but he sets the goal before us, and also directs us on the right way to it." This way is also a struggle.

Complex as his ideas were, it is easy to see how the later history of Calvinism has often been obscured by scholars' failure to distinguish among (1) Calvinism as the beliefs of Calvin himself, (2) the beliefs of his followers, who, though striving to be faithful to Calvin, modified his teachings to meet their own needs, and (3) more loosely, the beliefs of the Reformed tradition of Protestant Christianity, in which Calvinism proper was only one, albeit the most prominent, strand.

The Reformed churches in the 16th century were referred to in the plural to indicate, along with what they had in common, their individual autonomy and variety. They consisted originally of a group of non-Lutheran Protestant churches based in towns in Switzerland and southern Germany. These churches were jealous of their autonomy; and Geneva was not alone among them in having distinguished theological leadership. Ulrich Zwingli and Heinrich Bullinger in Zurich and Martin Bucer in Strasbourg also had a European influence that combined with that of Calvin, especially in England, to shape what came to be called "Calvinism."

Long after Calvin's death in 1564, the churchmen in Geneva continued to venerate him and aimed at being faithful to his teaching under his successors, first among them Theodore de Bèze. But during what can be appropriately described as a Protestant "Counter Reformation," the later Calvinism of Geneva, abandoning Calvin's more humanistic tendencies and drawing more on other, sterner aspects of his thought, was increasingly intellectualized. Indeed, it grew to resemble the medieval Scholasticism that Calvin had abhorred.

Predestination now began to assume an importance that had not been attributed to it before. Whereas Calvin had been led by personal faith to an awed belief in predestination as a benign manifestation of divine providence, predestination now became a threatening doctrine: God's decree determined in advance an individual's salvation or damnation. What good, one might wonder, were one's own best efforts if God had already ruled? In 1619 these tendencies reached a climax at the Synod of Dort in the Netherlands, which spelled out various corollaries of predestination, as Calvin had never done, and made the doctrine central to Calvinism.

Calvinist theologians, meanwhile, apparently finding Calvin's loose rhetorical style of expression unsatisfactory, began deliberately to write like Scholastic theologians, in Latin, and even appealed to medieval Scholastic authorities. The major Calvinist theological statement of the 17th century was the *Institutio Theologiae Elencticae* (3 vols., Geneva, 1688) of François Turretin, chief pastor of Geneva. Although the title of this work recalled Calvin's masterpiece, it was published in Latin, its dialectical structure followed the model of the great *Summas* of Thomas Aquinas, and it suggested at least as much confidence as Thomas in the value of human reason. The lasting effect of this shift is suggested by the fact that "Turretin," in Latin, was the basic theology textbook at the Princeton Seminary in New Jersey, the most distinguished intellectual center of American Calvinism until the middle of the 19th century.

Historians have continued to debate whether these developments were essentially faithful to Calvin or deviations from him. In some sense they were both. Later Calvinist theologians, as they abandoned Calvin's more humanistic tendencies and emphasized his more austere and dogmatic side, found precedents for these changes in the contrary aspects of his thought. They were untrue to Calvin, of course, in rejecting his typically Renaissance concern with balancing contrary impulses. One must remember, however, that these changes in Calvinism occurred during a period of singular disorder in Europe, caused by, among other things, a century of religious warfare. As a result, there was a widespread longing for certainty, security, and peace.

One or another aspect of Calvin's influence has persisted not only in the Reformed churches of France, Germany, Scotland, the Netherlands, and Hungary but also in the Church of England, where he was long as highly regarded as he was by Puritans who had separated from the Anglican establishment. The latter organized their own churches, Presbyterian or Congregational, and brought Calvinism to North America 300 years ago.

Even today these churches, along with the originally German Evangelical and Reformed Church, remember Calvin—that is, the strict Calvin of Geneva—as their founding father. Eventually Calvinist theology was also widely accepted by major groups of American Baptists; and even Unitarianism, which broke away from the Calvinist churches of New England during the 18th century, reflected the more rational impulses in Calvin's theology. More recently, Protestant interest in the social implications of the Gospel and Protestant Neo-Orthodoxy, as represented by Karl Barth and Reinhold Niebuhr, reflect the continuing influence of John Calvin.

Calvin's larger influence over the development of modern Western civilization has been variously assessed. The controversial "Weber thesis" attributed the rise of modern capitalism largely to habits encouraged by Puritanism, but Max Weber (1864–1920) avoided implicating Calvin himself. Much the same can be said about efforts to link Calvinism to the rise of early modern science; Puritans were prominent in the scientific movement of 17th-century England, but Calvin himself was indifferent to the science of his own day.

A somewhat better case can be made for Calvin's influence on political theory. His own political instincts were highly conservative, and he preached the submission of private persons to all legitimate authority. But, like Italian humanists of the 15th and 16th centuries, he personally preferred a republic to a monarchy; and in confronting the problem posed by rulers who actively opposed the spread of the Gospel, he advanced a theory of resistance, kept alive by his followers, according to which lesser magistrates might legitimately rebel against kings. And, unlike most of his contemporaries, Calvin included among the proper responsibilities of states not only the maintenance of public order but also a positive concern for the general welfare of society. Calvinism has a place, therefore, in the evolution of liberal political thought. His most durable influence, nevertheless, has been religious. From Calvin's time to the present, Calvinism has meant a peculiar seriousness about Christianity and its ethical implications.

William J. Bouwsma, 65, is Sather Professor of History at the University of California, Berkeley. Born in Ann Arbor, Michigan, he received an AB (1943), an MA (1947), and a PhD (1950) from Harvard. He is the author of, among other books, *Venice and the Defense of Republican Liberty* (1968) and *John Calvin: A Sixteenth-Century Portrait* (1988).

Reprinted with permission from *The Wilson Quarterly*, New Year's 1989 Edition, pp. 68–75. Copyright © 1989 by William J. Bouwsma. Reprinted by permission of the author.

Who Was Henry VIII and When Did It All Go Wrong?

Suzannah Lipscomb looks beyond the stereotypes that surround our most infamous monarch to ask this question.

SUZANNAH LIPSCOMB

We all think we know Henry VIII (r. 1509–47) and all there is to know about him. The Holbein portraits, the profusion of television dramas and films, the novels and histories set in his world make him ubiquitous. A whole set of clichés, truisms and fallacies accompany that famous silhouette. As a character, the king both repulses and fascinates us. His vast girth, larger than life persona, grandeur, pomp, arrogance and appetites make us strangely proud of this hypermasculine, fabled monarch.

Yet much of what we think we know about Henry VIII is just that—fable. We think of him in stereotypes. In 2007, in her column in *The Observer,* Victoria Coren wrote with heavy sarcasm: 'If you type "wife-killing" into Google, the first listing is a reference to Henry VIII, of wife-killing notoriety. Oh, *that* Henry VIII.' Popular perceptions of Henry VIII, according to focus groups consulted by the market research agency BDRC for Historic Royal Palaces, are that he was a fat guy who had six, or maybe eight wives, and that he killed a lot of them. In April 2007, next to a tomb in Oxford's Christ Church cathedral, where the heads of female figurines had broken off, I heard one man comment to another, 'Henry VIII has a lot to answer for, hasn't he?'

Myths and half-truths have accrued around Henry VIII through the distorted pictures given by filmmakers. Each film makes its own Henry and tells us far more about the preoccupations of each generation of filmmakers than they do about the king's character. Recent scholarship has shown that the Henrys of the 1930s, 1960s and 2000s differ wildly because they were designed to appeal to the different cultural imperatives of each era. Charles Laughton's Henry of 1933 in *The Private Life of Henry VIII* was an immature, sexually coy, sympathetic victim of his wives' machinations. Made for a culture that revered royalty, he is a comic, overly sentimental manchild, to be pitied and petted. By 1969, in *Anne of the Thousand Days,* Richard Burton could play Henry as a good-looking, suave, alpha male. He may have been arrogant and self-centred, but this was the pre-feminist, James Bond era—such a macho, lovable rascal was an unproblematic hero. In the 21st century, Henry VIII changed again. Still an alpha male, this time Ray Winstone played him as a gangster-king, 'the Godfather in tights', according to the television series' director Peter Travis. Winstone's Henry mixes sensitivity with aggression; he's easily led, has temper tantrums; and can be brutally aggressive, as in the disturbingly fictitious rape scene that writer Peter Morgan also added to the more recent film, *The Other Boleyn Girl.* As the critic Mark Lawson noted when the series came out, this Henry responds to sexual politics *after* the revolution—it is hard on Henry and soft on his women. *The Tudors,* a British television series made with more than one eye on the US market, plays into the Zeitgeist in another way. Testament to a cultural obsession with male body image, Jonathan Rhys-Meyers' Henry VIII looks like footballer David Beckham, but is otherwise characterised very similarly to the infantile king of *The Private Life.* Henry VIII's screen appearances have seeped into the collective consciousness—but this does not make them any more reliable, or true, as representations of a historic figure.

Another thing obscuring our relative ignorance about Henry as an individual is that what we mistake for knowledge about the king is in fact knowledge of what was around him. This year will see a spate of biographies of Henry VIII to mark the 500th anniversary of his accession and coronation, but it is striking that hitherto it has been his wives, courtiers and children who have been constantly revisited. Even where the information was more specifically concerned with Henry, it is not rare to find a recap of his tumultuous marital history, a plethora of details about his court, or a catalogue of his activities substituting for a true understanding of his character and motivations. That Henry VIII was a warrior or jouster only sheds light on his personality when we understand the cultural significance of these activities. Henry VIII has seemed like a rather large void at the centre of a maelstrom of information about early Tudor society.

Finally, perhaps the greatest problem with the popular impression of Henry VIII's character is that it is immutable. To understand a king who reigned for 38 years through one clichéd snapshot that is not dynamic and does not show change over time is hardly credible. Too often, we take our understanding of Henry in his last days and use it as a blueprint for the rest of his life and his reign, ascribing to him, for instance, character flaws in his early years that were not manifest until much later on. As such, he has become a caricature, a cipher.

So how can we get at a more profound understanding of this enigmatic man? There are obviously problems with putting historical figures on the psychiatrist's couch. Even ignoring the fact that the approach could, at worst, be thoroughly anachronistic, historians lack the sort of evidence that would most helpfully inform such a study. We have limited access to Henry VIII's thoughts, motivations and emotions—there are, for example, no helpful confessional diaries for the period of Anne Boleyn's arrest and execution. The historian Eric Ives has called Henry's psychology 'the ultimate unresolvable paradox of Tudor history'. Yet, we do have many contemporary reports of the king's behaviour and speech, such as those of the Imperial ambassador, Eustace Chapuys. We also have some of Henry's letters and the theological treatises he worked on and we possess a whole panoply of state papers, royal proclamations and Acts of Parliament. We can also situate the man in his time. Together, such evidence allows us to make cautious judgements about Henry VIII's character.

My research for Hampton Court Palace in the run-up to the 500th anniversary has suggested one fruitful way of getting to know the king. This is to recognise, and seek to understand, the stark differences between the early and the later king.

Henry VIII's accession in 1509 was received with rapturous praise. William Blount, Lord Mountjoy wrote in a letter to the great humanist Desiderius Erasmus on May 27th:

> When you know what a hero [the king] now shows himself, how wisely he behaves, what a lover he is

of justice and goodness, what affection he bears to the learned, I will venture that you need no wings to make you fly to behold this new and auspicious star. If you could see how all the world here is rejoicing in the possession of so great a prince, how his life is all their desire, you could not contain your tears of joy. The heavens laugh, the earth exults, all things are full of milk, of honey, of nectar. Avarice is expelled from the country. Liberality scatters wealth with bounteous hand. Our King does not desire gold or gems or precious metals, but virtue, glory and immortality.

It is not difficult to understand the tendency to such hyperbole in the inaugural period of the new reign. Nevertheless, as a young man, and for at least the first 20 years of his reign (he was just weeks away from his 18th birthday when he became king), Henry was consistently and unequivocally judged to be peerless in appearance, aptitudes and accomplishments.

For a start, Henry was clearly good-looking. The Venetian ambassador Sebastian Giustinian described him as 'the handsomest potentate I ever set eyes on' and remarked on his 'round face so very beautiful, that it would become a pretty woman'. The chronicler Edward Hall rhapsodised that:

> The features of his body, his goodly personage, his amiable visage, princely countenance, with the noble qualities of his royal estate, to every man known, needs no rehearsal, considering that, for lack of cunning, I cannot express the gifts of grace and of nature that God has endowed him with all.

Henry was gifted in other ways too. He demonstrated great intelligence and mental acuity. Erasmus wrote glowingly that even 'when the King was no more than a child . . . he had a vivid and active mind, above measure to execute whatever tasks he undertook . . . you would say that he was a universal genius.' As a skilful linguist, Henry spoke French, Spanish and Latin. He was a talented musician and composer. To entertain a visiting embassy from France in July 1517, Henry sang and played on every musical instrument available. In his report on the event, Francesco Chieregato, the Apostolic Nuncio in England, remarked that Henry was 'a most invincible King, whose acquirements and qualities are so many and excellent that I consider him to excel all who ever wore a crown.'

Henry's achievements also extended to physical activities. Ambassadors noted how beautifully he danced, while an observer of the 1513 campaign against France recalled the king practising archery with the archers of his guard, and how 'he cleft the mark in the middle, and surpassed them all, as he surpasses them in stature and personal graces.' He was fond of tennis, 'at which game it was the prettiest thing in the world to see him play; his fair skin glowing through a shirt of the finest texture', and was also 'a capital horseman, and a fine jouster'. Henry delighted in hunting, tiring eight or 10 horses a day before exhausting himself. Ambassador Giustinian judged Henry in 1515 as:

> not only expert in arms, and of great valour, and most excellent in his personal endowments, but . . . likewise so gifted and adorned with mental accomplishments of every sort that we believe him to have few equals in the world.

This energetic attitude towards sports was an essential part of his character and his youthful ebullience was sustained throughout his 20s and 30s. Contemporary reports suggest that Henry was spirited, mirthful and exuberant, 'young, lusty and courageous . . . [and] disposed to all mirth and pleasure'. He devoted his time to the pursuit of fun and revelled in entertainments, masques, banqueting and merrymaking. Court festivities were held on an astonishingly grand and lavish scale. To mark May Day in 1515, the king and his guard gathered at a wood near Greenwich Palace dressed all in green as Robin Hood and his Merry Men. Attended by 100 noblemen on horseback who were 'gorgeously arrayed', singers and musicians playing from bowers, and sweetly singing birds amassed for the occasion, Henry's court enjoyed a sumptuous open-air banquet, before processing back to Greenwich for a jousting tournament.

1536 was Henry's *annus horribilis*. In the course of one year he suffered threats, betrayals, rebellion, injury, grief and anxieties on a terrific scale.

Such flamboyance was also reflected in the magnificent finery of his wardrobe. The records unlocked by the costume historian Maria Hayward include frequent references to brocade, ermine, satin, velvet and huge, conspicuous jewels, including a round cut diamond that was described by one observer as 'the size of the largest walnut I ever saw'. As Henry was extremely charismatic and had great stage-presence, this combination of boisterousness and opulence was strangely compelling. Perhaps most surprisingly of all, commentators almost universally described his nature as warm and benevolent. In 1519, summing up four years at the English court, Giustinian enthused about how Henry was so 'affable and gracious', a man who 'harmed no one'. Ten years later,

Erasmus would call him 'a man of gentle friendliness, and gentle in debate; he acts more like a companion than a king.' Henry appears in his early years to have been friendly, affectionate and generous in gifts and attention.

What a contrast this is to reports of Henry VIII in later life. The most obvious change was in the king's appearance. Between the ages of 23 and 45 his waist and chest measurements increased gradually from 35 to 45 inches. After his 45th birthday in 1536, he quickly became gross—by 1541, his waist measured 54 inches, his chest 57. But this was the least of the changes. Instead of being known for the ease of his companionship and gentle graciousness, the older Henry was reputed to be irritable, capricious and capable of great cruelty. Comments were made about his increasing irascibility and *mal d'esprit*: 'The King was irritated and . . . his ministers were at a loss to account for it.' Others commented on his mercurial unpredictability: 'People worth credit say he is often of a different opinion in the morning than after dinner.' His volatile moods were a source of anxiety for his counsellors. He was violent with some—he would 'beknave' his erstwhile closest confidant and chief minister Thomas Cromwell twice a week, hitting 'him well about the pate'. Others he berated—after Cromwell's execution in 1540, Henry blamed his advisers for having 'upon light pretexts, by false accusations . . . made him put to death the most faithful servant he ever had'. Some of this stemmed from the inflamed condition of a varicose ulcer in the king's leg, probably reopened by a jousting accident in 1536. This ulcer brought him constant and debilitating pain, together with infections, fevers and discharges that produced a putrid smell. This undoubtedly had an impact on his temper, although cannot in itself explain its violent capriciousness.

By 1540, Charles de Marillac, the French ambassador, would describe Henry VIII as fearful, inconstant and 'so covetous that all the riches in the world would not satisfy him'. According to Marillac, Henry's inability 'to trust a single man' meant that 'he will not cease to dip his hand in blood' and 'every day edicts are published so sanguinary that with a thousand guards one would scarce be safe'. Such savagery was a particular feature of the reign after 1536. There are some notable exceptions from early in his reign, but Henry's tendency towards the cruel dispatching of those who had wronged him— including those very close to him—reached its apogee in his last decade. The method of dealing with miscreants also changed. After 1536, of all the high-status individuals executed at the king's behest, only the leaders of the Pilgrimage of Grace and the conspirators of the Exeter plot were tried and executed by judicial process. Everyone else of high status accused of high treason was convicted and executed on the basis of parliamentary attainder—that is, an act passed through Parliament that declared the accused guilty and condemned them to death without recourse to a common law trial. Attainders did not need to cite specific evidence or name precise crimes. Victims of this method included Thomas Cromwell, his fifth wife, young Catherine Howard, and the septuagenarian Margaret Pole, Countess of Salisbury, whose death on charges of treason when 'so infirm and weakened by interrogation that she had to be carried to the scaffold in a chair', the historian Greg Walker has called 'the nadir of royal vindictiveness'. Despite her royal blood, she was clearly no real threat to the realm.

Henry had become a misanthropic, suspicious and cruel king, and his subjects began (discreetly, for such words were illegal) to call him a tyrant. In his early years, Henry's charisma and egoism had been directed into a little showing-off while jousting (on one occasion he presented himself before the queen and the ladies with 'a thousand jumps in the air'), but the ends to which these qualities were now deployed had changed. Now they fuelled a vastly more repressive and harsh regime.

The idea of a king whose life was a tale of two halves helps enormously in reaching a more accurate understanding of Henry VIII's character. The next challenge is to work out how, when and why this change occurred. Scholars have suggested a variety of psychological turning points. Miles F. Shore, a professor of psychiatry at Harvard Medical School, plumped for 1525–27, when he hypothesised that Henry had experienced 'a crisis of generativity' caused by the reality of middle age and his inability to live up to his youthful narcissistic fantasies of omnipotence. Arthur Salisbury MacNulty suggested around 1527 and linked this to a head injury sustained by Henry in 1524. He cautiously reasoned that a cerebral injury could explain Henry's shift in behaviour and character from Jekyll to Hyde. The psychologist J.C. Flügel positioned the change around 1533, when he thought that Henry had undergone 'a marked transformation' and become 'vastly more despotic'.

To me, the evidence suggests that we should consider a slightly later date. Although the change was partly the result of a cumulative process, the year 1536 contained all the ingredients necessary to catalyse, foster and entrench this change. It was Henry VIII's *annus horribilis*. In the course of one year, the 45-year-old king suffered threats, betrayals, rebellion, disappointments, injury, grief and anxieties on a terrific scale. A near-fatal fall from his horse in January 1536 left this great athlete of the tiltyard injured and unable to joust again, when for Henry the pursuit of physical masculine activity was strongly linked to his sense of self. This injury was also the key to his later obesity. Henry's wife, Anne Boleyn, suffered a miscarriage of a male child on the same day as his first wife's funeral. In March 1536, Parliament passed an Act that was to have enormous repercussions—the Act for the Dissolution of the Smaller Monasteries. At the same time, Henry received a book, written by Reginald Pole, his own cousin, which viciously attacked Henry's role as the Supreme Head of the Church of England. In May, Anne was 'discovered' to be an adulteress with a number of men of the king's privy chamber and the confession of a key defendant provoked her rapid arrest, trial and execution on May 19th. Almost immediately, Henry remarried to Jane Seymour (Hans Holbein's famous head and shoulders portraits of the pair date from this time and this portrait of Henry strongly influenced Holbein's full-length portrait of a year later.) In July, soon after Henry had forced his daughter Mary to swear to her own illegitimacy, Henry's only son, the illegitimate Henry Fitzroy, Duke of Richmond and Somerset, died aged 17, leaving the king entirely heirless. The summer of 1536 saw a number of defiant religious innovations, including the publication of the Ten Articles, the first doctrinal statement of the new Church of England. These religious changes led, in October, to a series of linked uprisings that formed the largest peacetime rebellion against an English monarch, which Henry's small armies could not have defeated if it came to battle, and the pope issued a bull which threatened to make the invasion and overthrow of Henry's throne legitimate. Henry responded to all these blows by extreme reaction—decisively reasserting his power and raging against his enemies—but he was, nevertheless, broken by the tumultuous events of this one year. Looking at how and why Henry VIII changed will help us better to understand this mysterious and inscrutable king.

Further Reading

Lacey Baldwin Smith, *Henry VIII: The Mask of Royalty* (Academy, 1987); Thomas S. Freeman and Susan Doran, *Tudors and Stuarts on Film: Historical Perspectives* (CUP, 2009); Maria Hayward, *Dress at the Court of King Henry VIII* (Maney, 2007); David Starkey, *Henry: Virtuous Prince* (HarperPress, 2008); Greg Walker, *The Private Life of Henry VIII* (The British Film Guide 8, BFI, 2003); Alison Weir, *Henry VIII: King and Court* (Vintage, 2001); Derek Wilson, *In the Lion's Court: Power, Ambition and Sudden Death in the Reign of Henry VIII* (Hutchinson, 2001).

SUZANNAH LIPSCOMB is Research Curator at Hampton Court Palace. Her new book, *1536: The Year that Changed Henry VIII*, is published by Lion Hudson.

Women in War

In the roughly organized armies of 16th century Europe, there was literally a woman with every man. They were partners in pillage.

JOHN A. LYNN

"When you recruit a regiment of German soldiers today, you do not only acquire 3,000 soldiers; along with these you will certainly find 4,000 women and children." So observed Johann Jacob von Wallhausen in his 1615 treatise on war, Kriegskunst zu Fuss. During the 16th and 17th centuries, great crowds of camp women were not unusual; they were the rule. Not mere camp followers, women were an essential element of military forces in the field, providing many services to the troops. In fact, the presence of these women helps explain the very existence of early modern European armies and the conduct of war.

The tasks performed by camp women did include prostitution, but also traditional women's work like laundry, meal preparation and petty commerce, and even heavy camp labor— contemporary woodcuts often illustrate a soldier paired with a woman, who is usually bent under a heavier load than that borne by her male companion. The most important contribution of women in this era, however, was the seizing and managing of pillage. Without pillage, armies could not exist.

During the 16th and 17th centuries, European rulers, including Philip II of Spain and Louis XIII of France, commonly fielded armies they could not afford to pay or supply. Troops from the Spanish army of Flanders, for instance, charged in 1594 that they had not been paid for 100 months. Even when men did receive their pay, it was often insufficient to sustain them. A 1574 document complained that whereas a frugal soldier would need 10 pattards per day just for food, he received only four. Although soldiers were supposed to be fighting to earn money, one observer of the Thirty Years' War (1618–48) wrote, "If you will consider how their wages are paid, I suppose, you will rather think them Voluntaries, at least very generous, for doing the greatest part of their service for nothing." Some commanders even saw an advantage to paying troops irregularly. "To keep the troops together, it is a good thing to owe them something," observed the great Spanish general Ambrosio Spinola. His harsh logic held that troops would be less likely to desert if they expected to receive back pay in the future. However, while underpaying troops might keep an army together,

it practically guaranteed a breakdown in discipline, as troops turned to plunder as a form of compensation.

Troops with empty pockets and empty stomachs took matters into their own hands. Some responded by mutiny; the Spanish army of Flanders, commanded by such great generals as the dukes of Alva and Parma, suffered more than 45 mutinies between 1572 and 1607, including the horrendous 1576 Sack of Antwerp.

Most troops sought sustenance and compensation on campaign by pillaging the civilian communities that lay in their paths. "It is deplorable that our soldiers dedicate themselves to pillage rather than to honourable feats," wrote Pierre de Brantôme of his experience during the French Religious Wars (1662–74). "But it is all due to their not being paid." Princes might issue high-sounding declarations condemning troops for abusing civilian populations, but the bitter reality was that if those same rulers actually eliminated such excesses, they would have had to disband their armies as unaffordable.

The practice of allowing soldiers to pillage permeated the era. It was accepted as a distasteful but practical necessity. "One finds enough soldiers when one gives them the freedom to live off the land, and allowing them to pillage supports them without pay," concluded the annual register of current affairs, the Mercure François, in 1622. French monarch Louis XIV (r. 1643–1715) offered the same observation in his memoirs for the year 1666: "Of late, some commanders are found who have made great armies subsist for a long time without giving them any pay other than the license of pillaging everywhere."

Pillage and its associated savagery—beatings, torture, rape and murder—certainly warranted condemnation, even when inflicted on civilians loyal to the enemy, However, raiders made little distinction between friend and foe, even victimizing the loyal subjects of the government served by the soldiers. One observer described shameful conduct by the Florentine Black Bands as they marched through friendly territory in 1527: "[They are] worse than Turks. In the Valdarno, they have sacked three Florentine villages, raped women and perpetrated other very cruel things." Troops fielded by the Bourbon kings of

France notoriously ravaged the French countryside during the first half of the 17th century.

Because pillage was officially outlawed—if actually tolerated—the take from plunder was not tallied in royal accounts, even though it constituted a high proportion of military personnel expenses. Consequently, the true size of the pillage economy will always remain more or less unknown. This is further compounded by the fact that pillage supported not only soldiers, but also the vast array of civilians who accompanied them in the field, including camp women, who mastered the brutal business of plundering.

A military force in the field during the early modern period did not resemble an army as we know it today. Soldiers constituted only part of a campaign community, in which they lived symbiotically with male and female noncombatants. Officers and soldiers employed servant boys. Teamsters hauled wagons and cannon using draught animals supplied by private contractors. Entrepreneurs supplied bread to armies, sending their own staffs, including bakers, into the field. A large collection of other tradesmen—blacksmiths, wheelwrights, carpenters—served the community. Merchants and sutlers sold essentials and amenities to the troops.

Comprising such a varied multitude, a campaign community rivaled in complexity and size all but the largest towns of the day. A force of 25,000 soldiers with its accompanying supporters represented a larger population than that of contemporary Bordeaux, Strasbourg, or Turin. It is no exaggeration to describe military camps as cities on the march.

The campaign communities, moreover, formed a world apart, living according to their own rules, which were often quite hostile to civilian society—and vice versa. A mercenary principle drove enlistment; most common soldiers joined the ranks because they had few other options and hoped to fare better on campaign. A German woodcut dating from the 1530s makes this point with a poem attached to an illustration of a would-be Landsknecht, the much-feared, heavily armed Germanic mercenary of the 16th century: A tailor complains, "I must sit long hours for little pay with which I can hardly survive," so he decides to try his luck in "the open field to the sound of pipes and drums." The Englishman Sydnam Poyntz confessed a similar reason for enlisting in the 1620s: "My necessitie forced mee, my Money being growne short, to take the manes of a private soldier." Women opted for camp life with much the same rationale.

This need to survive and a desire to prosper ensured that men and the women who joined them on campaigns would prey upon the unfortunate civilian communities that lay in their paths. Troops quartered in civilian homes abused their hosts; pillagers stole, raped and murdered. The result of such violence was a pervasive animosity toward armies that, in turn, inspired the campaign community to reject the civilian world, its mundane life and its standards of propriety.

Although common soldiers came from the peasantry and urban working classes themselves, they announced their separation from such origins by sporting distinctive and often outlandish apparel. Most extreme was the bizarre multicolored and slashed garb of Landsknechts, though soldiers of other nations

adopted their own extreme fashions. An early 17th century description of Spanish infantry claimed, "It is the finery, the plumes and the bright colors which give spirit and strength to a soldier so that he can with furious resolution overcome any difficulty or accomplish any valorous exploit." These sons of the laboring classes transformed themselves from subservient sparrows to aggressive peacocks.

Campaign communities lived by codes that were libertine and brutal. Soldiers of the early modern era were known for drinking, gambling, wenching and fighting. The novelist Johann Jacob Christoffel von Grimmelshausen, who had fought in the Thirty Years' War, summed up the soldiers' lifestyle with its violence, suffering and poverty:

Their whole existence consisted of eating and drinking, going hungry and thirsty, whoring and sodomizing, gaming and dicing, guzzling and gorging, murdering and being murdered, killing and being killed, torturing and being tortured, terrifying and being terrified . . . pillaging and being pillaged.

Within this hard and hostile community, women performed a broad range of tasks. The most obvious, but by no means the most characteristic, employment was prostitution. The term "camp follower" is often regarded as synonymous with prostitute, and there is no question that prostitutes plied their trade with the troops. Many military authorities favored having them in camp for reasons of public order and efficiency. Public order argued that soldiers who relied on camp prostitutes for sex would be less likely to trouble respectable women; according to Mathieu de la Simonne, writing in the 1620s, "It is good for the local inhabitants, it is said, because their wives, daughters and sisters will be more in security." Efficiency justified bringing along a limited number of prostitutes to satisfy the men's urges instead of dragging along a far greater number of wives who would encumber armies.

Over time, however, tolerance of camp prostitution declined. Rising rates of venereal disease led commanders to see prostitutes as dangers to health, and the strict moral codes brought about by the Reformation and Counter-Reformation advocated marriage and condemned prostitution outright. Frederick William, the great elector of Brandenburg, banned prostitutes from his army by an article of war in September 1656, as did Louis XIV from French forces in the 1680s.

The great majority of camp women belonged to two other categories: wives and so-called "whores"—the unmarried female partners of soldiers. These women were not prostitutes, as each accompanied a single man, yet contemporary accounts often refer to them as "whores," and the officer in charge of keeping order among camp women on the march was known in German as a Hurenweibel, or whoremaster. The nature of the relationship between a soldier and his whore is suggested by the German practice of "May marriages," agreements to stay together for the campaign season, which traditionally began in May. Dionysius Klein, writing at the end of the 16th century, described such liaisons and their rationales:

German soldiers, no sooner an expedition arrives, saddle themselves with frivolous and loose women with whom they contract "May marriages," whom they drag here and there just as millers do their sacks. The soldiers enhance the situation by pretending that in war they cannot get along without women; they are needed to take care of clothes, equipment and valuables; and in cases of illness, injury or any other personal harm, the women are needed to nurse and take care of them.

Wives and whores applied themselves to traditional and necessary women's work. Laundering, for one, was almost exclusively a feminine chore that soldiers regarded as unmanly. In *The Life of Courage: The Notorious Thief, Whore and Vagabond,* Grimmelshausen has his female antiheroine, Courage, declare, "I refused to let [my husband] stay in the castle without me for fear he would be eaten up by lice, as there were no women to keep the men clean." Basic needlework also fell to women, who repaired clothes, stitched shirts and sewed linens. Nursing, too, was considered a particularly feminine talent. When Robert Venables, one of Cromwell's favored generals during the English Civil Wars, was censured for including his wife and allowing some soldiers to bring their wives on his disastrous expedition to the West Indies in 1654–55, he replied that experience in the Irish wars had demonstrated "the necessity of having that sex with an army to attend upon and help the sick and wounded, which men are unfit for." Cooking, although not narrowly defined as a woman's task, also fell to camp women.

Such gender-defined work was so valuable to an army's health and well-being that a certain number of useful women remained with regiments in the field even after most wives and whores were driven from camps in the late 17th century. From then until the French Revolution, a contingent of 15 to 20 women usually marched in the train of a French regiment, while the British brought along about six wives per 100 soldiers until the late 18th century.

Camp women also scrambled to earn whatever they could through petty commerce. Some became suffers (vivandières in French), peddling food, liquor, tobacco and sundries to officers and men. And camp women could be extremely creative in garnering money by more extraordinary schemes. During the occupation of Freiburg by the Swedes in the 1630s, one citizen complained of "the soldiers' abominable wives," who trespassed in local gardens, cut produce as soon as it appeared, and had the gall to sell what they did not consume in the Freiburg market.

Men with female partners enjoyed an advantage. Sir James Turner, in his Pallas Armata (1683), argued that during the 1624–25 Spanish siege of Breda, in the Netherlands, "The married Soldiers fared better, look'd more vigorously, and were able to do more duty than the Batchellors; and all the spite was done the poor women was to be called their husbands' mules by those who would have been glad to have had such mules themselves."

Turner's use of the term "mules" points to the heavy labor these formidable women performed. An anonymous handwritten German manuscript of 1612 detailed the load carried by women on the march:

Seldom is one found who does not carry at least 50 or 60 pounds. [The] soldier … loads straw and wood on her, to say nothing of the fact that many of them carry one, two or three children on their back. Normally, however, aside from the clothing they are wearing, they carry for the man one pair of breeches,

one pair of stockings, one pair of shoes. And for themselves the same number of shoes and stockings, one jacket, two Hemmeter [shifts], one pan, one pot, one or two spoons, one sheet, one overcoat, one tent and three poles. They receive no wood for cooking in their billets, and so they pick it up on the way. And to add to their fatigue, they normally lead a small dog on a rope or even carry him in bad weather.

The presence of so many women in the train of the army constituted a sizable labor pool that field commanders were quick to exploit. They even participated, according to Wallhausen, in the hard physical labor of siege work: "The whores and the boys [of the camp] also helped in binding fascines, filling ditches, digging pits and mounting cannon in difficult places."

The most important contribution made by camp women lay beyond their traditional women's work, petty commercial ventures and taxing manual labor. First and foremost, they took part in pillaging, without which early modern forces could not have maintained themselves on campaign. Grimmelshausen's antiheroine Courage boasted, "No one could match me at foraging." Peter Hagendorf, author of the only extant diary by a common soldier in the Thirty Years' War, reported how wives, his own included, pillaged the fallen city of Magdeburg in 1631 even after the fires that would destroy the city had broken out:

A cry then came from throughout the city as houses all fell on each other. Many soldiers and their wives who were searching to steal something died. God indeed protected [my wife]. After an hour and a half, she came out of the city accompanied by an old holy woman, who helped her carry bedding. She also brought me a large tankard with four liters wine. In addition, she found two silver belts and clothes, which I was able to cash in for 12 thaler in Halerstadt.

But women did more than steal; there is good reason to believe they guarded the booty and held the money gained by selling it. In woodcuts showing Landsknechts and their women, the men carry the weapons, ready for battle, while women are often shown with fat purses. Free from the immediate risks of fighting in the front rank, they held the money for their fighting men. The preceding description of May marriages confirms that women carried their men's clothing and other personal items, including their "valuables." A poem accompanying a 16th century woodcut claims that among a whore's duties was guarding the plunder:

Do well with me, my pretty lass

And stay with me in the Landsknechts

You'll wash my shirts

Carry my sacks and flasks

And if some booty should be mine

You shall keep it safe and fine

So when we put paid of this crew

We'll sell the booty when we are through.

Among artisan couples in the civilian community, women were similarly entrusted with holding goods and managing funds. Masters' wives regularly made sales and tended the till.

If the business maintained a market stall, this was the wife's preserve, for the husband was needed back at the shop. Pillage was a form of this early modern family economy.

Pillage was also the business of the army. Because the campaign community was based on mercenary principles, versus those of state service or patriotism, its members were easily seduced by greed. In his 1516 colloquy "Of a Soldier's Life," the great Dutch humanist Desiderius Erasmus confronted a soldier with the charge, "It was not the Love of your Country, but the Love of Booty that made you a Soldier," to which the soldier replied, "I confess so, and I believe very few go into the Army with any better Design." He also admits, "The Hope of Booty made me valiant." In fact, only a few common soldiers and their women profited, but it was just enough to tempt others in a kind of lottery psychology. When Erasmus inquires of his soldier, "Well, have you brought home a good Deal of Plunder then?" the soldier replies with a shrug, "Empty Pockets."

The unintended consequence of such unrealistic hopes of riches was the survival of military forces on campaign. Before European states developed the capacity to maintain their armies in the field, it was pillage that sustained them. The fact that women were key agents in securing and managing pillage explains the need for great numbers of them in the campaign community, as well as the radical reduction in their numbers after 1650.

Ultimately, pillaging and the abuses inescapably associated with it imposed limits on the reliability, efficiency and size of armies. To overcome these limits, European states developed the political power and administrative means to command revenues and tap credit sufficient to maintain their armies. Rulers curbed pillage by holding officers responsible for their soldiers' conduct and by imposing and enforcing stricter codes of discipline, but such efforts would have been fruitless were it not for major improvements in military administration and logistics, which in turn required advances in the state's ability to mobilize and disperse resources. These critical military and political changes affected different countries at different times, but in general the transformation occurred during the latter half of the 17th century. With distinct national twists, they were the work of Louis XIV in France, Frederick William the Great Elector (1640–1688) in Brandenburg-Prussia and Peter the Great (1682–1725) in Russia.

These monarchs' accomplishments demonstrate that war was the engine that drove state formation in Europe. Thus the history of camp women and their involvement in pillage merges with far greater issues—the rise of the modern army and the emergence of the modern state.

For further reading, **JOHN A. LYNN** recommends: *Battle Cries and Lullabies: Women in War from Prehistory to the Present,* by Linda Grant De Pauw.

Test-Your-Knowledge Form

We encourage you to photocopy and use this page as a tool to assess how the articles in *Annual Editions* expand on the information in your textbook. By reflecting on the articles you will gain enhanced text information. You can also access this useful form on a product's book support website at www.mhhe.com/cls.

NAME: DATE:

_____

TITLE AND NUMBER OF ARTICLE:

_____

BRIEFLY STATE THE MAIN IDEA OF THIS ARTICLE:

_____

_____

LIST THREE IMPORTANT FACTS THAT THE AUTHOR USES TO SUPPORT THE MAIN IDEA:

_____

WHAT INFORMATION OR IDEAS DISCUSSED IN THIS ARTICLE ARE ALSO DISCUSSED IN YOUR TEXTBOOK OR OTHER READINGS THAT YOU HAVE DONE? LIST THE TEXTBOOK CHAPTERS AND PAGE NUMBERS:

_____

LIST ANY EXAMPLES OF BIAS OR FAULTY REASONING THAT YOU FOUND IN THE ARTICLE:

_____

LIST ANY NEW TERMS/CONCEPTS THAT WERE DISCUSSED IN THE ARTICLE, AND WRITE A SHORT DEFINITION:

We Want Your Advice

ANNUAL EDITIONS revisions depend on two major opinion sources: one is our Advisory Board, listed in the front of this volume, which works with us in scanning the thousands of articles published in the public press each year; the other is you—the person actually using the book. Please help us and the users of the next edition by completing the prepaid article rating form on this page and returning it to us. Thank you for your help!

ANNUAL EDITIONS: Western Civilization, Volume 1, 16/e

ARTICLE RATING FORM

Here is an opportunity for you to have direct input into the next revision of this volume.
We would like you to rate each of the articles listed below, using the following scale:

1. **Excellent: should definitely be retained**
2. **Above average: should probably be retained**
3. **Below average: should probably be deleted**
4. **Poor: should definitely be deleted**

Your ratings will play a vital part in the next revision.
Please mail this prepaid form to us as soon as possible.
Thanks for your help!

RATING	ARTICLE
	1. More than Man's Best Friend
	2. Uncovering Secrets of the Sphinx
	3. Journey to the Seven Wonders
	4. The Coming of the Sea Peoples
	5. I, Pillar of Justice
	6. Before Tea Leaves Divination in Ancient Babylonia
	7. Troy's Night of the Horse
	8. The Historical Socrates
	9. Good Riddance, I Say
	10. Outfoxed and Outfought
	11. Mighty Macedonian: Alexander the Great
	12. Etruscan Women: Dignified, Charming, Literate and Free
	13. Rome's Craftiest General: Scipio Africanus
	14. Did Captured ARK Afflict Philistines with E.D.?
	15. Who Wrote the Dead Sea Scrolls?
	16. From Jesus to Christ
	17. An Inconvenient Woman
	18. The Elusive Eastern Empire

RATING	ARTICLE
	19. The Lost Secret of Greek Fire
	20. Islam's First Terrorists
	21. Al-Kimiya Notes on Arabic Alchemy
	22. The Church in the Middle Ages
	23. What Did Medieval Schools Do for Us?
	24. 1215 and All That
	25. The Fourth Crusade and the Sack of Constantinople
	26. Monsoons, Mude and Gold
	27. How a Mysterious Disease Laid Low Europe's Masses
	28. Joan of Arc
	29. Christian Humanism: From Renaissance to Reformation
	30. The Luther Legacy
	31. Explaining John Calvin
	32. Who Was Henry VIII and When Did It All Go Wrong?
	33. Women in War

BUSINESS REPLY MAIL
FIRST CLASS MAIL PERMIT NO. 551 DUBUQUE IA

POSTAGE WILL BE PAID BY ADDRESSEE

McGraw-Hill Contemporary Learning Series
501 BELL STREET
DUBUQUE, IA 52001

ABOUT YOU

Name _____ Date _____

Are you a teacher? ❑ A student? ❑
Your school's name _____

Department _____

Address _____ City _____ State _____ Zip _____

School telephone # _____

YOUR COMMENTS ARE IMPORTANT TO US!

Please fill in the following information:
For which course did you use this book?
_____

Did you use a text with this ANNUAL EDITION? ❑ yes ❑ no
What was the title of the text?
_____

What are your general reactions to the Annual Editions concept?
_____

Have you read any pertinent articles recently that you think should be included in the next edition? Explain.
_____

Are there any articles that you feel should be replaced in the next edition? Why?
_____

Are there any World Wide Websites that you feel should be included in the next edition? Please annotate.
_____

May we contact you for editorial input? ❑ yes ❑ no
May we quote your comments? ❑ yes ❑ no

NOTES

NOTES

NOTES

NOTES

NOTES

NOTES